DISCOURSE COMPREHENSION
Essays in Honor of Walter Kintsch

DISCOURSE COMPREHENSION
Essays in Honor of Walter Kintsch

Edited by

Charles A. Weaver, III
Baylor University

Suzanne Mannes
University of Delaware

Charles R. Fletcher
University of Minnesota

LEA LAWRENCE ERLBAUM ASSOCIATES, PUBLISHERS
1995 Hillsdale, New Jersey   Hove, UK

Lawrence Erlbaum Associates, Inc., Publishers
365 Broadway
Hillsdale, New Jersey 07642

Cover design by Cheryl Minden
Group photo credit: David Fendrich

Library of Congress Cataloging-in-Publication Data

Discourse comprehension : essays in honor of Walter Kintsch / edited
by Charles A. Weaver, III, Suzanne Mannes, Charles R. Fletcher.
    p.   cm.
Includes bibliographical references and index.
ISBN 0-8058-1534-1 (alk. paper).—ISBN 0-8058-1535-X (pbk. : alk. paper)
1. Discourse analysis—Psychological aspects. 2. Comprehension.
I. Kintsch, Walter, 1932–   . II. Weaver, Charles A. III. Mannes,
Suzanne. IV. Fletcher, Charles Randall.
P302.8.D574 1995
401′.41—dc20   94-21936
                                                          CIP

Printed in the United States of America
10 9 8 7 6 5 4 3 2 1

Contents

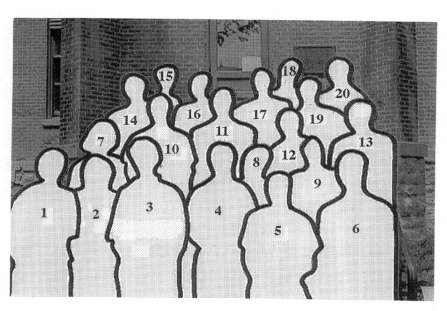

1. Roger Ratcliff	6. Charles A. Weaver, III	11. Peter G. Polson	16. Arthur M. Glenberg
2. Gail McKoon	7. Susan R. Goldman	12. Charles R. Fletcher	17. Wolfgang Schönpflug
3. Bennet B. Murdock	8. Morton Ann Gernsbacher	13. Franz Schmalhofer	18. Bruce K. Britton
4. Walter Kintsch	9. Suzanne Mannes	14. Arthur C. Graesser	19. Charles A. Perfetti
5. W. K. Estes	10. James G. Greeno	15. Rolf A. Zwaan	20. Ernest F. Mross

Preface

This book had its genesis in a rather innocent conversation that Suzanne Mannes and I had at the meeting of the Psychonomic Society in St. Louis in November 1992. Had Walter Kintsch reached the point in his career that we, his former students and colleagues, should honor him with a conference and perhaps an edited book? We had seen the excellent volumes that had recently been produced for Bill Estes and Endel Tulving, and we decided a similar festschrift for Walter was overdue. With good, albeit somewhat naive, intentions, we drew up a list of potential contributors. We tentatively set June 1993 as the date to schedule this conference.

As I began calling these individuals around Christmas 1992, several things dawned on me. First was the enormity of the undertaking—I had to get commitments from extremely busy individuals, despite the fact that I could not give them a firm date (we were still working on that), a firm "yes" from a publisher (we were working on that, too), or a firm list of others who would be involved. One of my colleagues who had arranged a similar conference several years ago told me that what he did was to tell each person on his list that every other person had agreed to come, even though he had not yet talked to the others. He just hoped he got enough affirmative responses to make the statement true (which, by the way, he did). Fortunately, I needn't have worried about that.

The second thing that struck me was the absolutely overwhelming enthusiasm I encountered. Despite the fact that I could provide none of the details, virtually everyone I contacted jumped at the chance to be involved. Randy Fletcher was asked to join us as an editor; he brought with him an abundance of editorial experience and energy.

That's when the pieces started falling together. We learned from Peter Polson that Walter would be awarded the American Psychological Association's "Distinguished Scientific Contribution" award in 1993. Walter was celebrating his 60th birthday in 1993, as well. Finally, the Institute for Cognitive Science, founded in 1968 at the University of Colorado (and then called the Institute for the Study of Intellectual Behavior), turned 25 in 1993. Walter has been the director there since 1983, so this was an important personal milestone. If we needed any other possible encouragement, Boulder was also serving as the host for the meeting of Cognitive Science Society in June 1993. We were able to set up a conference coinciding with this meeting. Knowing Walter's modesty, we waited until he was skiing (at the Winter Text Conference) to inform him.

Sometimes the gods are kind. On June 16 and 17, 1993, over 100 individuals from more than 10 countries attended the conference—Discourse Comprehension: Strategies and Processing Revisited. Essays in honor of Walter Kintsch—held in Boulder, Colorado. Most of the authors in the present volume spoke at this conference. In addition, we were delighted to have Art Glenberg and Bruce Britton speak, though they could not contribute chapters. We were also able to secure chapters from Susan Goldman, Vimla Patel, Kurt Reusser, and Mark McDaniel and Gil Einstein, even though they were unable to speak. The 2-day conference was a huge success, and Suzanne, Randy, and I wish to thank all who participated.

When we began making plans for an edited book centered around this conference, Suzanne, Randy, and I set a primary goal: to acknowledge the wide variety of researchers and research areas Walter has influenced. As a consequence, one of the more unusual elements of this volume is the diversity of the contributors. Many of us are students of Walter Kintsch in the formal sense; others are perhaps "adopted children," who have worked with Walter but for whom he has not served as an advisor in the conventional sense. Yet others are colleagues who have played a large role in the development of Walter's research as it has been formed over a period of years. Indeed, one of Walter's greatest achievements is the extent to which he has influenced research worldwide. Therefore, a significant number of authors are Walter's colleagues from Europe.

During the many phases of Walter's career, all of these individuals at some time or another gave critical input to different aspects of his work. They would all agree that the influence was mutual. As a testament to Walter's productivity and influence, the list of potential contributors could easily have been twice as long. We regret that we were not able to incorporate all of those additional scholars.

ACKNOWLEDGMENTS

A project of this magnitude could not have been completed without assistance from a number of individuals. First, we wish to thank those involved in organizing the conference. Walter's wife Eileen put countless hours into everything from menu selection to finding addresses for Walter's former students and colleagues.

Also, her skilled editorial work can be seen throughout the volume. Eileen was assisted in her organizational duties by Martha Polson, the associate director of the Institute of Cognitive Science at the University of Colorado. Martha provided funding, resources, and personnel, without which we could not have hosted the conference. Between the two of them they performed virtually all of the organizing duties. We are sincerely grateful.

We also wish to thank those contributors who freely gave their time to speak at the conference, write for the book, or both. We not only asked the writers to meet (almost) impossible deadlines, we asked them to review each other's work. We believe this resulted in a more coherently organized volume (after all, nothing would offend Walter more than an incoherent text prepared in his honor!). To the extent we accomplished these goals, much of the credit goes to the authors themselves.

We wish to thank Judi Amsel and Larry Erlbaum of Lawrence Erlbaum Associates for their support. They were very receptive to the idea of a festschrift honoring Walter Kintsch, and provided us with additional resources to produce this volume. Dave Salierno handled the production work for LEA, and did an outstanding job.

Charles A. Weaver, III
Suzanne Mannes
Charles R. Fletcher

I would like to thank Lewis M. Barker, my one-time mentor and present colleague, for his advice and encouragement over the years. Most academics consider themselves fortunate if they have one academic mentor as gifted as Walter Kintsch. I was lucky enough to have two.

Also, I wish to thank my good friend and fellow Kintschian Ernie Mross, who may be the only person who can claim the dubious honor of sharing either an office or a house with each of the three editors. In all seriousness, Ernie continues to be a valuable colleague, a trusted friend, and a heck of a center fielder.

My co-editors and friends, Suzanne Mannes and Randy Fletcher, have done a marvelous job in preparing this volume. They were a co-editor's dream—they worked with each individual author, securing reviews and organizing writing schedules, and provided invaluable feedback to me and the authors. I cannot imagine having undertaken this task without their help. It has been a privilege.

I also wish to thank my family: my wife, Lisa, and my children, Austin and Lindsay. Lisa has been with me from the start. The latter two are more recent additions. Thanks to them all for their patience and encouragement throughout this project. Needless to say, without their support we could not have produced this work.

Finally, I am grateful to Walter Kintsch for the many things he taught me, both professionally and personally; for the things he said and (perhaps as importantly) didn't say; and, most of all, for the example he has provided. It is with great pride that I tell people, "I am a student of Walter Kintsch."

Charles A. Weaver, III

In addition to all the folks Chuck has mentioned as having a critical role in the execution of this project, particularly the contributors themselves, there are a few I would like to acknowledge myself. David Fendrich and James E. Hoffman have provided untold moral support. David, in everything I do, and Jim in my recent academic endeavors. You guys really keep me going. I thank you. I also wish to thank Ernie Mross, first for serving for years as a personal consultant, and more recently for serving as a most gracious host. Were it not for Ernie's generosity in giving of his time and home, much of what we have accomplished would not have come to pass.

As has Chuck, I wish to thank Walter. He gave me the courage to do things, like "outhouse" and many unnamed chutes, that I would not have otherwise attempted. Most importantly he did so with genuine enthusiasm, delight, and everlasting patience. For the things he has taught me both in and out of the classroom, I thank him. I also wish to thank Eileen for being a part of my life, for her unconditional support and encouragement, and for providing me with a feeling of family whenever mine is far away.

Suzanne Mannes

I'd like to begin by thanking Chuck Weaver and Suzanne Mannes for doing the really hard work of finding a publisher and securing commitments from all of the authors before they asked me to co-edit this volume. I would also like to thank Linda Fletcher, my incredibly understanding and supportive spouse, for putting up with too many evenings and weekends alone so that I could hide in my office and get some work done. I would be lost without her!

Last, but certainly not least, I would like to say "thank you" to Walter Kintsch. I'll never forget the first time Walter critiqued one of my manuscripts. The first words out of his mouth were, "Well, this isn't really very good!" and I have to admit that he was right! Three years later, as I neared the end of my graduate career, Walter called me to his office to discuss yet another manuscript. All he said was, "This is perfect—send it to the journal like this!" In the years between these incidents, Walter gave me a lot of freedom to pursue my own research interests. When I did things well, he was generous with his praise. When I made mistakes, he made certain that I learned from them. Under his tutelage, the journey from "this isn't really very good" to "this is perfect" was, indeed, a pleasure.

Charles R. Fletcher

Chapter 1

Walter Kintsch: A Brief Biography

Peter G. Polson
University of Colorado

This chapter presents a brief biography focusing on Walter Kintsch's scientific contributions to cognitive psychology and cognitive science. It describes the major themes underlying Walter's research on text comprehension, memory for text, and utilization of information in text. In addition, the chapter characterizes the intellectual context in which he made these contributions.

THE BEGINNING

Of Rats and Humans

Walter received his doctorate from the University of Kansas in 1960 under the direction of Edward Wike. Walter's early papers were in the area of animal learning, focusing on the interactions between learning and incentive motivation, an important theoretical issue at the time. A typical title was "Runway Performance as a Function of the Amount of Reinforcement and Drive Strength," which was published in the *Journal of Comparative and Physiological Psychology* in 1962.

In that era, there was a single field of experimental psychology. Many experimental psychologists did both human and animal learning experiments. Researchers studying learning and memory were guided by the behaviorist paradigm defined by Watson, Skinner, Hull, and Spence. At the same time, Miller (1956),

Chomsky (1957), Newell, Shaw, and Simon (1957), and others were building the foundations of cognitive psychology and cognitive science.

Becoming a Mathematical Psychologist

During the academic year 1960–1961, Walter was a postdoc in the laboratory of William K. Estes, who was then at Indiana University. Walter changed his focus to memory and quickly established himself as a mathematical psychologist, a group developing mathematical models of basic psychological processes. Many of the models were formalized as finite Markov chains (Kemeny & Snell, 1959). The scope of these models included experimental paradigms like paired-associates learning, probability learning, discrimination learning, and concept identification (Restle & Greeno, 1970). Most of us today would recognize many of this group as leading researchers in cognitive psychology, including William K. Estes, Gordon Bower, Jim Greeno, and Walter.

From Math Models to Cognitive Models

By the mid-1970s, most mathematical psychologists identified themselves as cognitive psychologists. In retrospect, this transformation was not accidental. Many of the mechanisms in Markov models of associative learning and concept identification (Bower, 1962; Kintsch & Morris, 1965; Restle, 1962) anticipated many of the processes later incorporated into cognitive theories and could not easily be rationalized within the behaviorist framework. Gregg and Simon (1967) argued that a much more useful way to frame the mechanisms assumed by Markov models was in terms of the information-processing paradigm.

A Vision of the Future

It was in this intellectual environment that Walter began his research on text comprehension. Walter, influenced by research in linguistics and artificial intelligence, set out to develop a theory of comprehension and memory for sentences, whole paragraphs, and short stories. At the time, some of Walter's senior colleagues thought such an attempt was extremely premature.

Experimental paradigms still showed the influence of the behaviorist era, even though the foundations of what was to become modern cognitive psychology were clearly established. There was little research on memory for sentences and stories, although there were important exceptions like the early research in psycholinguistics (Fodor & Garett, 1967; Sachs, 1967). Barlett's (1932) research on memory using Native American folk stories was well known but had not been replicated or extended. A superb summary of this transition era between behaviorism and the information-processing paradigm is contained in one of the early textbooks on cognitive psychology (Kintsch, 1970).

THE NEXT 25 YEARS

The remaining chapters in this volume honor Walter for his research on comprehension, memory, and utilization of information in text. His efforts over the last 25 years have led to the development of detailed formal process models, in some cases implemented as computer simulations, that describe the cognitive processes involved in reading and the utilization of knowledge. His research has defined the theoretical and empirical paradigms that have led to our deep understanding of this area.

The Highlights

In this brief biography, I focus on four major contributions: *The Representation of Meaning in Memory* (Kintsch, 1974), a *Psychological Review* paper entitled "Towards a Model of Text Comprehension and Production" (Kintsch & van Dijk, 1978), *Strategies of Discourse Comprehension* (van Dijk & Kintsch, 1983), and a *Psychological Review* paper entitled "The Role of Knowledge in Discourse Comprehension: A Construction-Integration Model" (Kintsch, 1988). In each instance, I present my views on the lasting impact of each contribution.

Kintsch (1974): The Representation of Meaning in Memory. If you reread the first few chapters that describe the theory and its background, which I did recently, it is amazingly current, even though 20 years have elapsed since these chapters were written. It is superb cognitive science before the field was clearly defined, let alone legitimized by Sloan Foundation grants, a professional society, and journals. Walter's research drew on important work in linguistics, artificial intelligence, and, to a lesser extent, philosophy. However, in Walter's hands, key concepts from these fields were transformed, sometimes drastically, into the components of a psychological theory. He pruned away many issues that even today are the focus of research in these other fields. For example, he explicitly refused to embark on the project of developing a parser that maps the surface structure of text into an underlying propositional representation. The development of such a parser still defines, 20 years later, important unsolved problems in artificial intelligence and computational linguistics. He was also equally willing to put aside many formal and conceptual issues in logic and semantics that are important topics in modern linguistics and philosophy.

Walter clearly stated that his goals were to develop and test a psychological theory of the representation of meaning in memory. There were some strong negative reactions. Several well-known researchers in linguistics and philosophy were unamused. The 1974 book received a small number of savage reviews. These reactions to Kintsch(1974) are a good illustration of why truly excellent interdisciplinary work is so difficult.

Research results from other fields have had and will continue to have important implications for cognitive psychology. However, successful utilization of borrowed concepts requires both the background to understand them and the imagination to transform and then incorporate them into an empirically testable, psychological theory. Psychology's empirical and theoretical methodologies have nothing to contribute to many of the issues central to these other fields.

Kintsch (1974) summarized an extensive series of experiments done by him and his early students here at Colorado. These results established that the basic unit for the storage of meaningful information in long-term memory was the proposition and that the meaning of sentences and short paragraphs could be represented as a network of propositions.

Kintsch and van Dijk (1978): Toward a Model of Text Comprehension and Production. This paper described the processes involved in text comprehension and the processes involved in recalling and summarizing text. The theory was an important advance over Kintsch (1974) in terms of both scope and level of detail of the process descriptions. The Kintsch and van Dijk model provided a detailed description of how information is extracted from text and how a persistent representation of the gist along with less a reliable representation of details is stored and then retrieved from memory.

The paper describes the synthesis of three important lines of research. The first was van Dijk's work on text linguistics, which had an important influence on the 1974 book. The 1978 version of the theory incorporated mechanisms, originally proposed by van Dijk, representing the gist of the text in memory. The second was the incorporation of text comprehension processes into the standard model of the human information-processing system that had been articulated by Atkinson and Shiffrin (1968), Newell and Simon (1972), and others. Comprehension processes were characterized in the context of a generic information-processing architecture incorporating short- and long-term memory stores. Third, quantitative predictions were derived from the theory based on assumptions incorporated into Markov models of all-or-none learning.

van Dijk and Kintsch (1983): Strategies of Discourse Comprehension. This monograph expanded and refined the framework presented in Kintsch and van Dijk (1978). It made explicit the notion that text comprehension involves and results in multiple representations of a text. They introduced the concept of a situation model of the information contained in the text. The situation model is one of the key ideas used in Kintsch and van Dijk's accounts of how information contained in the text is used in problem-solving activities. The theory also describes how information in large texts, longer articles, book chapters, and the like is stored in long-term memory and how that knowledge is utilized. A very detailed analysis of the process of solving algebra word problems derived from the 1983 book was published by Kintsch and Greeno (1985).

Kintsch (1988): The Role of Knowledge in Discourse Comprehension: A Construction-Integration Model. This paper describes a synthesis of Walter's previous research with important ideas adapted from connectionism. The model is an important departure from the basic theoretical architecture underlying all of Walter's previous work. All of his earlier theoretical contributions were consistent with the information-processing paradigm and the symbolic nature of cognition (Newell, 1980; Vera & Simon, 1993). The construction-integration model is a hybrid of Walter's earlier work cast in the symbolic mode with important ideas borrowed from connectionist models. This paper presents novel reinterpretations of many of his previous results, as well as accounting for other important results from the text comprehension literature.

Walter pointed out that his previous models never solved in a principled fashion a basic and difficult computational problem in language comprehension, the *combinatorics*. Individual words have multiple meanings. The different meanings of words can each be combined into sentences with multiple interpretations. It was the combinatorics, in addition to incorrect conceptualizations of language, that led to the failures of early attempts in the late 1950s and early 1960s at mechanical language transition. These combinatorics bedevil computational linguists to this day.

One possible solution to these combinatorial problems was the evolution of a set of theoretical ideas that Walter refers to as "smart rules." Expectation driven processes based on scripts (Schank & Ableson, 1977), frames (Minsky, 1975), and the like have been proposed as possible solutions of the combinatorics within the symbolic paradigm. However, attempts to write smarter and smarter rules that solve the combinatorial problems of comprehension inevitably fail because smart rules are too brittle.

The construction-integration model combines propositional representations and context-free rules with features of the connectionist paradigm, spreading activation and massive parallelism. The resulting framework accounts for a wide range of psychological phenomena ranging from the impact of contexts on word sense disambiguation to the utilization of knowledge in problem solving. In the last few years, Walter—with Suzanne Mannes, Stephanie Doane, and others of us here at Colorado—has extended the construction-integration model further into the area of knowledge utilization dealing with problems of action planning in human–computer interaction (Mannes & Kintsch, 1991).

WALTER'S IMPACT

Walter's research on text comprehension has had a huge impact on cognitive psychology and cognitive science. Most of the major contributions of Kintsch (1974), Kintsch and van Dijk (1978), and van Dijk and Kintsch (1983) have been incorporated into the foundations of modern theories of memory for meaningful material and text comprehension. A majority of the chapters in this volume rest on theoretical and methodological foundations drawn in large part from Walter's research. His methodological and theoretical contributions have given us a clear instance of superb cognitive science and thus helped define this interdisciplinary field.

Varieties of propositional representations developed in Kintsch (1974) are now the standard notation for the analysis of text material and for the scoring of recall protocols in experiments studying memory for texts. Refinements and variations of the Kintsch and van Dijk (1978) and van Dijk and Kintsch (1983) models of text comprehension are the standard models of comprehension processes today. The construction-integration model (Kintsch, 1988), a new framework for the analysis of the comprehension and retention of meaningful materials, is too new for us to be able to predict its ultimate impact.

Synthesis Based on Transformations

Many of the important episodes in development of modern cognitive psychology have been attempts by various researchers to borrow important ideas from artificial intelligence, linguistics, or another field, and to show that they can find psychological evidence for analogs of these mechanisms. Two good illustrations are the early work in psycholinguistics motivated by transformational grammar (Sachs, 1967) and the memory research on scripts and frames (Bower, Black, & Turner, 1979).

Although Walter was influenced by research in other fields, he never just borrows concepts. Walter's theoretical contributions are based on his profound understanding of the evolution of our ideas about mind and cognition, including philosophy, the psychology of the 19th and early 20th centuries, the Hull–Spence framework, and mathematical psychology. Although Walter has extensive knowledge of relevant work in linguistics and artificial intelligence, his use of those ideas has been shaped by his knowledge of psychology and by his goal to build psychological theories. His major contributions are a true synthesis of often conflicting concepts of mind drawn from different fields in which the original ideas are transformed in the process. Concepts drawn from these other fields are profoundly transformed by his goal to develop a psychological theory of text comprehension.

Service

Walter has an impressive record of service to his profession and the University of Colorado. He has served on grant review panels and has been or is a consulting editor for many top journals. Let me enumerate the highlights. He was editor of the *Journal of Verbal Learning and Verbal Behavior* from 1976 to 1980. He was a member of the governing board of the Psychonomics Society from 1979 to 1984 and chaired the governing board in 1984. He was a founding member and is now serving a second term on the governing board of the Cognitive Science Society, and he chaired the board in 1984. He completed a 6-year term as editor of the *Psychological Review* at the end of 1993. In 1983, he was appointed and still serves as director of the Institute of Cognitive Science at the University of Colorado at Boulder.

Honors

Walter has received many prestigious awards in recognition of his research contributions. He was elected to the Society of Experimental Psychologists in 1974. He was a Fellow of the Center for Advanced Study in the Behavioral Sciences from 1981 to 1982. In 1984 he received the University of Colorado's highest award for research accomplishments, the Lectureship on Research and Creative Work. The American Educational Research Association awarded Walter and van Dijk their outstanding book award in 1984 for *Strategies of Discourse Comprehension*. In 1987 he received a Merit award from the National Institutes of Mental Health. In the academic year 1991–1992 he was a visiting scientist at the Max Planck Institut fur Psychologische Forschung. Walter is a Fellow of the American Psychological Association, and in 1993 he received the APA's award for Distinguished Scientific Contributions.

A BALANCED LIFE

One of Walter's most impressive accomplishments is his ability to balance the numerous competing demands of his successful professional career with his personal life. I have come to respect and envy his efficiency and his resource allocation skills. Walter manages his editorial and administrative functions with incredible skill and efficiency. Consider the example of his action letters. They are models of brevity. Walter's week is always structured so that he spends a significant fraction of his time on his research and writing—in spite of the many other demands on him. Family, skiing, mountain climbing, and musical events also receive a share of his time. Walter and his wife, Eileen, frequently attend concerts in the Boulder–Denver area.

BIOGRAPHY

Walter was born in Temeschwar, Romania, on May 30, 1932. The Kintsch family was part of a large, ethnic German community that had lived in that part of the Balkans for many generations. Late in World War II, the Kintschs fled to Austria. Walter's original academic training was as a grade-school teacher, and he taught in one-room schools in the mountains of Austria from 1951 to 1955. In 1955 he came to the University of Kansas in Lawrence, Kansas, where he received his master's in psychology in 1956. He then returned to Austria and studied psychology at the University of Vienna. He returned to the University of Kansas in the fall of 1957, and he received his doctorate in 1960. It was also there that he met and married Eileen Hoover.

Walter was a National Institutes of Mental Health postdoctoral fellow in William K. Estes's laboratory at Indiana in the 1960–1961 academic year. In 1961 Walter, joined the Department of Psychology at the University of Missouri-Columbia. He was there until 1965 when he went to the University of California at Riverside. During the academic year 1967–1968, he was a visiting associate professor at the Department of Psychology at Stanford. In 1968, he joined the Department of Psychology at the University of Colorado as full professor, where he has been ever since. The Kintschs have two daughters, Anja, born in 1968, and Julia, born in 1971.

REFERENCES

Atkinson, R. L., & Shiffrin, R. M. (1968). Human memory: A proposed system and its control processes. In K. W. Spence & J. T. Spence (Eds.), *The psychology of learning and motivation: Advances in research and theory* (Vol. 2, pp. 89–195). New York: Academic Press.

Bartlett, F. C. (1932). *Remembering*. Cambridge, England: Cambridge University Press.

Bower, G. H. (1962). A model of response and training variables in paired-associates learning. *Psychological Review, 69*, 34–53.

Bower, G. H., Black, J. B., & Turner, T. J. (1979). Scripts in memory for text. *Cognitive Psychology, 11*, 177–220.

Chomsky, N. (1957). *Syntactic structures*. The Hague: Mouton.

Fodor, J. A., & Garett, M. F. (1967). Some syntactic determinants of sentential complexity. *Perception and Psychophysics, 2*, 289–296.

Gregg, L. W. & Simon, H. A. (1967). Process models and stochastic theories of simple concept formation. *Journal of Mathematical Psychology, 4*, 246–276.

Kemeny, J. G., & Snell, J. L. (1959). *Finite Markov chains*. Princeton, NJ: Van Nostrand.

Kintsch, W. (1970). *Learning, memory, and conceptual processes*. New York: Wiley.

Kintsch, W. (1974). *The representation of meaning in memory*. Hillsdale, NJ: Lawrence Erlbaum Associates.

Kintsch, W. (1988). The role of knowledge in discourse comprehension: A construction-integration model. *Psychological Review, 95*, 163–182.

Kintsch, W., & Greeno, J. G. (1985). Understanding and solving word arithmetic problems. *Psychological Review, 92*, 109–129.

Kintsch, W., & Morris, C. J. (1965). Application of a Markov model to free recall and recognition. *Journal of Experimental Psychology, 69*, 200–206.

Kintsch, W., & van Dijk, T. A. (1978). Towards a model of text comprehension and production. *Psychological Review, 85*, 363–394.

Mannes, S. M., & Kintsch, W. (1991). Routine computing tasks: Planning as understanding. *Cognitive Science, 15*, 305–342.

Miller, G. A. (1956). The magical number seven, plus or minus two: Some limits on our capacity for processing information. *Psychological Review, 63*, 81–97.

Minsky, M. (1975). A framework for representing knowledge. In P. H. Winston (Ed.), *The psychology of computer vision* (pp. 211–277). New York: McGraw-Hill.

Newell, A. (1980). Reasoning, problem-solving, and decision processes: The problem space as a fundamental category. In R. Nickerson (Ed.), *Attention and performance* (Vol. 8, pp. 693–718). Hillsdale, NJ: Lawrence Erlbaum Associates.

Newell, A., Shaw, J. C., & Simon, H. A. (1957). Empirical explorations of the logic theory machine. In *Proceedings of the Western Joint Computer Conference* (pp. 218–230). New York: IRE.

Newell, A., & Simon, H. A. (1972). *Human problem solving.* Englewood Cliffs, NJ: Prentice-Hall.

Restle, F. (1962). The selection of strategies in cue learning. *Psychological Review, 69,* 329–343.

Restle, F., & Greeno, J. G. (1970). *Introduction to mathematical psychology.* Reading, MA: Addison-Wesley.

Sachs, J. D. S. (1967). Recognition memory for syntactic and semantic aspects of connected discourse. *Perception and Psychophysics, 2,* 437–442.

Shank, R. C., & Ableson, R. (1977). *Sprits, plans, goals, and understanding.* Hillsdale, NJ: Lawrence Erlbaum Associates.

van Dijk, T. A., & Kintsch, W. (1983). *Strategies of discourse comprehension.* New York: Academic Press.

Vera, A. H., & Simon, H. A. (1993). Situated action: A symbolic interpretation. *Cognitive Science, 17,* 7–48.

Chapter 2

Where Do Propositions Come From?

Charles A. Perfetti
M. Anne Britt
University of Pittsburgh

Thanks to Walter Kintsch, and the research field that was launched by his work (Kintsch, 1974), we know where propositions go: They go to the textbase. They get remembered, understood, integrated, or forgotten. But where do they come from?

This question has seemed either too trivial or too inscrutable to have received much attention in text processing. One searches in vain through most of the text processing literature, including Kintsch's seminal 1974 book and the more recent construction and integration theory (Kintsch, 1988), for more than a passing reference to this question.

We want to examine the reason for this neglect before modifying the question so that we can suggest an answer. But first we have to reveal the short form of the answer: Propositions come from sentences. And how do they come from sentences? There do seem to be some prepropositional processes that operate on words, phrases, and sentences, whether spoken or written, in such a way as to yield something like propositions. These processes as a group are handily referred to as "parsing." That's where propositions come from.[1]

Why has the question been neglected? Partly because it was difficult, and partly because the question itself might have been invisible. There was nothing much in the mid-1970s that seemed likely to answer the question. The only

---

[1]There is a deeper meaning to the question of where propositions come from. In this question, one wants to know about the epistemic origins of meanings, the representational systems of sentences compared with images, and the like. Our goal here is modestly restricted to propositions understood as text objects.

parsing ideas available to psychologists were those of Kimball (1973), who published his seven principles of parsing in 1973, only a year before the publication of Kintsch's *The Representation of Meaning in Memory*. And without much in the way of data, Kimball's paper was published in *Cognition*, a journal then known for its psycholinguistic sympathies, but not quite in the mainstream of the new work on text processing.

Of course, there is another very interesting reason. Propositions seemed to be just the right level of analysis for understanding text processes. The questions were about how people represented the meaning of texts. These questions entailed attention, not to sentence processes, but to processes that operate on the meanings of sentences. The propositional part of sentence meanings was a very logical place to start.

To start with a proposition, however, is to start where some important and far-from-trivial processes leave off. To that extent, propositional accounts are incomplete even as models of sentence comprehension. Of course, some researchers who have worked on text understanding have targeted the propositional level as much too narrow a topic. That's the way it is: One researcher's minutiae are another researcher's too-big-to-work-on problem.

PROPOSITIONS ACCORDING TO USER'S GUIDES

There are really two parts to the question of where propositions come from. The answer to the substantive part is that propositions come from parsing. The answer to the methodological part is complex and perpetually tentative: Propositions come from a set of rules or heuristics developed by researchers. Note that these two questions are related: Researchers make informed guesses about what counts as a proposition. There are not enough sure-fire parsing algorithms to do that for them. But even if there were, the human judgment factor would still be involved.

Consider Sentence 1, taken from Turner and Green (1978), which is the most comprehensive "user's guide" to the "propositionalizing" of texts:[2]

(1) *Lyle stayed in Paris for 3 months.*

The propositional analysis offered by Turner and Green for this sentence yields three propositions, expressed in simplified form, omitting names for arguments:

---

[2]One might object that this is an old system, and may not be used in recent work. But any differences, as near as we can tell, do not affect the point we make about constituents and whether they translate to propositions.

1. STAY (Lyle, Paris)
2. NUMBER OF (Months, 3)
3. EXTENT OF ((Stay, Lyle, Paris), (Number of months, 3))

Numbering the propositions, of course, allows a shorthand notation for embedding such that Proposition 3 can be written:

3. EXTENT OF (1, 2)

Can this list of propositions have come from a parser? We can imagine a parser that would give the following constituent analysis: *(Lyle ((stayed) (in Paris)) (for 3 months))*. The verb phrase (VP) (stayed in Paris for 3 months) has only two constituents, *(stayed)* and *(in Paris)*. The second prepositional phrase (PP) (for 3 months) is not a constituent of the VP, but an adjunct, a constituent attached high to the sentence. Or at least it appears to be (see Fig. 2.1A). This attachment corresponds to the semantic scope of the propositional analysis: Proposition 1 is embedded in Proposition 3.

However, suppose the parser, instead of producing an adjunct constituent when it encounters "for 3 months," produces a structure with two PPs inside the VP, as shown in Fig. 2.1B. This parsing alternative would not support the three propositions given in Turner and Green. In fact, it would support at most two:

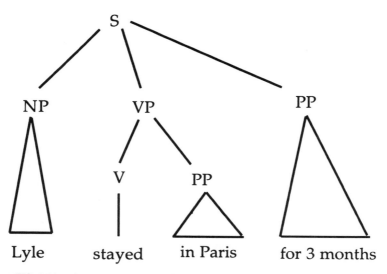

FIG. 2.1A. A tree structure parse for Sentence 1 showing an adjunct reading of the PP "for 3 months."

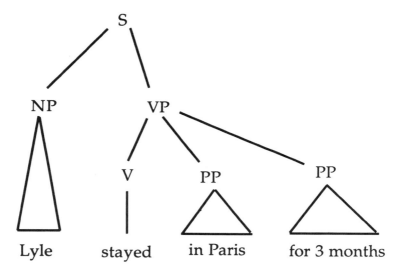

FIG. 2.1B.   A tree structure parse for Sentence 1 showing a verb argument interpretation of the PP "for 3 months."

1. STAY (Lyle, Paris, Some months)
2. NUMBER OF (Months, 3)

There remains the question of whether the quantifier 3 is a separate proposition, as has been customary in text analysis, or whether it should be expressed as part of the first proposition. (That amounts to asking whether or not there are really two propositions here—or only one.) This is a question that can be handled only with some degree of arbitrariness. However, at least one parsing procedure (1A) can yield part of the proposition list that is said by text analysis to underlie Sentence 1.

Now consider the related Sentence 2:

(2) *Lyle pushed Paris out of his mind for 3 months.*

Unlike Sentence 1, Sentence 2 has a multiple argument VP. *Push*, unlike *stay*, seems to require both something pushed and someplace where it gets pushed to. *Paris* then becomes a theme argument (it is the affected object) and *out of his mind* becomes a goal object. (The source object is implicit: *in Lyle's mind*). Fig. 2.2 shows a tree diagram for this sentence. The key point is that both *Paris* and *out of his mind* are now internal to the VP; they are both arguments of the verb. *For 3 months* remains external; it appears not to be an argument of the verb.

How would the rules of propositional text analysis handle this case? Here are two possibilities, accepting the convention about quantifiers being separate propositions:

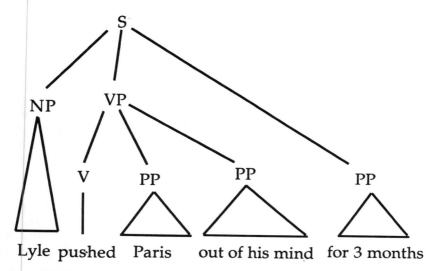

Lyle pushed Paris out of his mind for 3 months

FIG. 2.2. A tree structure parse for Sentence 2 showing an adjunct reading for the PP "for 3 months" and a verb argument interpretation of the PP "out of his mind."

Solution A:

1. PUSH (Lyle, Paris, Out of his mind)
2. NUMBER OF (Months, 3)
3. EXTENT OF (1, 2)

Solution B:

1. PUSH (Lyle, Paris)
2. GOAL (1, Out of mind)
3. NUMBER OF MONTHS (3)
4. EXTENT OF (2,3)

We suspect that many text researchers would prefer Solution B to Solution A.[3] However, Solution A would come closer than Solution B to what is yielded by syntactic analysis. Moreover, there is an empirical prediction that, according to a syntactically based hypothesis, a person reading Sentence 2 would assemble

---

[3]Actually, we have some indication that text analysis researchers do prefer the two-argument predicate for this sentence. We asked three experts to propositionalize this sentence. Only one expert honored the constituent boundary of push as a three place predicate [PUSH (Lyle, Paris, out-of-mind)], Solution A. Both of the other two experts constructed more propositions than grammatical constituents, Solution B. Additionally, it is interesting to note that there was considerable variance in the number of propositions constructed. The three experts parsed this sentence into three, five, and seven propositions. Besides differences due to predicate boundary segmentation, other differences were mainly due to the degree of specificity.

propositions that look more like those in A than those in B. Put another way, the parsing operations would produce constituents that resemble A more than B.

The point is, in principle, a parsing procedure could be used to produce constituents and these constituents could then become propositions. Only when a constituent is controlled by a verb—that is, when it is part of the VP—does it become an argument of that verb inside a proposition. Even with such help from the parser, however, there would still be decisions to be made on other grounds. For example, adverbs, adjectives, and quantifiers are typically considered in text analysis to be predicates that take arguments. But there is nothing in the grammar itself that encourages a decision to treat all of these the same in propositions.

Let's step back from the examples to see the main points: The analysis of propositions as practiced in text research requires decisions about what counts as propositions. But there are both direct and indirect constraints on what can count as propositions. An indirect source of constraints is the grammar of English (assuming the parser is informed by the grammar), and the direct source is the set of human parsing operations, or parsing principles, that yield constituent structures for sentences. The extent to which these constraints are implicitly honored in text research is difficult to determine without a more exhaustive study of propositionalized texts. There are likely to be some diverging analyses, lists of propositions that are not likely to be supported by syntactic processes. To the extent this is true, the psychological reality of propositions, at least in their specific details, can be questioned.

To be clear: The empirical successes of propositionally based text analysis has been dramatic. There is a wealth of data demonstrating that text reading times and text recalls are well predicted by a theory that includes a propositional textbase. It is possible that this success has capitalized in part on approximations to psychological units provided by propositions. Perhaps success would be even more dramatic with propositions defined slightly differently, more in accord with grammar-informed parsing ideas.

We summarize the state of affairs this way: The analysis of propositions was important to advance research in text comprehension. There was little point in waiting around for someone to figure out where propositions came from. Syntactic analysis would have required some arbitrary decisions anyway. A good pragmatic approach was undertaken, the analysis of propositions became a fairly reliable enterprise, and text research flourished.

Propositions with Syntax

Interestingly, some of the recent research in text comprehension, especially Kintsch's recent work, gives an enlarged role to syntax. Kintsch has argued that syntactic structures can affect the importance, and hence the memory, of propositions, drawing on Gernsbacher's (Gernsbacher & Shroyer, 1989) experiments with definite reference and Givon's (1992) observations about the processing functions of grammatical devices. When the construction-integration model is syntax-enhanced by increasing the activation weights of propositions, the ability of that model to predict recall is improved (Kintsch, 1992). The question can no longer be whether syntax matters for text processing. The only question is how much work will be given to syntax. The use of a few selected syntactic devices to increase the power of the construction-integration model—for example, increasing activation for *this egg* relative to *an egg*—demonstrates only the tip of the iceberg. There is a whole wealth of syntax in text. Every single word has it.[4]

Consider in this context the force of some examples studied by McKoon, Ward, Ratcliff, and Sproat (1993, p. 61):

(3) *However, lately he's taken up deer hunting.*
(4) *However, lately he's taken up hunting deer.*

Both of these sentences would contain a proposition such as:

HUNT (he, Deer)

The difference between a gerundive nominal compound ("deer hunting") and a participle + object ("hunting deer") is completely lost to propositional analysis. The data, however, show some interesting differences in how the two sentences are processed. McKoon et al. found that the referent, "deer," was more accessible when initially mentioned in the participle + object ("hunting deer") construction than when initially mentioned in the gerundive nominal compound ("deer hunting") construction. How a discourse entity was introduced syntactically influenced how accessible the entity was for later reference.

The general point is that it does make a difference how you say things. *The baron freed the serfs* and *The serfs were freed by the baron* may be propositionally identical, but it has long been clear that the expression of the proposition one way rather than the other is motivated by discourse features assumed by the speaker/writer (Perfetti & Goldman, 1976). Moreover, the reader is sensitive to the form of expression. Readers not only remember how things are said, but their processing of current sentences depend on the expression of previous sentences about the same topic. Whether the propositional format loses something important about this is not clear. It may be reasonable to maintain that there are multiple levels of representation for the reader, one of which is blind to the form of information, dedicated to representing meaning, and one of which is able to remember how things were said.

---

[4]Individual words carry information about their suitability for syntactic structures—syntactic category information, syntactic argument information, and discourse-relevant syntactic information.

Conclusion

So far, we have suggested two things: First, syntax could be called on to do more in providing propositions. And, second, propositional representations are incomplete for the job of understanding texts. We do not endorse the more radical proposal that the level of propositions can be done away with altogether (Johnson-Laird, 1983). But it is worth noting that if there are three levels of information that readers use in text—syntactic, propositional, and situational—it is far from clear that the propositional one should be privileged. A level of narrowly construed text meaning independent of the levels below (syntax) and above (situational) seems odd in some ways. An interpreted syntactic level (not propositional, but lexical-syntactic) appears to be essential anyway. And so does an interpreted, language-free representation. The propositional is a level of representation that sticks close to the words of sentences but neither to their syntax nor to their implications. In fact it does not stick very close to the words either. Idioms are paraphrased down to some compatible meaning. The example we used in Sentence 2 about Lyle pushing Paris out of his mind would have to be recast into a predicate like "tried to forget". The literal meaning of pushing, which is tied closely to the syntax, is lost to text analysis. This is a significant loss to the extent that phrasing is more than a mere packaging for propositions. Nevertheless, we do not wish to overstate these problems. The form-free propositional level of representation has been quite useful and we assume it is approximating a functionally important level of text understanding. At minimum, however, this functional level can be enriched by analysis of sentence forms and some serious consideration of the functional consequences of these forms.

PARSING IN TEXTS

So where do propositions come from, besides heuristics and user's guides? Do we know enough about parsing to actually help text analysis? The question of how parsing works is a daunting one, and if there were a thorough answer, propositions would not be so mysterious. Indeed, we could run parsing algorithms instead of using intuition.

We want to address a softer question: How does parsing work as part of text processing? Short of parsing algorithms, are there some principles that can connect syntactic information to higher level text information? For that we turn to some of our own research.

The next section provides an informal account of how parsing operations might go on when a person is reading a text. Accordingly, we do not argue which of several parsing proposals is the best, nor do we try to review the empirical states of affairs. Suffice it to say that the situation is complex, with a growing convergence of evidence that syntactic parsing principles play a role, but that frequency-based decision rules at several levels also play a role. (For evidence related to parsing principles, see Frazier & Rayner, 1982, and Mitchell, 1989;

for evidence on the role of frequency, see Taraban & McClelland, 1988, and Tanenhaus, Carlson, & Trueswell, 1989.)

PARSING AND PROPOSITIONS

To examine how parsing provides propositions, consider Sentences 5 and 6. Beneath each sentence is a list of its propositions, as we would imagine them, based on various propositionalizing heuristics.

(5) *He dropped the book on the chair before leaving.*
1. DROPPED (He, Book)
2. GOAL (1, Chair)
3. LEAVE (He)
4. BEFORE (1, 3)

(6) *He dropped the book on the battle before leaving.*
1. DROPPED (He, Book)
2. ATTRIBUTE (Book, Battle)
3. LEAVE (He)
4. BEFORE (1, 3)

The propositional difference between these two sentences lies mainly in Proposition 2: For Sentence 5, this proposition expresses where the book was dropped—on the chair. In Sentence 6, this proposition specifies the kind of book. There is, however, a real question about whether Sentence 5 is properly analyzed.[5] The listing of propositions in Sentence 5 follows the conventions we believe most text analysis researchers would follow. In contrast to Sentence 5, however, we think that Proposition 1 has got to include the Goal argument itself: Either as DROPPED (He, Book, Chair) or, indirectly, as DROPPED (He, Book, GOAL). Notice that if Proposition 1 has no third argument, then there is not a proper scope for the BEFORE proposition. Accordingly, we believe the correct analysis is not the one in the listing for Sentence 5 but one that has the GOAL in Proposition 1.[6]

---

[5]One of our three experts constructed a three place predicate, as in DROPPED (he, book, chair), leading to an interpretation of the location as an argument of the verb. In contrast, the other two experts constructed a two place predicate, as in Sentence 5.

[6]We believe that a decision among these alternatives can be motivated if one can distinguish arguments from adjuncts. If chair is an argument, then it should be in Proposition 1. And there is no motivation for embedding an empty GOAL argument without the additional assumption that it is an optional argument. So a GOAL is indicated in the top level proposition, reflecting that in this particular case, there is going to be a GOAL expressed. By contrast, the thing dropped, the book, is an obligatory argument. So the only question for the proposition is the specification of the argument. Our suggestion is that it is exactly this kind of connection between syntax and semantics that ought to be part of text analysis.

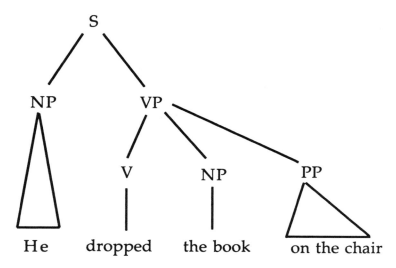

FIG. 2.3A. A tree structure parse for Sentence 5 showing a verb argument interpretation of the PP "on the chair."

If we are correct, there are additional differences between Sentences 5 and 6. It is not just the content of one of the arguments, but the richness of the propositions (more arguments in Proposition 1 for Sentence 5 than Sentence 6, and perhaps the number of propositions (one more in Sentence 6 than Sentence 5) that are different.

Now that we have struggled through the propositions using heuristics, let's see where we go using syntax instead. Parse trees for Sentences 5 and 6 are shown in Figs. 2.3A and 2.3B. These trees are final-parse representations. They show the result of parsing operations, not the intermediate steps. It is the steps toward the final product that are of interest in parsing. The central research question for parsing is how it is that one gets from a string of written or spoken words to representations such as those shown in Figs. 2.3A and 2.3B.

The syntactic difference between Sentences 5 and 6 is localized in the VP. For Sentence 5, the PP "on the chair" is attached directly to the VP. This represents its status as an argument of the verb *dropped*. It is equal, in its syntactic position, to *drop*'s other argument, "the book." In Fig. 2.3B the location of the PP is different. "On the battle" is attached to the noun phrase, not the VP. (And the NP "the book" is embedded under the same NP node.) Note that the entire NP is not "the book" but rather "the book on the battle."

An important fact emerges from this example: There is a mismatch between what counts as an argument in propositional analysis and what counts as an argument in syntactic analysis. For Sentence 6, in the propositional system, "the book" is an argument. (See Proposition 1.) But in the syntactic system, "the book" is not an argument. "The book on the battle," however, is an argument.

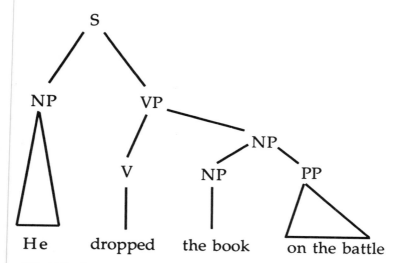

FIG. 2.3B. A tree structure parse for Sentence 6 showing a noun modifying reading of the PP "on the battle."

It is clear that the different meanings of the two sentences are roughly captured by their different propositions. But it is less clear whether the different configurational "meanings" of their syntactic structures are captured by the propositions. That depends on which propositions are claimed to be contained in the two sentences. And it is not clear whether the number of propositions is the same in the two cases. That too depends on which analysis one takes as correct, because on one analysis, Sentence 6 has one more proposition than Sentence 5. Notice that this is very important for text processing, because the number of propositions to be processed in one cycle is a key parameter in the text processing models (Kintsch, 1988; Kintsch & van Dijk, 1978). Finally, there is question about the decompositionality of meaning. The propositional system decomposes quite a bit, yielding smaller units of language, as when it gives "book" as an argument rather than "the book on the battle." The syntactic analysis allows a decomposition—"the book" is a constituent—but it does not allow this constituent to be an argument, because it only allows the entire (NP) to be attached to the (VP) as an argument.

The moral here is not that one ought to use the syntax to define propositions. Rather, it is that some interpretive principles are needed to get from the syntax to propositions. More generally, what is needed is a three-step system with principles defined at each level: Parsing Principles → Syntactic Structures → Interpretive Principles → Propositions → Integration Principles → Text Representation. Our impression is that text research has actually attended carefully to the integration principles and has also tried to attend to interpretive principles. There is considerable discussion in Kintsch (1974) and Turner and Green (1978) about these issues. But it may be that a new round of attention is due.

Before There Are Propositions

We turn now to the question of what is going on during the processing of a sentence
to yield propositions. We return to Sentences 5 and 6 and the corresponding
diagrams in Figs. 2.3A and 2.3B. The final structures shown in Figs. 2.3A and 2.3B
are different, as previously noted. But there is now ample evidence that there was
a point during processing when they were the same. In particular, part of the tree
shown in Fig. 2.3A for the "chair" sentence is temporarily built for the "battle"
sentence (Britt, Perfetti, Garrod, & Rayner, 1992; Ferreira & Clifton, 1986). The
reader gets temporarily "garden pathed" in the "battle" sentence.

Although garden path phenomena are well known, it is worthwhile to try to
lay out the details a bit, because we are then going to show how text features
can and cannot influence these details.

The key assumption is that readers and listeners attempt to attach every word,
as it is read or heard, to some preexisting configurational structure. This structure
does not have to be a parse tree, but a tree is a good representation of what the reader
is taking account of in this process. With the word "he," the reader begins to build
a sentence, constructing both the S node and the NP node dominated by S (the
subject NP). When the word "dropped" is encountered, its status as a verb causes
the NP to be "closed" and causes the VP to be built. "The book" is taken as a NP
and attached to the VP as an argument of the verb. The parsing problem comes in
the next operation: Instead of keeping the NP open, "on" is attached as a preposition,
opening a PP attached to the VP in the position of an argument of the verb. If the
next word is something like "chair," then this works fine, because "chair" could
serve as a goal argument for "dropped." But "battle" is a very poor argument, and,
when the reader realizes this, a repair of the parsing must be made. Figure 2.4
illustrates the representation at the point that "battle" is encountered. It is identical
to what the reader would have constructed for the "chair" sentence.

The reason for the misstep in the "battle" sentence is a matter of theoretical
preference. The most general account of all garden paths comes from Frazier's
(1979) minimal attachment theory, which says that the parser always makes the
simplest decision at each choice point. It never builds a node that it is not forced
to. On this account, the key misstep has occurred not on "battle" but earlier on "the
book." The parser has built the simple NP node there. It has not assumed it would
need an embedded NP node. There are alternative accounts for what happens in
such sentences (Perfetti, 1990; Taraban & McClelland, 1988), although none as
general as minimal attachment, which explains a wide range of attachment
phenomena. However, it is likely that any account will have to accommodate
frequency effects (Tanenhaus et al., 1989; Taraban & McClelland, 1988).

Evidence for this garden path effect comes from reading time data that show
sentences with PPs as NP modifiers ("dropped the book on the battle") take longer
to read in key regions compared with sentences with VP-attached PPs ("dropped
the book on the chair"). Readers either stumble over "the battle" immediately or

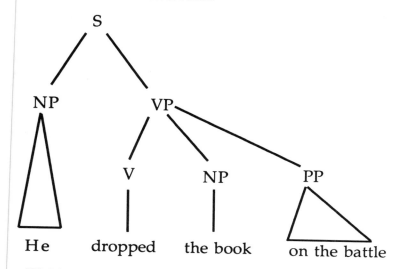

FIG. 2.4. A tree structure parse for Sentence 6 showing a verb argument reading of the PP "on the battle." Notice that the attachment is made directly to the VP rather than to an intermediate NP as in Fig. 2.3B.

stumble in the next phrase. These are usually small differences in reading time, and there is no reason to believe that the problems readers have reach consciousness on such sentences.

The existence of these effects is quite important for comprehensive accounts of text processing. These garden path effects are not so much about resolving structural ambiguities, although they do stimulate an account for this (e.g., Frazier & Rayner, 1982). They are more generally about confirming a level of syntactic processing in sentences. The propositions really do come from processing work that occurs *while* a reader reads a sentence. This level of syntactic analysis may be independent of some other processes, that is, there may be a level of autonomous syntax. In order to suggest that this level includes more than configurational information, we refer to it as the *syntactic-lexical* level of processing. It uses information about words and information about syntactic configurations. The question of whether this level can include other information is addressed in the next section. For now, the important empirical fact for text processing is that there is life before propositions. The reader cannot go from words to concepts to propositions. There is something else in between.

CAN A DISCOURSE MODEL HELP A PARSER?

So there is a level of syntactic-lexical processing that produces something like propositional representations. Is there an influence in the opposite direction? Is the syntactic-lexical level influenced by the reader's semantic representation of the text?

Empirical answers to this question are based on the following research strategy: Observe a garden-path effect on a sentence in isolation. This is evidence for a process controlled by syntactic-lexical principles. Then arrange a biasing text that requires the garden path (less preferred) reading. If the garden path effect is eliminated, that is, there is no reading time evidence that the syntactically preferred reading was considered when the discourse context supported the alternative reading, then conclude that information from the text representation can influence parsing. The general question here is autonomy: Is there an autonomous level of syntactic-lexical processing?

The empirical answers to this question are mixed. Some studies point to an affirmative answer (Altmann & Steedman, 1988; Crain & Steedman, 1985), others to a negative answer (Ferreira & Clifton, 1986; Rayner, Garrod, & Perfetti, 1992). Others draw a more complex picture, finding evidence for text influences for the PPs represented in Sentences 5 and 6, but not for reduced relative sentences such as Sentence 7 (Britt et al., 1992).

(7) *The coffee spilled on the rug was difficult to conceal.*

Sentence 7 produces a garden path beginning at the verb *spilled* as the reader first tries to interpret *spilled* as the main clause's active verb rather than as the past participle of a relative clause (cf. "The coffee that was spilled . . ."). Britt et al. found that context did not prevent this garden path, but context could prevent the kind of garden path indicated in Sentences 5 and 6. This differentiated pattern of results conforms to a model that makes distinctions between major and minor phrase boundaries and allows some tentative parsing decisions for the latter but not the former (Britt et al., 1992; Perfetti, 1990).

The complex pattern of results across different studies reflects differences in measurement and differences in the construction of text passages. We do not attempt to sort things out precisely. As a conservative reading of the situation we suggest this: Influences of text information on *online* parsing decisions are not especially easy to obtain.[7] This suggests that such influences may be limited, although the possibility that text materials must be constructed just-so to obtain such effects must be kept in mind.

Our goal here is to make the general case for why these effects might be limited. The heart of this case is that there is a limit on the kinds of information available. The locus of influences of text representation on syntactic-lexical processing is limited to the semantic argument structure and the checking of the discourse model for referents. The limitations of text information are in a mismatch between the kind of information a text representation has and the kind of information a parser needs.

---

[7]We emphasize "online." The question is whether there is a brief moment of processing in which the syntactic principle controls parsing even when it turns out to be incorrect. Fine-grain measures such as eye-fixations are best.

The parser must build constituents and attach them. For this it needs information about syntactic and lexical categories and constraints on constituent attachment. There are essentially two types of information needed: The first type is information about configuration constraints; for example, sentences in English have NP + VP structures; VPs have V + Complement structures; self-embedding is permitted, and so forth. These constraints reflect individuals' knowledge about the categorical and hierarchical structure of their language. We refer to these as *constituent processes*, and assume they operate according to a combination of top-down and bottom-up processes. Top-down processes are exemplified by rules that create S nodes, and immediately S-dominated NP and VP slots; bottom-up processes are syntactic triggers, as when a determiner (e.g., *the*) triggers the opening of a NP node.

The second type of information is lexical: knowledge that, to use our previous examples, *drop* is the kind of verb that must take a single argument, a theme (affected object), and may take a second argument, a goal; and *put* is the kind of verb that must take two arguments, a theme and a goal, and that the second argument in English is expressed by a PP. There is other lexical information involving semantic categories that may or may not be part of syntactic structure building, but is critical in filtering structures that might be incorrect.[8] The level of argument structure, however, is especially interesting because it sits on the semantic-syntactic interface. The arguments of propositional analysis should bear a close relationship to the arguments of syntactic analysis. (For linguistic treatments of this issue, see Grimshaw, 1990; Williams, 1981).

What Does a Text Model Have That Is Helpful?

Given that a parser needs configurational and lexical information, what does a text model have that would provide such information? Fig. 2.5 shows a rough sketch of the kind of information a text model might have.

There are two aspects of a text model: its *contents* and its *dynamics*. Its contents include *referents* or concepts introduced in the text, and *relations*, or propositions that connect referents and predicates. Its dynamics include a variety of discourse processes that control the availability of referents—*focus, contrastiveness, definiteness*, and perhaps others. These dynamic features are much more complex than Fig. 2.5 can indicate (see Grosz & Sidner, 1986). In text processing terms, these dynamic features can be said to influence the same

---

[8]For example, animacy considered as a semantic attribute of nouns is important in filtering out the active reading of a sentence that begins "The gun believed . . ." It is possible that the syntactic constituent builder tries to build such a structure and then rejects that structure on the basis of mismatching semantic attributes (guns are not the kinds of thing that can believe). If so, then garden paths may be avoided: "The gun believed to be the murder weapon was found in the trash." Evidence on this is mixed (Ferreira & Clifton, 1986; King & Just, 1991; Tanenhaus et al., 1989). Again the question is only one of timing. Such information must be used eventually.

Elements of a Discourse Model
I. Contents of the Model
A. Referents
- objects
- persons

B. Relations
- Propositions
- Relations between objects
- 2nd order propositions
- Relations between propositions

C. Discourse Features
- Knowledge of Source (Speaker/Writer)
- Discourse History

II. Dynamic Properties (The Camera Lens Model of Discourse)
A. Focus/Background (In Focus/Out of Focus)
- part of model momentarily in high activation

B. Contrastiveness (Zoom)
- of two equally focused elements, one is marked by the discourse

C. Definiteness (Resolution)
- Elements are individuated by discourse markers

FIG. 2.5.   Description of the type of information that might be contained in a text model.

activation parameter. For example, Kintsch's use of increased activation weight for the determiner "this" can be considered as using a "focus" dynamic.

Notice there are other facts about a text or a discourse that a reader can represent (i.e., *discourse features*). For example, knowledge about the source, about why it was written and so on, are clearly important for an enriched representation of the text. However, there is no reason to believe that such information can be useful to the parsing process.

Among the types of content information available from a text representation, the best candidate for information the parser can use is information about persons and objects mentioned in the text, that is, information about referents. To see how this information can be useful, consider again the garden path Sentence 8, related to Sentence 6 but clearly disambiguated by syntactic information. (Sentence 6, strictly speaking, is syntactically ambiguous.)

(8) *He dropped the book on the battle on the chair.*

The garden path here is a bit more dramatic than in Sentence 6, because if the reader has attached "on the battle" to the VP as an argument of "drop" there is no place left to attach "on the chair." This triggers a reanalysis, if one has not taken place already based on the unlikelihood of "battle" as an argument of "dropped."

To avoid the garden path, "on the battle" must be immediately attached as a modifier to "the book." This means that "on the battle" must be interpreted as a referring expression. Crain and Steedman (1985) pointed out that the interpretation of such phrases as referring expressions had to be motivated by referential uncertainty. If there were only one book in the discourse model, there would be no reason to refer to "the book on the battle"; "the book" would be sufficient. Only in a situation in which more than one book has been introduced would there be a reason for the extended modifier.

So here is a clear candidate for text-based information that can help parsing. If the text model includes two books, one on a battle and one on something else, then the parser may not close the NP started with "the book" until it gets enough information to secure the reference, which requires keeping the NP open while the modifying expression is processed. Britt et al. (1992) showed that such information is in fact used online. A garden path for those like Sentence 8 was completely eliminated when a discourse context preceding the target sentence mentioned two objects. This effect was found with both self-paced word-at-a-time reading and eye fixations.

We think there is a range of possibilities for referential information to influence parsing. Not only does the discourse model represent the number of referents, but it may represent sets of discourse objects in a rather precise set-relational manner (Ni & Crain, 1990). Referential information is something that the syntactic-lexical level can use, and it appears to do so. It can use it at least to overcome the relatively benign garden paths created by these examples of ambiguous PPs. For reduced relatives such as Sentence 7, evidence has been more difficult to find (Britt et al., 1992; Ferreira & Clifton, 1986; Rayner et al., 1992). (But see Altmann & Steedman, 1988; King & Just, 1991; Tanenhaus et al., 1989; for positive evidence based on sentence semantics, although not discourse.)

We see little beyond referential information that can be useful. The propositional content of the discourse model does not seem to be a likely source of information useful to the parser. We note, however, that this remains to be seen.

What about the dynamics of the discourse? Here, there is evidence that bringing a referent into focus can influence not parsing itself, but the process of repairing parsing errors. Rayner et al. (1992) presented garden path examples such as Sentence 9:

(9) *She decided to take the cheese from the farmer out of her bag to eat for lunch.*

The garden path in Sentence 9 involves the PP "from the farmer," which is first interpreted as an argument of "take" and attached to the VP. It must be reanalyzed to attach to the extended NP "the cheese from the farmer." Based on the assumption that referential presuppositions influence the pragmatics of a referring expression, one might expect that two kinds of cheese are necessary in order to use "the cheese from the farmer" as a referring expression. However, in this study the manipulation involved not the number of referents but the "focus" of the referent. In both conditions the prior text began thus: "Mary usually tried to do the week's shopping on a Saturday morning. So she started out by going down the road, where she bought some delicious cheese from the local farmer." In one condition (nonfocused) there were then two sentences prior to the target Sentence 9. In the focused condition, there was only one sentence prior to the target. Eye-fixation data showed that the garden path remained on the first analysis of the sentence in both conditions, that is, readers had trouble with the PP and the following disambiguating phrase ("out of her bag"). But there were fewer regressions, indicating fewer repairs, in the focus condition than in the nonfocus condition.

In summary, the reader's text model has important referential information and also dynamic information. Both have the potential to influence processes at the syntactic-lexical level. Referential information can affect the initial decision to use a PP as a noun modifier, avoiding a garden path. Referential focus can influence, at minimum, the speed with which referential information can be used to repair a momentary attachment error.

There are, however, some further constraints on the helpfulness of the text model. We think its information is less privileged than certain information from the lexicon that must be used in making configurational decisions.

THE LEXICAL INTERFACE

Recall the discussion of arguments. *Drop* and *put*, for example, differ in their argument structure, information found in the lexical representation on the verb. A verb's argument structure may affect parsing by making a phrase attachment optional or obligatory. For example, the verb *drop* can take a PP as a goal argument, as in Sentence 10a, but is also acceptable without a filled goal argument as in Sentence 10b. Compare this with the verb *put*, which requires a filled goal argument to be grammatical. Sentence 10c is grammatical, but Sentence 10d is not grammatical due to the unfilled goal argument. Thus we say that the goal is an optional argument of *drop* but is an obligatory argument of *put*.

(10a) He dropped the book on the chair.
(10b) He dropped the book.
(10c) He put the book on the chair.
(10d) *He put the book.

Britt (1991) examined whether a verb's preference for an obligatory or optional goal argument would influence the parser's decision to attach the PP as an argument of the verb. For example, will the parser initially interpret a potential goal PP as filling the argument role in Sentences 11c and 11d because the verb requires a goal argument? Is this preference less assertive when the verb permits but does not require the argument, as in Sentences 11a and 11b?

(11a) He dropped the book on the chair before leaving.
(11b) He dropped the book on the battle onto the chair.
(11c) He put the book on the chair before leaving.
(11d) He put the book on the battle onto the chair.

Britt had subjects read sentences with either a verb that preferred an optional goal argument (e.g., *drop*) or a verb that preferred an obligatory goal argument (e.g., *put*). For each verb type a pair of PPs was constructed. The first sentence of each pair was created to be successfully interpreted according to the parser's initial preference for building a structure, as in Sentences 11a and 11c. These sentences have a VP attachment reading where the preposition is interpreted as introducing a goal argument (e.g., the book ended up on the chair). Here the PP is attached as a goal argument and should be read faster. The second of each pair was written to ensure failure as a goal argument interpretation. For instance, the PP "on the battle" in Sentences 11b and 11d fails as a goal location. These sentences are considered NP-modifying sentences because they are best interpreted with a NP attachment reading where the preposition is interpreted as a topic of the NP (e.g., the book was about the battle).

These pairs of sentences were embedded in a discourse that supported the correct final interpretation. A discourse that supports the verb-argument reading is one that establishes a clearly unique referent for the NP "the book." When reading the NP, the subject successfully returns a unique referent and there is no need for further modifying. A discourse that supports the NP-modifying reading is one that creates more than one possible referent for the NP "the book." When reading the NP, the subject encounters an ambiguous referent for the NP "the book," and further modifying is needed to distinguish which book is being referred to. Attaching the PP as a NP-modifier will successfully create a unique NP.

Britt found that the NP-modifying sentences (11b and 11d) took longer to read than the verb-argument sentences for both verb types when preceded by a context that created a unique referent for the NP (see Fig. 2.6). This difference was expected because the single referent context is verb-argument supporting. The critical comparison is when the sentences follow a context that supports a NP-modifying reading. Is the failure to find a unique referent enough to eliminate the parser's initial preference for verb-argument attachments? Britt found that following NP-modifying context the NP-modifying sentences with obligatory verbs were again read slower than the verb-argument sentences. However, the NP-modifying sentences with optional verbs were not read faster than the verb-argument sentences. The need to secure a unique referent can influence initial attachments of a PP, but only when the argument is not required for grammaticality. Referential ambiguity does influence the reader's immediate assignment of an ambiguous PP, but only when allowed to do so by a verb's argument structure. When the verb requires a goal argument in order to be grammatical, the ambiguous PP is taken to fill that argument even if the target NP is referentially ambiguous.

Thus, one significant syntactic constraint on where propositions come from is the lexical restrictions available from the verb frame. This lexical information guides the syntactic interpretations of a sentence. A verb requiring a PP will assign the first PP, meeting certain restrictions, to that argument. Unless semantically or pragmatically anomalous, this analysis will be the final analysis of the sentence. Our claim is then that propositional predicates should map onto these syntactic arguments.

A MODEL FOR SENTENCE PARSING IN DISCOURSE

The experiments presented show that a sentence's discourse context can influence parsing. There are, however, considerable limits on this influence. The parser can use referents from the discourse to delay attachments, except in cases where

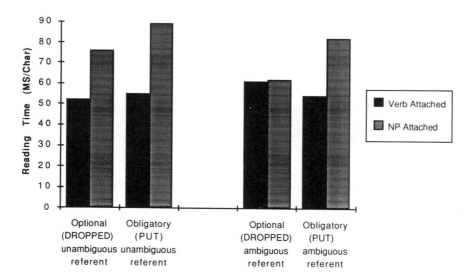

FIG. 2.6.   Results from Britt (1991) Experiment 2 showing the influence of verb argument structure and referential status on per character reading times of the critical segment ("the chair before" or "the battle onto") of the verb argument and noun modifying sentences.

a verb's argument structure requires the constituent as an argument. Our efforts to understand discourse influences in parsing have lead us to some speculation about how propositions are constructed.

The discoveries that both discourse information and verb argument structure influence parsing have led us to think about parsing in two stages. Perfetti (1990) and Britt (1991) described models that divide the work of parsing into phrase construction and argument filling. (See Abney, 1991, for a similar proposal.) These models propose that simple phrases, such as NPs and PPs, are constructed according to phrase structure rules and then they are attached to open noun or verb arguments. Phrases are opened by triggering features that are part of the syntactic information in the lexicon (e.g., determiners and prepositions) and are closed by encountering a new word that cannot be part of the current phrase (i.e., late closure). In our current model (Britt, Gabrys, & Perfetti, 1993), the decision to close a phrase also uses information about the referential ambiguity of a NP and whether an obligatory argument is waiting to be filled. Completed phrases are attached to the open arguments of VPs and perhaps some NPs. Arguments are filled when there is a match between a completed phrase and an open argument. Thus a decision about how to attach a PP is based on the argument structure information, the meaning of the preposition, and the referential status of the NP in the discourse context.

Propositions are created in the discourse model from completed NPs and filled argument frames. An EXIST proposition is created for each new NP and a predicate is created for each verb frame and PP. Referents for pronouns and definite NPs are obtained by an anaphoric search through the discourse model.

Table 2.1 provides an illustration of the operations of the model on Sentence 8. Reading the first word, *He*, causes a noun marker to be retrieved from the lexicon. In the constituent builder, this opens an NP and attaches the pronoun to the NP. In the argument filler, a sentence frame is opened because this is the first word of a new sentence. Because the word is a pronoun, a discourse model search is initiated that returns (or creates) a referent. The second word, *dropped*, retrieves a verb marker, which leads to the closing of the NP because a verb cannot be added to the NP. In the argument filler, the verb frame is retrieved and *He* is assigned as the agent of the verb. The third word *the* opens an NP. Because there are no new closed phrases, there are no new actions in the argument filler or the discourse model. Next, the fourth word *book* is added to the NP.

The fifth word *on*, is critical for the illustration of the parser's interaction with the discourse model. The preposition cannot be included in the NP (*the book*), so the NP is closed. In the discourse model, "the book" triggers a search for a referent. If the search returns a unique referent for "the book," the NP is closed and sent to the argument filler where it is attached as the object of the verb, *drop*. This will result in "the book" being understood as the object that was dropped, and the PP, once completed, will be understood as specifying the location of the book after it was dropped. If, however, the search fails to return a unique referent for "the book," a complex NP has to be created. The open PP

TABLE 2.1
Operations of the RI Parser on an NP Attached Sentence in
Two Referent Context for an Optional Argument

Lexical Access	Constituent Builder	Argument Filler	Discourse Model
He	Open NP_1		Find NP referent
	Attach $N-NP_1$		(1 retrieved)
dropped	Open VP	Assign NP_1-S	
		Assign VP-S	
the	Open NP_2		
	Attach $D-NP_2$		
book	Attach $N-NP_2$		
on	Open PP_1	Assign NP_2-VP	Find NP referent
	Attach $P-PP_1$		(2 retrieved)
the	Open NP_3		
	Attach $D-NP_3$		
battle	Attach $N-NP_3$		
onto	Open PP_2	Assign PP_1-NP_2	Find NP referent
	Attach $P-PP_2$		(1 retrieved)
	Attach NP_3-PP_1		

Note. "On the battle" is correctly assigned to NP "the book" as an NP modifier.

can then be attached to this complex NP, which then is attached as the object of the verb, as shown in Table 2.1. This will result in the interpretation that *the book on the battle* is the object that was dropped. Parsing proceeds in this manner until the sentence ends, at which point, the discourse model will contain referents for the NPs that have been constructed.

Although our work to date has been concerned with how a discourse model can provide information for a parser, we can begin to ask the reverse question, that is, how parsing can influence the construction of a discourse model. For example, parsing of simple NPs such as "the book" produces different referential objects than parsing complex NPs such as "the book on the battle." A later pronoun will pick out different referents from the discourse model in the two cases. Similarly, parses of two-argument verbs, such as *put*, produce different object relations than parses of single argument verbs, such as *drop*. The consequences of such differences are open to empirical test. Further work like that of McKoon et al. (1993) might suggest the discourse model consequences of parsing on the later activation of propositions.

CONCLUSION

Text research has flourished following Kintsch's (1974) ground-breaking work. The progress in text research was partly enabled by a pragmatic decision to ignore syntax. Semantics-before-syntax not only enabled rapid progress on theories of meaning representation, but also reflected the lack of well-motivated parsing principles. More recent work in text processes (Kintsch, 1992) reintroduces the importance of syntax, and, combined with progress in parsing research, presents an important opportunity for figuring out where propositions come from. More generally, we can look forward to learning more about the semantics-syntax interface in the understanding of sentences in texts.

ACKNOWLEDGMENTS

We would like to thank William K. Estes and Gareth L. Gabrys for their helpful comments on an earlier version of this chapter.

REFERENCES

Abney, S. P. (1991). Parsing by chunks. In R. C. Berwick, S. P. Abney, & C. Tenny (Eds.), *Principle-based parsing: Computation and psycholinguistics* (pp. 257–278). Boston: Kluwer Academic.

Altmann, G., & Steedman, M. (1988). Ambiguity, parsing strategies, and computational models. *Language and Cognitive Processes, 3*, 73–97.

Britt, M. A. (1991). *The role of referential uniqueness and argument structure in parsing prepositional phrases*. Unpublished doctoral dissertation, University of Pittsburgh.

Britt, M. A., Gabrys, G., & Perfetti, C. A. (1993). A restricted interactive model of parsing. In *Proceedings of the 15th Annual Conference of the Cognitive Science Society* (pp. 260–265). Hillsdale, NJ: Lawrence Erlbaum Associates.

Britt, M. A., Perfetti, C. A., Garrod, S., & Rayner, K. (1992). Parsing in discourse: Context effects and their limits. *Journal of Memory and Language, 31*, 293–314.

Crain, S., & Steedman, M. (1985). On not being led up the garden path: The use of context by the psychological syntax processor. In D. R. Dowty, L. Karttunen, & A. M. Zwicky (Eds.), *Natural language parsing: Psychological, computational, and theoretical perspectives* (pp. 320–358). Cambridge, England: Cambridge University Press.

Ferreira, F., & Clifton, C., Jr. (1986). The independence of syntactic processing. *Journal of Memory and Language, 25*, 348–368.

Frazier, L. (1979). *On comprehending sentences: Syntactic parsing strategies*. Bloomington, IN: Indiana University Linguistics Club.

Frazier, L., & Rayner, K. (1982). Making and correcting errors during sentence comprehension: Eye movements in the analysis of structurally ambiguous sentences. *Cognitive Psychology, 14*, 178–210.

Gernsbacher, M. A., & Shroyer, S. (1989). The Cacioppo use of the definite this in spoken narratives. *Memory and Cognition, 17*, 536–540.

Givon, T. (1992). The grammar of referential coherence as mental processing instructions. *Linguistics, 30*(1), 5–55.

Grimshaw, J. (1990). *Argument structure*. Cambridge, MA: MIT Press.

Grosz, B., & Sidner, C. (1986). Attention, intensions, and the structure of discourse. *Computational Linguistics, 12*, 175–204.

Johnson-Laird, P. N. (1983). *Mental models*. Cambridge, MA: Harvard University Press.

Kimball, J. (1973). Seven principles of surface structure parsing in natural language. *Cognition, 2*, 15–47.

King, J., & Just, M. A. (1991). Individual differences in syntactic processing. *Journal of Memory and Language, 30*, 580–602.

Kintsch, W. (1974). *The representation of meaning in memory.* Hillsdale, NJ: Lawrence Erlbaum Associates.

Kintsch, W. (1988). The role of knowledge in discourse processing: A construction-integration model. *Psychological Review, 95*, 163–182.

Kintsch, W. (1992). How readers construct situation models for stories: The role of syntactic cues and causal inferences. In A. F. Healy, S. M. Kosslyn, & R. M. Shiffrin (Eds.), *From learning processes to cognitive processes: Essays in honor of William K. Estes* (Vol. 2, pp. 261–278). Hillsdale, NJ: Lawrence Erlbaum Associates.

Kintsch, W., & van Dijk, T. A. (1978). Towards a model of text comprehension and production. *Psychological Review, 85*, 363–394.

McKoon, G., Ward, G., Ratcliff, R., & Sproat, R. (1993). Morphosyntactic and pragmatic factors affecting the accessibility of discourse entities. *Journal of Memory and Language, 32*, 56–75.

Mitchell, D. C. (1989). Verb guidance and other lexical effects in parsing. *Language and Cognitive Processes, 4*, SI123–154.

Ni, W., & Crain, S. (1990). *How to resolve structural ambiguities.* Paper presented at North East Linguistic Society, Pittsburgh, PA.

Perfetti, C. A. (1990). The cooperative language processors: Semantic influences in an autonomous syntax. In D. A. Balota, G. B. Flores d'Arcais, & K. Rayner (Eds.), *Comprehension processes in reading* (pp. 205–230). Hillsdale, NJ: Lawrence Erlbaum Associates.

Perfetti, C. A., & Goldman, S. R. (1976). Discourse memory and reading comprehension skill. *Journal of Verbal Learning and Verbal Behavior, 14*, 33–42.

Rayner, K., Garrod, S., & Perfetti, C. A. (1992). Discourse influences during parsing are delayed. *Cognition, 45*, 109–139.

Taraban, R., & McClelland, J. R. (1988). Constituent attachment and thematic role assignment in sentence processing: Influences of content-based expectations. *Journal of Memory and Language, 27*, 597–632.

Tanenhaus, M. K., Carlson, C., Trueswell, J. C. (1989). The role of thematic structures in interpretation and parsing. *Language and Cognitive Processes, 4*, SI77–104.

Turner, A., & Green, E. (1978). Construction and use of a propositional textbase. *JSAS Catalogue of Selected Documents in Psychology*, No. 1713.

Williams, E. (1981). Argument structures and morphology. *Linguistic Review, 1*, 81–114.

Chapter 3

A General Model of Classification and Memory Applied to Discourse Processing

W. K. Estes
Harvard University

This chapter approaches the topic of discourse comprehension from the perspective of general models of memory and cognition. Thus, I can best set the stage for discussion of some specific problems by giving a brief sketch of the evolution of current theory of discourse comprehension and production as viewed from my standpoint.

A series of notable milestones marks the development of models of text and discourse processing (henceforth, for brevity, just discourse processing) over the past two decades. First was the assumption that information gained from discourse is represented in memory in the form of propositions, introduced into general theories of memory by Anderson and Bower (1973) and Rumelhart, Lindsay, and Norman (1972), then quickly adapted to the interpretation of discourse comprehension by Kintsch (1974). Kintsch added the key idea that the propositions stored in memory during processing of a passage form a network structure in which connections between propositional nodes correspond to shared arguments. And for a period, research focused on testing the "reality" of propositional representations as distinguished from sentence memories (Kintsch, 1974; Kintsch & Glass, 1974) and the assumption that representations are accessed by search through the propositional network (McKoon & Ratcliff, 1980; Ratcliff & McKoon, 1978). The next major advance was the outline of a comprehensive model for the organization of propositional information at higher (macro) and lower (micro) levels with dominance relations representing the relative importance of particular propositions for comprehension (Kintsch & van Dijk, 1978; van Dijk & Kintsch, 1983). Most recently, we have seen the beginning of modeling of construction and recovery processes in terms of spreading activation (Kintsch, 1988) and weight adjustment (Kintsch, 1992).

The main emphasis throughout this series of developments has been on identifying learned strategies for comprehension: that is, selection of some items of information rather than others from a verbal input for representation in memory, and choice of a mode of encoding that makes the representation amenable to cognitive processing. The pioneering formulation of Kintsch (1974) was based on a model for episodic memory together with the conception that an individual's ability to form propositional networks is constrained by capacity limits on short-term memory, but in more recent years there have been few inputs from concurrent developments in general models of memory and memory processing. This chapter tries to bring out some resources that contemporary models may have to contribute to research and theory in the domain of discourse processing.

A COMPOSITE MEMORY MODEL
FOR CLASSIFICATION

I use as a vehicle an array-model for classification that derives from the category learning model of Medin and Schaffer (1978). At the heart of the model are two assumptions: Objects and events are encoded in memory in terms of their features, or attribute values; and access to memory is based on similarity relations between perceived and stored representations. The first assumption is shared with the episodic model of Kintsch (1974). It is the second assumption, including a particular algorithm for similarity computation, that distinguishes the array model from Kintsch's and also from other, more current, episodic memory models (e.g., Gillund & Shiffrin, 1984; Murdock, 1982; Ratcliff, 1978; Raaijmakers & Shiffrin, 1981). The model has been elaborated and applied to various classification tasks by many investigators, but I limit attention here to a simplified "core model" (Estes, 1986; 1994).

Categorization as a Constituent of Comprehension

To introduce the model in the context of discourse processing, I use the task of comprehending the following passage of text:

> Glass and plastic objects are alike in some respects but different in others. Among the objects present in a particular scene, a plastic water bottle is transparent, light, and pliant; a glass window is also transparent, but heavy and brittle; a glass vase is opaque, heavy, and brittle.

According to current models of discourse comprehension, the information given concerning the objects in the scene is embodied in three propositions, each of which has a predicate (the verb "to be," which is suppressed in my representation), and several arguments. In each case, one of the arguments is a noun (the name of an object) and the others are adjectives (property labels). Together, the propositional representations form a network in which the nodes corresponding to the first and second and the second and third propositions are close together, because of the shared arguments, and the nodes for the first and third propositions further apart, because they share no arguments.

Up to a point, the representation assumed in the array model is quite similar. Each object is represented by its combination of three features, and similarity relations among the representations correspond precisely to the distances among them in the propositional network based on argument overlap. In the propositional network, the first proposition in the passage plays the role of a macroproposition, which imposes a structure on the whole representation. In the array model, the terms "glass" and "plastic," which are arguments of the macroproposition, take on the role of category labels, and it is assumed that the information gained from processing the passage increases the learner's ability to classify objects as glass or plastic.

The memory representation in the array model after the learner has read the text passage once has the form illustrated in Table 3.1. The entries under Object are descriptions—in terms of feature combinations—of the objects mentioned in the passage, and entries in the right-hand part of the table signify that the bottle was mentioned once, with its category designated as Plastic, and the window and the vase were mentioned once each, with the category designated as Glass. (If the passage were studied more than once, all that would change in the array would be the frequencies entered for the Plastic and Glass categories.)

To show how similarity relations constitute the basis of processing of the array when the learner is prompted to interrogate memory in the course of a task,

TABLE 3.1
Categorization of Objects on the Basis of Learning from Text

Memory Array		
	Category	
Object	*Plastic*	*Glass*
Bottle: transparent, light, pliant	1	0
Window: transparent, heavy, brittle	0	1
Vase: opaque, heavy, brittle	0	1

Categorization Test
New Object: opaque, light, pliant   [Plastic or Glass?]

Similarity to Plastic $= s*1*1 = s$
Similarity to Glass $= s*s*s + 1*s*s = s^3 + s^2$

Probability (Plastic) $= s/(s + s^3 + s^2) = 1/(1 + s^2 + s)$
        If $s = .10$, Probability (Plastic) $= 1/(1 + .1 + .01) = .90$

the lower part of Table 3.1 exhibits a categorization test on which the learner is given a description of a new object—its features being opaque, light, and pliant—and is asked whether the object is more likely to be glass or plastic. The first step in generating an answer is to compute the similarity of the new object to each of those stored in the array by means of an algorithm termed the *product rule*. For this computation, the features are regarded as values of three binary-valued attributes. The similarity of any two patterns (object representations) is the product of their similarities on the three attributes, the similarity on any one attribute having a value of unity when there is a match and a value s (a parameter with a value between 0 and 1) when there is a mismatch. Thus, comparing the new object to the bottle, the similarity is $s * 1 * 1 = s$ (the asterisk signifying multiplication as in computer programs) because the objects differ on the first attribute but match on the other two. Similarly, the similarities of the new object to window and vase are s^3 and s^2, respectively. The total, "global" similarity of the new object to each category is the sum of its similarities to the stored representations in that category, namely s for Plastic and $s^3 + s^2$ for Glass, respectively. Finally, the probability that the learner assigns the new object to the category plastic is given by the total similarity of the object to that category divided by the sum of its similarities to both categories, that is,

$$s/(s + s^3 + s^2) = 1/(1 + s^2 + s).$$

If the value of s is small, the probability of categorizing the new object as Plastic is large; for example, as shown in Table 3.1, if s is equal to .10, the categorization probability is .90.

Pattern Completion

A valuable property of the array model is that the same memory array that provides the basis for categorization also can be interrogated to serve other cognitive functions (Estes, 1993). Consider, for example, pattern completion, a function that has been important in the development of discourse models (Kintsch, 1974). Suppose that a person who has read the Glass–Plastic passage and formed the memory array shown in Table 3.1 encounters in a continuation of the passage a partial description of a new object that is light and pliant. What is the probability that the person will infer that the object is transparent? To derive an answer from the model, we assume that the person computes the similarity of each of the possible completions—light, pliant, transparent and light, pliant, opaque—to the memory array, obtaining $1 + s + s^3$ and $s + s^2 + s^3$, respectively. The desired probability is, then the first of these similarities divided by the sum of the two, that is,

$$\text{Probability (transparent)} = (1 + s + s^3)/(1 + s + s^3 + s + s^2 + s^3).$$

It is easy to work out that this probability must be between .5 and 1, closer to 1 as s becomes smaller. For an intermediate value of s, say .5, the probability is .62. Thus, completing patterns by what might be termed probabilistic inference can be accounted for in terms of the model with no additional assumptions.

Recognition

Beyond the ability to classify objects, we might be interested in learners' performance if tested for recognition of the propositions corresponding to the stored representations. In terms of the array model, we view recognition simply as a special case of categorization in which the categories are New and Old rather than substantive categories like Plastic and Glass. To prepare for similarity computations on the example of Table 3.1, we need only reorganize the memory array in the manner shown in Table 3.2. We assume that as each proposition is abstracted from the text passage during processing, its memory representation is classified, not only as Plastic or Glass, but also as Old, or the equivalent, distinguishing it henceforth from propositions that are encoded for the first time on a recognition test and should be called New. In the memory array of Table 3.2, each of the propositions from Table 3.1 is entered with a frequency of 1 in the Old category. The only entry in the New category represents any background information the learner may have at the start of the experiment concerning the kind of stimuli that may occur, and it is assumed that any test object, new or old, has some average similarity, s_0, to the background representation.

TABLE 3.2
Recognition of Objects on the Basis of Learning from Text

	Memory Array	
		Category
Object	Old	New
Background		1
Bottle: transparent, light, pliant	1	
Window: transparent, heavy, brittle	1	
Vase: opaque, heavy, brittle	1	

Old–New Recognition Tests

    Old Object: transparent, light, pliant   [Old or New?]
Similarity to Old = $1 + s^2 + s^3$
Probability of Old Response = $(1 + s^2 + s^3)/(1 + s^2 + s^3 + s_0) = .83$
    New Object: opaque, light, pliant   [Old or New?]
Similarity to Old = $s + s^3 + s^2$
Probability of Old Response = $(s + s^3 + s^2)/(s + s^3 + s^2 + s_0) = .36$

Note. Computations assume $s = .10$ and $s_0 = .20$.

Predictions for typical Old/New recognition tests are shown at the bottom of Table 3.2. For a test with a description of a bottle (an Old object), similarity to the Old array is computed just as in the categorization examples, and probability of an Old response (a *hit* in the currently standard terminology of recognition research) is this similarity divided by this similarity plus similarity to the New category, and, as shown in Table 3.2, for the parameter values $s = .10$ and $s_0 = .20$, equals .83. For a test on a description of a rattle (a New object), a similar computation yields a probability of Old (a *false alarm*) equal to .36.

The difference between the hit and false alarm probabilities is due in great part to the fact that the Old proposition is included in the memory array, so its similarity to itself makes a large contribution to its total similarity to the Old array. The same would be true of tests on other combinations of old and new objects, but the specific predictions would depend on argument overlap between test and stored propositions, reflected in the array model by similarity relations. Suppose, for example, that a different new object was tested—say a paperweight having the features transparent, light, and brittle, and therefore sharing more arguments with propositions in the Old array than was the case for rattle. Similarity to the Old array would be $2s + s^2$, yielding a false alarm probability of .51 for the parameter values in this example.

One might choose to test for recognition by means of a forced-choice rather than an old–new test, for example, by presenting descriptions of vase and paperweight and asking which member of the pair occurred in the study passage. The probability of (correctly) choosing the vase is given by its similarity to the Old array divided by that value plus the similarity of paperweight to the Old array,

$$P(\text{Correct}) = (1 + s^3 + s)/(1 + s^3 + s + 2s + s^2) = .85.$$

Recall

When treating problems of discourse comprehension, one is often interested in recall rather than recognition. In this example, we might ask, for example, whether activation of the representation of bottle would be more likely to lead to recall of window or recall of vase. To predict the probability of recalling window, we compute the similarity of its representation to that of bottle, obtaining s^2, because there are mismatches on two attributes, and divide this quantity by the sum of the similarities of window and vase to bottle,

$$P(\text{window}) = s^2/(s^2 + s^3) = 1/(1 + s),$$

which, for the s value used previously equals .91. Qualitatively, the prediction on the basis of similarity agrees with the expectation we would draw from discourse theory on the basis of argument overlap; however, if an estimate of the value of s is available, the array model enables us to replace a qualitative with a quantitative prediction.

AN ANALYSIS OF PRIMING OF PROPOSITIONS
IN MEMORY FOR TEXT

To bring out a possible role for the array model in the analysis of text processing, I draw on a study by Guindon and Kintsch (1984) in which subjects read text paragraphs and then were tested for recognition of target words that had appeared in primary (macro) or secondary (micro) propositions of the text. A sample paragraph used in Guindon and Kintsch's Experiment 1 is:

> Extra powerful shoulders that could give a decathloner an advantage in throwing the discus and shot can slow him in the sprints and hurdles. Thus, he must try to keep tight tapered calves of a sprinter even as he builds up strong hands for throwing the discus, shot, and javelin, and a barrel chest to pump air for endurance. A decathloner must develop a well-rounded athletic body that avoids overspecialization. (p. 510)

The propositions into which this passage can be analyzed are more diverse in form than those of the Glass, Plastic example; however, we can prepare for applications of the array model by forming a predicted memory array of basically the same form as that shown in Table 3.2. In that table, the predicates of the propositions were redundant (all being instances of the verb *to be*) and therefore were omitted from the representation. In the Decathlon passage, both the predicate and the arguments of the propositions should be included in the representation, so the entries in the Old memory array take the following form:

has, decathloner, shoulder
give, decathloner, advantage
.
.
.
develop, decathloner, body
avoid, body, overspecialization.

The next to last item is the macroproposition of the passage and the others (including the omitted, intervening, entries) are micropropositions.

In the array representation, the macroproposition has no special distinction, unless it proves to be the proposition with the largest total similarity to the Old array. As in the previous, simpler, example, the total similarity of each proposition to the full Old array can be computed and forms the basis for predictions about recognition or recall. With plausible assumptions about similarities among predicates and arguments (which I do not go into in detail), the macroproposition does turn out to have the largest total similarity. I doubt this relation will hold in general, although the macroproposition will usually have one of the largest total similarities because of its argument overlap (or similarity) with many of the other propositions. I would expect the special status of the macroproposition to emerge during processing of the text passage rather than being dictated by structural considerations. In the discourse-processing models of Kintsch and his associates (Kintsch, 1974, 1988; Kintsch & van Dijk, 1978), it is assumed that the macroproposition of a passage generally undergoes more processing cycles than subsidiary propositions. In terms of the array model, more processing cycles would be translated into the storage of multiple representations of the macro-proposition in the memory array, owing to more recalls or rehearsals during processing. In my treatment of the Guindon and Kintsch (1984) experiment, I start with the simplifying assumption that all propositions are stored with single representations during processing, then consider the consequences of relaxing that assumption.

To set the stage for this analysis, the top of Table 3.3 provides a stripped-down paraphrase of the text passage of Guindon and Kintsch's Experiment 1 in the form of four propositions, the first three being micropropositions and the last one the macroproposition of the paragraph, drawn from the summary sentence at the end. Following Guindon and Kintsch's treatment, I list under Prime and Target the elements of each proposition that enters into the analysis, namely, the predicate and one argument. The entries under Frequency signify that, initially, I assume that a single representation of each proposition is stored in the Old memory array.

The reason for the designations Prime and Target is that Guindon and Kintsch were concerned with priming effects. It has been well established (Meyer & Schvaneveldt, 1971; Ratcliff & McKoon, 1978, 1981) that if two successive test

TABLE 3.3
Partial Propositional Representation of Text Passage Used by Guindon and
Kintsch (1984) and Format of Memory Tests

	Text	
Proposition Type	Prime and Target	Frequency
Macro	develop, body	1
Micro	build, hands	1
Micro	give, advantage	1
Micro	pump, air	1
	Tests	
Test Type	Word Pair	Similarity
Intact Macro	develop, body	$1 + 3s^2$
Intact Micro	build, hands	$1 + 3s^2$
Re-paired Micro	give, air	$2s + 2s^2$
New	contribute, family	$4s^2$

words come from the same proposition of a study passage, reaction time for a recognition response to the second word is shorter than if they come from different propositions (or if the first does not come from the passage). Guindon and Kintsch's interpretation, somewhat akin to that of Ratcliff and McKoon (1988), is that when perception of the first member of a pair (the prime) on a test activates a memorial unit that also includes the second member (the target), recognition of the target is facilitated. An interpretation in terms of the array model is similar up to a point, but differs in that the recognition response is assumed to depend, not only on activation of a memorial representation of the target, but also on the current state of the entire memory array, the most important aspect being similarity relations between both prime and target and other elements of the memory array. We can make this somewhat abstract characterization more concrete by working through some predictions of the array model for Guindon and Kintsch's study.

In the lower part of Table 3.3, I give word pairs used on typical recognition tests in that study, the first word of each pair being a prime and the second word a target. The Macro row gives the verb and object of the macroproposition of the text, the Micro row the verb and object of one of the micropropositions, the Different row the verb from one microproposition and the object from another, and the New row a verb and object neither of which had appeared in the text passage. On any test trial, subjects were presented with one of the test word pairs and indicated whether they recognized it as old (that is, as having appeared in the study passage) or thought it to be new. Guindon and Kintsch's data showed best recognition for intact macropropositions, with recognition poorer for intact and re-paired micropropositions. The latter two cases did not differ significantly, but the investigators suggest that the lack of an advantage for intact over re-paired micropropositions may have been an artifact of the way the passage was constructed.

Quantitative predictions for the recognition tests can be generated from the array model by the same computations that were illustrated for the Glass–Plastic example. Referring now to the lower part of Table 3.3, we compute the total similarity of each test pair to the Old array (shown under Prime and Target in the upper part of Table 3.3). Assuming, for simplicity, a single similarity value s for each mismatch between any two pairs with respect to either the predicate or the argument (prime or target), we obtain for the Intact Macro a sum of 1 (the similarity of develop, body to its own representation in the memory array) plus three entries of s^2, because the entry develop, body mismatches both components of each of the other entries in the memory array with respect to both components. The other similarities shown in the right-hand column of the Tests portion of the table are obtained similarly. The result of equal total similarities, and therefore equal predicted probabilities of correct responses to intact macro- and micropropositions is not in line with Guindon and Kintsch's data. The fault may lie with the simplifying assumption of equal weights (entries in the Frequency column of Table 3.3). As noted earlier, it would be expected that the macroproposition would receive more processing cycles (or rehearsals) than the microproposition. In Table 3.4, we see the result of assuming that the macroproposition receives one, two, or four processing cycles (columns R1, R2, and R4, respectively). The predicted percentages of Old responses, computed with the parameter values $s = .2$ and $s_0 = .2$, show that an advantage for the macroproposition over the microproposition appears in the R2 column and increases as the number of processing cycles for the macroproposition increases, whereas the difference between the intact and re-paired microproposition decreases. The predictions for measures of recognition accuracy (the d' measure of signal detectability theory) show similar trends.

In general, the predictions from the array model are qualitatively in line with those derived from the discourse-processing model. A potentially important difference is that the array model yields quantitative predictions, not only for the relationships studied by Guindon and Kintsch, but also for others that might be of interest, for example, recognition of the different test pairs as a function of degree of semantic similarity between arguments or of the length of the study passage.

The derivation of predictions regarding passage length can be explicated with the aid of Table 3.5. Let us assume that the text passage of Guindon and Kintsch (1984) is replaced with a passage that includes the four propositions listed in the upper part of Table 3.3 together with additional propositions, n in number, which have no argument overlap with the first four or with each other. Also, we assume that the macroproposition receives four processing cycles during reading of the text, so the memory array of Table 3.3 is replaced by the one shown in Table 3.5. The total similarities to the memory array computed for the test types of Table 3.3 are changed only by the addition of the term ns^2 (each test pair differing

TABLE 3.4
Theoretical Predictions for Test Types of Table 3.3

Test Type	Similarity		
Percent "Old"	R1	R2	R4
Intact Macro	85	91	95
Intact Micro	85	85	86
Re-paired Micro	71	72	75
New	44	50	58
Recognition Accuracy (d')			
Intact Macro	1.19	1.34	1.44
Intact Micro	1.19	1.04	.88
Re-paired Micro	.70	.58	.48

Note. Columns R1, R2, and R3 give predictions for cases when the Intact Macro received one, two, or three processing cycles and therefore had one, two, or three representations, respectively, stored in the memory array.

TABLE 3.5
Augmentation of Guindon and Kintsch (1984) Example with
Additional Unrelated Micropropositions
(Four Processing Cycles Assumed for Macroproposition)

	Old Memory Array	
Proposition Type	Features (Prime and Target)	Frequency
Macro	develop body	4
Micro	build hands	1
Micro	give advantage	1
Micro	pump air	1
Unrel. Micros.		n
	Tests	
Test Type	Word Pair	Similarity
Intact Macro	develop body	$4 + 3s^2 + ns^2$
Intact Micro	build hands	$1 + 6s^2 + ns^2$
Re-paired Micro	give air	$2s + 5s^2 + ns^2$
New	contribute family	$7s^2 + ns^2$

from each of the additional unrelated microproposition in both arguments and, therefore, having similarity s^2 to each). Using the new similarity expressions, we can now compute predicted probabilities of hits (correct Old responses) to each of the test types shown in Table 3.5 just as was done in generating Table 3.4. For values of n ranging from 0 to 20, these predictions are displayed in Fig. 3.1. Naturally, the predicted percentages of hits (correct old responses) to the intact macroproposition and microproposition increase with n, simply because of the growth in size of the memory to which total similarity of each is computed when we generate the prediction. But, for the same reason, percentages of old responses to the repaired microproposition, and even to new propositions, grow with n and converge toward the value for the intact microproposition as n becomes large. These trends do not, however, signify that accuracy of recognition of a proposition increases when it is imbedded in a larger memory array. If we pair the values shown in Fig. 3.1 for the macroproposition, intact microproposition, and re-paired microproposition with corresponding values for new propositions and compute the familiar measure of recognition accuracy, the d' index of signal detectability theory, we obtain the trends shown in Fig. 3.2, all of which decline uniformly as n increases. Thus, in the terminology of discourse processing, we must predict that accuracy of recognition of stored propositions will generally decline as a function of the length of the passage in which they occur, but so also will false recognitions of actually new propositions that are formed by recombining constituents of propositions that are present in the memory array (re-paired micropropositions).

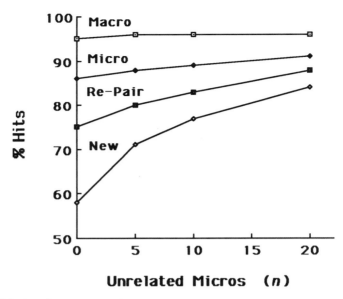

FIG. 3.1. Percentages of Old responses to different types of test items as a function of length of study passage, indexed by the number (*n*) of unrelated micropropositions added to the base passage represented in the upper portion of Table 3.3.

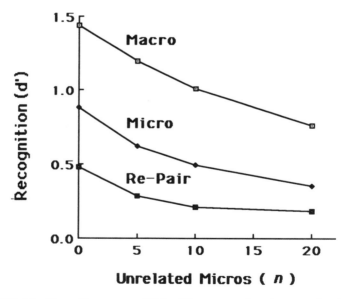

FIG. 3.2. Recognition accuracy (d′) for different types of test items as a function of length of study passage, indexed by the number (*n*) of unrelated micropropositions added to the base passage represented in the upper portion of Table 3.3.

CONCLUDING REMARKS

This examination of some aspects of discourse comprehension in the framework of a family of models of classification and memory suggests the following overall conception of the roles of different memory processes during discourse processing. In the early stages of comprehension of a text, the propositional constituents of the evolving textbase and situational model are represented in an array format as distinct items in a relatively short-term memory system. There they are retrievable by memory searches as needed for incorporation into larger units. However, as time passes, the propositional representations lose their individual identities, leaving only a residual, composite memory from which information is accessible by means of parallel similarity computations. The power of these computations comes into play when our attention shifts from problems of understanding how text is comprehended to predicting how the information gained by comprehension can be used later in new contexts.

It is not to be expected that general models of classification and composite memory will displace the more specific models of comprehension, but they may offer a valuable additional resource in the continuing development of models for all aspects of discourse processing.

ACKNOWLEDGMENTS

Preparation of this chapter was supported by Grant BNS 90-09001 from the National Science Foundation.

REFERENCES

Anderson, J. R., & Bower, G. H. (1973). *Human associative memory.* Washington, DC: Winston.

Estes, W. K. (1986). Array models for category learning. *Cognitive Psychology, 18,* 500–549.

Estes, W. K. (1993). Concepts, categories, and psychological science. *Psychological Science, 4,* 143–153.

Estes, W. K. (1994). *Classification and cognition.* New York: Oxford University Press.

Gillund, G., & Shiffrin, R. M. (1984). A retrieval model for both recognition and recall. *Psychological Review, 91,* 1–67.

Guindon, R., & Kintsch, W. (1984). Priming macropropositions: Evidence for the primacy of macropropositions in the memory for text. *Journal of Verbal Learning and Verbal Behavior, 23,* 508–518.

Kintsch, W. (1974). *The representation of meaning in memory.* Hillsdale, NJ: Lawrence Erlbaum Associates.

Kintsch, W. (1988). The role of knowledge in discourse comprehension: A construction-integration model. *Psychological Review, 95,* 163–182.

Kintsch, W. (1992). How readers construct situation models for stories: The role of syntactic cues and causal inferences. In A. F. Healy, S. M. Kosslyn, & R. M. Shiffrin (Eds.), *From Learning*

Processes to Cognitive Processes: Essays in honor of William K. Estes (Vol. 2, pp. 261–278). Hillsdale, NJ: Lawrence Erlbaum Associates.

Kintsch, W., & Glass, G. (1974). Effects of propositional structure upon sentence recall. In W. Kintsch (Ed.), *The representation of meaning in memory* (pp. 140–150). Hillsdale, NJ: Lawrence Erlbaum Associates.

Kintsch, W., & van Dijk, T. A. (1978). Towards a model of text comprehension and production. *Psychological Review, 85*, 363–394.

McKoon, G., & Ratcliff, R. (1980). Priming in item recognition: The organization of propositions in memory for text. *Journal of Verbal Learning and Verbal Behavior, 19*, 369–386.

Medin, D. L., & Schaffer, M. M. (1978). Context theory of classification learning. *Psychological Review, 85*, 207–238.

Meyer, D. E., & Schvaneveldt, R. W. (1971). Facilitation in recognizing pairs of words: Evidence of a dependence between retrieval operations. *Journal of Experimental Psychology, 90*, 227–234.

Murdock, B. B., Jr. (1982). A theory for the storage and retrieval of item and associative information. *Psychological Review, 89*, 609–626.

Raaijmakers, J. G. W., & Shiffrin, R. M. (1981). Search of associative memory. *Psychological Review, 88*, 93–134.

Ratcliff, R. (1978). A theory of memory retrieval. *Psychological Review, 85*, 59–108.

Ratcliff, R., & McKoon, G. (1978). Priming in item recognition: Evidence for the propositional structure of sentences. *Journal of Verbal Learning and Verbal Behavior, 17*, 403–417.

Ratcliff, R., & McKoon, G. (1981). Automatic and strategic priming in recognition. *Journal of Verbal Learning and Verbal Behavior, 20*, 204–215.

Ratcliff, R., & McKoon, G. (1988). A retrieval theory of priming in memory. *Psychological Review, 95*, 385–408.

Rumelhart, D. E., Lindsay, P. H., & Norman, D. A. (1972). A process model for long term memory. In E. Tulving & W. Donaldson (Eds.), *Organization of memory* (pp. 197–246). New York: Academic Press.

van Dijk, T. A., & Kintsch, W. (1983). *Strategies of Discourse Comprehension*. New York: Academic Press.

Chapter 4

Primacy and Recency in the Chunking Model

Bennet B. Murdock
University of Toronto

In episodic memory, primacy refers to superior performance (greater accuracy, shorter latency) on items at the beginning of the list, whereas recency refers to superior performance on items at the end of the list. These effects also show up in studies of discourse processing (Kintsch, 1974). Presumably they are telling us something important about human memory, and they should be of interest to those studying both discourse processing and episodic memory.

PRIMACY AND RECENCY

There is considerable evidence to show that in serial recall you find an extensive primacy effect, whereas in item recognition you get an extensive recency effect. With primacy, performance is best for items early in the list and declines as you go toward the end of the list. With recency, performance is best for items at the end of the list and declines as you go toward the beginning of the list.

The presentation format in these studies is the same in both cases. A short list of items is presented (or read) sequentially, and each list is tested immediately after presentation or following a short delay. Here, the analysis is restricted to single-trial studies; only a single presentation of the list is involved. The dependent variable is generally accuracy for recall but latency for item recognition because error rates for item recognition are generally too low to be very informative (Sternberg, 1969).

Illustrative data for serial recall are shown in Figs. 4.1 and 4.2. Figure 4.1 shows data from Parkinson (1972) where 8-item lists of letters were recalled

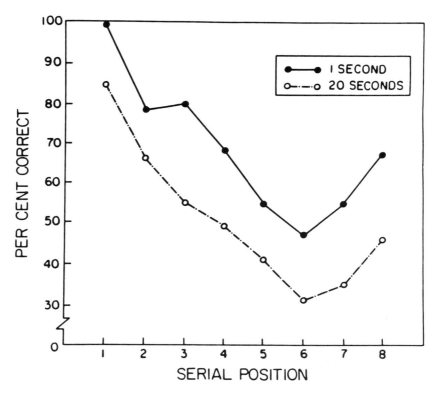

FIG. 4.1.   Serial recall of an 8-item list following a 1- or 20-sec delay. Data from Parkinson (1972).

either immediately or after 20 sec of interpolated shadowing. In both cases, there was extensive primacy extending over the first six serial positions and a small (but by no means atypical) recency effect over the last two serial positions.

Figure 4.2 shows data from Drewnowski and Murdock (1980) from a memory-span experiment. Subjects were tested individually and an adaptive procedure was used. After each correct recall list length was increased by one, but after each incorrect recall list length was decreased by one. The data were partitioned in terms of the number of words presented ("List length"); for auditory and visual presentation, there were monotonic primacy effects for all list lengths.[1]

Illustrative data for recognition are shown in Figs. 4.3 and 4.4. Figure 4.3 shows reaction time as a function of set size (m) on an immediate (right-hand

---

[1]The absence of a recency effect here reflects the particular method of scoring; see the original article for details.

Corballis (1967) tested recall and recognition (postcued) in the same experiment, but he only gave a few recall tests. Whereas his recognition data showed clear recency (and a 1-item primacy effect), all he reported for recall was that recall generally was in the forward order.

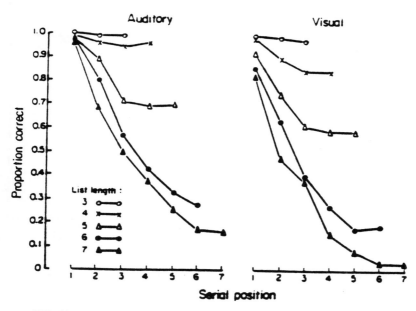

FIG. 4.2. Performance on a memory-span task with auditory or visual presentation. Data from Drewnowski and Murdock (1980).

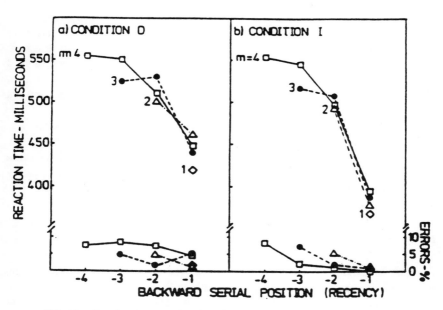

FIG. 4.3. Reaction times as a function of backward serial position in a Sternberg task for an immediate (I) or delayed (D) Condition. Data from Monsell (1978).

51

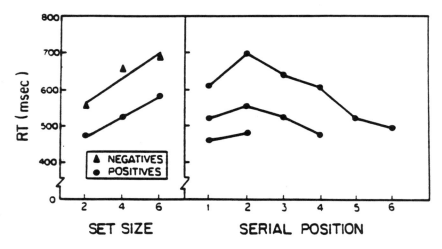

FIG. 4.4.   Reaction times as a function of serial position for 2-, 4-, and 6-item lists. Data from Murdock & Franklin (1984).

panel) and delayed (left-hand panel) test in a Sternberg task reported by Monsell (1978). For all set sizes and for both conditions there was a monotonic recency effect (reaction time increased so "strength" decreased) and, for both conditions, the different set-size functions lay on top of one another. Thus, older items were associated with longer latencies.

Figure 4.4 shows item-recognition data from Murdock and Franklin (1984). Subjects were instructed to remember both the items and their order and were randomly tested on one or the other. The figure shows the data from the item tests for set sizes 2, 4, and 6; here there is a monotonic recency effect with a (not uncommon) one-item primacy effect. If the curves were right-justified, then the recency portions (but not the primacy portions) would again more or less fall on top of one another.

Here then is a sample of the evidence for primacy in serial recall and recency in item recognition; what is the explanation for this difference? One might say this is evidence for two separate memory systems. But, instead, this interaction can be dealt with in terms of the chunking model, that part of TODAM (a theory of distributed associative memory) that deals with serial-order effects.

THE CHUNKING MODEL

The chunking model (Murdock, 1992) is designed to explain serial organization and chunking, but it should apply to serial recall and item recognition as well. Chunks function as higher order cognitive units, but they can be unpacked into their constituents (or their constituents can be recognized) as well. A single word would be a chunk. Although it consists of a number of letters, it functions as a unit—but we can spell it if we have to. At a higher level, a proposition probably functions as a unit, but again we can break it down into its constituents. The importance of chunks has been known ever since the seminal paper of Miller (1956).

This chapter presents a very brief technical account of the chunking model, followed by a nontechnical account. These sections are followed by an account of some simulations wherein an attempt is made to show that the model can mimic the primacy/recency pattern in the data just discussed.

Technical

Items are represented as random vectors (vectors of random variables) after Anderson (1973). The basic operations are convolution for associations, correlation for recall, and the dot product for item and association recognition. Items, pairs of items, or chunks can all be stored in a common memory vector so these operations characterize the storage and retrieval of item, associative, and serial-order information (Murdock, 1993).

Convolution and correlation are operations that combine two N-dimensional vectors into a single vector of dimension $2N - 1$ (for illustrations, see, e.g., Eich, 1985). The dot (or inner) product of two vectors is the comparison process; the result is a single number. The corresponding elements of the two vectors are multiplied and the cross products summed to get the result. All this is possible because of the initial representation assumption (i.e., that items are represented as random vectors). Although the details vary, this assumption is common in distributed-memory models (e.g., Humphreys, Bain, & Pike, 1989) and connectionist models (e.g., McClelland & Rumelhart, 1985).

For the chunking model, multiple convolutions, n-grams, and chunks are needed. For items A and B, $\mathbf{a} * \mathbf{b}$ denotes a two-way convolution ($\mathbf{a}$ and $\mathbf{b}$ are hypothetical item vectors corresponding to the A and B items), $\mathbf{a} * \mathbf{b} * \mathbf{c}$ would denote a three-way convolution, $\mathbf{a} * \mathbf{b} * \mathbf{c} * \mathbf{d}$ a four-way convolution, so an n-way multiple convolution is just the convolution of n items. An n-way multiple convolution is still a vector, whereas in a matrix or connectionist model that uses outer products an n-way outer product is no longer a vector or a matrix but a higher-order entity with Nn elements.

An n-gram is the n-way autoconvolution of the sum of n item vectors. If $G(n)$ denotes an n-gram, $\mathbf{f}_i$ is the i-th item vector, and α is the forgetting parameter, $0 \le \alpha \le 1.0$, then

$$\mathbf{G}(n) = (\sum_{i=1}^{n} \alpha_i \mathbf{f}_i)^{*n}$$

where the "$*n$" notation denotes an n-way autoconvolution. That is, $\mathbf{f}^{*n} = \mathbf{f} * \mathbf{f} * \ldots * \mathbf{f}$ (n times).

A chunk is defined as the sum of n-grams 1 to n. Thus, if $C(n)$ denotes a chunks size n then

$$C(n) = \sum_{i=1}^{n} G(i) = \sum_{i=1}^{n} (\sum_{j=1}^{i} \alpha_j f_j)^{*i}$$

A chunk is still a vector because it is composed of the sum of n-grams that are themselves vectors.

Retrieval works by the filter principle. The filter principle says that, if we have a multiple convolution of n items and a second multiple convolution composed of a subset of m of these items, then correlating the latter with the former retrieves the remainder. Specifically, if we use X to symbolize multiple convolution (like Σ for multiple summation) then

$$\underset{i=1}{\overset{m}{X}} f_i \quad \# \quad \underset{i=1}{\overset{n}{X}} f_i \quad = \quad \underset{i=m+1}{\overset{n}{X}} f'_i$$

where the prime (i.e., f') denotes an approximation.

If there is a chunk (the sum of n-grams) the delta vector (a "unity" vector) retrieves the first item, the first item retrieves the second item, the convolution of the first two items retrieves the third item, and so on. This works because the chunk consists of an engram ($n = 1$), a digram ($n = 2$), a trigram ($n = 3$), and so on, and at each step the only items retrieved are single items (Murdock, 1992).

These operations go on in *working memory*, a system of a small number of registers designed for vector processing. The place of working memory in the system architecture is shown in Fig. 4.5 along with the perceptual (P), response (R), and "query" (Q) system. The P-, Q-, and R-systems, in conjunction with working memory, map inputs into outputs. Only the Q system and working memory are modeled by TODAM.

Nontechnical

Items can be represented as a list of features, which is hardly a novel idea (e.g., Bower, 1967; Flexser & Tulving, 1978; Underwood, 1969; Wickens, 1972). An association is a "holistic entity" (e.g., Asch, 1969; Rock & Ceraso, 1964) or blend of two items, not a link or a connection between two distinct nodes. Multiple associations are composites of three or more items, still a "holistic entity."[2]

N-grams can be thought of in a simple algebraic way. For a list A, B, C, D, ... an engram would be a, a digram would be $(a + b)^2$, a trigram would be

---

[2]After a mathematical psychology meeting here in Boulder in 1983, I asked Walter whether a proposition consisted of three pairwise associations or one three-way association. He unhesitatingly selected the latter, so perhaps that was the real start of the chunking model.

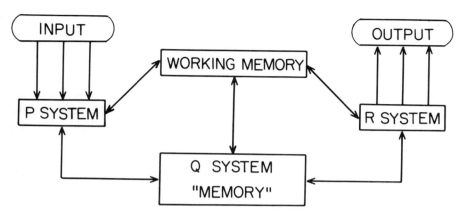

FIG. 4.5. System architecture for the chunking model, which shows the relations between the perceptual (P), Query (Q), and Response (R) system and working memory. Figure 2 from Murdock (1983).

$(a + b + c)^3$, and so forth. Thus, instead of autoconvolutions of sums of item vectors, n-grams can be thought of as the n-th power of the sum of n items.

This analogy does not hold at the microlevel (i.e., the attributes themselves), but it does make it easy to understand and remember the components of n-grams. Thus, in expanded form an engram is simply a, a digram is $a^2 + b^2 + 2ab$, a trigram is $a^3 + b^3 + c^3 + 3(a^2b + a^2c + ab^2 + b^2c + ac^2 + bc^2) + 6abc$, and so on. These components are what underlie recall and recognition.

The forgetting parameter α operates on items within n-grams and on n-grams within chunks. For items within n-grams, if the sum of the first j items is $\mathbf{F}_j$, then

$$\mathbf{F}_j = \alpha\mathbf{F}_{j-1} + \mathbf{f}_j$$

Thus, an n-gram would be a, a digram would be $(a\alpha + b)^2$, a trigram would be $(\alpha^2a + \alpha b + c)^3$, and so forth. For n-grams within chunks,

$$\mathbf{C}_j = \alpha\mathbf{C}_{j-1} + \mathbf{G}_j$$

so this implies $\mathbf{C}(1) = a$, $\mathbf{C}(2) = \alpha a + (\alpha a + b)^2$, $\mathbf{C}(3) = \alpha^2a + \alpha(\alpha a + b)^2 + (\alpha^2a + \alpha b + c)^3$, and so on.

Why does α operate on items and n-grams in working memory? It prevents saturation. In a distributed-memory model, you cannot keep adding things without a compensating "subtraction" (attenuation) or you will soon run into overflow problems. There has always been a forgetting parameter in TODAM so the same logic must apply to working memory as well. In a way, α is a modification of the displacement notion of the buffer model of Atkinson and Shiffrin (1968). To say one item displaces another would be tantamount to saying $\alpha = 0$, but if $\alpha > 0$ then the prior item is attenuated but the new item is superimposed.

For recall, the filter principle can be thought of as being like division following multiplication. If a is divided by one, we get a. If ab is divided by a we get b, if abc is divided by ab we get c, and so forth. In a sense, convolution is like multiplication and correlation is like division. However, there is an important difference; with multiplication and division we get $a, b, c, \ldots$, whereas with convolution and correlation we get $a', b', c', \ldots$ (i.e., approximations, not exact results). This poses a problem.

For serial recall, each retrieved item is combined (by convolution) with all items retrieved to date in order to form the next retrieval. What do we plug in, a or a'? b or b'? c or c'? This question is answered when the simulations are presented.

How does recognition work? If you work out the details of a chunking-building routine, you will see that you need the sum of the n items (technically, $\sum_{i=1}^{n} \alpha_i \mathbf{f}_i$, where $\alpha_i = \alpha^{n-i}$) in order to form $\mathbf{G}(n)$, the highest order n-gram in the chunk. When the chunk is formed, this term (summation) can be found in one of the registers in working memory (Murdock, 1992). Thus, for item recognition, all you have to do is compute the dot product of the probe item with this particular register in working memory and you have all the necessary ingredients for a standard signal-detection analysis of recognition memory. That is, the old- and new-item means and variances can be computed (or obtained from the simulations) from which you can obtain d' values (for each serial position at each list length) to compare with experimental data.

The critical reader may have noted that there is more going on here than I have described. That is, there are more terms in n-grams and chunks than the particular multiple convolution you need to retrieve the next item. Some of this is noise and can be disregarded. More correctly, it increases the variance but does not affect the means; this comes through in the simulations. However, some retrieval components are not noise and they pose problems for deblurring (i.e., mapping a' into a, b' into b, etc.). We return to this point in the next section where the simulations are described.

SIMULATIONS

Procedure

The independent variable in these simulations was set size, and each different set size constituted a single chunk. Because set size ranged from one to seven, we had $\mathbf{C}(1)$, $\mathbf{C}(2)$, $\mathbf{C}(3)$, ..., $\mathbf{C}(7)$. Each chunk was formed in working memory using the flowchart shown in Fig. 10.1 of Murdock (1992). That is, for each set size, we set up the requisite number of item vectors, formed the n-grams, and added them together to form the chunk. On each replication a single chunk was formed and then we tested for recall and recognition. This too was all done in working memory.

There are four parameters in the model: N, the number of features in each item vector, α, the working memory forgetting parameter, p, the encoding probability (the proportion of features in each item vector that were actually encoded in the n-grams),[3] and ρ, the interitem similarity. The values of the parameters we used in the simulation were $N = 229$, $\alpha = .8$, $p = .5$, and $\rho = 0$. These parameter values were selected on the basis of previous work (Murdock, 1993) and many pilot runs; they are reasonable but by no means necessarily optimal.[4]

We have found that, for any but the smallest chunks, normalization is essential to prevent the simulation from blowing up. We used scale factors for n-grams and chunks that would normalize them to 1.0 had p been 1.0, and we also used a retrieval scale factor as well. For further details, see Murdock (1993).

For recall, we used the procedure already described. Starting with the delta vector, we used (the multiple convolution of) the items recalled to date as the retrieval cue for the next item. Scoring was by the best match. We computed the resemblance (similarity) of the retrieved information to each of the list items and assumed the item with the highest dot-product value was the item recalled.[5] With large N the possibility of a tie was negligible, but if all dot-product values were negative we scored an omission.

We used the list item as the plug-in for the next retrieval cue if the best match was the correct item; otherwise we used whatever had been retrieved. This could flip back and forth, so even if there was an error or an omission we could get back on track (i.e., recall later items). A clean-up operation was used before scoring; all items recalled or retrieved to date were subtracted from the retrieved information before the scoring. (One of the registers in working memory accumulated the retrievals.) This clean-up operation served to reduce (though not eliminate) the recall of items previously recalled and so implemented a sampling-without-replacement scheme. However, in the scoring algorithm all list items were always potential candidates for the best match, so we hope that the chunking model is not vulnerable to the problems noted by Mewhort, Popham, and James (1994) and Nairne and Neath (1994) for the chaining model of Lewandowsky and Murdock (1989).

For recognition, for each set size we probed each serial position and used a new-item probe as well. Each probe item (old or new) was compared by means

---

[3]This is necessary for learning to occur with repetition; see Murdock and Lamon (1988).

[4]If ρ, the interitem similarity, is greater than zero, then the noise level increases so accuracy decreases but the general pattern of the results is not affected.

[5]This is a scoring algorithm only, and we do not assume all list items are available in memory for a direct comparison. For a process account we would need a deblurring network, but we do not model the R system any more than we model the P system.

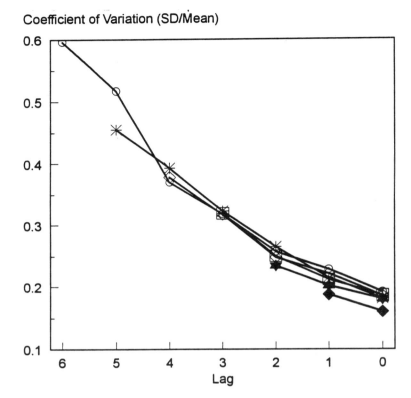

FIG. 4.6.   Coefficient of variation (SD/Mean) as a function of lag from a simulation
of the chunking model.

of the dot product with the register in working memory that contained the summed
item information used to form the highest-order n-gram in the chunk. The dot
product is a measure of strength or familiarity, and we can sum these values
over replications to get the old- and new-item means and variances we need for
a d' analysis. There were 500 replications of the complete design, which took
about 4 days to run on a SPARC2.

Results

The recognition results are shown in Figs. 4.6 and 4.7. Figure 4.6 shows the
coefficient of variation (standard deviation over the mean) for each lag in each
set size, where lag is the number of items from the end of the list. Figure 4.7
shows d' for each lag in each set size where d' is the old-item mean divided by
the square root of the average of the old- and new-item variances (the old-item

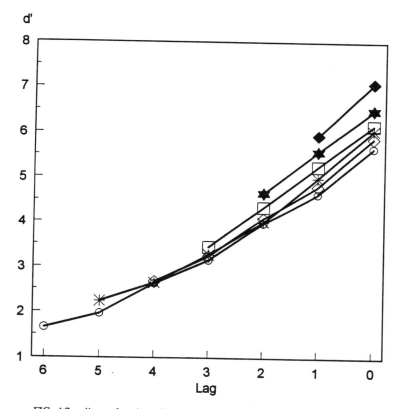

FIG. 4.7.   d′ as a function of lag from a simulation of the chunking model.

variance for that serial position). By using lag as the independent variable we mimic Figure 4.3 so the curves are right-justified.

As can be seen, all the curves show pure recency and they essentially fall on top of one another. Thus, except for the absence of a primacy effect (Fig. 4.4) they show exactly the same pattern of results as Figs. 4.3 and 4.4.[6] Of course, these data are "strength" values and Figs. 4.3 and 4.4 are latencies, so we need some strength-to-latency mapping. However, these results imply that a rather simple (possibly linear) strength-to-latency mapping might suffice.

In a way, these results are not too surprising. After all, α almost guarantees a recency effect. That is, if the memory vector (or a register in working memory) is decremented by α every time a new item is presented, the last item will be at full strength and the strength of previous items will fall off proportionally to the

---

[6]We can get a 1-item primacy effect if we also correlate the probe item with the chunk because the chunk always includes the first item. However, for these parameter values this primacy effect is much larger than it should be.

Recall Probability

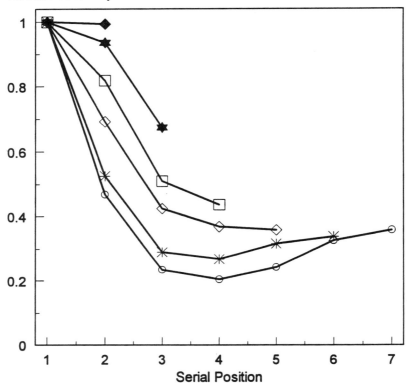

FIG. 4.8. Probability of recall as a function of serial position for lists of 1–7 items from a simulation of the chunking model.

distance from the end of the list. However, it is reassuring to see how clearly this effect emerges considering all the information in the chunk. Still, the real question is recall; what do the serial-position curves for correct recall look like?

The recall data are shown in Fig. 4.8, separately for each list length. As can be seen, performance on the first item is always perfect but the curves fan out from there. At all subsequent serial positions, recall probability is inversely proportional to list length, the same pattern that was shown in Fig. 4.2. There is a slight recency effect for the two longest lists (6 and 7 items), but not quite as sharp as in Fig. 4.1. However, it is absent as often as it is present in the many simulations that we have done, so it is not a consistent effect. Qualitatively at least these simulation results seem to be in good agreement with the experimental data shown in Fig. 4.2.

However, further analyses of these data revealed two problems. First, Lee and Estes (1977) found that, in a Brown-Peterson paradigm, intralist intrusions show symmetric distance functions where a distance function is the distance (if any) that a recalled item has migrated from its original position (see also Nairne, 1990). However, analyses of these simulation data show no such pattern. (The intrusions generally show recency effects but not symmetry.) Of course, no interpolated activity preceded recall, but there is still no particular reason why interpolation should change things.

The second problem is the conditional probability functions. In serial recall, if you plot the probability that Item i is recalled as a function of whether or not Item $i - 1$ is recalled, the curves steadily diverge until you reach the end of the list, but then the curves come together and the probability that the last item is correctly recalled is independent of whether or not the next-to-last item had been recalled (Murdock, 1968).[7] The simulation data show the divergence pattern, but they show no sign of coming together as they should. A second (backward) pass through the list might give the desired result, but this was not implemented in the simulations.

DISCUSSION

Kintsch and Welsch (1991) showed that the construction–integration model can handle a primacy–recency interaction reported by Gernsbacher, Hargreaves, and Beeman (1989). This interaction occurs in recognition memory for sentences where there is a recency effect on an immediate test but a primacy effect on a delayed test. We have shown here that the chunking model predicts a recency effect on an immediate recognition test. If a recall-like process mediated recognition performance on a delayed test, then the chunking model too would predict this interaction. This is the same explanation of the interaction suggested by Kintsch and Welsch (1991).

As it has been presented here, the chunking model deals with unrelated items but, as is well known, propositions are the building blocks in discourse processing (Kintsch, 1974). But perhaps a proposition is only a special kind of a chunk; in the simplest case, a relation (R) and several arguments (say a and b). But order information must be preserved in a proposition (aRb is not the same as bRa). Just as we can unpack a chunk into its constituents or use it as a higher order unit, so propositions in connected discourse seem to have similar properties. As I have argued before (e.g., Murdock, 1993), there are provocative parallels between chunks and propositions, and the chunking model might tell us something about how propositions are represented and stored in memory.

What implications does this have for discourse processing and text comprehension? If a proposition were represented as a chunk as formulated by the chunking model, then it in turn could serve as a higher order unit in more complex

---

[7]McDowd and Madigan (1991) found independence for auditory presentation but dependence for visual presentation, so the effect is apparently modality dependent.

processing. Then we would have to concern ourselves with how argument repetition or predication could lead to text comprehension. This would also necessitate consideration of the interaction between episodic and semantic memory as in Kintsch's construction-integration model (Kintsch, 1988).

In summary, this chapter has attempted to show that primacy and recency are salient aspects of serial recall and item recognition, respectively. The chunking model uses summed n-grams to form a chunk and different retrieval operations for recall and recognition. The simulation results show that the model seems to capture the main features of the data, but there are still a few rough edges.

ACKNOWLEDGMENTS

This reaearch was supported by Grant APA 146 from the Natural Sciences and Engineering Research Council of Canada. I would like to thank Mike Kahana and an anonymous reviewer for helpful comments.

REFERENCES

Anderson, J. A. (1973). A theory for the recognition of items from short memorized lists. *Psychological Review, 80,* 417–438.

Asch, S. E. (1969). A reformulation of the problem of associations. *American Psychologist, 24,* 92–102.

Atkinson, R. C., & Shiffrin, R. M. (1968). Human memory: A proposed system and its control processes. In K. W. Spence & J. T. Spence (Eds.), *The psychology of learning and motivation: Advances in research and theory* (Vol. 2, pp. 89–195). New York: Academic Press.

Bower, G. H. (1967). A multicomponent theory of the memory trace. In K. W. Spence & J. T. Spence (Eds.), *The psychology of learning and motivations: Advances in research and theory* (Vol. 1, pp. 229–325). New York: Academic Press.

Corballis, M. C. (1967). Serial order in recognition and recall. *Journal of Experimental Psychology, 74,* 99–105.

Drewnowski, A., & Murdock, B. B. (1980). The role of auditory features in memory span for words. *Journal of Experimental Psychology: Human Learning and Memory, 6,* 319–332.

Eich, J. M. (1985). Levels of processing, encoding specificity, elaboration, and CHARM. *Psychological Review, 92,* 1–38.

Flexser, A. J., & Tulving. E. (1978). Retrieval independence in recognition and recall. *Psychological Review, 85,* 153–171.

Gernsbacher, M. A., Hargreaves, D. J., & Beeman, M. (1989). Building and accessing clausal representations: The advantage of first mention versus the advantage of clause recency. *Journal of Memory and Language, 28,* 735–755.

Humphreys, M. S., Bain, J. D., & Pike, R. (1989). Different ways to cue a coherent memory system: A theory for episodic, semantic, and procedural tasks. *Psychological Review, 96,* 208–233.

Kintsch, W. (1974). *The representation of meaning in memory.* Hillsdale, NJ: Lawrence Erlbaum Associates.

Kintsch, W. (1988). The use of knowledge in discourse processing: A construction-integration model. *Psychological Review, 95,* 163–182.

Kintsch, W., & Welsch, D. M. (1991). The construction-integration model: A framework for studying memory for text. In W. E. Hockley & S. Lewandowsky (Eds.), *Relating theory and data: Essay on human memory in honor of Bennet B. Murdock* (pp. 367–386). Hillsdale, NJ: Lawrence Erlbaum Associates.

Lee, C. L., & Estes, W. K. (1977). Order and position in primary memory for letter strings. *Journal of Verbal Learning and Verbal Behavior, 16,* 395–418.

Lewandowsky, S., & Murdock, B. B. (1989). Memory for serial order. *Psychological Review, 96,* 25–57.

McClelland, J. L., & Rumelhart, D. E. (1985). Distributed memory and the representation of general and specific information. *Journal of Experimental Psychology: General, 114,* 159–188.

McDowd, J., & Madigan, S. (1991). Ineffectiveness of visual distinctiveness in enhancing immediate recall. *Memory and Cognition, 19,* 371–377.

Mewhort, D. J. K., Popham, D., & James, G. (1994). On serial recall: A critique of chaining in TODAM. *Psychological Review, 101,* 534–538.

Miller, G. A. (1956). The magical number seven, plus or minus two: Some limits on our capacity for processing information. *Psychological Review, 63,* 81–96.

Monsell, S. (1978). Recency, immediate recognition memory, and reaction time. *Cognitive Psychology, 10,* 465–501.

Murdock, B. B. (1968). Serial order effects in short-term memory. *Journal of Experimental Psychology Monograph Supplement, Part 2, 76,* 1–15.

Murdock, B. B. (1983). A distributed memory model for serial-order information. *Psychological Review, 90,* 316–338.

Murdock, B. B. (1992). Serial organization in a distributed memory model. In A. F. Healy, S. M. Kosslyn, & R. M. Shiffrin (Eds.), *From learning theory to connectionist theory: Essays in honor of William K. Estes* (Vol. 1, pp. 201–225). Hillsdale, NJ: Lawrence Erlbaum Associates.

Murdock, B. B. (1993). TODAM2: A model for the storage and retrieval of item, associative, and serial-order information. *Psychological Review, 100,* 183–203.

Murdock, B. B., & Franklin, P. E. (1984). Associative and serial-order information: Different modes of operation? *Memory & Cognition, 12,* 243–249.

Murdock, B. B., & Lamon, M. (1988). The replacement effect: Repeating some items while replacing others. *Memory and Cognition, 16,* 91–101.

Nairne, J. S. (1990). Similarity and long-term memory for order. *Journal of Memory and Language, 29,* 733–746.

Nairne, J. S., & Neath, I. (1994). A critique of the retrieval/deblurring assumptions of TODAM. *Psychological Review, 101,* 528–533.

Parkinson, S. R. (1972). Short-term memory while shadowing: Multiple-item recall of visually and of aurally presented letters. *Journal of Experimental Psychology, 92,* 256–265.

Rock, I., & Ceraso, J. (1964). Toward a cognitive theory of associative learning. In C. Scheerer (Ed.), *Cognition: Theory, research, promise* (pp. 110–146). New York: Harper & Row.

Sternberg, S. (1969). Memory-scanning: Mental processes revealed by reaction-time experiments. *American Scientist, 57,* 421–457.

Underwood, B. J. (1969). Attributes of memory. *Psychological Review, 76,* 559–573.

Wickens, D. D. (1972). Characteristics of word encoding. In A. W. Melton & E. Martin (Eds.), *Coding processes in human memory* (pp. 191–215). Washington, DC: Winston.

Chapter 5

Understanding Concepts in Activity

James G. Greeno
Stanford University and the Institute for Research on Learning

This chapter presents a preliminary framework for theoretically analyzing concepts and conceptual understanding. This introductory section gives a brief overview of current theories of concepts in cognitive science. As I understand the situation, we have theoretical analyses of concepts, knowing concepts, and understanding concepts developed in two general frameworks, which I call *denotational* and *procedural* frameworks.

THE DENOTATIONAL FRAMEWORK

Denotational analyses of concepts have been developed most fully; they focus on activities of classification (Smith, 1989, 1990). Cognitive psychologists have studied learning and knowing concepts by presenting sets of stimuli that participants learn, or have learned, to label according to their membership in categories (e.g., Bower & Trabasso, 1964; Bruner, Goodnow, & Austin, 1956; Estes, 1994; Greeno & Scandura, 1966; Hull, 1920; Medin & Schaffer, 1978; Murphy & Medin, 1985; Rosch, 1973; Shepard, Hovland, & Jenkins, 1961; Smith & Medin, 1981; Smith, Shoben, & Rips, 1974). Other examples, from research on cognitive development, involve concepts such as number conservation and class inclusion (e.g., Piaget, 1941/1965). In number conservation, for example, children are shown a display of two kinds of objects and are tested to see whether they correctly classify the display as an example of "more" of one kind or of "the same."

These psychological theories of classification analyze concepts in the way that they have been analyzed traditionally in empiricist philosophy, in a tradition that can be traced from Aristotle through Hume to Frege, Russell, Tarski, and Montague (Barwise & Etchemendy, 1989). In these theories concepts correspond to set-theoretic entities in a domain of objects, events, and situations, and are the denotations of terms in formal or natural languages. A similar treatment of meaning in linguistics is the theory of semantic components (H. H. Clark & E. V. Clark, 1977). A psychological hypothesis is that concepts are represented mentally as sets of features or sets of examples. These representations are part of the cognitive basis for understanding language, and for recognizing specific objects, events, and situations as being members of a categories, and thereby supporting actions in those situations that are appropriate for the categories.

THE PROCEDURAL FRAMEWORK

Procedural analyses of concepts have been developed more recently in cognitive science. As an example, consider models of solving word problems in arithmetic and algebra (Cummins, Kintsch, Reusser, & Weimer, 1988; Kintsch & Greeno, 1985; Nathan, Kintsch, & Young, 1992; Riley & Greeno, 1988; Staub & Reusser, chap. 16, this vol.; Weaver & Kintsch, 1992). These models represent understanding of mathematical concepts such as *addition, subtraction, multiplication, division*, and *rate* in the form of procedures and schemata. Nathan et al. illustrated their model with a distance–rate–time problem involving airplane flight. The model computes symbolic expressions that represent a coherent textbase, a situation model that includes propositions—such as that overtaking corresponds to flying equal distances—and a problem model in which quantities are organized by a schema of distance, rate, and time, which is used to generate equations.

Other examples of procedural analyses of concepts are models of knowing the concept of *subtraction*, in the form of procedures for solving multidigit subtraction problems, which include several varieties of partial knowledge that simulate incorrect answers on some problems (Brown & Burton, 1980) and an account of how those "bugs" could be acquired in learning from examples (Van Lehn, 1990). Another example is the analysis of knowing the concept of *acceleration* in physics, represented as a procedure for computing the acceleration of a body in motion at a point by representing its velocity at successive moments as vectors and computing the acceleration as their difference (Heller & Reif, 1984).

These procedural models of understanding concepts in human cognition are consistent with treatments of concepts that are common in artificial intelligence and computational linguistics. Knowledge representational systems, language understanding systems, and knowledge-based expert systems all provide formats for representing knowledge of concepts in ways that support their use in constructing representations and making inferences (Rumelhart & Norman, 1988).

The procedural view of concepts and understanding subsumes the denotational view. Classification can be represented procedurally, and an analysis of knowing a concept in order to classify stimuli incorporates the features that define a concept in some form, either as explicit tests (e.g., Feigenbaum, 1963; Hunt, Marin, & Stone, 1966), as features of examples that are compared to the stimulus to be classified (e.g., Reitman & Bower, 1973), or as elements of a network of features that settles into a pattern that corresponds to recognition of a member of the category (e.g., Estes, 1994).

COMPONENTS OF A THEORY OF CONCEPTS

A theory of concepts needs to specify assumptions about what constituents of concepts are, an epistemological assumption that states how concepts are known or understood, and a method of diagnosing constituents of conceptual understanding; that is, a way or ways of inferring from behavior which constituents of a concept a person or group's understanding includes.

In denotational theories, concepts correspond to categories, and constituents of concepts are the properties and relations of objects, events, and situations that are relevant to the categories they belong in. Knowing a concept corresponds to having abilities to evaluate truth conditions for membership in the concept category. Diagnoses of conceptual understanding are based on presenting test items that participants are asked to classify, and inferences are made about which constituent features of a concept play a role in the person's classification. For example, in Piagetian experiments on conservation of number, the concept of a number is considered, in Russell's (1938) sense, as a category of sets in which the members can be put in one-to-one correspondence, and the physical space occupied by the set is irrelevant. When children say that there are more objects when the set occupies more space, the inference is made that their understanding of the concept includes the property of spatial extent, which, when they are older, will not be relevant to their classifying sets by their cardinalities.

In procedural analyses, concepts correspond to procedures and data structures used in solving problems and making inferences. Knowing concepts corresponds to ability to execute those procedures with those data structures. Constituents of concepts, then, are components of those procedures and data structures, including schemata that are interpreted in performing tasks. Diagnoses are made by having participants perform tasks and then inferring what procedures and data they use in their performance.

Examples include the analyses of the concepts of subtraction and acceleration, mentioned earlier. Diagnoses of students' procedures for solving subtraction problems are obtained using the diagnostic program DEBUGGY (Burton, 1982); the similarities and differences of a student's procedure and a procedure for correct subtraction characterize the student's understanding of the concept of subtraction.

Related examples, also involving instruction, are the diagnostic models incorporated in interactive tutorial programs, such as those developed by Anderson and his associates (e.g., Anderson, Boyle, Corbett, & Lewis, 1990) in the domains of geometry, algebra, and LISP programing. The programs produce diagnoses of students' current states of understanding in terms of procedures that produce correct solutions of problems and present texts intended to aid students in acquiring lacking or mistaken components.

A SITUATIVITY-THEORETICAL FRAMEWORK[1]

Constraints, Affordances, Abilities, and Attunements

The preliminary framework for a theory of concepts presented here is designed to give an account of conceptual understanding that functions in activity by defining the constituents of concepts as *constraints, affordances*, and *abilities* of activity, and understanding of a concept as *attunements* to the concept's constituent constraints, affordances, and abilities.

The idea of constraints is from philosophical situation theory (Barwise & Perry, 1983; Devlin, 1991). A constraint is a regularity that holds in some domain, usually dependent on some conditions. Technically, a constraint is a dependency relation between two *situation types*, where a situation type is a class of situations that share some property or relation. An example, used by Barwise and Perry (following Dewey, 1938), is the constraint "Smoke means fire." That is, if a situation is of the type that has smoke, then that situation is also of the type that has fire. Constraints support activity by enabling actions to have results that an agent can anticipate. For example, a constraint in driving is "Turning the steering wheel changes the direction of the car's motion," so a driver can get the car to change its direction by turning the steering wheel.

The idea of affordances is from ecological psychology (Gibson, 1979/1986). An affordance is a resource in the environment that supports an interactive activity by an agent. An example used by Gibson is the affordance that a chair provides for the activity of sitting. Affordances are relations between environments and agents. For an object or system in the environment to afford an activity by an agent, the agent needs to be appropriately equipped and capable. An object or system in the environment affords an activity by an agent if the agent has an

---

[1]I use the term *situativity theory* to refer to a combination of philosophical situation theory, ecological psychology, ethnography, and situated automata that is emerging in cognitive science. I use the neologism, reluctantly, because the main alternative term, *situated cognition*, misleads people to think that there are some kinds of cognition that are situated and some that are not. Rather, I assume, as do other working with this approach, that being situated—that is, situativity—is a general characteristic of cognition, and that the theory of cognition should consider activity fundamentally as an interaction of agents in situations.

ability to engage in the activity by interacting with the object or system. For example, to sit in a chair, individuals need to be the right size for the chair, and needs to be able to bend their knees and hips appropriately. This idea of ability has been discussed by Shaw, Turvey, and Mace (1982) and by Snow (1992).[2] An affordance and an ability mutually define each other and comprise a potential for an activity in which an agent interacts with a system in the environment. The affordance is the contribution of the system in the environment, and the ability is the contribution of the agent.

In situation theory, the term *attunement* refers to a property of an agent, specifically, a regularity in the agent's activity that corresponds to a constraint of the environmental system that the agent interacts with. In this use, the term attunement refers to an aspect of *ability*, as I have defined it here. Attunement has an advantage over ability in that it makes the relation with the environment more salient. I use attunement more or less synonymously with ability, but with more focus on the dependence of activities on constraints and affordances of the environment, and less on the agent as such. We can also use attunement more symmetrically, because adjustments can be made in properties of environmental systems, as well as in properties of people's actions, to achieve better interactions. In my discussion here, however, I mainly attend to attunements of agents to constraints and affordances of systems in the environment.

Consider the example of steering a car. A complex and subtle system of constraints relate rotations of the steering wheel to changes in the car's direction. One general constraint is that greater rotation results in greater change of the car's direction, but the details of that relation differ depending on the car, its speed, whether it is accelerating or decelerating, and the condition of the road and the tires. The shape of the steering wheel is designed to afford its rotational movement by persons of average size, with the ability to grasp the wheel and move their arms in the directions needed to make the wheel rotate. Successfully steering the car depends on the driver's activity being attuned to these constraints and the affordance of the steering wheel, along with the related constraints and affordances involved in changing the speed of the car using the brake and accelerator pedals. All of these regularities are conditional on the car's steering and speed-regulating mechanisms being in good working order.

Concepts in Practices

Communication is a key aspect of human activity. People communicate to coordinate their actions, agree on plans and goals, monitor their progress, and explain their actions to others. In such communication, people refer to significant aspects of their activity. It can be significant to refer to the choice of one action

---

[2]Although Shaw et al. used the term *effectivity* and Snow used the term *aptitude* to refer to this concept.

rather than another, to a quality of an action, to a condition that makes an action desirable or necessary, to the use or quality of some material that is used, to a quality of a product that is being prepared, and so on. People who participate in a domain of practice learn to use terms that facilitate their activity.

I propose to consider the concepts of a domain of practice as the meanings of terms that practitioners use in their communication in and about their activities. I also propose, as an assumption to use in theoretical analyses, that the meanings of conceptual terms in a domain of activity are families of constraints, affordances, and abilities that practitioners of the activity attend to and find useful to discuss. In other words, the constituents of concepts in a domain are constraints, affordances, and abilities that practitioners refer to when they communicate in and about their activities. Viewed in this way, the constituents of a concept will not be a closed set, except under very special circumstances. Rather, nearly all concepts will be constituted by open-ended families of constraints and affordances, consistent with arguments by Lakoff (1987) and, earlier, Wittgenstein (1953).

To study the concepts of a practice, we can conduct a kind of ethnographic inquiry. This involves studying practitioners' discourse to identify the meanings of terms that they use to refer to actions, functions, resources, and circumstances of their activities. We could, for example, conduct an ethnographic study of the concepts of driving by studying discourse that occurs in different communities, such as ordinary drivers, taxi drivers, drivers who test performance of cars, and engineers who design cars. It is likely that we would find substantial differences in the meanings of terms such as *steering* in these different communities.

Two distinctions are important for this account of conceptual understanding. One distinction is between *symbolic* and *nonsymbolic* functions of activity. Many activities have functions of interacting with physical systems as well as functions of representing the systems and agent-physical system interactions symbolically. It is useful, then, to distinguish between nonsymbolic constraints, affordances, and abilities (the regularities and resources of the environment and of agents for interacting with the physical systems) and symbolic constraints, affordances, and abilities (the regularities and resources of systems of symbols and of agents for constructing and interpreting symbolic representations of the physical systems and representations of the nonsymbolic aspects of the activity). For example, in driving, nonsymbolic functions include physical interactions involved in steering the car, and symbolic functions include communication about driving and interpretation of symbols that are provided in the environment, such as speedometer readings and road signs.

A second distinction involves functions of activity that I call *instrumental* and *theoretical*. Instrumental functions are concerned with getting things done. Symbolic functions often serve instrumental functions, as with planning, coordinating, performing, and evaluating activities in the domain. Theoretical functions, which

Dewey (1938) called *reflective inquiry*, are primarily symbolic and are concerned with the meanings of conceptual terms in the domain. In discussions that are primarily theoretical, meanings of conceptual terms are the main topic. Often, statements are treated as hypotheses or conjectures, and the participants in conversation evaluate them in relation to other statements that are considered as evidence or general principles to which the participants are committed. Many discussions have functions that are both instrumental and theoretical, involving communication that is directly about an activity but also with functions of clarifying meanings of conceptual terms.

Understanding Concepts

I have proposed that a concept is a family of constraints, affordances, and abilities that practitioners in a domain refer to in their communication in and about their activities. The companion to this is a proposal that understandings of a concept are attunements to constraints, affordances, and abilities that are constituents of that concept.

Diagnosing someone's understanding of a concept involves inferences about which of the constituent constraints, affordances, and abilities of the concept the person is attuned to. Analyzing whether someone is attuned to a constraint, affordance, or ability is done by observing and analyzing whether the person's actions are consistent with that constituent. Parsimony would require that simpler hypotheses, not involving that attunement, are insufficient to account for the performance in some of the situations where the person's activity is consistent with the constraint, affordance, or ability. One kind of inquiry asks about someone's understanding of a concept, presupposing a prior analysis of the constituents of the concept in the activity that is examined. In another kind of inquiry, discourse of practitioners is observed and analyzed to discover what concepts of their practice are.

Understanding in Instrumental and Theoretical Functions of Activity. One of my theoretical goals is to provide a framework for characterizing implicit understanding, such as the understanding of the concept *number* that is assessed in Piaget's conservation test and other situations (e.g., Gelman & Gallistel, 1978). The distinction between instrumental and theoretical functions of activity seems to provide a promising approach. Attunement to constraints and affordances of theoretical functions of discourse about the meaning of a conceptual term involves a more explicit form of understanding than attunement to constraints, affordances, and abilities of instrumental functions of discourse and other symbolic representational activity, or to constraints, affordances, and abilities of nonsymbolic activity.

People can be attuned to constraints, affordances, and abilities of an instrumental activity, such as driving a car, whether or not they are attuned to constraints, affordances, and abilities of the activities of discussing the meanings of linguistic terms and other symbols that are used in theoretical discourse in the domain, and vice versa. As an example, the concept of *turning radius* can be used to refer to the radius of a car's path turning as sharply as it can. In steering a car successfully, drivers must be attuned to the constraint that the term *turning radius* refers to, but they do not need to be attuned to the constraints of using the term in discourse. In that case, we could say that the drivers understand the concept turning radius, in the instrumental sense, whether or not they understand the concept theoretically. On the other hand, a person could know the technical definition of a car's turning radius and know how to represent the trajectory of the car in its tightest turn without being attuned to the constraints involved in driving the car successfully to avoid obstacles in a difficult driving exercise. We would say, then, that this person understood the concept of turning radius theoretically, but did not have particularly strong understanding of the concept instrumentally.

Understanding in Nonsymbolic and Symbolic Aspects of Activity. If we consider only instrumental activities in a domain, we can distinguish between being attuned to constituent constraints, affordances, and abilities of a concept that support performance of the primary activity and being attuned to symbolic constraints, affordances, and abilities that support communication, discourse and other symbolic representations of the activity. In the example of driving, those who drive very well in varied conditions may or may not be able to describe accurately many of the maneuvers that they accomplish routinely. An analysis of their understanding would attribute understanding of concepts of steering, acceleration, and so on, in terms of the constraints, affordances, and abilities of successful performance that they are attuned to, and would also note representational constraints, affordances, and abilities that they are not attuned to. On the other hand, driving teachers need to be much more skillful in representing properties of driving activities symbolically, both to support their understanding of students' progress and to communicate with student drivers in order to get them to attend to aspects of driving that are important for their learning. Such a person's understanding of concepts such as steering and acceleration would include attunements to constraints, affordances, and abilities of attending to and representing the attunements of student drivers—that is, to properties of students' performance regarding how they are attuned to constraints, affordances, and abilities of driving.

The distinction between attunements to constraints, affordances, and abilities of nonsymbolic aspects of activity and of representational aspects of activity also applies to theoretical functions. Someone can be well-attuned to constraints, affordances, and abilities of constructing and interpreting conceptual representations in a domain without being well-attuned to the discourse practices of practitioners of theoretical activity in the domain, or conversely.

Concepts that Originate in a Community of Specialized Practitioners Can Be Understood by Other People. A previous section proposed that concepts are evolved by communities of practitioners in their discourse in and about activities. This section discusses varieties of understanding that include attunements to the constituent constraints, affordances, and abilities of concepts, without necessarily including abilities to participate in the kind of discourse that occurs in the communities where the concepts evolved.

Although these proposals may seem to be in conflict, they are easily reconciled. We can identify meanings of concepts by studying the discourse activity of a community of specialized practitioners in a domain. According to proposals discussed earlier, such meanings are families of constraints, affordances, and abilities that the practitioners refer to in communicating in and about their activities. The constituent constraints, affordances, and abilities include some that are involved in how the domain specialists do what they do, and some that are involved in how they talk about and otherwise symbolically represent what they do.

With the results of such an inquiry, we can proceed to study activities of people who are not members of the community of specialized practice that we studied to identify the meanings of concepts of the domain. When we find that activities of those other people are attuned to some of the constraints, affordances, and activities that are constituents of a concept, we can say that those attunements constitute understanding of the specialists' concept. If the constituents that they are attuned to are mainly limited to constraints, affordances, and abilities that do not consider meanings of symbolic representations, we would say that their understanding of the concept is largely implicit; but it is understanding, even so.

Often, the communities whose discourse we use to identify meanings of concepts are recognized in the society as specialists in the domain, and we assess the conceptual understanding of people who are not members of that community of recognized specialists regarding the concepts of the specialized practitioners. This is especially the case in academic subjects, where we find the meanings of concepts in communities of academic specialists, and assess the understanding of students. Of course, educational goals and educational assessments include concerns with students' abilities to participate in discourse about concepts as well as activities that require attunements to instrumental constituents of concepts, but students' attunements to instrumental constituents are important components of understanding that can be a basis on which more explicit theoretical understanding can be learned.

Relation to Procedural and Denotational Frameworks

The situativity framework is a generalization of the two frameworks discussed in the first section, the denotational and the procedural frameworks. The generalization is due to the fact that procedural representations are a special case of constraint satisfaction. Any procedure can be represented as a set of *if–then* production rules, each of which can be interpreted as a constraint that is satisfied when that production is executed. Furthermore, any denotational analysis can be formulated as a procedure. In addition to constituents that can be interpreted as procedures, however, analyses in terms of constraints, affordances, and abilities can also include constituents that are not specified procedurally. Those constituents specify a function of activity, without specifying how that function has to be performed. An assumption of attunement to a constraint, then, corresponds to assuming that the activity includes a member of a class of procedures that all have that functional characteristic.

EXAMPLES

This section briefly discusses four examples of concepts to illustrate some of the ideas in the theoretical overview. The first example, in the domain of basketball, illustrates discourse that refers to constraints, affordances, and abilities in activity. This example illustrates research that studies what concepts are in a practice, rather than whether someone understands concepts that the researchers already know about. We identified a concept in the discourse of a coach and a player that involves a pattern of action during a game. The main goal of the discourse was to improve the player's ability in a certain kind of game situation, but the discourse also established significant components of conceptual meaning.

The second example emphasizes attunements to constraints of symbolic representations. The activity of the example included reasoning about the quantitative properties of a physical device that we have used in research on understanding the mathematical concept of linear function, and I discuss excerpts of a dialogue between students working on tasks involving use of equations to represent relations among quantitative properties of the physical system.

In the third example, two teachers constructed an explanation of a constraint on quantities in a word problem. Their task had a salient theoretical function, in that it involved constructing a representation that would convey a constituent of the meaning of the concept of rate to students. The representation that they constructed was an enactment in which they played the roles of objects moving in opposite directions by walking toward each other and colliding.

The fourth example, from an exercise in engineering education, also illustrates theoretical functions of discourse. Engineering students had the task of analyzing the operation of a bathroom scale. Their discourse involved attunements to constraints of the physical system that they were analyzing, as well as constraints in the conceptual domain of physics that they had learned as part of their pre-professional training. Their discourse was explicitly theoretical in that statements involving theoretical terms were explicitly evaluated as hypotheses.

A Concept in a Discourse of Practice[3]

An earlier section mentioned that to identify concepts of a practice, we can study the discourse of practitioners and analyze constraints, affordances, and abilities that they refer to when they communicate in and about their activities. This example illustrates a result of such a study.

I discuss a concept that Christian Rohrer and I found in a sample of discourse that we recorded in which a basketball coach was working with a player. We videotaped a coaching session in which the coach and player watched videotape of a previous game for about 40 min., and then worked on shooting drills for about 25 min. In our study, we have reviewed this videotape and the telecast, and the radiocast and public address announcements of a few other games for conceptual terms. In this small corpus, there are a few hundred different terms that were used conceptually.

The concept that I discuss here, *being ready to shoot*, was referred to in the conversation at least six times during the videotape viewing, and some additional times during the shooting drills. *Being ready to shoot* is an action that the coach wanted the player, a forward, to perform whenever she received a pass in her normal position. Rather than immediately passing the ball to another player or dribbling toward the basket, she should be in a position where she could take a shot. The following excerpt contains at least four references to the concept, which I show in italics. (Here, and in subsequent transcriptions, the symbol = indicates overlapping talk.)

[On the tape of the previous game, the player had just shot and missed.]
Coach: That was a good shot to take. Where was your girl? =Right.
Player: =She was doubling in.
Coach: Alright, then, *you should be ready to shoot. Are you ready here?*
Player: Uh, yeah, kinda, I guess.
Coach: Yeah, but don't just watch the play. *You get ready to shoot it. Get your feet squared up.* [The coach rewound the tape and watched the missed shot again.] That was good. That was fine. That was a good shot to take. C. got the rebound. [They watched tape for several seconds.] You're doin' a good job of gettin' open on the lane. [The ball was passed to this player.] *Square up here. Is this a shot?*
Player: Well, I had just missed. I didn't want to deck up another one, heh heh.
Coach: Yeah, heh, heh, don't worry about it, though. *If you're open, you don't have to take it but at least look like you're going to shoot, look at the basket, just to get her out on you. And then if you're lookin' up, just like you did that one time in the second half, as soon as you went like that* [the coach moved as in faking a

---

[3]The research discussed in this section was done with the collaboration of Christian P. Rohrer, and was supported by a grant from the Stanford University Office of Technology Licensing. We are grateful to the coach and player who agreed to let us record their work.

shot] *she came flying out and then you put it on the floor. You might get her flying out and then you can get it in to V.*

In one of the drills, the coach was playing the role of a defensive player, guarding the player. The player received a pass from another participant, then dribbled around the coach to take a shot. The coach said:

Coach: *You gotta hold your fake. I'm not even comin' out yet. Look like you're gonna shoot, react to me, when I come out then put it on the floor.*

It would be reasonable to say that the concept that we call *being ready to shoot* was constructed in the discourse of the coach with the player. We doubt that this was the first time that this concept was considered by either of the participants, but there is sufficient material in this conversation to identify several constituents of the concept:

(1A1)   Having the ball affords shooting/The player can shoot well.
(1C1)   If your guard is farther away, the chance of shooting successfully is greater.
(1C2)   If your guard moves closer to you, she will be farther away from other players, particularly your teammate playing center.
(1C3)   If your guard moves close enough to you to guard against a shot, that can provide space through which you can dribble to the basket.
(1A2)   Having the ball affords faking a shot/The player can fake shots convincingly.
(1C4)   If you fake a shot, your guard will probably move closer to you.

The coach's discussions with the player called attention to these and other constraints, affordances, and abilities. Although we did not observe the player's behavior over a long period, it seems clear that the coach's intention was to facilitate her becoming more strongly attuned to these constraints and affordances in her play during actual games. We could say that the discourse of the coach and player constructed significant understanding of the concept of being ready to shoot. The understanding of the concept that occurred in the discourse included identifying examples of activity that were attuned to the main constituents and examples that were not, and attending to states of affairs in situations that were instances of the situation types that are related in the constituent constraints and affordances of the concept.

This example illustrates discourse with both instrumental and theoretical functions. The main goal of the discourse was to foster improvement in the player's activity in games, a matter of practical understanding in the sense of being attuned to constraints, affordances, and abilities that we identify, in our analysis, as constituents of the concept of being ready to shoot. At the same time, the discourse also specified the meaning of this concept in significant ways. The coach's calling attention to the relevant features of situations and actions in watching the tape and in the shooting drills called attention to relations among concepts in the family of constraints, affordances, and abilities that constitute the concept. A considerable amount of the coach's talk was in the form of conditional statements (e.g., "If you're open, you don't have to take it, but at least look like you're going to shoot, look at the basket, just to get her out on you.") which refer to constraints directly (Barwise, 1989). These statements all consider constituents of *being ready to shoot* as relations among other concepts, such as a dependency between *looking at the basket*, or *faking a shot*, and *getting your guard to come out* and *passing to the center or driving toward the basket*. And by presenting these various features in a single discourse segment, including explicit reference to some of the strategic and causal relations among the features, the coach and the player constructed a configuration of constraints as the meaning of the concept. This discourse was not intentionally theoretical, however; for example, they did not consider alternative definitions of terms, construct new representations of constituents, or treat statements as representations of hypotheses that were evaluated by evidence.

Constructing Meanings of Symbolic Representations of Linear Functions[4]

This example focuses on conceptual understanding involved in constructing and interpreting symbolic representations of a concept. A community that has a concept in its practices also has conventions for symbolically representing situations that involve that concept and related concepts. Such representational practices include constructing and interpreting symbols that refer to the concept's constituent constraints and affordances, and there are constraints, affordances, and abilities for the activities of constructing and interpreting symbols. Understanding the concept, therefore, can include attunements to the constraints, affordances, and abilities of those symbolic practices.

The example involves research in which I am collaborating with Randi Engle and Laura Kerr, continuing a study in which I collaborated with Joyce Moore and Rory Mather. We have analyzed reasoning by pairs of students about quantitative properties of a simple physical device that we designed to study understanding of the concept of *linear function*. The system, which we call *winches*, included a yard-long board with two parallel tracks, each with a groove and a ruler that marked the distance from one end of the track. Each track had a small metal block that slid along the groove, with a string tied to the block that wound around a spool, turned by a handle at the end of the track. There were spools of

[4]This research was supported by National Science Foundation grants BNS-8718918 and MDR-9053605.

different sizes, any of which could be used to wind the string for either track. The system was designed to embody linear functions of the form $y = mx + b$, where b is the starting position of a block, m is the circumference of the spool, the distance the block moves with each turn of the handle, x is the number of turns, and y is the block's final position.

Attunements to Constraints, Affordances, and Abilities in Quantitative Reasoning. In previous research (Greeno, in press; Moore & Greeno, 1991) we found that middle-school and high-school students have significant implicit understanding of the concept of linear function, as evidenced by their abilities to reason successfully about quantities such as the position a block would reach when the handle is turned a given number of times, or the number of turns that would be needed for one block to catch up with the other block, when the block that starts farther ahead has a smaller spool.

We analyzed understanding the concept of linear function in this situation as attunement to several constraints and affordances, including the following. Some of the constraints involve quantitative properties of the winch, for example, that the distance that a block moves on each turn is a constant, equal to the spool size, and the total distance a block moves in r turns is the combination of r segments, each equal to the spool size. Some constraints involve arithmetic, including the operations of addition and multiplication and their inverses. And some of the constraints involve relations between arithmetic and winch quantities, for example, that the numerical position of a block after a turn is the arithmetic sum of its previous numerical position plus the numerical size of the spool, and the numerical position of a block after r turns is the sum of its initial position, plus the multiplicative product of r times the numerical size of the spool.

Different attunements to these constituents of the concept of linear function were evidenced by the different methods that students used to make inferences. Some pairs of students inferred the successive positions of the blocks by pointing to positions along the rulers. Marking incremental distances by pointing only requires attunement to the constraints that the distance moved on each turn is constant, and that segments of movement combine to form the total movement. The inference of each position could be made by counting the appropriate number of 1-in. intervals, rather than by using numerical addition. Affordances and abilities for this method include the 1-in. marks on the rulers and the ability to measure distances and the number of turns by counting.

Some other pairs constructed numerical tables with symbols for positions of the blocks after successive turns. Construction of such a table would involve attunement to the constraint that successive positions can be inferred by adding numbers, but would not necessarily involve attunement to the constraint involving arithmetic multiplication, because the multiplicative relation of number of turns times spool size is satisfied as a consequence of the way the table is constructed. Affordances and abilities included paper and a pencil for writing the table, numbers that afford the operation of addition as well as counting, and the abilities to write numerical symbols, to add and count numerically, and to interpret numerical symbols as positions of the blocks.

Some pairs of students gave answers directly and reported that they did mental arithmetic to answer questions. This would involve attunement to the constraints that the distance moved in several turns can be inferred by multiplying the number of turns times the spool size and the final position can be inferred by adding the numerical distance moved plus the numerical initial position. Affordances and abilities included numbers that afforded arithmetic operations and abilities to choose the operations to infer the required quantities and to perform those operations, and to interpret the results of the operations as values of the quantitative attributes of winch events.

Attunements to Constraints, Affordances, and Abilities of Constructing and Interpreting Mathematical Representations. Understanding the concept of linear function also can include knowing how to construct and interpret standard mathematical representations of linear function, such as tables, equations, and graphs. To study this, we prepared workbooks for pairs of students with problems and questions about the winch that also asked the students to construct arithmetic and algebraic representations of quantitative properties of winch events and to write explanations of their representations. The example discussed here is from a study in which the mathematical representations were tables and equations. Participants were six pairs of middle-school students taking different levels of mathematics.

Conceptual understanding in these tasks involves attunement to several kinds of constraints and affordances concerned with the instrumental functions of constructing and interpreting representations.

- One kind is constraints, affordances, and abilities of the system and events that are represented, and of activities of making inferences about the system. In this case, these are the constraints of quantitative relations of the winch, of arithmetic, and of coordinating quantitative relations with arithmetic, which were discussed previously.

- A second kind is syntactic constraints and affordances of the system of symbols, such as conventions for writing numerical symbols in tables, for writing equations, and for drawing graphs.

- A third kind is semantic constraints and affordances for interpreting the meanings of symbols as referring to properties, relations, and events of the system that is being represented. The semantic constraints in this situation include referring relations between symbols and quantitative properties of winch events and referring relations between symbols and arithmetic entities, that is, numbers and operations. Because of the coupling of arithmetic and the winch's quantitative properties, the referring relations involving winch quantities and arithmetic can be merged, and symbolic expressions often refer simultaneously to winch properties and to entities of arithmetic.

The first several problems in the workbook all involved situations with a block starting at zero on the track. First, students constructed tables representing positions of blocks after different numbers of turns with different spools. When asked how far a block would move if it was attached to a 3-spool and the handle was turned 4 times, all pairs gave an answer of 12, with most explaining that it was necessary to multiply the number of turns by the spool size.

Problem 7 introduced notation for equations. The text presented an expression called a "word equation,"

$$\text{turns} \times \text{spool size} = \text{distance moved.}$$

Then the text noted that the name of a quantity could be replaced by a letter, displayed the equation

$$\text{turns} \times \text{spool size} = d,$$

and indicated that the other words also could be replaced by letters, giving what was called a "symbol equation." Answering the questions that followed involved constructing symbols and their semantic interpretations.

Students were asked to write a symbol equation for "turns × spool size = distance moved." Five of the six pairs wrote "T × S = D," or a near variant. Constructing this "symbol equation" involved substituting letters for the words that the text presented, presumably with the same semantic interpretations that the words had. These interpretations included references to the quantitative attributes named by the words and to arithmetic relations of multiplication and equality of numbers, in some combination that may have differed among the student participants.

Next, students were asked to solve the problem, "The block is at 20 and the spool is a 4. How many times was the handle turned?" Five of the six pairs represented the arithmetic operation of dividing 20 by 4 to infer the answer, 5 turns, using numerals and a symbol for division. Most of the pairs did this without significant elaboration, but the conversation by a seventh-grade pair showed some details of the semantic construction. The conversation included references to five turns as a quantity, as well as to the arithmetic operations of multiplication and division, from which we infer that the students were attuned to the correspondence of the arithmetic operations and the quantitative relations.

Mark: Okay, you divide this time. So that twenty divided by four . . . unless . . . is a four . . . divided by twenty or twenty divided by four?
Doug: (reading) "The block is at twenty . . ."
Mark: I think it's four into twenty. That's what I guess [wrote, "20 ÷ 4"]
Doug: So the spool is a four?
Mark: Mhm.
Doug and Mark: [rereading] "The spool is a four."
Mark: So it's times five [wrote "5 turns" in the arithmetic expression, producing

"20 ÷ 4 = 5 turns"]. So it took five tu——
Doug: Wait, twenty . . .
Mark: So, five turns, right?
Doug: Wait a sec, that . . . wait, let me see.
Mark: Right, cause five times four is twenty.

After some more conversation, including Doug writing the arithmetic expression himself, they agreed on the answer.

Mark was apparently attuned to a constraint of the relation of multiplication and division, when he said, "Okay, so you divide this time," responding to the request to find "How many times was the handle turned?" given a distance moved and a spool size. The arguments of a division operation corresponding to the relation of turns, spool size, and distance, require the distance as the dividend and spool size as the divisor, to infer the number of turns. Mark settled on that relation after some uncertainty, and wrote an arithmetic representation of it. When he wrote "5 turns" we infer that he was simultaneously referring to the arithmetic relation of dividing numbers and to the winch-event quantity of the number of turns. Doug did not accept Mark's representation immediately, and Mark referred to the multiplicative fact, $4 \times 5 = 20$, we suppose, to support his proposal.

Next, the students were asked to make up word and symbol equations "for how you did this," four of the pairs wrote words with an operator symbol and the equality symbol for the word equation, for example, "distance ÷ spool size = turns," and wrote letters, the operator symbol, and the equality symbol for the symbol equation, for example, "d ÷ s = t." Mark and Doug had the following dialogue:

Mark: Okay, so, um . . .
Doug: Four divided by twenty equals D.
Mark: Spool size divided by [wrote "spool size ÷"].
Doug: Nope. Not quite. The =place on the ruler divided by . . . =
Mark: =Well, what do you call = Ok, so distance divided by sp . . . [drew a line through "spool size ÷"]
Doug: Distance divided by spool size.
Mark: Distance divided by spool size equals turns [wrote "distance ÷ spool size = turns"]. Okay, so that's the word equation [wrote "word" with a box around it].
Doug: Okay, and then what's the symbol equation?
Mark: Symbol [wrote "symbol" with a box around it]. D divided by SS equals T (wrote "D ÷ SS = t")
Doug: [laughing] Equals T?
Mark: Uh huh.

This segment shows that some work had to be done to satisfy semantic constraints. The assignment of arguments for division had to be sorted out again, and it took some work to identify the word to use for the distance the block moved ("place on the ruler," then "distance"). The syntactic constraints of the division expression appeared to cause no difficulty, and substitution of letters for words to form a "symbol equation" was similarly uneventful.

Questions in the workbook proceeded to more complicated situations involving transformations of the equation and equations that included nonzero starting positions. Students varied considerably in their success as the problems became more complicated, and the characterization of their conceptual understanding of symbols that we are developing is quite complex. An example of one such problem was discussed by Greeno, Engle, Kerr, and Moore (1993). But the material presented here serves to illustrate that understanding of a concept includes attunement to constraints of constructing and interpreting symbolic representations of the concept that need to be learned, that students have significant attunements to some of those constraints, and that the processes of reasoning and learning involved in constructing meaning of symbolic expressions can be interesting and complex.

Constructing an Understanding of Composition of Velocities[5]

The third example discussed here involves the concept of *velocity*. The example comes from research conducted by Hall (1993). Two mathematics teachers constructed an explanation of the solution of a standard algebra word problem about vehicles in motion: "Tom can drive to Bill's house in 3 hours, and Bill can drive to Tom's house in 4 hours. If they both leave at noon, driving toward each other, when will they meet?"

The teachers were asked to construct an explanation that did not depend on algebraic formulas. In contrast to the previous example, in which students were asked to construct representations in a notation that is standard in mathematics and mathematics education, these teachers were to construct a representation that did not use the standard symbolic resources. Their activity, in doing this, involved discourse with a significant theoretical function of constructing meaning. The teachers constructed a semantic interpretation that extended their understanding of the meaning of the concept *rate*, by relating one of its constraints to a type of event in which they participated and therefore had first-person experience.

The constituent of the concept of velocity that is central here is a constraint on the composition of velocities in compound motion, that is, focusing on the relation between the two objects that are both moving. The specific constraint that is involved is the following:

(3C1)   If two objects are moving toward each other along a path, then the distance along the path between the objects decreases at a rate equal to the sum of the magnitudes of their respective velocities.

Another constraint that is critical in solving this problem is that a velocity is inversely proportional to the time it takes to traverse a fixed distance:

[5]This research, by Rogers P. Hall, was supported by a postdoctoral fellowship from the Program in Cognitive Studies for Educational Practice of the James S. McDonnell Foundation.

(3C2)   If an object moves a distance d in a time t, its (average) velocity is d/t.

Their symbolic work also was attuned to constraints of a kind of representation in which properties and relations of a symbolic expressions are the same as properties and relations of the system it represents. This kind of representation can be called *analogous* (Plyshyn, 1978), *intrinsic* (Palmer, 1978), or *demonstrative* (H. H. Clark & Gerrig, 1990).

(3C3)   To represent a property or relation of some system demonstratively, objects in the symbolic expression have a property or relation that is interpreted as being the same property or relation in the represented system.

The teachers began by choosing an arbitrary distance between Bill's and Tom's houses, 60 km, and performed calculations involving fractions of that distance. After several minutes, they wrote several algebraic expressions (recognizing that this was for their own understanding, rather than for the explanation without formulas that they were trying to construct), and chose the equation $\frac{7}{12} T = D$ from the several expressions they had on the white board for finding a solution algebraically.

The teachers then returned to constructing a solution appropriate for students. One of the teachers organized an activity for them both to engage in, which went as follows:

Teacher S: Ok, cause if, if you use more of an example. Ok. Stand over there. [Teacher J walked to the other side of the white board.] Ok.
You walk towards me . . . [J did exaggerated walk to S]
Now, let's say it takes you . . . three seconds, ok? [S pushed J, who stumbled back past his starting position]
Now, for me to walk to you . . . [S walked to J with measured steps]
I'm slower , so it takes me about four seconds to walk over to you. Right? [They both laughed. J pushed S back to his starting location, then mocked hitting him].
But now . . . and, and =if we walk towards each other.
Teacher J: =Yeah, right ⟨pretty good⟩ [S and J walked toward each other].
Teacher S: Then it's be like we're goin sup-er, =we're goin like super, I'm going superfast. [They collided].
Teacher J: =WHOA! We're goin faster! RIGHT!

The teachers needed to construct a representation to explain how the numerical relation: :"$\frac{1}{3} T + \frac{1}{4} T = \frac{7}{12} T$" was appropriate for solving the problem. This algebraic expression refers to a combination of velocities by adding their numerical magnitudes, obtaining a magnitude that is greater than the magnitude of either of the separate velocities. They created a representation that referred to that property demonstratively, that is, the greater magnitude of the velocity of approach with both of the teachers moving is a property of the event that the expression represented, the greater magnitude of the velocity of approach of two vehicles when they are both moving. Hall argued that the first-person character of this model may have been a critical feature, providing Teacher J with a strong experience of the contrasting rates of Teacher S's approach.

The teachers proceeded to construct a series of transformations from their enactment of the combination of velocities to support understanding of the symbolic algebraic expression for sum of one-fourth and one-third. In this, they used a diagram showing the path between two points, hand gestures that repeated the demonstration of combining velocities, and the word "combined" to indicate the quantitative relation corresponding to the arithmetic relation of adding the magnitudes of velocities. The construction of the enactive representation extended the teachers' understanding of the meaning of the concept rate, providing a strong semantic interpretation for the arithmetic operation of adding numbers, for which "$^7/_{12}$" represents the result. Potentially, use of this kind of representation in a mathematics class would provide a meaningful context in which to present, or guide, students toward discovering the additive relation between velocities represented by the standard algebraic formula.

In this example, affordances and abilities that played an important role included use of the white board, diagrams, and algebraic symbols, as well as the concepts of arithmetic and algebra. They also included use of the participants' bodies to enact a symbolic representation in which they could experience a problematic quantitative relation directly.

Reconciling Concepts of Force and Measured Weight in an Engineering Exercise[6]

The last example to be discussed included theoretical discourse, in which statements that referred to meanings of concepts were treated hypothetically. In this example, proposals about constraints that are constituents of concepts were evaluated both on grounds of their consistency with general theoretical principles, and empirically, by considering their implications for a situation and conducting experiments.

The activity that we observed and analyzed was designed by Margot Brereton to give engineering students opportunities to analyze and design systems earlier than they have in the traditional engineering curriculum. In the exercise discussed here, the task was to analyze the mechanisms of two kitchen scales and two bathroom scales. The students were given a list of suggested questions. They investigated behavior of the scales for a few minutes, then took the scales apart

---

[6]This research was done in collaboration with Margot Brereton, Jason Lewis, Charlotte Linde, Jeremy Roschelle, and Reed Stevens, and was supported by the Synthesis Coalition, a consortium of schools of engineering funded by the National Science Foundation.

and examined their internal parts. We consider the activity of three students who volunteered to test the exercise. They received course credit for participating, but their performance was not graded.

This example extends the theoretical discussion of the example of teachers in the previous section. They constructed an enactment that provided meaning for a standard technical representation. The students in this example coordinated meanings of concepts of physics that they expressed technically (although not in formulas) with experiences that they had previously with weighing themselves on bathroom scales and with observations that they took in the situation when two of them weighed themselves.

The discussion was an example of theoretical discourse that focuses on relations between meanings—in this case meanings of the concepts of *force* and *measured weight*. The concept of force was referred to directly with the term "force." The concept of measured weight was referred to with the term "weight," and terms such as "50 pounds," for referring to readings of the scale.

In their activity, they changed the meaning of force that they considered as applying to the concept of measured weight with a bathroom scale, moving from a meaning of force acting on a point mass, to a meaning of force measured at a point on an extended object that depends on the magnitudes and directions of other forces exerted on the object, on the positions at which those forces are applied, and on distortions of the object such as bending. This shift occurred after the students discussed an implication of the meaning of force acting on a point mass, which they could not reconcile with their experience and observations.

In the segments of activity that I discuss, the students responded to one of the questions given in the exercise materials. The question asked whether a bathroom scale gives the same reading whether it is on a hard floor or a soft carpet.

The main goal of the participants' activity was construction of an explanation of the scales. In general, I hypothesize that when people construct an explanation, their discourse is primarily a progressive series of agreements (a) about constraints and affordances of the system that they are trying to explain, and (b) about constraints and affordances that apply to the explanation that they are trying to produce. (The explicit discussion by these participants was about [a], the operation of the scales.) Contributions to the discourse, in H. H. Clark and Schaefer's (1989) sense, include presentations of candidate constraints and affordances, and acceptance, modification, or rejection of those constraints by the participants as a group, in the process of constructing the common ground of constraints and affordances that then constitute the explanation that has been constructed.

My discussion of the students' inquiry is organized by four issues.

Issue 1: Does Measured Weight Depend on the Supporting Surface?   First, the participants considered the proposition that measured weight might differ, depending on the kind of surface on which a scale is supported. The following candidate constraints were considered prominently:

(4C1)   The measured weight of a person on a scale depends on the weight of the person, and is independent of the surface that supports the scale.

(4C1') The measured weight of a person on a scale is different if the scale is supported on a soft surface than on a hard surface.

Statements of these constraints were treated as hypotheses, subject to empirical test. They also were considered in relation to other constraints involving the concept of force.

In the transcriptions of the students' conversation, I refer to the participants as Right, Middle, and Left, indicating their positions on the videotape. Right tentatively presented an assertion that readings differ depending on the surface supporting the scale, Left commented that such a difference would be "weird," and Middle affirmed the assertion authoritatively.

Right: [Right was reading the sheet of questions.] Oh, that's an interesting question. I heard that, ah, like bathroom scales, if you try it on carpet and you try it on hard floors=
Left: Oh, yeah, that's really weird=
Middle: =Yeah=
Right: =you get different readings. I don't know if they are, are they?=
Middle: =Um-hm [while shaking her head up and down].
Left: I think that's true.
Middle. [authoritatively] That's true.

Middle's contention made the assertion a serious proposition. It was testable in the situation, and the students eventually tested it.

Issue 2: Does the Concept of Force Imply Constraint (4C1)? The second issue that the participants considered involved possible relations between Constraint (4C1) and alternative meanings of the concept of force. One constituent they considered is an implication of Newton's third law:

(4C2)   When objects are at rest, with some objects supported by other objects, the forces between those objects are balanced, that is, they sum to zero.

The relation that was considered is that (4C2) implies (4C1); that is, the constraint that forces must balance implies that the measured weight of a person is independent of the surface supporting the scale.

In their conversation, the participants constructed a conceptual problem. They recognized that the softer surface of a carpet can be compressed, but it was an open question whether that difference would be consistent with differences between scale readings. Right invoked a principle of *balance of forces* to argue that the scale readings should not differ, and Left apparently concurred.

Middle: ... Cause if you think about it, carpet, carpet has give to it, you know, it's never, it's never like [Middle pounded on the table with her hand] there's, like, air and there's, like, padding there so it's never a rigid surface necessarily=
Left: The way I conceptualized it, is, is like it's totally in between the carpet and the thing, so it's just measuring=
Right: =yeah, as soon as it reaches that cushion, then the balance of forces must be the same.
Left: But there must be some weird thing where the carpet supports different parts of the=
Right: =well, the carpet has to support the whole scale and your weight=
Left: =yeah=
Right: =right, so there the force going up from the carpet=
Left: =it, it should be the same=
Right: =should equal the scale and your weight and then the force going down on the scale, the spring has to take up all the weight=
Left: =uh huh=
Right: There's no way=
Left: But I mean, it does, I, I,

This was theoretical discourse of an interesting kind. The students apparently considered a constraint on their explanation that it should be consistent with concepts they knew from physics, in this case, the concept of force and constraint (4C2). Right expressed a constraint, that forces would have to be balanced, and he believed this implied that the scale reading should be independent of the surface. Left expressed agreement, with some uncertainty.

Issue 3: Does an Absorbed Force Result in a Decrease of Measured Weight?
The third issue was consideration of another alternative constraint—whether some of the force between an object and the surface of another object that supports it can be absorbed in the material of the supporting object.

(4C3)   The material of a supporting object can absorb some of the force between it and another object that rests on it.

Constraint (4C3) was presented as a counter to the proposal that (4C2) implied (4C1); apparently its proposer considered that (4C3) might be consistent with (4C1'). An effort was made by the other participants to explain that compression of the carpet material would have only a temporary effect on the measured weight.

Right and Left had proposed an analysis that would imply Constraint (4C1). Middle did not accept that analysis. Recall Middle's authoritative assertion of

Constraint (4C1'). Middle previously had mentioned that the carpet was not a rigid surface (it had "give to it"). Middle extended that analysis, using the concept of *absorption of force*. Left responded to Middle's proposal about absorption by developing a more elaborate explanation that the balance of forces should apply when the system reached equilibrium after the cushioning effect of the carpet went away. Left used an available piece of paper to draw a diagram, explaining to Middle why absorption would not affect the reading.

> Middle: Well, doesn't carpet kinda, I mean, doesn't carpet, ah, absorb it, otherwise walking on carpet would be just like walking on this [Middle pounded on the table again].
> Left: Right. What we're saying is= [Left took a pen and folded back a page on the sketchpad.]
> Right: =it absorbs it temporarily=
> Left: It's like totally in between, like you can walk on the cushy carpet and you'll go down, but if you put—you'll still weigh the same amount, so if you put a scale underneath, you know, you'd weigh the same amount, like, say you put carpet on your scale, you get a certain reading. [Left had drawn a diagram with a representation of a scale with carpet under it, and another version where a piece of carpet is on the scale, between the top of the scale and a person standing on it.]
> Middle: =Oh, I see=

Middle apparently accepted the analysis that the cushioning effect is a transient, regarding the constraint that forces have to balance at equilibrium, (4C2). This left the group with the problem of reconciling (4C2) with the possibility that measured weight depends on the supporting surface. Right proposed that it does not, and introduced an appeal to experience ("I've tried it, but I weighed the same") that conflicted with Middle's earlier confident assertions of a dependence as a matter of fact.

Issue 1: Does Measured Weight Depend on the Supporting Surface? The next few episodes resolved the issue between (4C1) and (4C1') empirically. The organizer gave the participants a towel ("my simulated soft carpet"). Left weighed himself with and without the towel under the scale and got different readings. Right, remaining unconvinced, also weighed himself with and without the towel under a scale. He used the other bathroom scale, however, which was relatively unaffected by the surface, and the readings were similar. They continued to experiment, and eventually got a reading that confirmed the phenomenon of differences in readings. They also found that the readings can differ depending on where on the scale the person stands.

> Left: Try it again.
> Right: Let me try it again.
> Left: Maybe it depends on how you stand.

Middle: Yeah.
Left: Try and stand on the very center.
Right: One-thirty-eight again.
Left: Okay, when you stand on it on the carpet, try standing in the center.
Right: One-forty-five again here ⟨⟩ standing in the center, one-thirty-eight.
Left: Okay
Middle: How bizarre.
Left: That's really weird. Here, try it with this scale.

———

Middle: Hah. ⟨that's weird⟩
Left: You lost twenty pounds with this one. Did you see that it went down to one-oh-five.

Issue 4: Does Measured Weight Depend on the Distribution of Forces Applied to the Surface of the Scale?   After accepting that Constraint (4C1′) was correct, the students had to find a way to explain it. In principle, they might have considered giving up belief in the implication of Newton's third law, (4C2), but they did not. Instead, they considered a more general concept of force. Left proposed a possible connection between where the person stands on the scale and measured weight because of "where the mechanism is located." Previously, the students had implicitly considered force as acting on a point mass, an imaginary object with no physical extent. A scale, however, does have physical extent, and the behavior of the scale under a load can depend on where the force is applied. In other words:

(4C4)   The force measured at a point on an extended object depends upon not only the magnitudes and directions of other forces exerted on the object, but also on the positions at which the forces are applied and distortions of the object by those forces.

Left: Like, wriggle around, like, it must be a different, um, mechanism.
Right: The way, yeah,
Left: Where the mechanism is located, or something.
Right: That doesn't even make sense to me, because
Left: It doesn't.
Right: It should all be the same.
Left: Right.
Right: No matter what mechanism, by theory.

Right did not see a way to reconcile the conflict between the theoretical principle, Constraint (4C2), and the phenomenon. Left then introduced another constituent of the concept of force, the idea of moments.

Left: There must be another weird moment or < > that messes it up.
Right: Maybe, oh, yeah, maybe moment-wise, that's different.

Left: Because it will support it differently.

Middle: Maybe, yeah, maybe it's unevenly distributed.

Left: See, here, they expect it to be supported at these four points, maybe, because, like, you're supporting it here, it changes how, the, it must change how the mechanism responds.

Right seemed more inclined to accept Constraint (4C4) when it was phrased more technically, with the idea of *moments*. He proceeded to experiment with the effect of standing in different places on the scale, and confirmed that this was relevant.

Right: Wow, hold on, hold on. When I'm stepping like this, and then I weigh, oops. See, I step on the center and I weigh a whole lot less than when I step on the sides, I weigh a whole lot more.

I'm going to see if it's the same here.

One-thirty-six ⟨I did⟩ How strange. This scale is off. One-fifty-four. That's a huge difference. Yeah, one-thirty-six. It's got to be the moments.

The participants determined that readings with the towel differed, depending on how the person's weight was distributed on the scale. This supported the suggestion that moments of force are important. Later, when they took the scale apart, they found how the mechanism makes the reading depend on the supporting surface and the distribution of weight.[7]

Summary.   The participants assembled a set of constraints that related the concept of force to behavior of the scales. They opened a possibility for resolving a theoretical dilemma. Initially, they faced a contradiction between a principle (that forces balance) and a candidate phenomenon (that the readings of a scale differ depending on the supporting surface and the distribution of weight on the scale). They identified a way in which the phenomenon could be consistent with the principle of balanced forces by considering another constituent of the concept of force, that of moments of force, which is consistent with the finding that the reading differed depending on where the person placed his weight.

A major achievement of the conversation was to construct meaningful connections between technical terms, such as "forces in balance" and "moments," and the behaviors of the physical systems in the situation: the scales, including the numerical symbols that indicated measured weights, the towel, and the bodies of the participants as they weighed themselves. The participants took different roles in achieving these connections. Right was most firmly committed to an understanding that was consistent with the conventional meanings of technical terms. Middle attended strongly to qualitative properties of materials in the situation. Left

---

[7]There are bars along the sides of the scale, supported near the corners, that are bent by the weight of a person standing on the scale. If the scale is on a soft surface, the corners of the scale usually compress the surface unevenly, and the distortion of the bars is affected to produce an inaccurate reading.

made significant efforts to integrate these two domains of phenomena and discourse. They established significant common ground and made noticeable progress in the content of their understanding, moving from an undifferentiated concept of the force caused by a person's body resting on the scale to a more differentiated concept that takes account of the distribution of force at different locations on and inside the scale. Their interaction, therefore, provides a positive example of theoretical communication, in which comprehension was constituted in discourse.

Affordances and abilities involved in this reasoning would play an important role in a more complete analysis. Affordances were provided, obviously, by the scales that the students examined, and by pens and paper that were available for use in drawing diagrams. The participants' attunements to their own and each others' abilities were apparent in their selections of topics and levels of technical discourse, as well as in their agreements to each others' presentations of information based on experience or technical knowledge.

CONCLUSIONS

I have presented a sketch of a framework for studying concepts and their understanding, in which concepts are considered as products and instruments of social practice. I have presented four examples that illustrate how this framework can be used to analyze meanings of concepts and their understanding by participants in activity and discourse. The examples illustrate informal analyses of concepts in terms of constraints, affordances, and abilities involved in activities, and analyses of understanding concepts in terms of attunements to those kinds of constituents. The examples also illustrate distinctions among different kinds of understanding involved in some different ways in which constraints, affordances, and abilities function in activity. This chapter has discussed distinctions between nonsymbolic and symbolic functions in activity, and between instrumental and theoretical functions, particularly in discourse.

The empirical materials in these examples were obtained in situations that we can call *arranged conversations*. The conversational groups had two or three members. In some cases, the task they worked on was organized for the purposes of our research; in other cases, we observed activity that was organized for other purposes. In all cases, however, the conversations of participants provided us, as researchers, with a text that we can analyze and interpret. In my interpretations, I have identified events in the conversations that I believe provide evidence that the participants were attuned to constraints, affordances, and abilities that are constituents of concepts, and, therefore, provide illustrations of the idea of conceptual understanding that I am developing.

It would be possible to analyze the texts of transcribed conversations more systematically. One way would be to translate segments of the text into propositions and examine ways in which the contents of conversations are organized, considering issues that are examined in the analysis of written texts, in which Kintsch (e.g., 1974) plays a leading role. The resulting analyses could show how a common ground of information is constructed in productive conversations. The propositional structures of such analyses could be considered in relation to the constituent constraints, affordances, and abilities of analyses of conceptual meanings, providing detailed analyses of the construction of conceptual understanding in discourse.

Another direction in which this framework can be developed more systematically involves use of computational formalisms. We have done some computational modeling of reasoning about quantitative properties of the winches, in the form of simulations of reasoning processes (Moore & Greeno, 1991). Those models provide a procedural characterization of understanding, analogous to those discussed in the section on the procedural framework, although we interpret the model as describing states of affairs in the interactions of agents with the material and conceptual resources of situations, rather than necessarily as contents of mental states and operations. We are also developing computational models that can provide more direct support for claims about the content of conceptual understanding. In this work, we are using the programing language PROSIT (Borota et al., 1992) which is in development at the Center for the Study of Language and Information. Programs written in PROSIT have the form of a set of constraints and assertions, and the program computes other assertions that are implied by the constraints. In the programs we are writing, we include constraints that we hypothesize participants are attuned to and assertions that hold in the situation that we are analyzing, and the program computes other assertions that we can compare with states of affairs that we observe empirically. As these programs develop, we will be able to show that attunements to sets of constraints that we hypothesize are sufficient to account for states of affairs that we observe in reasoning and problem solving.

The framework of treating concepts as products and instruments of social practice, constituted by constraints and affordances of activity, raises questions that are somewhat different than those that have been addressed in the denotational and procedural frameworks. Consider the following questions:

1. One question about concepts—perhaps the primary question in this framework—concerns how concepts emerge and evolve in communication that occurs in and about practices. The examples that I have discussed in this chapter suggest some general possibilities.

- Concepts can develop in order to focus attention on important properties of action.
- Explanations of phenomena can be constructed by assembling representations of constraints, affordances, and abilities that are constituents of general concepts, and understanding of general concepts can be extended by requiring explanations to be consistent with phenomena that are explained.

- Conceptual understanding of symbolic representations can involve coordinating constituent constraints and affordances from multiple domains, including the domain of phenomena being represented as well as domains of general concepts that symbolic expressions also refer to.

These general possibilities, in turn, raise further questions that could be addressed in research.

2. How can the use of concepts in coaching and other communication help learners in becoming attuned, instrumentally and theoretically, to important constraints and affordances of activity?

3. What kinds of interactional and informational processes can be involved in the construction of instructions and explanations in discourse that depend on and extend participants' understanding of concepts?

4. How can understandings of concepts in different domains interact? That is, how can attunement to constraints and affordances in one kind of activity, including understanding of symbolic representations of those constraints and affordances, provide resources for becoming attuned to constraints and affordances in another kind of activity?

These questions are, of course, not entirely new. Even so, they treat concepts and their understanding more broadly than psychologists typically have. Some issues, such as Question 4 here, involve research topics that are currently active (in this case, analogical reasoning) in a somewhat different perspective. Other issues, such as Questions 2 and 3 here, suggest ways of relating questions about individuals' understanding of concepts with questions about social interaction in conversational discourse and the learning of social practices.

I believe that the results presented here, of applying this framework informally to a few examples, are encouraging for further work. The idea, of considering constituents of concepts as constraints, affordances, and abilities that are referred to in communication in and about social practice, seems to apply reasonably well to these examples. More systematic development of a theory based on this idea is needed to arrive at a more definite conclusion about its merits. I hope this initial preliminary discussion might encourage some colleagues to participate in that enterprise.

ACKNOWLEDGMENTS

This chapter was prepared with the support of Grant MDR9154119 from the National Science Foundation. I thank Margot Brereton, Randi Engle, Charles Fletcher, Gary Hatfield, Laura Kerr, and Jeremy Roschelle for comments on earlier versions.

REFERENCES

Anderson, J. R., Boyle, C. F., Corbett, C. F., & Lewis, M. W. (1990). Cognitive modelling and intelligent tutoring. *Artificial Intelligence, 42*, 7–50.

Barwise, J. (1989). *The situation in logic.* Stanford, CA: Center for the Study of Language and Information.

Barwise, J., & Etchemendy, J. (1989). Model-theoretic semantics. In M. Posner (Ed.), *Foundations of cognitive science* (pp. 207–245). Cambridge, MA: MIT Press/Bradford.

Barwise, J., & Perry, J. (1983). *Situations and attitudes.* Cambridge, MA: MIT Press.

Borota, J., Frank, M., Ito, A., Nakashima, H., Peters, S., Reilly, M., & Schütze, H. (1992). *The PROSIT language v1.0.* Unpublished manuscript, Center for the Study of Language and Information, Stanford University.

Bower, G. H., & Trabasso, T. (1964). Concept identification. In R. C. Atkinson (Ed.), *Studies in mathematical psychology* (pp. 32–94). Stanford, CA: Stanford University Press.

Brown, J. S., & Burton, R. R. (1980). Diagnostic models for procedural bugs in basic mathematical skills. *Cognitive Science, 4*, 370–426.

Bruner, J. S., Goodnow, J. J., & Austin, G. A. (1956). *A study of thinking.* New York: Wiley.

Burton, R. R. (1982). Diagnosing bugs in a simple procedural skill. In D. Sleeman & J. S. Brown (Eds.), *Intelligent tutoring systems* (pp. 157–184). New York: Academic Press.

Clark, H. H., & Clark, E. V. (1977). *Psychology and language.* New York: Harcourt Brace Jovanovich.

Clark, H. H., & Gerrig, R. J. (1990) Quotations as demonstrations. *Language, 66*, 764–805.

Clark, H. H., & Schaefer, E. F. (1989). Contributions to discourse. *Cognitive Science, 13*, 259–294.

Cummins, D., Kintsch, W., Reusser, K., & Weimer, R. (1988). The role of understanding in solving word problems. *Cognitive Psychology, 20*, 439–462.

Devlin, K. (1991). *Logic and information.* Cambridge, England: Cambridge University Press.

Dewey, J. (1938). *Logic: The theory of inquiry.* New York: Henry Holt.

Estes, W. K. (1994). *Classification and cognition.* New York: Oxford University Press.

Feigenbaum, E. A. (1963). The simulation of verbal learning behavior. In E. A. Feigenbaum & J. Feldman (Eds.), *Computers and thought* (pp. 297–309). New York: McGraw-Hill.

Gelman, R., & Gallistel, C. R. (1978). *The child's understanding of number.* Cambridge, MA: Harvard University Press.

Gibson, J. J. (1986). *The ecological approach to visual perception.* Hillsdale, NJ: Lawrence Erlbaum Associates. (Original work published 1979)

Greeno, J. G. (in press). Research to reform education and cognitive science. In L. A. Penner, G. M. Batche, H. M. Knoff, D. L. Nelson, & C. D. Spielberger (Eds.), *Contributions of psychology to mathematics and science education.* Washington, DC: American Psychological Association.

Greeno, J. G., Engle, R. A., Kerr, L. K., & Moore, J. L. (1993). Understanding symbols: A situativity-theory analysis of constructing mathematical meaning. In *Proceedings of the Fifteenth Annual Conference of the Cognitive Science Society* (pp. 504–509). Hillsdale, NJ: Lawrence Erlbaum Associates.

Greeno, J. G., & Scandura, J. M. (1966). All-or-none transfer based on verbally mediated concepts. *Journal of Mathematical Psychology, 3*, 388–411.

Hall, R. (1993). *Representation as shared activity: Situated cognition and Dewey's cartography of experience.* Unpublished manuscript, School of Education, University of California, Berkeley.

Heller, J. I., & Reif, F. (1984). Prescribing effective human problem-solving processes: Problem description in physics. *Cognition and Instruction, 1*, 177–216.

Hull, C. L. (1920). Quantitative aspects of the evolution of concepts. *Psychological Monographs, 28* (Whole No. 20).

Hunt, E. B., Marin, J., & Stone, P. I. (1966). *Experiments in induction.* New York: Academic Press.

Kintsch, W. (1974). *The representation of meaning in memory.* Hillsdale, NJ: Lawrence Erlbaum Associates.

Kintsch, W., & Greeno, J. G. (1985). Understanding and solving word arithmetic problems. *Psychological Review, 92*, 163–182.

Lakoff, G. (1987). *Women, fire, and dangerous things: What categories reveal about the mind.* Chicago, IL: University of Chicago Press.

Medin, D. L., & Schaffer, M. M. (1978). Context theory of classification learning. *Psychological Review, 85*, 207–238.

Moore, J. L., & Greeno, J. G. (1991). Implicit understanding of functions in quantitative reasoning. In *Proceedings of the Thirteenth Annual Conference of the Cognitive Science Society* (pp. 221–226). Hillsdale, NJ: Lawrence Erlbaum Associates.

Murphy, G. L., & Medin, D. L. (1985). The role of theories in conceptual coherence. *Psychological Review, 92*, 284–316.

Nathan, M. J., Kintsch, W., & Young, E. (1992). A theory of algebra-word-problem comprehension and its implications for the design of learning environments. *Cognition and Instruction, 9*, 329–389.

Palmer, S. E. (1978). Fundamental aspects of cognitive representation. In E. Rosch & B. B. Lloyd (Eds.), *Cognition and categorization* (pp. 259–303). Hillsdale, NJ: Lawrence Erlbaum Associates.

Piaget, J. (1965). *The child's conception of number.* New York: Norton. (First published in French, 1941)

Pylyshyn, Z. (1978). Imagery and artificial intelligence. In W. Savage (Ed.), *Perception and cognition: Issues in the foundation of psychology* (pp. 19–55). Minneapolis, MN: University of Minnesota Press.

Reitman, J. S., & Bower, G. H. (1973). Storage and later recognition of exemplars of concepts. *Cognitive Psychology, 4*, 194–206.

Riley, M. J., & Greeno, J. G. (1988). Developmental analysis of understanding language about quantities and of solving problems. *Cognition and Instruction, 5*, 49–101.

Rosch, E. (1973). On the internal structure of perceptual and semantic categories. In T. E. Moore (Ed.), *Cognitive development and the acquisition of language* (pp. 111–144). New York: Academic Press.

Rumelhart, D. E., & Norman, D. A. (1988). Representation in memory. In R. C. Atkinson, R. J. Herrnstein, G. Lindzey, & R. D. Luce (Eds.), *Stevens' handbook of experimental psychology, second edition: Vol. 2. Learning and cognition* (pp. 511–587). New York: Wiley.

Russell, B. (1938). *The principles of mathematics* (2nd ed.). New York: Norton.

Shaw, R., Turvey, M. T., & Mace, W. (1982). Ecological psychology: The consequences of a commitment to realism. In W. Weimer & D. Palermo (Eds.), *Cognition and the symbolic processes* (Vol. 2, pp. 159–226). Hillsdale, NJ: Lawrence Erlbaum Associates.

Shepard, R. N., Hovland, C. I., & Jenkins, H. M. (1961). Learning and memorization of classifications. *Psychological Monographs, 75*, 1–41.

Smith, E. E. (1989). Concepts and induction. In M. Posner (Ed.), *Foundations of cognitive science* (pp. 501–526). Cambridge, MA: MIT Press/Bradford.

Smith, E. E. (1990). Categorization. In D. N. Osherson & E. E. Smith (Eds.), *An invitation to cognitive science. Vol. 3: Thinking* (pp. 33–53). Cambridge, MA: MIT Press.

Smith, E. E., & Medin, D. L. (1981). *Categories and concepts.* Cambridge, MA: Harvard University Press.

Smith, E. E., Shoben, E. J., & Rips, L. J. (1974). Structures and process in semantic memory. *Psychological Review, 81*, 214–241.

Snow, R. E. (1992). Aptitude theory: Yesterday, today, and tomorrow. *Educational Psychologist, 27*, 5–32.

Van Lehn, K. (1990). *Mind bugs: The origins of procedural misconceptions.* Cambridge, MA: MIT Press/Bradford.

Weaver, C. A., III, & Kintsch, W. (1992). Enhancing students' comprehension of the conceptual structure of algebra word problems. *Journal of Educational Psychology, 84*, 419–428.

Wittgenstein, L. (1953). *Philosophical investigations.* New York: MacMillan.

Chapter 6

The Minimalist Hypothesis: Directions for Research

Gail McKoon
Roger Ratcliff
Northwestern University

According to the minimalist hypothesis (McKoon & Ratcliff, 1992), the only inferences routinely generated during reading (without special goals or strategies), are those based on quickly and easily available information and those required for local coherence of the text being read. The minimalist hypothesis summarizes the past 20 years of text processing research. During that time, little uncontestable evidence has been found to support the notion that readers engage in the constructive processes that would be required to generate a large number and variety of inferences. Most of the data that does show constructive inferences has been collected in situations where readers could plausibly be thought to use special efforts, goals, or strategies directed toward the kind of inference under investigation. For the great majority of experiments, in which there is no reason to think such efforts took place, the minimalist hypothesis is a description of the few kinds of inferences that might be drawn in the absence of special goals or strategies.

Of course, readers often engage in reading for a special purpose—to learn, to criticize, to gain information for decision making, and so on. But in most experiments, they have no such purpose. The data collected in these experiments—the data summarized by the minimalist hypothesis—will hopefully provide the basis from which we can eventually gain an understanding of the kinds of inferences that are added when readers make special efforts toward some particular goal. The minimalist hypothesis describes the initial information provided by the retrieval system to construct an initial representation of a text that in turn could provide a foundation on which constructionist representations could be built. The hope is to understand which inferences are provided initially and which require additional processing. Of course, the theoretical picture is not likely to be this simple; such complications as continuously available kinds of information, partial information (McKoon & Ratcliff, 1986), and parallel processing are to be expected. But we have hope that such issues as the time course of availability of different kinds of information, the automaticity of some kinds of processes, and the interdependence of various kinds of inferences can be sorted out.

At this writing, a year has gone by since the minimalist hypothesis was proposed and it has become clear that this hypothesis has more to offer than was originally intended. Although we meant the hypothesis to be a summary of the current state of text processing research, we also hoped that it would provide a challenge to investigators to examine inference processes with renewed intensity and increased methodological rigor. We hoped that constructionist theories would begin to specify what inferences should be generated with what kinds of cognitive processes, in counterpoint to the minimalist hypothesis. Instead, constructionist efforts have most often treated the minimalist hypothesis as a target, criticizing the hypothesis on all conceivable grounds. In most cases, the attacks on minimalism offer no constructive impetus to new research.

To give an example, consider the well-known inference about an actress who falls from a 14th-story roof (McKoon & Ratcliff 1986, 1989a, 1989d). McKoon and Ratcliff (1992) claimed that the failure of readers to explicitly encode the inference that the actress died was a contradiction of constructionist theories of reading. Instead of developing an account of this result or providing new empirical information about it, constructionists began an argument among themselves over whether their view, as formulated in the past, should or should not predict the "died" inference (e.g., against: Glenberg & Mathew, 1992; for: Magliano & Graesser, 1991). Such an argument points to the incoherence of the constructionist view.

Constructionist theorists have also become revisionists with respect to the conditions under which constructionist inferences are generated. In the past literature, from Bransford, Barclay, and Franks in 1972 to Glenberg (Glenberg & Mathew, 1992; Glenberg, Meyer, & Lindem, 1987), Graesser (Graesser, 1981; Magliano & Graesser, 1991), Singer (Singer, 1979; Singer, Halldorson, Lear, & Andrusiak, 1992), and Trabasso (Trabasso & Sperry, 1985; Trabasso & van den Broek, 1985) in the 1990s, constructionists have discussed their experimental results as though they reflected inferences generated during encoding, in the absence of special efforts, goals, or strategies on the part of the reader. There has never been any suggestion that special circumstances existed in their experiments, or that such circumstances were required for the encoding of constructionist inferences (except see Johnson-Laird, 1980, 1983). When we labeled their position as postulating automatic encoding of inferences (McKoon & Ratcliff, 1992) and argued that the data could not support such a claim, we find suddenly that Glenberg (Glenberg & Mathew, 1992) "does not think most mental modelers would hold that mental models are constructed automatically (at least not all of the time)," while Garnham (1992, sec. 1.1) in contradiction implies that it has always been the case that "constructionist processes play an essential role in inferences that are made automatically."

Equally confusing is the constructionist response to our characterization of their hypothesis as: "the mental representation of a text automatically specifies, in some complete way, the real-life situation described by the text" (McKoon & Ratcliff, 1992, p. 458). We thought this a fair rewording of Bransford, Barclay, and Franks's original hypothesis that comprehension results in the "construction of a holistic description of the overall situation being communicated" by a text (Bransford, Barclay, & Franks, 1972, p. 202), and because most constructionists would align themselves with Bransford, Barclay, and Franks, we thought our characterization to be a fair rendition of current constructionist positions. Apparently, not all constructionists agree (cf. Garnham, 1992, 1993a, 1993b, 1993c; Glenberg & Mathew, 1992). But, without exact distinctions among which inferences are and are not required to communicate the situation described by a text, their agreement or disagreement does not provide any useful insights.

What has become apparent is that the "constructionist position" is not a position at all. One could have assumed that many of those engaged in research on text processing in recent decades shared an underlying theoretical view, the constructionist view originally put forward by Bransford et al. (1972). The assumption of a shared view was reasonable given that there was little discussion of any alternative view and, indeed, little discussion of any disagreement of any kind. However, instead of a unified view, it now appears that constructionism is a collection of informal views that differ on various dimensions. Each view is apparently molded by data collected from whatever methodology the holder of that view believes to reveal underlying text representations. We do not, of course, expect constructionists to provide a complete and detailed theory of inference generation overnight. Rather, we intended the minimalist hypothesis to prompt new research that would lead to revisions in both the minimalist hypothesis and constructionist views. At the end of this chapter, we point to some intriguing examples of such research (and see Graesser, Singer, & Trabasso, 1993; Graesser & Zwaan, chap. 7 in this vol.). We hope for research that will extend and elaborate the minimalist hypothesis until, perhaps, it will no longer be declared minimalist. But this can happen only through cumulative research, not through argument.

First, however, we need to clarify some of the methodological constraints on empirical research specified by the minimalist hypothesis and define some of the particular problems for study that the hypothesis suggests. In so doing, we show that some criticisms of the hypothesis have been misguided.

METHODOLOGICAL RULES

The minimalist hypothesis describes the kinds of inferences that will be generated during reading when the reader engages in no special efforts, goals, or strategies. Special strategies can be set up for the reader through instructions, payoffs, or problem-solving kinds of texts (cf. Bransford et al., 1972, Exp. 3; Potts, 1974). In the absence of such strategies, the minimalist hypothesis states that only two kinds of inferences will be generated during reading: those based on easily and quickly available information and those required to establish local coherence. Such a severe limit on inference processes implies an equally severe limit on experimental procedures. The minimalist hypothesis can be tested only by examining the encoding of inferences under conditions in which the experimental procedures allow all processes *but* those of encoding during reading to be excluded as explanations of the results.

Online Tests. These are popular, but unfortunately the logical possibilities for interpretation of their results are not universally understood. When a target item immediately follows a text, responses to the target may be determined by backwards context-checking processes (Forster, 1981) or by processes in which the target and the context interact (Norris, 1986; Ratcliff & McKoon, 1988). Either way, it is important to note that the preceding context can potentially include *all* preceding information and that context includes not only individual pieces of information but also the meanings that result when those pieces are combined. It is not possible, for example, to test for context checking by comparing whole texts against texts with some sentences deleted (Singer et al., 1992) or against texts with the same words recombined into different meanings (Whitney, Ritchie, & Crane, 1992) because the preceding context has necessarily changed.

Because of the context checking and interactive processing possibilities, online results can rarely tell us whether the information represented by a target item was available during reading *before* the target was actually presented for test. All they can usually tell us is how quickly the relation between target and context is available when the context and target are both in short-term memory at the same time, which happens when the target is presented. For example, Onifer and Swinney's (1981) results do not necessarily indicate that both meanings of an ambiguous word are available during reading (as suggested by Singer, Graesser, & Trabasso, 1993); logically, all that can be concluded is that the relation between the ambiguous word and a test word is quickly available (see Ratcliff & McKoon, 1988). However, it is theoretically possible to rule out context checking and interactive processing explanations of online results. We know of two occasions on which this has been done (noting that on both occasions the results supported the minimalist hypothesis; Dopkins, Klin, & Myers, 1993; McKoon & Ratcliff, 1992), and we strongly urge that further studies be conducted as tests of the minimalist hypothesis.

Reading Time. Another popular measure of comprehension processes is reading time for a word, phrase, or sentence. Sometimes (cf. Huitema, Dopkins, Klin, & Myers, 1993; Myers, O'Brien, Albrecht, & Mason, 1993; Rayner &

Morris, 1991) a slow down in reading rate is used simply to indicate that processing is more difficult for one linguistic unit than another. But when reading time is used to measure comprehension, a serious problem arises: Readers always have the option to trade off speed and accuracy. As the minimalist hypothesis emphasizes, readers can read for speed, sacrificing accurate and complete understanding; or they can read for complete understanding, sacrificing speed; or they can engage in more microscopic tradeoffs. Without some measure of degree of understanding, reading time is uninterpretable except as an indication that the reader has chosen some particular point on a speed/accuracy trade-off function. What is required for many purposes is the combination of reading time *and* a measure of comprehension. On the basis of reading time data alone, it is not correct to decide that some inference is established in the mental representation of a text during comprehension (as has been done by, for example, Graesser et al., 1993, pp. 20, 39; O'Brien, 1987; O'Brien, Shank, Myers, & Rayner, 1988).

Multiple regression analysis of reading times is sometimes suggested as an alternative to more traditional controlled experiments (Graesser & Kreuz, 1993; Magliano & Graesser, 1991). Graesser, Magliano, and Haberlandt (in press, p. 8) say that "it is important to appreciate the broad capabilities of the reading-regression methodology," and point to the valuable contributions of this methodology in demonstrating the robust effects of such variables as number of letters per word, word frequency, imagery, and the serial positions of sentences in texts (p. 9). It has yet to be shown, however, that this methodology will allow investigation of questions of more subtle interest about inference processes (see Kliegl, Olson, & Davidson, 1982).

Facilitative Effects as Opposed to Inhibitory Effects. A frequently encountered mistake in the interpretation of data is the assumption that differences in some measure are due to For example, consider these two texts from experiments by Singer (Singer, in press; Singer et al., 1992):

(1) Wendy aspired to be able to play the grand piano. Her training included doing weights every day. Are pianos heavy?

(2) Peter went to the store for onions for the salad. Peter couldn't keep from crying. Do onions make eyes tear?

Such texts are odd, perhaps incoherent, according to undergraduate judges (and according to Graesser et al., 1993; Magliano & Graesser, 1991; and Singer et al., 1993, have been vehement in their warnings against the use of such texts). In addition, the combinations of the texts with their questions are odd. Any kind of processes (e.g., those measured by reading time or postreading question answering time) might be slowed by the oddness, and therefore any differences in processing times between these texts and less odd texts cannot be attributed to facilitation of processing for the less odd texts.

A similar problem applies to these two texts from Sanford and Garrod (1981):

(3) John was not looking forward to teaching math. The bus trundled slowly along the road. He hoped he could control the class today.

(4) John was on his way to school. The bus trundled slowly along the road. He hoped he could control the class today.

Sanford and Garrod found that the third sentence of the second text was read more slowly than the third sentence of the first text. They and others (Keenan, 1992) attribute this difference to an inference generated during reading of the first sentence of the second text, the inference that John is a school boy. This inference then conflicts with him controlling the class, slowing reading time. But the difference in reading times could equally well have come about because processing in the first text was facilitated by the information that John was a teacher in its first sentence. From the minimalist point of view, one goal for research is to separate out these kinds of confoundings by investigating whether inferences like John being a schoolboy are quickly and easily available from a sentence like *John was on his way to school.*

Subjects' Intuitions.   Many procedures rely on subjects' intuitions, or give subjects the motivation, time, and opportunity to adopt strategies specific to the task they are given. Such procedures include free and cued recall, verbal protocols, story summaries, ratings of various kinds, and question answering under conditions in which there is no speed pressure (Bransford et al., 1972; Glenberg & Mathew, 1992; Graesser et al., 1993; Magliano & Graesser, 1991; Singer et al., 1993). What we know about these procedures from the past 20 years of research and from current theories about memory retrieval processes is that they allow subjects to edit their responses or to construct responses based on information that they otherwise had not encoded and would not have encoded. Corbett and Dosher (1978) and Singer (1978) showed that performance in cued recall is best explained by retrieval processes working to construct a link from the cue back to the to-be-remembered material. McKoon and Ratcliff (1986) showed that free recall responses contained inferences that did not appear in an online test or in a later speeded recognition test. McKoon and Ratcliff (1986, 1989a, 1989d) and Potts, Keenan, and Golding (1988) showed that subjects' ratings of the likelihood of a predictable event did not predict whether the inference would be drawn during reading: For events rated extremely likely, there was no evidence for inference during reading under some retrieval conditions, and two sets of events rated equally likely to occur were not equally strongly inferred during reading. Finally, McKoon (in preparation) showed that subjects' answers to questions about the goals of characters in stories do not accurately predict the occurrence of inferences about those goals during reading. Conversely, there exist inferences that *are* encoded during reading that would never show up in question answering, recall, or verbal protocols (cf. Barton & Sanford, 1993; Erickson & Mattson, 1981; Greene, Gerrig, McKoon, & Ratcliff, in press; Greene, McKoon, & Ratcliff, 1992; McKoon, Greene, & Ratcliff, 1993; McKoon, Ratcliff, Ward, & Sproat, 1993; McKoon, Ward, Ratcliff, & Sproat, 1993; Rayner & Frazier, 1987; Taraban & McClelland, 1988; Ward, Sproat, & McKoon, 1991). For those who advocate the use of subjects' intuitions as a research strategy (Glenberg & Mathew, 1992; Graesser et al., 1993; Magliano & Graesser, 1991; Singer et al., 1993; Suh & Trabasso, 1993), the task is to model how such intuitions are constructed, to theoretically relate the intuitions to data obtained from other procedures for investigating comprehension, and to explain how subjects' intuitions will reveal such subtle aspects of comprehension as might be predicted by the minimalist hypothesis—for example, the argument structures of verbs or the combinations of meaning that make the anomaly of surviving dead unnoticeable (Barton & Sanford, 1993).

Speeded Item Recognition.   One paradigm in which subjects' intuitions and retrieval strategies can be kept from affecting their responses is speeded item recognition. When a single test word is embedded in a list of other test words, it is very unlikely that subjects can guess the purpose of the experiment, and therefore unlikely that they can adopt strategies specific to the variables under investigation. It is also unlikely that they can engage in retrieval strategies beyond fast automatic ones (automatic as defined by Posner & Snyder, 1975) because their response times are kept well within the automatic range. It might be argued that recognition responses to single words tap only some superficial representation of a text in memory (Graesser & Kreuz, 1993; Graesser et al., 1993; Magliano & Graesser, 1991; Morrow, Bower, & Greenspan, 1989, 1990; Morrow, Greenspan, & Bower, 1987; Zwaan & Graesser, 1993a, 1993b), but several results show this to be incorrect. Despite claims to the contrary (Graesser et al., 1993, p. 23; Whitney & Waring, 1989), recognition data have shown evidence of schemalike structures in memory for text (Allbritton, McKoon, & Gerrig, 1994; McKoon & Ratcliff, 1980b; McKoon, Ratcliff, & Seifert, 1989; Seifert, McKoon, Abelson, & Ratcliff, 1986), evidence of the encoding of what-happens-next inferences (McKoon & Ratcliff, 1986, 1989a, 1989d), evidence of the encoding of inferences connecting widely separated pieces of text information (Greene et al., in press; McKoon & Ratcliff, 1992), evidence of the encoding of causal connections not explicitly stated by the text (McKoon, Greene, & Ratcliff, 1993), evidence that contextually appropriate aspects of meaning are encoded (McKoon & Ratcliff, 1988), and evidence of inferences related to discourse models (McKoon, Ratcliff, Ward, & Sprout, 1993; McKoon, Ward, Ratcliff, & Sproat, 1993; Ward et al., 1991). It should also be pointed out that constructionist theorists show no hesitation over accepting the results of recognition procedures when those results are consistent with their position (Glenberg et al., 1987; Graesser et al., 1993; Singer et al., 1993; Suh & Trabasso, 1993; Trabasso & Suh, 1993).

"Naturalistic" Texts.   It is sometimes argued (Graesser, Magliano, & Haber-landt, in press; Magliano & Graesser, 1991) that the choice of textual materials is a critical methodological issue, that "naturalistic" texts are better in some way than texts written by experimenters. How this argument might be supported empirically is unclear, because Graesser, Person, and Johnston (in press) found no effects of their theoretically interesting variables on reading times for natu-ralistic texts (on first reading). Empirical support aside, choice of text is not an issue of preference. Instead, it should be the goal of any theory of inference to explain what inferences are generated under what conditions. Constructionist theories must explain why some kinds of inferences (e.g., those studied by Cor-bett, 1984; Dopkins et al., 1993; Glenberg et al., 1987; Greene et al., in press; Greene et al., 1992; Huitema et al., 1993; McKoon, Greene, & Ratcliff, 1993; McKoon & Ratcliff, 1986, 1989a, 1989c, 1989d, 1992; Murray, Klin, & Myers, 1993; Myers et al., 1993; Potts et al., 1988) are generated from experimenter-written texts and other inferences are not. And constructionist theorists must explain why they accept as support for their position some results from experi-menter-written texts (e.g., Glenberg et al., 1987; Singer, 1993, in press; Suh & Trabasso, 1993; Trabasso & Suh, 1993) yet reject results from experimenter-written texts that do not support their position.

The argument for rejection of results from nonnatural materials is a general one that appears in many contexts (cf Neisser, 1978). It could form the basis of rejection for much of the research in the areas of visual and auditory perception, memory, decision making, and problem solving. Our reasons against such rejec-tion are the same as those previously put forward by others in other contexts (see Banaji & Crowder, 1991).

FALSIFICATION

The minimalist hypothesis applies to several different kinds of inferences and it is important to separate them in discussing whether the hypothesis can be falsified by empirical data. In the following sections, we separate inferences based on easily available information from those triggered by local incoherence, and we separate inferences based on knowledge given explicitly in the text from infer-ences based on general knowledge not stated in the text. Throughout these sec-tions, we discuss situations in which the reader has no special goals or strategies.

Locally Coherent Text

1. Suppose that some inference is encoded during reading into the mental representation of a text and that the text contains no coherence break that could have triggered the inference. Then, according to the minimalist hypothesis, the inference could only be generated from information that is quickly and easily

available. To be quickly available, the information could be in short-term memory, it could be in long-term memory for previously encoded parts of the text, or it could be well-known general knowledge. Consider the case where the information is general knowledge. In this case, it is possible to show that the minimalist hypothesis is wrong, and in fact, we have already done so in experiments presented in McKoon and Ratcliff (1989d).

In those experiments, we first showed that an inference about someone being hurt was encoded, to some degree, during reading of a sentence about that person diving into an empty swimming pool and hitting concrete. The evidence that the inference was encoded was obtained from a delayed memory test, so that the problems of interpretation of online tests were avoided, and the test required speeded responses in a situation where subjects could not guess the goals of the experimenter, thus avoiding strategic retrieval processes that could have constructed the inference at the time of the test. Given evidence from the delayed memory test that the inference was encoded and retrievable in certain retrieval contexts, then the minimalist hypothesis must predict that the relation between the inferred information (getting hurt) and the information in the text (diving into concrete) should be available immediately during reading (i.e., within say 250 ms of reading the information on which the inference was based; this would be defined as automatic availability in the Posner & Snyder, 1975, sense of automaticity). Our data showed that it was not (see also Murray et al., 1993). Thus, we ourselves have falsified one prediction of the minimalist hypothesis (noting that, because evidence for encoding of the inference depends on the retrieval context at test time, constructionist predictions are also contradicted). In discussing this finding previously (McKoon & Ratcliff, 1992), we pointed out that it might be accommodated by Kintsch's construction-integration model (Kintsch, 1988), illustrating how the minimalist hypothesis can be modified by the addition of explicit processing mechanisms.

The kind of evidence that cannot, by itself, falsify the minimalist hypothesis is evidence that some relation is (or is not) available immediately online. For example, the relation between bug and insect appears to be available immediately even when the sentence context indicates that the other meaning of bug is intended (Onifer & Swinney, 1981). Because there is no evidence that the wrong meaning supports an inference encoded into the text representation, there is no contradiction of the minimalist hypothesis. Similar reasoning applies to online results discussed by Singer et al. (1993) and to results from experiments by Swinney and Osterhout (1990); Till, Mross, and Kintsch (1988); and Dell, McKoon, and Ratcliff (1983) (but not McKoon & Ratcliff, 1980a).

2. Easily available information can come not only from general knowledge but also from the text being read. Text information can reside in long-term memory like general knowledge, if it was read far back in the text, or it can reside in short-term memory, if it has just been read or if it has been brought back into short-term memory for some reason (cf. Fletcher, 1986; Fletcher, Arthur,

& Skeete, chap. 11 in this vol.; Fletcher & Bloom, 1988; Kintsch & van Dijk, 1978; van den Broek, 1988, 1990a, 1990b). For short-term memory, the minimalist hypothesis explicitly (McKoon & Ratcliff, 1992) assumes that information is processed in cycles, as described by Kintsch (Kintsch & van Dijk, 1978; also Fletcher & Bloom, 1988), such that the propositions residing in short-term memory on any given cycle are a function of both recency and topicality or salience (contra claims by Singer et al., 1993). Clearly, the encoding of inferences based on text information residing in short-term memory cannot contradict the minimalist hypothesis because short-term memory information is assumed by definition to be easily available, although the degree of availability of a concept in short-term memory may vary (see discussion later).

For text information in long-term memory (information that has not been reinstated into short-term memory), empirical evidence about its use in inference generation is only suggestive (Huitema et al., 1993; McKoon & Ratcliff, 1992; Murray et al., 1993; Myers et al., 1993) and it is discussed later in the context of new directions for research.

Locally Incoherent Text

1. Inferences that are not based on easily available information must be triggered, according to the minimalist hypothesis, by local incoherence. For example, our data (McKoon & Ratcliff, 1992) suggest that readers try to understand the relation between Sentences 5 and 6.

> (5) The engine of their old car blew up, and Karen and Felix had to buy a new car.
>
> (6) Karen decided fix up the basement.

These sentences are obviously locally incoherent (simple argument repetition alone does not provide coherence, a point missed by some, Graesser et al., 1993, p. 43; Singer, in press; Suh & Trabasso, 1993; but noted previously by Keenan, Baillet, & Brown, 1984).

What is difficult is defining local coherence for situations beyond the obvious ones. As we pointed out previously (McKoon & Ratcliff 1992), there currently is no definition of local coherence. Arbitrary definitions designed to contradict the minimalist hypothesis provide no real solution to the problem. For example, it is not productive to decide that Sentences 7 and 8 or Sentences 9 and 10 are locally coherent just in order to use data from their texts to falsify the minimalist hypothesis (Graesser et al., 1993; Singer et al., 1993; Suh & Trabasso, 1993; Trabasso & Suh, 1993). These pairs of sentences represent possible coherence breaks, and as such must be carefully considered when attempting to model processing of their texts. These pairs of sentences exemplify the need for empirical explorations of various bases for coherence, with the goal of arriving at a definition against which minimalism could be tested.

(7) Betty felt sad.

(8) Betty saw her friend knitting.

(9) Jimmy was very sad.

(10) Jimmy's mother told him that he should have his own savings.

2. It has been pointed out that the minimalist hypothesis can be saved from falsification by attributing contradictory findings to "strategies" adopted by subjects especially to produce those findings. Unlike some critics of the hypothesis (Keenan, 1992; Singer et al., 1993; Zwaan & Graesser, 1993a), we do not think this will be so easy. On the one hand, there are experiments where the materials given to subjects might easily be thought to invoke special strategies (Bransford et al., 1972; Potts, 1974), and the instructions and test conditions used in some experiments (e.g., Morrow et al., 1989; see also Wilson, Rinck, McNamara, Bower, & Morrow, 1993) are another instance where special strategies might be used by subjects. But most psycholinguistic experiments cannot be so easily classed as invoking special strategies. How could it be argued, for example, that Glenberg et al.'s (1987) subjects—reading stories about girls picking flowers and other such topics—were engaging in strategies, whereas our subjects (McKoon & Ratcliff 1992)—reading about CIA agents and cowboy shoot-outs—were not?

More importantly, what any theory must do is to explain the varied and complex sets of results from all those experiments in which subjects most likely did not have special goals, experiments in which the texts constructed by the experimenters were not very interesting and the only strategy subjects engaged in was designed to get themselves out of the experiment as quickly as possible with some minimally acceptable level of performance. Dismissing the varied and complex results from these experiments (as suggested by Graesser, Magliano, & Haberlandt, in press; Magliano & Graesser, 1991) is to miss the power of text comprehension processes. In most experiments, subjects do not necessarily have the "NEED TO KNOW" (Graesser et al., 1993; Singer et al., 1993, p. 34) postulated by some constructionist theorists, yet the complex patterns of data offer the possibility of important theoretical constraints. Even with "puzzling sequence(s) of propositions that satisfy a researcher's counterbalancing constraints" (Graesser et al., 1993, p. l8), there are powerful data to be explained.

Directions for Research

The minimalist hypothesis emphasizes the *processes* of inference generation. It is this emphasis that in large part determines the methodological rules that must be followed in future research to test or falsify the hypothesis. However, as mentioned earlier, our original intention was to focus research on the specific kinds of inferences suggested by the minimalist hypothesis. Inference generation is assumed to depend on the ease with which supporting information becomes available or the difficulty of establishing local coherence. Thus the obvious questions for research become what kinds of information are easily available and how easily local coherence is constructed.

Given the evidence available in current research, we have no understanding of why some kinds of information are easily available in support of inferences and others are not. For example, sentences about milking animals on farms are understood as references to cows, information that can be shown to be quickly available (McKoon & Ratcliff, 1989b; Roth & Shoben, 1983), but sentences about stirring coffee are not understood as references to spoons (Corbett & Dosher, 1978; McKoon & Ratcliff, 1981), and information about spoons is not quickly available in the stirring coffee context. The minimalist hypothesis explains this in the processing sense that it predicts the failure of encoding when information is not quickly available. But it does not take the second step of explaining why one kind of information is available and the other not. Constructionist theories do not offer any explanation at all: Either neither piece of information, cows or spoons, would be required in a situation model for the text or both would be required; there is no a priori reason to distinguish between them.

There are a number of intriguing candidate kinds of information that might be easily available and encoded from general knowledge during reading. Instantiations of stereotypical aspects of meaning are one kind of inference suggested by the cow example (see also McKoon & Ratcliff, 1989b). "John rides the bus in the morning" might, through conceptual combinations among *John, riding a bus*, and *morning*, quickly evoke the concept school (Sanford & Garrod, 1981). A story about a surgeon might quickly evoke an instantiation of a person of the male sex (Keenan, 1992).

It is important to understand that, from the minimalist point of view, instantiations will not necessarily represent "correct" interpretations of a text. Because we assume that reading is a collection of processes for which speed and accuracy can be traded off against each other (Greene et al., 1992; McKoon, Greene, & Ratcliff, 1993), information that is quickly available may not be fully checked for accuracy. Such a tradeoff is suggested by the comprehension failures exhibited in the Moses illusion (Bredart & Modolo, 1988; Erickson & Mattson, 1981; van Oostendorp & de Mul, 1990; Reder & Kusbit, 1991) and in Barton and Sanford's (1993) example about burying the survivors of an airplane crash.

It is also important to understand that information that is quickly and easily available might represent quite complex mixtures. For example, the causal chain that explains how antibiotics combat infection might be quite long, and part of the general knowledge of most readers, but the causal connection between having an infection and curing it with antibiotics that is encoded during reading might be some shorthand like *fix, antibiotics, infections* (see Keenan et al., 1984). For

6. THE MINIMALIST HYPOTHESIS

another example, the meanings of verbs might include contingencies with respect to the syntactic structures in which they are expressed; *cramming a closet with books* might mean something quite different from *cramming books into a closet* (Levin, 1993; McKoon & Ratcliff, 1989c).

Just as some pieces of information in general knowledge can be quickly and easily accessible from a text being read, so can some pieces of information in long-term memory for the text being read. Salience is the term we have used to describe the accessibility of a concept or event in the discourse model of a text (cf. McKoon & Ratcliff, 1992). During reading, the discourse model is assumed to contain all the concepts and events of the text, though, in general, concepts mentioned recently would be assumed to be more accessible than concepts mentioned farther back in a text. Accessibility is determined by many interacting factors, including syntactic position in a sentence (McKoon, Ratcliff, Ward, & Sproat, 1993; McKoon, Ward, Ratcliff, & Sproat, 1993; Ward et al., 1991); semantic position relative to a verb (McKoon & Ratcliff, 1989c); connections to other concepts via semantic, pragmatic (McKoon & Ratcliff, 1981), associative, argument repetition, and perceived topicality links (McKoon & Ratcliff, 1992; McKoon, Ward, Ratcliff, & Sproat, 1993; Ward et al., 1991); and so on. During reading, all of these factors interact to give text concepts in both short- and long-term memory different degrees of accessibility. In addition, the accessibility of a concept or event depends on the particular cue with which it is referenced (cf. McKoon, Ward, Ratcliff, & Sproat, 1993). For example, *surgeon* might be more accessible relative to the cue *he* than the cue *she*. The retrieval process involved in accessing some discourse concept or event in long-term memory is understood in terms of the current global memory models (the resonance metaphor used in Gillund & Shiffrin, 1984; Hintzman, 1986; Murdock, 1983; Ratcliff, 1978; Ratcliff & McKoon, 1988). (It should be noted that we see the notion of a discourse model as an update of the 1978 Kintsch and van Dijk model; the only difference is that we are attempting to better define the representation constructed during processing, in the same spirit as Fletcher & Bloom, 1988; Kintsch, 1992; van den Broek, 1990b).

As with information from general knowledge, information from the text being read may not be "correctly" interpreted. For example, inferences to instantiate a concept as the referent of a pronoun should succeed just to the extent that the correct referent is sufficiently more salient than other possible referents with respect to the pronoun as a cue. When the referent is not sufficiently more salient, then the speed/accuracy trade-off situation applies; we assume readers can sacrifice accuracy for speed, leaving some references unresolved (Greene et al., 1992; Greene et al., in press; McKoon, Greene, & Ratcliff, 1993).

When is textual information in long-term memory sufficiently salient that it becomes involved in the processing of information currently being read? One possibility is that information about the main characters in a story is always sufficiently salient. McKoon and Ratcliff (1992, see also Murray et al., 1993;

O'Brien & Albrecht, 1992) found evidence that different pieces of information about a main character were connected together even when separated by large distances in surface structure. However, this cannot be assumed to be true quite in general. McKoon and Ratcliff (1992), in a different set of much shorter stories, found that subjects appeared not to encode the inconsistency of two propositions about a main character when the propositions were separated by only a few sentences, and other failures of readers to notice inconsistencies are well documented (cf. Epstein, Glenberg, & Bradley, 1984). Perhaps, a suggestion about how these results might be reconciled is offered in recent experiments by Huitema, Myers, and their colleagues (Huitema et al., 1993; Myers et al., 1993). They used short texts each with a main character, very much like the short stories used by McKoon and Ratcliff (1992), but they found evidence that readers did notice the inconsistency between information given about the character early in the text and information given later in the text. For example, in one story, Dick wants to take a vacation for sun and swimming but later Dick buys a plane ticket for Alaska (Huitema et al., 1993). It may be that the general knowledge that connects vacations, sun, and swimming to plane tickets adds to the accessibility of the proposition about a vacation from the proposition about buying a plane ticket. In other words, *Dick*, by itself, in the earlier proposition might not be sufficiently accessible from Dick, by itself, in the later proposition. But *Dick* plus *vacation, sun*, and *swim* might be sufficiently accessible from *Dick* plus *plane ticket*. In Myers et al. (1993), accessibility of the earlier information was increased in a different way; the information was discussed in several sentences with strong emphasis. Again, readers appeared to notice a later inconsistency. These results are intriguing; they suggest broader explorations of the variables that govern salience and consideration of the possibility that such variables are more powerful than we might have thought.

A particularly appealing outcome of such explorations might be to reduce the importance of the problem of defining local coherence. Our original thought (McKoon & Ratcliff, 1992) was that incoherence in the sense of disconnected pieces of information is a rare occurrence. Discourse (written or spoken) is produced from the message that the writer or speaker wants to convey, and we can assume that the message is usually coherent. It may be made coherent through connections among propositions in short-term memory or through easily accessible pieces of general knowledge, or it may be made coherent through salient connections to earlier parts of the discourse. Perhaps it is rare for all of these mechanisms to fail. If so, the research strategy would be, not to look for instances of incoherence, but instead to investigate how quickly and easily the different kinds of information required to establish coherence become available.

Consider the following paragraph from some recent experiments by Dopkins et al. (1993):

The atmosphere on the luxury liner was getting tense. Several valuable items had disappeared from the cabins. When he heard about the problem, the captain began an investigation in order to nab the thief. After two days of considering the evidence, the captain had the purser brought to his office.

Dopkins et al. investigated comprehension of the purser. This concept was not mentioned before the last sentence in the text. Although the definite article *the* might suggest an anaphor, no explicit referent exists in the discourse model. So this might be thought to provide an instance of incoherence. But there are a number of possibilities about how *the purser* might be connected to the rest of the text. General knowledge might provide a simple connection between luxury liners and the purser as one of the employees on the liner. General linguistic knowledge might provide more information, that is, that people are *brought* to some location by an authority figure for some purpose. The "purpose" argument of *brought* is left unfilled, and this gap might function as an anaphor to cue a referent. Dopkins et al.'s data support such a suggestion: *thief*, a part of the possible referent *to nab a thief*, is facilitated in an online test following the *purser* sentence. These several kinds of processing might conspire to provide coherence.

If the paragraph is changed to provide different information about the purser, then the conspiracy of processes also changes:

While strolling the deck with the purser, the captain noticed that the atmosphere on the luxury liner was getting tense. Several valuable items had disappeared from the cabins. When he heard about the problem, the captain began an investigation in order to nab the thief. After two days of considering the evidence, the captain had the purser brought to his office.

Now, when *the purser* is encountered in the last sentence, anaphoric processes connect it to the most salient (with respect to *the purser* as cue) earlier mentioned discourse entity, the purser encountered in the first sentence. And apparently, according to Dopkins et al.'s data, there is no further processing of the purser to connect it to *thief*.

This analysis (following closely that of Dopkins et al.) provides an intriguing example of how coherence can be investigated. The challenge is to find and tease apart other such conspiracies of coherence, and to map out their processes and the structures of information upon which they depend.

We are still left, however, with a different kind of incoherence, the incoherence that arises when readers fail to encode connections given to them explicitly (Noordman & Vonk, 1992; Vonk & Noordman, 1990) or when readers appear to encode contradictory pieces of information, such as the animals entering Moses's Ark two by two (Erickson & Mattson, 1981; van Oostendorp & de Mul, 1990). The minimalist account of such incoherence is simple: Readers, in trading off speed for accuracy in processing, mistake the quantity of easily available connections between Moses and the Ark for quality. But, as with other inferences, the minimalist account does not specify for what kinds of information or under what textual conditions this quantity/quality tradeoff should apply. Constructionist accounts fare even worse. Mental models might be stretched to keep the actress falling off the 14th-story roof alive (Glenberg & Mathew, 1992), but we cannot envision a mental model of the surviving dead from an airplane crash (Barton & Sanford, 1993).

CONCLUSION

This chapter has outlined minimalist hypothesis considerations of comprehension processes and methodologies for testing those processes. We hope to have emphasized our original goal, to promote investigation of inference processes with renewed intensity and increased methodological rigor. The large amount of recent research on inference processes, in journals and in the chapters of this book, leads us to be optimistic that much will be learned about comprehension processes in the next few years.

ACKNOWLEDGMENTS

The research described in this chapter was supported by NIDCD grant ROI-DCOI240 and AFOSR grant 90-0246 (jointly funded by NSF) to Gail McKoon and by NIHM grants HD MH44640 and MHOO871 to Roger Ratcliff.

REFERENCES

Allbritton, D. W., McKoon, G., & Gerrig R. (1994). *Metaphor-based schemas and text representations: Making connections through conceptual metaphors.* Manuscript submitted for publication.

Banaji, M. R., & Crowder, R. G. (1991). Some everyday thoughts on ecologically valid methods. *American Psychologist, 46,* 78–79.

Barton, S. B., & Sanford, A. J. (1993). A case-study of anomaly detection: Shallow semantic processing and cohesion establishment. *Memory and Cognition, 21,* 477–487.

Bransford, J. D., Barclay, J. R., & Franks, J. J. (1972). Sentence memory: A constructive versus interpretive approach. *Cognitive Psychology, 3,* 193–209.

Bredart, S., & Modolo, K. (1988). Moses strikes again: Focalization effect on a semantic illusion. *Acta Psychologica, 67,* 135–144.

Corbett, A. T. (1984). Pronominal adjectives and the disambiguation of anaphoric nouns. *Journal of Verbal Learning and Verbal Behavior, 23,* 683–695.

Corbett, A. T., & Dosher, B. A. (1978). Instrument inferences in sentence encoding. *Journal of Verbal Learning and Verbal Behavior, 17,* 479–491.

Dell, G. S., McKoon, G., & Ratcliff, R. (1983). The activation of antecedent information during the processing of anaphoric reference in reading. *Journal of Verbal Learning and Verbal Behavior, 22,* 121–132.

Dopkins, S., Klin, C., & Myers, J. L. (1993). Accessibility of information about goals during the processing of narrative texts. *Journal of Experimental Psychology: Learning, Memory and Cognition, 19*, 70–80.

Epstein, W., Glenberg, A. M., & Bradley, M. M. (1984). Coactivation and comprehension: Contribution of text variables to the illusion of knowing. *Memory and Cognition, 12*, 355–360.

Erickson, T. D., & Mattson, M. E. (1981). From words to meaning: A semantic illusion. *Journal of Verbal Learning and Verbal Behavior, 20*, 540–551.

Fletcher, C. R. (1986). Strategies for the allocation of short-term memory during comprehension. *Journal of Memory and Language, 25*, 43–58.

Fletcher, C., & Bloom, C. P. (1988). Causal reasoning in the comprehension of simple narrative texts. *Journal of Memory and Language, 27*, 235–244.

Forster, K. I. (1981). Priming and the effects of sentence and lexical contexts on naming time: Evidence for autonomous lexical processing. *Quarterly Journal of Experimental Psychology, 33A*, 465–495.

Garnham, A. (1992). Minimalism versus constructionism: A false dichotomy in theories of inference during reading. *Psycoloquy.*

Garnham, A. (1993a). Dichotomy or not dichotomy?: That is the question: Reply to Keenan on Garnham on Reading-Inference. *Psycoloquy.*

Garnham, A. (1993b). An impartial view of inference making: Reply to Zwaan & Graesser on Garnham on Reading-Inference. *Psycoloquy.*

Garnham, A. (1993c). Space: the final frontier?: Reply to Haberlandt on Garnham on Reading-Inference. *Psycoloquy.*

Gillund, G., & Shiffrin, R. M. (1984). A retrieval model for both recognition and recall. *Psychological Review, 91*, 1–67.

Glenberg, A. M., & Mathew, S. (1992). When minimalism is not enough: Mental models in reading comprehension. *Psycoloquy.*

Glenberg, A. M., Meyer, M., & Lindem, K. (1987). Mental models contribute to foregrounding during text comprehension. *Journal of Memory and Language, 26*, 69–83.

Graesser, A. C. (1981). *Prose comprehension beyond the word.* New York: Springer.

Graesser, A. C., & Kreuz, R. J. (1993). A theory of inference generation during text comprehension. *Discourse Processes, 16*, 145–160.

Graesser, A. C., Magliano, J. P., & Haberlandt, K. (in press). Psychological studies of naturalistic text. In H. Van Oostendorp & R. A. Zwaan (Eds.), *Naturalistic text comprehension.* Norwood, NJ: Ablex.

Graesser, A. C., Person, N. P., & Johnston, G. S. (in press). Three obstacles in empirical research on aesthetic and literary comprehension. In R. J. Kreuz & M. S. MacNealy (Eds.), *Empirical approaches to literature and aesthetics.* Norwood, NJ: Ablex.

Graesser, A. C., Singer, M., & Trabasso, T. (1993). *Constructing inferences during narrative text comprehension.* Unpublished manuscript.

Greene, S. B., Gerrig, R., McKoon, G., & Ratcliff, R. (in press). Unheralded pronouns and the management of common ground. *Journal of Memory and Language.*

Greene, S. B., McKoon, G., & Ratcliff, R. (1992). Pronoun resolution and discourse models. *Journal of Experimental Psychology: Learning, Memory, and Cognition, 18*, 266–283.

Hintzman, D. (1986). "Schema abstraction" in a multiple-trace memory model. *Psychological Review, 93*, 411–428.

Huitema, J. S., Dopkins, S., Klin, C. M., & Myers, J. L. (1993). Connecting goals and actions during reading. *Journal of Experimental Psychology: Learning, Memory, and Cognition, 19*, 1053–1060.

Johnson-Laird, P. N. (1980). Mental models in cognitive science. *Cognitive Science, 4*, 71–115.

Johnson-Laird, P. (1983). *Mental models.* Cambridge, MA: Harvard University Press.

Keenan, J. M. (1992). Thoughts about the minimalist hypothesis: Commentary on Garnham on Reading-Inference. *Psycoloquy.*

Keenan, J. M., Baillet, S. D., & Brown, P. (1984). The effects of causal cohesion on comprehension and memory. *Journal of Verbal Learning and Verbal Behavior, 23*, 115–126.

Kintsch, W. (1988). The role of knowledge in discourse comprehension: A construction-integration model. *Psychological Review, 95*, 163–182.

Kintsch, W. (1992). How readers construct situation models for stories: The role of syntactic cues and causal inferences. In A. F. Healy, S. M. Kosslyn, & R. M. Shiffrin (Eds.), *Essays in honor of William K. Estes*. Hillsdale, NJ: Lawrence Erlbaum Associates.

Kintsch, W., & van Dijk, T. A. (1978). Toward a model of text comprehension and production. *Psychological Review, 85*, 363–394.

Kliegl, R., Olson, R. K., & Davidson, B. J. (1982). Regression analysis as a tool for studying reading processes: Comment on Just and Carpenter's eye fixation theory. *Memory and Cognition, 10*, 287–296.

Levin, B. (1993). *English verb classes and alternations: A preliminary investigation*. Chicago: University of Chicago Press.

Magliano, J. P., & Graesser, A. C. (1991). A three-pronged method for studying inference generation in literary text. *Poetics, 20*, 193–232.

McKoon, G. (1993). Manuscript in preparation.

McKoon, G., Greene, S. B., & Ratcliff, R. (1993). Discourse models, pronoun resolution, and the implicit causality of verbs. *Journal of Experimental Psychology: Learning, Memory, and Cognition, 19*, 1–13.

McKoon, G., & Ratcliff, R. (1980a). The comprehension processes and memory structures involved in anaphoric reference. *Journal of Verbal Learning and Verbal Behavior, 19*, 668–692.

McKoon, G., & Ratcliff, R. (1980b). Priming in item recognition: The organization of propositions in memory for text. *Journal of Verbal Learning and Verbal Behavior, 19*, 369–386.

McKoon, G., & Ratcliff, R. (1981). The comprehension processes and memory structures involved in instrumental inference. *Journal of Verbal Learning and Verbal Behavior, 20*, 671–682.

McKoon, G., & Ratcliff, R. (1986). Inferences about predictable events. *Journal of Experimental Psychology: Learning, Memory, and Cognition, 12*, 82–91.

McKoon, G., & Ratcliff, R. (1988). Contextually relevant aspects of meaning. *Journal of Experimental Psychology: Learning, Memory, and Cognition, 14*, 331–343.

McKoon, G., & Ratcliff, R. (1989a). Assessing the occurrence of elaborative inference with recognition: Compatibility checking vs. compound cue theory. *Journal of Memory and Language, 28*, 547–563.

McKoon, G., & Ratcliff, R. (1989b). Inferences about contextually-defined categories. *Journal of Experimental Psychology: Learning, Memory, and Cognition, 15*, 1134–1146.

McKoon, G., & Ratcliff, R. (1989c). *Inferences based on lexical information about verbs*. Presented at 30th Annual Meeting of Psychonomic Society, Atlanta.

McKoon, G., & Ratcliff, R. (1989d). Semantic association and elaborative inference. *Journal of Experimental Psychology: Learning, Memory, and Cognition, 15*, 326–338.

McKoon, G., & Ratcliff, R. (1992). Inference during reading. *Psychological Review, 99*, 440–466.

McKoon, G., Ratcliff, R., & Seifert, C. (1989). Making the connection: Generalized knowledge structures in story understanding. *Journal of Memory and Language, 28*, 711–734.

McKoon, G., Ratcliff, R., Ward, G., & Sproat, R. (1993). Syntactic prominence effects on discourse processes. *Journal of Memory and Language, 32*, 593–607.

McKoon, G., Ward, G., Ratcliff, R., & Sproat, R. (1993). Morphosyntactic and pragmatic factors affecting the accessibility of discourse entities. *Journal of Memory and Language, 32*, 56–75.

Morrow, D., Bower, G., & Greenspan, S. (1989). Updating situation models during narrative comprehension. *Journal of Memory and Language, 28*, 292–312.

Morrow, D. G., Bower, G. H., & Greenspan, S. L. (1990). Situation-based inferences during narrative comprehension. In A. C. Graesser & G. H. Bower (Eds.), *Inferences and text comprehension*, 123–135. New York: Academic Press.

Morrow, D. G., Greenspan, S. L., & Bower, G. H. (1987). Accessibility and situation models in narrative comprehension. *Journal of Memory and Language, 26,* 165–187.

Murdock, B. B. (1983). A distributed memory model for serial-order information. *Psychological Review, 90,* 316–338.

Murray, J. D., Klin, C. M., & Myers, J. L. (1993). Forward inferences in narrative text. *Journal of Memory and Language, 32,* 464–473.

Myers, J. L., O'Brien, E. J., Albrecht, J. E., & Mason, R. A. (1993). *Maintaining global coherence during reading.* Manuscript submitted for publication.

Neisser, U. (1978). Memory: What are the important questions? In M. M. Gruneberg, P. E. Morris, & R. N. Sykes (Eds.), *Practical aspects of memory* (pp. 3–24). London: Academic Press.

Noordman, L. G. M., & Vonk, W. (1992). Readers, knowledge and the control of inferences in reading. *Language and Cognitive Processes, 7,* 373–391.

Norris, D. (1986). Word recognition: Context effects without priming. *Cognition, 22,* 93–136.

O'Brien, E. J. (1987). Antecedent search processes and the structure of text. *Journal of Experimental Psychology: Learning, Memory, and Cognition, 13,* 278–290.

O'Brien, E. J., & Albrecht, J. E. (1992). Comprehension strategies in the development of a mental model. *Journal of Experimental Psychology: Learning, Memory, and Cognition, 18,* 777–784.

O'Brien, E. J., Shank, D. M., Myers, J. L., & Rayner, K. (1988). Elaborative inferences during reading: Do they occur on-line? *Journal of Experimental Psychology: Learning, Memory, and Cognition, 14,* 410–420.

Onifer, W., & Swinney, D. A. (1981). Accessing lexical ambiguities during sentence comprehension: Effects of frequency of meaning and contextual bias. *Memory and Cognition, 9,* 225–236.

Posner, M. I., & Snyder, C. R. (1975). Attention and cognitive control. In R. L. Solso (Ed.), *Information processing and cognition: The Loyola symposium* (pp. 55–85). Hillsdale, NJ: Lawrence Erlbaum Associates.

Potts, G. R. (1974). Storing and retrieving information about ordered relationships. *Journal of Experimental Psychology, 103,* 431–439.

Potts, G. R., Keenan, J. M., & Golding, J. M. (1988). Assessing the occurrence of elaborative inference: Lexical decision versus naming. *Journal of Memory and Language, 27,* 399–415.

Ratcliff, R. (1978). A theory of memory retrieval. *Psychological Review, 85,* 59–108.

Ratcliff, R., & McKoon, G. (1988). A retrieval theory of priming in memory. *Psychological Review, 95,* 385–408.

Rayner, K., & Frazier, L. (1987). Parsing temporarily ambiguous complements. *Quarterly Journal of Experimental Psychology, 39A,* 657–673.

Rayner, K., & Morris, R. K. (1991). Comprehension processes in reading ambiguous sentences: Reflections from eye movements. In G. Simpson (Ed.), *Understanding word and sentence.* Amsterdam: North Holland Press.

Reder, L. M., & Kusbit, G. W. (1991). Locus of the Moses Illusion: Imperfect encoding, retrieval, or match? *Journal of Memory and Language, 30,* 385–406.

Roth, E. M., & Shoben, E. J. (1983). The effect of context on the structure of categories. *Cognitive Psychology, 15,* 346–378.

Sanford, A. J., & Garrod, S. C. (1981). *Understanding written language.* New York: Wiley.

Seifert, C. M., McKoon, G., Abelson, R. P., & Ratcliff, R. (1986). Memory connections between thematically similar episodes. *Journal of Experimental Psychology: Learning, Memory, and Cognition, 12,* 220–231.

Singer, M. (1978, August). *The role of explicit and implicit recall cues.* Paper presented at the meeting of the American Psychological Association, Toronto.

Singer, M. (1979). Processes of inference during sentence encoding. *Memory and Cognition, 7,* 192–200.

Singer, M. (1993). Minimalism: A hedged analysis of restricted inference processing: Commentary on Garnham and on Glenberg & Mathew on Reading-Inference. *Psycoloquy.*

Singer, M. (in press). Constructing and validating motive bridging inferences. *Journal of Memory and Language.*

Singer, M., Graesser, A.C., & Trabasso, T. (1993). *Minimal or global inference in comprehension?* Unpublished manuscript.

Singer, M., Halldorson, M., Lear, J. C., & Andrusiak, P. (1992). Validation of causal bridging inferences in discourse understanding. *Journal of Memory and Language, 31,* 507–524.

Suh, S. Y., & Trabasso, T. (1993). Inferences during reading: Converging evidence from discourse analysis, talk-aloud protocols, and recognition priming. *Journal of Memory and Language, 32,* 278–301.

Swinney, D., & Osterhout, L. (1990). Inference generation during auditory language comprehension. In A. Graesser & G. Bower (Eds.), *The psychology of learning and motivation. Vol. 25: Inferences and text comprehension* (pp. 17–33). New York: Academic Press.

Taraban, R., & McClelland, J. (1988). Constituent attachment and thematic role assignment in sentence processing: Influences of content-based expectations. *Journal of Memory and Language, 27,* 597–632.

Till, R. E., Mross, E. F., & Kintsch, W. (1988). Time course of priming for associate and inference words in a discourse context. *Memory and Cognition, 16,* 283–298.

Trabasso, T., & Sperry, L. L. (1985). Causal relatedness and importance of story events. *Journal of Memory and Language, 24,* 595–611.

Trabasso, T., & Suh, S. (1993). Understanding text: Achieving explanatory coherence through on-line inferences and mental operations in working memory. *Discourse Processes, 16,* 3–34.

Trabasso, T., & van den Broek, P. (1985). Causal thinking and the representation of narrative events. *Journal of Memory and Language, 24,* 612–630.

van den Brook, P. (1988). The effects of causal relations and hierarchical position on the importance of story statements. *Journal of Memory and Language, 27,* 1–22.

van den Broek, P. (1990a). The causal inference maker: Towards a process model of inference generation in text comprehension. In D. A. Balota, G. B. Flores d'Arcais, & K. Rayner (Eds.), *Comprehension processes in reading* (pp. 423–445). Hillsdale, NJ: Lawrence Erlbaum Associates.

van den Brook, P. (1990b). Causal inferences and the comprehension of narrative texts. In A. C. Graesser & G. H. Bower (Eds.), *The psychology of learning and motivation: Vol. 25. Inferences and text comprehension* (pp.175–196). New York: Academic Press.

van Oostendorp, H., & de Mul, S. (1990). Moses beats Adam: A semantic relatedness effect on a semantic illusion. *Acta Psychologica, 74,* 35–46.

Vonk, W., & Noordman, L. G. M. (1990). On the control of inferences in text understanding. In D. A. Balota, G. B. Flores d'Arcais & K. Rayner (Eds.), *Comprehension processes in reading* (pp. 447–464). Hillsdale, NJ: Lawrence Erlbaum Associates.

Ward, G., Sproat, R., & McKoon, G. (1991). A pragmatic analysis of so-called anaphoric islands. *Language, 67,* 439–474.

Whitney, P., Ritchie, B. G., & Crane, R. S. (1992). The effect of foregrounding readers' use of predictive inferences. *Memory and Cognition, 20,* 424–432.

Whitney, P., & Waring, D. A. (1989, November). *Task effects on reader's use of elaborative inferences.* Paper presented at the meeting of the Psychonomic Society, Atlanta, GA.

Wilson, S. G., Rinck, M., McNamara, T. P., Bower, G. H., & Morrow, D. G. (1993). *Mental models and narrative comprehension: Some qualifications.* Manuscript submitted for publication.

Zwaan, R. A., & Graesser, A. C. (1993a). Reading goals and situation models: Commentary on Glenberg & Mathew on Reading-Inference. *Psycoloquy.*

Zwaan, R. A., & Graesser, A. C. (1993b). There is no empirical evidence that some inferences are automatically or partially encoded in text comprehension: A commentary on Garnham. *Psycoloquy.*

Chapter 7

Inference Generation and the Construction of Situation Models

Arthur C. Graesser
Rolf A. Zwaan
Memphis State University

Kintsch's models have distinguished three levels of cognitive representation that are achieved as a result of comprehending text (Kintsch, 1988; Kintsch, Welsch, Schmalhofer, & Zimny, 1990; Schmalhofer & Glavanov, 1986; van Dijk & Kintsch, 1983). The *surface code* preserves the exact wording and syntax of clauses. In most cases, comprehenders retain the surface code of only the most recent clause being processed. The *textbase* contains the explicit text propositions in a stripped-down form that preserves meaning, but not the exact wording and syntax of text. The textbase also includes a small number of inferences that are needed to establish text coherence. Finally, there is the referential *situation model* of what the text is about. A situation model is a mental representation of the people, setting, actions, and events that are explicitly mentioned or inferentially suggested by the text (Albrecht & O'Brien, 1993; Bower, 1989; Glenberg, Meyer, & Lindem, 1987; Johnson-Laird, 1983; Morrow, Bower, & Greenspan, 1987; Singer, 1990). Situation models may vary in abstractness from bare-bone conceptual sketches to lifelike renditions of episodes in the real world. Most inferences generated during text comprehension are part of the constructed situation model.

At this point in the science, researchers know far more about the construction of the surface code and the textbase than they know about the construction of the situation model. In an effort to provide a more balanced picture of comprehension activities, we have investigated the representation and processing of situation models. This chapter identifies some of the processes that we believe are central to the construction of situation models when narrative text is com-

117

prehended by adult readers. We identify classes of inferences that readers generate while they construct the situation models.

There are some useful metaphors for understanding the construction of situation models in the context of narrative text. For example, Bower (1989) used a *doll's house* metaphor. The mental doll's house contains a spatial layout of regions, objects, and actors. A mental flashlight is shined on various regions in the doll's house during comprehension (usually the most recent actor or action mentioned in the text). The mental flashlight lights up actors, objects, and properties in focal attention. Our favorite metaphor is a *stage in a theater.* A mental stage is constructed in working memory, under the guidance of a mental director who manipulates characters, props, a mental camera, and the agenda. The director solicits characters to fill roles, moves the characters on stage, governs interactions with other characters, and removes them from stage. Objects and components of the stage setting are also manipulated by the mental director. The manipulation of the actors, actions, and objects is organized by a plot that contains goals, plans, and causal chains. The director uses the camera to scan the constructed scenario. The camera zooms in on particular characters, spatial regions, character actions, unusual events, eye-catching states, and other hot spots throughout the course of comprehension. It takes time for the mental director to perform these cognitive operations. For example, it takes time to move a new character or object on the stage (Graesser, Hoffman, & Clark, 1980; Haberlandt, & Graesser, 1985; Kintsch, Kozminsky, Streby, McKoon, & Keenan, 1975), to move the mental camera from one character to another character (Bower, Black, & Turner, 1979), and to move the camera from one spatial region to another region (Bower, 1989; Morrow et al., 1987). The situation model may also include the communicative interaction between the director (i.e., narrator) and the audience. However, this pragmatic level is often not very visible to the reader.

A large number of inferences are potentially generated while readers construct situation models. Suppose, for example, that an adult reads a novel. The following classes of inferences are potentially constructed: The goals and plans that motivate characters' actions, character traits, characters' knowledge and beliefs, character emotions, the causes of events, the consequences of events and actions, properties of objects, spatial relationships among entities, and referents of nouns and pronouns. At the pragmatical level, readers potentially construct the attitudes of the writer, the goals of the writer, the stance of the narrator, and the appropriate emotional reactions of the reader. Researchers in discourse processing and cognitive psychology have attempted to identify and to explain which of these classes of inferences are normally generated during comprehension (Balota, Flores d'Arcais, & Rayner, 1990; Graesser & Bower, 1990; Graesser & Kreuz, 1993; Kintsch, 1993; McKoon & Ratcliff, 1992; Singer, 1988; Whitney, 1987).

This chapter presents our current views about the process of constructing situation models during narrative comprehension. The first section identifies those classes of inferences that are normally generated during the construction of a situation model. The second section identifies the information sources and processing mechanisms that produce the inferences. More specifically, we analyze the extent to which the inferences are *lexicon-based inferences* versus *novel situational inferences*. Lexicon-based inferences are directly inherited from the world knowledge that is housed within the explicit lexical items in the text (i.e., content words). Novel situational inferences are not inherited from any of the lexical items. Some of these novel inferences are produced by active manipulations of the mental director in a uniquely situated mental stage.

WHAT INFERENCES ARE GENERATED WHEN A SITUATION MODEL IS CONSTRUCTED?

Most of the inferences constructed during the comprehension of narrative text are knowledge-based inferences. Knowledge structures from long-term memory are activated during comprehension and a subset of this information is instantiated as inferences in the situation model. The activated knowledge structures include generic packages of world knowledge, such as scripts, frames, stereotypes, or schemata (Bower et al., 1979; Graesser & Clark, 1985; Mandler, 1984; Rumelhart & Ortony, 1977; Schank & Abelson, 1977). These generic knowledge structures are activated by content words, combinations of content words, and interpreted text constituents. Other knowledge structures are specific, referring to a particular experience or text comprehended in the past. Compared to generic knowledge structures, it presumably takes more time and processing resources to access and utilize information from specific knowledge structures because they are not over-learned and automatized. It should be noted that knowledge-based inferences do not include logic-based inferences derived from domain-independent formal reasoning (e.g., proposition calculus, predicate calculus, theorem proving) and quantitative inferences that are derived from formulas. Such inferences are difficult to derive, as everyone knows who has attempted to solve an analytical problem or an algebra problem.

Examples of knowledge-based inferences are presented in Table 7.1. While reading the story of "The Czar and His Daughters," the reader eventually comprehends the explicit action "the heroes fought the dragon" and potentially generates the following classes of knowledge-based inferences.

Superordinate goal. The inference is a goal that motivates an agent's intentional action.

Subordinate goal/action. The inference is a goal, plan, or action that specifies how an agent's intentional action is achieved.

Causal antecedent. The inference is on a causal chain (bridge) between the explicit clause being comprehended and the previous passage context.

Causal consequence. The inference is on a forecasted causal chain, unfolding from the explicit clause being comprehended. According to our classification scheme, these include physical events and new plans of agents, but not emotions.

Character emotion. The inference is an emotion experienced by a character in response to the action or event being comprehended.

State. The inference is an ongoing state, from the time frame of the story plot, that is *not* causally linked to the episodes in the plot. These include character traits, properties of objects, and spatial relationships among physical entities.

All of the inferences that are considered are "extratextual" inferences in the sense that they are inherited or derived from knowledge structures. We do not focus on "text-connecting" inferences that refer exclusively to explicit information in the text. Needless to say, the six classes of inferences in Table 7.1 do not exhaust the classes of knowledge-based inferences that are potentially generated during comprehension. Classification schemes are expected to vary according to the different theories of comprehension pursued by researchers.

An adequate explanation of situation model construction should accurately predict which classes of inferences are normally generated during comprehension. That is, a good theory would discriminate between those classes of inferences that are normally generated "online" (during comprehension) and those generated "offline" (during a later retrieval task, but not during comprehension). This section ultimately evaluates the adequacy of a number of theoretical explanations. However, before addressing theory, it is important to discuss briefly some critical methodological points.

TABLE 7.1
The Czar Story and Example Inferences

The Czar and His Daughters

Once there was a Czar who had three lovely daughters. One day the three daughters went walking in the woods. They were enjoying themselves so much that they forgot the time and stayed too long. A dragon kidnapped the three daughters. As they were being dragged off they cried for help. Three heroes heard their cries and set off to rescue the daughters. The heroes came and fought the dragon and rescued the maidens. Then the heroes returned the daughters to their palace. When the Czar heard of the rescue, he rewarded the heroes.

Inferences when comprehending the action "The heroes fought the dragon."
SUPERORDINATE GOAL: *The heroes wanted to free the daughters.*
SUBORDINATE GOAL/ACTION: *The heroes threw spears.*
CAUSAL ANTECEDENT: *The heroes saw the dragon.*
CAUSAL CONSEQUENCE: *The dragon died.*
CHARACTER EMOTION: *The dragon was angry.*
STATE: *The dragon has scales.*

Given that world knowledge structures furnish knowledge-based inferences, it is a good policy for researchers to ensure that readers have an adequate amount of world knowledge in tests of whether these inferences are generated online. There should be some validation that the inferences could be generated by readers if the readers had sufficient time to make the inferences. This is accomplished by collecting verbal protocols from a sample of readers as they comprehend the text, clause by clause. These verbal protocols consist of "think aloud" protocols (Ericsson & Simon, 1980; Trabasso & Suh, 1993), question-answering protocols (Graesser, 1981; Graesser, Robertson, & Anderson, 1981), and question-asking protocols (Collins, Brown, & Larkin, 1980; Olson, Duffy, & Mack, 1984). The verbal protocols expose potential knowledge-based inferences that can be used as test items in more rigorous experimental tests of the online status of inferences. The researcher has some assurance that the reader has the prerequisite world knowledge to generate the inferences.

We endorse a "three-pronged method" of investigating inference generation during the construction of situation models (Graesser, Bertus, & Magliano, in press; Graesser & Kreuz, 1993; Magliano & Graesser, 1991; Suh & Trabasso, 1992; Zwaan, 1993). The three-pronged method coordinates theories of discourse processing that make predictions about inference generation, the collection of verbal protocols to expose potential inferences, and the collection of online temporal measures that rigorously test whether a class of inferences is truly made online. An application of the three-pronged method is presented in this section.

Theoretical Explanations of Inference Generation

There are several theoretical positions that make specific claims about the online status of different classes of inferences. This section focuses on the six classes illustrated in Table 7.1: superordinate goals, subordinate goals/actions, causal antecedents, causal consequences, character emotions, and states. As it turns out, the online status of these six inference categories is quite diagnostic in discriminating the alternative theoretical positions.

For purposes of simplification, each inference class is assigned to either an online status or an offline status. A more accurate account would no doubt specify a probabilistic continuum between these two extremes. The continuum is a result of fluctuations in reading ability, reading goals, text materials, samples of inferences, and experimental tasks (van den Broek & Fletcher, 1993). The continuum might also be attributed to the possibility that inferences are activated to some degree rather than all-or-nothing (Gernsbacher, 1990; Kintsch, 1988; McKoon & Ratcliff, 1992; A. J. C. Sharkey & N. E. Sharkey, 1992). A more accurate manner of articulating the predictions would be that the set of online inferences have a stronger encoding than the set of offline inferences.

The present discussion of inference generation applies to normal reading conditions when readers are attempting to comprehend the text for no particular purpose. All bets are off for shallow reading conditions, such as skimming a text or proofreading a text for spelling errors. Similarly, all bets are off under conditions in which the reader is pursuing unusual reading goals, such as tracking the spatial locations of objects. When readers normally read narrative text, they want to comprehend the plot at sufficient depth to extract the main points of the story.

The predictions of six theoretical positions are summarized in Table 7.2. This subsection briefly presents the highlights of each theoretical position and also the rationale for the predictions. A more complete description of each theoretical position is presented elsewhere (Graesser et al., in press; Graesser, Singer, & Trabasso, 1994; Magliano & Graesser, 1991).

Explicit Textbase Position. This position predicts that none of the inferences in Table 7.1 are online because the explicit textbase constitutes the meaning representation. Kintsch's early theory of text representation is closest to this position (Kintsch, 1974). The *Zeitgeist* at that point in discourse processing research was to account for the processing of explicit text rather than inferences. The explicit textbase position is approximately correct in the case of expository texts on unfamiliar topics because there is virtually no knowledge to supply knowledge-based inferences (Britton & Gulgoz, 1991). However, narrative is a different kettle of fish because adult readers have a rich repertoire of world knowledge about the topics in narrative.

Minimalist Hypothesis. McKoon and Ratcliff (1992, chapter 6, this vol.) proposed this hypothesis to account for those inferences that are automatically (versus strategically) encoded during comprehension. The only inferences en-

TABLE 7.2
Predictions of Six Theoretical Positions Regarding the Online Status
of Six Classes of Inferences

	Class of Inference					
Theoretical Position	*Causal Antec.*	*Causal Conseq.*	*Superord. Goal*	*Subord. Goal*	*Charact. Emotion*	*State*
Explicit Textbase						
Minimalist Hypothesis	X*					
Current-State Selection						
Strategy	X		X			
Constructionist Theory	X		X		X	
Prediction-Substantiation						
Model	X	X	X		X	
Promiscuous Inference						
Generation Model	X	X	X	X	X	X

*"X" indicates whether a class of inferences is normally generated online.

coded automatically during reading are (a) those based on easily available information and (b) those required to make statements in the text locally coherent. The inferences associated with (a) do not make any discriminating predictions regarding the status of the six classes of inferences in Table 7.1. The inferences associated with (b) are most likely to include the causal antecedent inferences. The causal antecedent inferences establish a coherent bridge between an incoming clause and a previous clause that is resident in working memory. The other five classes of inferences in Table 7.1 are not normally needed to achieve local text coherence. Causal antecedent inferences therefore should have a higher likelihood of being constructed online than the other five classes (which are only strategically or probabilistically encoded).

Current-State Selection Strategy and the Causal Inference Maker Model. These are strategic models of narrative comprehension that specify the process of constructing causal chains and goal structures (Bloom, Fletcher, van den Broek, Reitz, & Shapiro, 1990; Fletcher, Arthur, & Skeate, chapter 11 in this vol.; Fletcher & Bloom, 1988; van den Broek & Lorch, 1993). These models were inspired substantially by Kintsch and van Dijk's (1978) classic model of comprehension. The Kintsch and van Dijk model had a systematic computational mechanism for generating inferences that were needed to establish local text coherence. The model relied heavily on argument repetition as a foundation for establishing local coherence; whenever an incoming clause had no noun-phrase argument that matched an existing argument in working memory, the reader attempted to construct an inference in order to establish local coherence. The current-state selection strategy and the causal inference maker model augmented the Kintsch and van Dijk model. According to these models, comprehenders attempt to establish causal coherence by constructing causal antecedent inferences and superordinate goal inferences during comprehension. These two inference classes should therefore have a higher strength of encoding than the other four inference classes in Tables 7.1 and 7.2.

Constructionist Model. This constructionist model, recently proposed by Graesser and his colleagues (Graesser et al., in press; Graesser & Kreuz, 1993; Graesser et al., 1994) resurrects the *effort-after-meaning* principle (Bartlett, 1932; Berlyne, 1971). This principle asserts that comprehenders attempt to construct meaning out of text, social interactions, and perceptual input. More specifically, the principle is elaborated with three critical assumptions. First, according to a *reader goal assumption*, the reader constructs inferences that address the reader's goals. This first assumption does not offer any discriminating predictions about which inference classes in Tables 7.1 and 7.2 tend to be generated online. Second, according to the *explanation assumption*, the reader attempts to explain *why* actions, events, and states are mentioned in the text (Schank, 1986; Trabasso & Suh, 1993). Answers to why-questions consist of the causal antecedents and superordinate goals (Graesser, 1981; Graesser, Lang, & Roberts, 1991; Graesser et al., 1981) so these inferences are predicted to be online. Third, according to a *coherence assumption*, the reader attempts to construct a meaning representation that is coherent at both global and local levels. Superordinate goals and character emotions are critical components in the global plot structures of narrative text (Dyer, 1983; Lehnert, 1981; Stein & Levine, 1991). Causal antecedent inferences are critical for establishing local coherence, as discussed earlier. Therefore, three inference classes are predicted to have an online status in the constructionist model: superordinate goals, causal antecedents, and character emotions.

Prediction-Substantiation Model. This model asserts that comprehension is expectation driven in addition to explanation-driven (Bower et al., 1979; DeJong, 1979; Dyer, 1983; Schank & Abelson, 1977). Readers generate expectations about future occurrences in the plot and these expectations influence the interpretation of clauses in a top-down fashion. For example, suppose that a story activates a revenge theme when the text states that *A kills B* and *C is a friend of B*; the comprehender would generate an expectation that *C will harm A*. As specified in Table 7.2, the prediction-substantiation model predicts that four inference classes are online.

Promiscuous Inference Generation Position. This extreme position states that all classes of inferences are generated online, as long as the comprehender has the prerequisite world knowledge to furnish the inference. The comprehender constructs a complete lifelike situation model that fills in all of the details about characters, props, spatial layout, actions, events, beliefs, goals, and so on. At the extreme, the mental director creates a high-resolution mental videotape of the narrative, along with details about the mental states of characters and the pragmatic exchange between author and reader. This position is perhaps a straw man because no researcher has seriously advocated it. The construction phase of Kintsch's *construction-integration* model would be compatible with the promiscuous inference generation position, whereas the integration phase would prune out (or deactivate) potential inferences that are not conceptually connected to other information (Kintsch, 1988).

Collection of Verbal Protocols to Extract Inferences

The second prong of the three-prong method involves the collection of verbal protocols to extract potential knowledge-based inferences. These protocols are collected for each sentence or clause in the order that the information is presented in the text. As mentioned earlier, there are different ways to collect verbal protocols: thinking aloud, question asking, question answering, and free associations.

Most of our research has collected question-answering protocols to expose inferences (Graesser, 1981; Graesser & Clark, 1985). After reading each clause (that refers to an action, event, or state), subjects answer questions about the clause. Three types of questions have been asked in most of our studies: why, how, and what-happens-next (WHN). These question classes were selected to expose particular classes of inferences. Why-questions elicit superordinate goals and causal antecedents. How-questions elicit subordinate goals/actions and causal antecedents; WHN questions elicit causal consequences and character emotions (i.e., those that are causal consequences). States are exposed by all of the question categories; they can be distinguished by content.

A *constructive history chart* was prepared for each inference that was elicited by the question-answering protocols. This chart identifies those explicit clauses in the text that elicited the particular inference, the type of question that elicited it, and the proportion of subjects who mentioned the inference in the question-answering task. The point in the story where the inference first emerged was particularly informative. In fact, all experiments that collected time-based behavioral measures tested an inference when it first emerged in the situation model, as manifested in the question-answering protocols.

All tests of the online status of inferences included the inferences extracted from the question-answering protocols. The different classes of inferences were equated on the proportion of subjects who generated the inferences in the question-answering protocols. Inference test words were also equated on a number of extraneous measures, such as word length, word frequency, and word class (i.e., noun, adjective, versus main verb).

Collection of Online Behavioral Measures

The third prong of the three-prong method involves the collection of time-based behavioral measures to test whether particular classes of inferences are truly generated online. These time-based behavioral measures have included word reading times (Graesser, Haberlandt, & Koizumi, 1987), sentence reading times (Millis, Morgan, & Graesser, 1990), naming latencies for test words presented after sentences (Long, Golding, & Graesser, 1992), and lexical decision judgments on test strings presented after sentences (Long et al., 1992; Long, Golding, Graesser, & Clark, 1990; Long & Golding, 1993; Magliano, Baggett, Johnson, & Graesser, 1993).[1] In some studies, there was precise control over the timing of word presentation by employing a rapid serial visual presentation (RSVP) task; the words in each sentence were presented very quickly on the computer

---

[1]Some researchers are concerned that lexical decision latencies are not perfect windows to online inference processes because "context checking" operations may be executed while lexical decisions are made. This context checking explanation has periodically been evaluated in follow-up studies with other tasks that allegedly are not contaminated by context checking (e.g., word naming latencies), or by imposing various controls over the stimulus materials. We have reasons for dismissing the plausibility of the context checking explanation, but it is beyond the scope of this chapter to address these reasons.

screen at a constant rate (e.g., 250 ms per word). There was control over the time interval between the presentation of the final word in the sentence and the presentation of an inference test word; this is called the stimulus onset asynchrony (SOA). Kintsch and his associates (Kintsch, 1988; Till, Mross, & Kintsch, 1988) also manipulated SOA interval in conjunction with the RSVP task. It is possible to compute an *inference encoding score* for each inference test word by subtracting the decision latency (or naming latency) of the test word in the inference context from the latency of the same word in an unrelated context, as specified in Formula 1.

$$\text{Inference encoding score} = \text{latency (unrelated context)} - \text{latency (inference context)} \qquad (1)$$

In one study, Magliano et al. (1993) tested whether causal antecedent and causal consequence inferences are generated online. The texts were short narrative passages, such as the Czar story in Table 7.1. Table 7.1 also presents an example causal antecedent and causal consequence inference. Magliano et al. manipulated inference class (causal antecedent versus causal consequence), RSVP rate (250 vs. 400 ms), and SOA interval (250, 400, 600, vs. 1,200 ms). Lexical decision latencies were collected on a test string after each sentence. The results supported the conclusion that causal consequences are not generated online because the inference encoding scores were consistently negative or close to zero. Causal consequences are not normally constructed online because there are too many alternative hypothetical plots that could be forecasted, and most of these would end up being erroneous when the full story is known (Graesser, 1981; Graesser & Clark, 1985; Kintsch, 1988; Potts, Keenan, & Golding, 1988). It also takes substantial cognitive resources to forecast multiple hypothetical plots (Johnson-Laird, 1983).

Magliano et al. (1993) did find that, unlike the causal consequences, causal antecedent inferences are constructed online. The results indicated that there was a threshold of 400 ms after stimulus presentation (either RSVP, SOA, or both) before causal antecedent inferences are generated. Inference encoding scores were above zero only in cells in which both the RSVP rate and SOA interval were 400 ms or higher; the scores were negative when either the RSVP rate or SOA interval was only 250 ms. Therefore, sufficient time is needed to interpret the sentence and construct the situation model before these causal antecedent inferences are generated.

Which Model of Inference Generation is Supported?

The constructionist theory has received the most support from available studies that have collected time-based behavioral measures. There is empirical support for the online construction of causal antecedent inferences (Graesser et al., 1987; McKoon & Ratcliff, 1989; Magliano et al., 1993; Potts et al., 1988; Singer, Halldorson, Lear,

& Andrusiak, 1992), superordinate goal inferences (Graesser et al., 1987; Long & Golding, 1993; Long et al., 1992; Long et al., 1990), and character emotion inferences (Gernsbacher, chapter 8, this vol.; Gernsbacher, Goldsmith, & Robertson, 1992). As predicted by the constructionist theory, the following inference classes are not normally generated online: causal consequences (Graesser et al., 1987; Magliano et al., 1993; McKoon & Ratcliff, 1989; Potts et al., 1988; Singer & Ferreira, 1983), subordinate goals/actions (Long & Golding, 1993; Long et al., 1990; Long et al., 1992), and states (Long et al., 1990; Seifert, Robertson, & Black, 1985). Therefore, the constructionist theory most accurately predicts the subset of inference classes that are online versus offline.

There are two processing mechanisms that dilute the elegant picture we have sketched with respect to online versus offline inferences. One processing mechanism consists of strategic comprehension that is driven by particular reader goals. Readers sometimes read texts for very particular goals and they construct inferences that address these goals. For example, the reader might read a short story for the purpose of forming a mental picture of the spatial setting. The reader would form spatial state inferences under these conditions even though spatial inferences are not constructed under naturalistic reading conditions (Zwaan & van Oostendorp, 1993). It should be noted that one of the key assumptions of the constructionist theory was the reader goal assumption. The fact that there are fluctuations in reader goals is not problematic theoretically.

A second processing mechanism consists of bottom-up activations of inferences from multiple information sources (Graesser & Clark, 1985; Kintsch, 1988; O'Brien, Shank, Myers, & Rayner, 1988). A potential inference receives more activation and strength of encoding to the extent that it is activated by multiple information sources (i.e., there is convergence) and it is compatible with the knowledge structures in working memory (i.e., it survives a constraint satisfaction mechanism). If we were to adopt a connectionist neural network architecture, an inference is constructed when it receives a sufficient amount of positive activation from multiple information sources, and negative inhibitory activation from few (if any) information sources. Kintsch's (1988) construction-integration model captures these convergence and constraint satisfaction mechanisms. The incidence of these activation-based inferences is assumed to be equivalent for the six classes of inferences in Tables 7.1 and 7.2.

In summary, we propose a hybrid explanation of inference generation during the construction of situation models. The hybrid is an amalgamation of Kintsch's construction-integration model (Kintsch, 1988) and the constructionist theory (Graesser et al., in press; Graesser & Kreuz, 1993; Graesser et al., 1994; Singer, Graesser, & Trabasso, 1994). The construction-integration model accounts for the activation-based inferences that are passively generated during comprehension. The constructionist theory handles the deeper inferences that are products of more active processing mechanisms that explain the explicit information, establish both global and local coherence, and address the readers goals.

WHERE DO INFERENCES COME FROM?

The previous section identified some classes of knowledge-based inferences that are normally generated during the construction of a situation model. This section examines the information sources and processing mechanisms that produce these inferences. More specifically, we contrast two sets of inferences: lexicon-based inferences versus novel situational inferences.

The lexicon-based inferences are directly inherited from the world knowledge that is stored in explicit content words in the text. The content words include nouns, adjectives, and main verbs. For example, suppose that the comprehender reads the sentence *The heroes fought the dragon* in the Czar story. Three lexical items are activated by this sentence: HERO, FIGHTING, and DRAGON. World knowledge is housed within each of these lexical items. We know, for example, that a hero is brave, protects victims, and fights villains. Some passage inferences are simply inherited (i.e., passed down, copied) from the world knowledge stored within the lexical items. For example, the state inference *the dragon has scales* was probably inherited from DRAGON, but not from HERO and FIGHTING. The causal consequence inference *the dragon died* was possibly inherited from all three lexical items.

The novel situational inferences do not directly match any information stored under the lexical items. Instead, they are products of more complex processing mechanisms, some of which are not well understood. Some of these mechanisms are summarized here.

1. *Compound cues.* Two or more lexical items together provide access to a generic or specific knowledge structure, which in turn passes down an inference (McKoon & Ratcliff, 1989, 1992; Reiser, Black, & Abelson, 1985). For example, the inference *X throws spears* is passed down from knowledge structure K; structure K was accessed by the compound cue FIGHTING DRAGON, but not by FIGHTING alone or DRAGON alone. Knowledge structure K might be a specific movie or story that a person comprehended in the past. Alternatively, it may be a generic knowledge structure, such as the script of "men fighting in the olden days."

2. *Synthesized explanations.* The novel inference is part of a synthesized causal chain or plan that explains why an action or event occurred. The synthesized explanation is a product of multiple steps of reasoning, which assemble fragments of knowledge from multiple information sources. For example, the inference *the heroes wanted to free the daughters* is a part of the following explanation of the explicit action *the heroes fought the dragon.*

> The daughters were victims of being kidnapped by the dragon so they wanted to get free. The heroes perceived the kidnapping. Given that they were heroes and heroes want to help victims, the heroes wanted to help the daughters achieve their

goals. The heroes therefore adopted the goal to free the daughters. They did this by fighting the dragon.

The inference is not directly stored in a particular lexical item, but is derived from explanatory reasoning that taps multiple information sources.

3. *Operations of the mental director.* Inferences are generated as the mental director performs operations in the mental stage. The director moves characters and props on, off, and within the stage. Properties come into focus as the director moves the mental camera and zooms on particular entities. These inferences are constrained by the unique situational context of the narrative. So we could potentially infer that *the heroes surrounded the dragon* when an animated image of the heroes fighting the dragon emerges in focal attention. This inference is not merely copied from the information stored within a particular lexical item.

We analyzed the inferences extracted by the question-answering protocols in light of the distinction between lexicon-based inferences and novel situational inferences. We segregated those inferences that were lexicon based from those that were novel situational inferences. This classification of inferences was reported in a detailed study of the knowledge associated with a sample of four short narrative texts (Graesser & Clark, 1985). These same passages had been used in the study that collected question-answering protocols to extract inferences (Graesser, 1981) and the studies that collected time-based behavioral measures to test whether inference classes are online (see previous section). Graesser and Clark used some "knowledge engineering" methods to extract empirically the world knowledge associated with each of the lexical items within the sample of narrative texts. The conceptual content of all of the lexical items in texts was therefore available. This permitted us to trace the lexical information sources of all knowledge-based inferences in the narrative texts. We could ultimately compare the encoding strength of lexicon-based inferences and novel situational inferences.

Analysis of the Knowledge Stored in Lexical Items

Researchers in linguistics, psycholinguistics, and lexicography have disagreed on what knowledge is stored in lexical items. At one extreme, there are those who claim that the lexicon is limited to phonological code, syntactic code, and those semantic features necessary for making syntactic computations (Chomsky, 1965).

    HERO
phonological code: \'he-(l)ro\
syntactic code: +noun
semantic code: +concrete, +animate, +human, +male

An intermediate position would add semantic features that are part of semantic theories that are alinguistic (Katz & Fodor, 1963; G. A. Miller, Beckwith, Fellbaum, Gross, K. Miller, & Tengi, 1990).

semantic code: *sense1*—the central male character in a novel, play, or story.

At the other extreme, there are those who include world knowledge in the lexicon (Alterman, 1985; Dahlgren, 1985; Graesser & Clark, 1985; Kintsch, 1988).

world knowledge: a hero is brave, a hero helps victims, a hero fights villains

We have adopted the latter position in our studies of the lexicon. The lexical entry for HERO includes a rich structure of world knowledge, which has been represented as "conceptual graph structures" (Graesser & Clark, 1985).

Graesser and Clark conducted a large-scale investigation of the world knowledge stored in 128 lexical items. The 128 items included all of the content words that were explicitly mentioned in the four short stories examined in the studies reported earlier. Graesser and Clark extracted the content of each lexical item by collecting free generation protocols and question-answering protocols from college students. When extracting the content of HERO, for example, one group of subjects furnished free generation protocols by listing all states, events, and actions that are typical of heroes. All propositions listed by two or more out of eight subjects were included in a set of "free generation" propositions for hero. Each of these free generation propositions was queried by another group of eight subjects who completed a question-answering task; these subjects answered a why-question and a how-question about each free generation proposition. The final list of propositions included all propositions produced by at least two subjects in either the free generation task or the question-answering task. On the average, a lexical item had 39 free generation propositions and 166 total propositions.

Graesser and Clark performed two additional analyses on the content of each lexical item. First, they organized the propositions into a conceptual graph structure. A structure consisted of the proposition nodes interconnected by labeled, relational arcs. It is beyond the scope of this chapter to describe these arc categories. Second, each of the propositions was scaled on several dimensions: how typical the proposition is for the lexical concept, how necessary the proposition is for the concept, how central the proposition is to the meaning of the concept, how distinctive the proposition is (i.e., is the proposition stored in many other GKSs?), the likelihood the proposition was generated in the free generation task, and structural centrality (i.e., the number of arcs directly connected to the proposition node in the conceptual graph structure). In summary, a very thorough analysis was performed on the lexical items associated with the four stories.

Graesser and Clark next investigated the extent to which the content of the lexical items could account for the inferences extracted by the question-answering protocols in the three-pronged methodology. Approximately 5,810 propositions would potentially be relevant to one of the stories, given that approximately 35 lexical items were relevant to a story and there were 166 propositions per lexical item. Of course, all of these 5,810 propositions would not be inherited as inferences during story comprehension. In fact, only 4% of these 5,810 propositions ended up being inferences. Most of the inferences were lexical-based inferences. Sixty-three percent of the inferences matched a proposition in at least one lexical item in the story; the other 37% of the inferences were novel situational inferences. Fifty-nine percent of the inferences matched a proposition in a lexical item that was active in working memory.

Graesser and Clark (1985) developed a model that predicted the subset of propositions stored in the lexical items that ended up being passage inferences. The model was based on the principles of convergence and constraint satisfaction. According to the convergence principle, propositions that intersect (i.e., match, overlap) between two or more information sources tend to become passage inferences. The information sources included the explicit text and the lexical items in working memory. The model assumed a processing mechanism in which all of these information sources are evaluated in parallel during the identification of intersecting nodes. The likelihood that an intersecting node in a lexical item became a passage inference was comparatively high (.43) compared to nonintersecting propositions (.04).

The principle of constraint satisfaction prunes out nodes from one information source that are incompatible conceptually with nodes from an information source of higher priority. Graesser and Clark identified the different types of incompatibility, such as direct contradictions, clashes in time frames, and clashes in plans of agents. They also proposed particular priority rules among information sources:

1. The explicit text has priority over the world knowledge in lexical items.
2. Lexical items in working memory have priority over lexical items that no longer reside in working memory.
3. Lexical items that convey actions and events (i.e., verbs) have priority over lexical items that convey static information (i.e., nouns).

Graesser and Clark reported empirical evidence for these constraint satisfaction mechanisms, but it is beyond the scope of this chapter to report these data. The general point to emphasize is that it is possible to test potential processing mechanisms by analyzing the content of the lexical items and by relating this content to the passage inferences that were extracted by verbal protocols during text comprehension.

Analysis of Propositions that Intersect
Between Two Lexical Items

We devoted some attention to the content of intersecting propositions, given the importance of the convergence principle in predicting lexicon-based inferences. Graesser and Clark (1985) reported that a proposition stored in a lexical item had a rather low likelihood (.03) of intersecting a proposition stored in another randomly selected lexical item. Thus, the content of any two randomly selected lexical items would not be very similar. On the average, only 5 out of the 166 nodes in a lexical item would match a node in one other lexical item.

We performed some analyses on intersecting propositions in order to identify the types of knowledge that overlaps between a pair of lexical items. We randomly selected a sample of 40 word pairs from Graesser and Clark's (1985) set of 128 lexical items. Each pair fit a noun-verb frame (e.g., *daughter-seeing, time-giving*). Clauses in narrative frequently have a noun-verb or noun-verb-noun combination of content words so such a sample would be reasonably representative of word combinations that appear in narrative texts. For each of these 40 pairs, we identified all proposition nodes that intersected. An intersecting proposition involved matching predicates. For example, the proposition "obey(daughter, parents)" from *daughter* would overlap "obey(X,Y)" in another lexical item. We also identified arguments that overlapped, as long as the arguments were not totally depleted semantically (e.g., X, Y, Z). Once the list of intersecting propositions was identified, we computed the number of times that a particular predicate overlapped in the sample of 40 lexical pairs. For example, the intersecting proposition "harm(X,Y)" was a match in 3 of the 40 pairs; *harm* is the predicate in this case. Frequent intersecting predicates were also segregated from infrequent intersecting predicates. A frequent intersecting predicate was part of an intersecting proposition in 10% or more of the 40 pairs, whereas an infrequent intersecting predicate was in 5% to 8% of the pairs.

There were 46 frequent intersecting predicates and 46 infrequent intersecting predicates. Predicates referring to emotions, sentiments, and evaluations were well represented (14/92 = 15%): *happy, angry, afraid, anxious, smile, fear, enjoy, like, love, care-for, good, bad, nice,* and *pleasant.* Significantly more of these predicates were among the frequent intersecting predicates than the infrequent intersecting predicates, 11 versus 3, respectively, chi-square(1) = 4.57, $p < .05$. Nine of the 92 intersecting predicates referred to events, typically cognitive and perceptual events: *see, feel, sense, smell, appear, learn, expect, experience,* and *perceive.* Ten of the intersecting predicates referred to states and attributes: *have, own, safe, know, alone, physical, easy, big, small,* and *round.* Fourteen of these 19 events and states referred to abstract phenomena, such as cognition and ownership, rather than physical concrete dimensions. In contrast, Graesser and Clark (1985) reported that only 40% of state and event nodes in the entire sample of 128 lexical items referred to abstract phenomena. There was a significant tendency for the intersecting events and states to be abstract phenomena, compared to the Graesser and Clark (1985) sample, chi-square(1) = 8.98, $p < .05$.

The lion's share of the intersecting predicates consisted of goals/actions. There were 59 goal/action predicates, which amounts to 64% of the intersecting predicates. Approximately half (49%) of these goal/action predicates referred to instrumental goals/actions, such as acquiring or retaining possession of resources (*get, obtain, gain, keep, take, buy, pay*), changing or retaining the location of a person or object (*move, go, change, run, walk, climb, escape, leave, stay, stand, set, remove, put, place*), intentional perceptions and cognitions (*watch, look-at, find, think, concentrate*), and procedural descriptions (*create, make, release*). Communication goals/actions consisted of 12% of these predicates (*talk, tell, ask, answer, yell, show, teach*). Main goals/actions, which comprised 39% of these predicates, referred to biological, personal, and social domains: *survive, win, improve, relax, relieve, avoid, hide, follow, give, offer, let, inherit, control, stop, free, fight, hurt, harm, threaten, protect, bore, treat*, and *frustrate*. When contrasting the instrumental goals with the main goals (and eliminating the communication goals), 56% of these predicates were instrumental goals and 44% were main goals. Graesser and Clark (1985) performed the same categorization on 1,374 goals in the entire sample of lexical items; in their analysis, 40% were instrumental goals and 60% were main goals. The distribution of intersecting goals significantly differed from the Graesser and Clark distribution, chi-square(1) = 5.39, $p < .05$. Therefore, there was a significant tendency for intersecting predicates to be instrumental goals/actions.

There were a few other informative findings. Some of the goal/action predicates were not analyzed because they were semantically depleted (*do, use, be, become, act*). All of these semantically depleted predicates were high frequency intersecting propositions. Similarly, a number of the intersecting arguments were semantically depleted (*person, self, each-other, thing, location*). Eight out of 10 of these semantically depleted items were parts of high-frequency rather than low frequency intersecting propositions. Twenty-one abstract and concrete nouns were semantically rich: *life, pressure, attention, danger, work, emotion, pregnancy, reality, right, society, affection, championship, pain, tension, car, money, house, ground, ear, weapon*, and *world*. Fourteen out of these 21 arguments are abstract, whereas only 36% of the lexical items in the Graesser and Clark sample were abstract. There was a significant tendency for the overlapping arguments to be abstract rather than concrete compared to the sample of 128 GKSs, chi-square(1) = 8.57, $p < .05$.

In summary, there were four major trends in our analyses of intersecting propositions and overlapping arguments when the 40 pairs of lexical items were examined. First, there was a tendency for the content of the intersecting propositions to be semantically depleted. Second, the intersecting propositions tended to have predicates and arguments that were abstract rather than concrete. Third, there was a tendency for intersecting propositions to be emotions, sentiments, and evaluations. Fourth, there was a tendency for intersecting propositions to be instrumental actions/goals rather than main actions/goals.

This subsection has identified particular predicates and arguments that frequently or occasionally intersect between lexical items. Given that there is a robust tendency for lexicon-based inferences to be intersecting statement nodes, these items are good candidates for being inferences when text is comprehended. In particular, it is likely that they would be among the activation-based inferences in Kintsch's construction-integration model.

A Reanalysis of Lexical Decision Latencies for Inference Words

The aforementioned analyses of the lexical items permitted us to distinguish between those passage inferences that were inherited from lexical items and those that were novel situational inferences. Once again, the lexicon-based inferences matched a proposition node in at least one lexical item from the explicit clause (that elicited the inference). A novel situational inference did not match a proposition node in any of the lexical items.

We reanalyzed the lexical decision data reported in Magliano et al. (1993) in order to compare the inference words that were lexicon-based with those that were novel situational inferences. That study had contrasted causal antecedent inferences and causal consequence inferences. Our reanalysis focused entirely on the causal antecedents because they were generated online; there was no evidence that causal consequence inferences were online. There was a manipulation of RSVP rate (250 vs. 400 ms) and SOA interval (250, 400, 600, vs. 1,200 ms) in that study. Magliano et al. reported that there was a threshold of 400 ms (both RSVP and SOA) before the inferences could be generated online. Therefore, we contrasted the cells in which there were minimal constraints on processing speed (i.e., both the RSVP and SOA were 400 ms or longer) and the cells that had high constraints on processing speed (i.e., either the RSVP or SOA was 250 ms). The critical dependent measure in these analyses was the inference encoding score (see Equation 1), following the practice of other researchers (Kintsch, 1988; Long et al., 1992; A. J. C. Sharkey & N. E. Sharkey, 1992).

The results of the reanalysis are shown in Table 7.3. The interesting news is the contrast between lexicon-based inferences and novel situational inferences. Surprisingly, the inference encoding scores in Table 7.3 are significantly lower for lexicon-based inferences than for novel situational inferences, −27 versus 12, respectively.[2] Most researchers would expect the lexicon-based inferences to be fastest because they are directly inherited from overlearned lexical items that are

---

[2]Interpretations of the negative inference encoding scores are provided by Magliano et al. (1993) and by Lorch, Balota, and Stamm (1986). The raw lexical decision latencies were approximately the same for lexicon-based inferences and novel situational inferences in unrelated contexts. Therefore, differences in inference encoding scores cannot be attributed to intrinsic properties of the words.

TABLE 7.3
Reanalysis of Inference Encoding Scores Derived from the Lexical Decision
Latencies for Causal Antecedent Inferences Reported by
Magliano, Baggett, Johnson, and Graesser (1993)

	Constraints on Processing Speed	
	Low[a]	High[b]
Lexicon-based Inferences	−13	−41
Novel situational Inferences	39	−16

[a]Both the RSVP rate and SOA interval were 400 ms or longer.
[b]The RSVP rate and/or the SOA interval was 250 ms.

activated by the content words in the explicit clause. In contrast, the novel situational inferences presumably are products of time-consuming constructive processes that operate on the contextually specific situation model.

One potential explanation of the counterintuitive results would appeal to compound cues (McKoon & Ratcliff, 1989, 1992; Reiser et al., 1985). According to such an account, inferences are constructed more quickly when they are products of compound memory cues (i.e., 2 or 3 lexical items as a compound) than single lexical items. Two critical conditions must be met, however, before this compound cue explanation can be taken seriously. The first is that the novel inferences in our sample were actually products of generic and specific knowledge structures that were accessed by compound cues. The alternative would be that the inferences were products of synthetic explanations or operations of the mental director, as discussed earlier, but not compound cues accessing knowledge structures. The second condition pertains to the relative speed of accessing knowledge structures. In order to account for the results, the speed would need to be faster in the case of compound cues than single lexical cues. More research is needed to evaluate the plausibility of these two conditions and the compound cue explanation.

Another explanation of the results is that the novelty of the novel situational inferences attracts the reader's focal attention and enhances their strength of encoding. The novel information is what contrasts the new unique situation from generic knowledge and from other specific situations stored in memory. The novel information provides distinctive indices for memory organization and retrieval (Kolodner, 1984; Schank, 1990). The novel information is most relevant and distinctive to the situation model, so it may play a more central role in guiding inference generation than generic, nondistinctive information. Moreover, there is some evidence that novel information is detected very quickly during perception and comprehension (Beiderman, Mazzanotte, & Rabinowitz, 1982; Loftus & Mackworth, 1978). This novelty explanation would be consistent with Berlyne's emphasis on the importance of novelty and uncertainty during meaning construction (Berlyne, 1971). However, more research is needed to assess the plausibility of this explanation of our results.

CLOSING COMMENTS

In this chapter, we have identified some of the inferences that are generated when readers construct situation models for narrative text. We have also identified the knowledge structures and processing mechanisms that furnish these knowledge-based inferences. These mechanisms of inference generation and situation model construction are far less mysterious today than they were 15 years ago, so we believe the field has shown some signs of progress.

When some of us began investigating knowledge-based inferences 15 years ago, there were colleagues who warned us that we may be going down the primrose path. The skeptics pointed out that most world knowledge is open-ended, imprecise, ill-defined, and vague, so the whole enterprise would end up sinking in quicksand. The skeptics urged us to concentrate on language comprehension mechanisms that were better understood and computationally specified, such as the construction of syntactic code and the explicit textbase. We chose to ignore the skeptics and attempt to unravel the mysteries of constructing situation models. Fortunately, we have managed to construct a working edifice and avoid getting buried in quicksand. We owe an enormous debt to Walter Kintsch, whose pioneering models provided the platform.

ACKNOWLEDGMENTS

This research was funded by contracts awarded to Arthur C. Graesser by the Office of Naval Research (N00014-88-0110 and N00014-90-J-1492). We would like to thank Bill Baggett, Eugenie Bertus, and Joe Magliano for their help throughout this project. We would also like to thank Randy Fletcher, Gail McKoon, and an anonymous reviewer for their comments on an earlier draft of this chapter.

REFERENCES

Albrecht, J. E. & O'Brien, E. J. (in press). Updating a mental model: Maintaining both local and global coherence. *Journal of Experimental Psychology: Learning, Memory, and Cognition.*

Alterman, R. (1985). A dictionary based on concept coherence. *Artificial Intelligence, 25,* 153–186.

Balota, D. A., Flores d'Arcais, G. B., & Rayner, K. (Eds.). (1990). *Comprehension processes in reading.* Hillsdale, NJ: Lawrence Erlbaum Associates.

Bartlett, F. C. (1932). *Remembering: A study in experimental and social psychology.* Cambridge, England: Cambridge University Press.

Berlyne, D. E. (1949). "Interest" as a psychological concept. *British Journal of Psychology, 39,* 184–195.

Berlyne, D. E. (1971). *Aesthetics and psychobiology.* New York: Appleton-Century-Crofts.

Biederman, I., Mezzanotte, R. J., & Rabinowitz, J. C. (1982). Scene perception: Detecting and judging objects undergoing relational violations. *Cognitive Psychology, 14,* 143–177.

Bloom, C. P., Fletcher, C. R., van den Broek, P., Reitz, L., & Shapiro, B. P. (1990). An on-line assessment of causal reasoning during comprehension. *Memory and Cognition, 18*, 65–71.

Bower, G. H. (1989). Mental models in text understanding. In A. F. Bennett & K. M. McConkie (Eds.), *Cognition in individual and social contexts* (pp. 129–144). Amsterdam: Elsevier.

Bower, G. H., Black, J. B., & Turner, T. J. (1979). Scripts in memory for text. *Cognitive Psychology, 11*, 177–220.

Britton, B. K., & Gulgoz, S. (1991). Using Kintsch's computational model to improve instructional text: Effects of repairing inference calls on recall and cognitive structures. *Journal of Educational Psychology, 83*, 329–345.

Chomsky, N. (1965). *Aspects of the theory of syntax.* Cambridge, MA: MIT Press.

Collins, A. M., Brown, J. S., & Larkin, K. M. (1980). Inferences in text understanding. In R. J. Spiro, B. C. Bruce, & W. F. Brewer. (Eds.), *Theoretical issues in reading comprehension* (pp. 385–404). Hillsdale, NJ: Lawrence Erlbaum Associates.

Dahlgren, K. (1988). *Naive semantics for natural language understanding.* Boston: Kluwer Academic.

DeJong, G. (1979). Prediction and substantiation: A new approach to natural language processing. *Cognitive Science, 3*, 251–273.

Dyer, M. G. (1983). *In-depth understanding: A computer model of integrated processing for narrative comprehension.* Cambridge, MA: MIT Press.

Ericsson, K. A., & Simon, H. A. (1980). Verbal reports as data. *Psychological Review, 87*, 215–251.

Fletcher, C. R., & Bloom, C. P. (1988). Causal reasoning in the comprehension of simple narrative texts. *Journal of Memory and Language, 27*, 236–244.

Gernsbacher, M. A. (1990). *Language comprehension as structure building.* Hillsdale, NJ: Lawrence Erlbaum Associates.

Gernsbacher, M. A., Goldsmith, H. H., & Robertson, R. R. (1992). Do readers mentally represent character's emotional states? *Cognition and Emotion, 6*, 89–112.

Glenberg, A. M., Meyer, M., & Lindem, K. (1987). Mental models contribute to foregrounding during text comprehension. *Journal of Memory and Language, 26*, 69–83.

Graesser, A. C. (1981). *Prose comprehension beyond the word.* New York: Springer-Verlag.

Graesser, A. C., Bertus, E. L., & Magliano, J. P. (in press). Inference generation during the comprehension of narrative text. In E. J. O'Brien & R. F. Lorch (Eds.), *Sources of coherence in text comprehension*, Hillsdale, NJ: Lawrence Erlbaum Associates.

Graesser, A. C. & Bower, G. H. (Eds.). (1990). *Inferences and text comprehension.* New York: Academic Press.

Graesser, A. C., & Clark, L. F. (1985). *Structures and procedures of implicit knowledge.* Norwood, NJ: Ablex.

Graesser, A. C., Haberlandt, K., & Koizumi, D. (1987). How is reading time influenced by knowledge based inferences and world knowledge. In B. K. Britton & S. M. Glynn (Eds.), *Executive control processes in reading* (pp. 217–252). Hillsdale, NJ: Lawrence Erlbaum Associates.

Graesser, A. C., Hoffman, N. L., & Clark, L. F. (1980). Structural components of reading time. *Journal of Verbal Learning and Verbal Behavior, 19*, 135–151.

Graesser, A. C., & Kreuz, R. J. (1993). A theory of inference generation during text comprehension. *Discourse Processes, 16*, 145–160.

Graesser, A. C., Lang, K. L., & Roberts, R. M. (1991). Question answering in the context of stories. *Journal of Experimental Psychology: General, 120*, 254–277.

Graesser, A. C., Robertson, S. P., & Anderson, P. A. (1981). Incorporating inferences in narrative representations: A study of how and why. *Cognitive Psychology, 13*, 1–26.

Graesser, A. C., Singer, M., & Trabasso, T. (1994). Constructing inferences during narrative text comprehension. *Psychological Review, 101*, 375–395.

Haberlandt, K., & Graesser, A. C. (1985). Component processes in text comprehension and some of their interactions. *Journal of Experimental Psychology: General, 114*, 357–374.

Johnson-Laird, P. N. (1983). *Mental models: Toward a theory of inference, language, and consciousness.* Cambridge, MA: Harvard University Press.

Katz, J. J., & Fodor, J. A. (1963). The structure of semantic theory. *Language, 39,* 170–210.

Kintsch, W. (1974). *The representation of meaning in memory.* Hillsdale, NJ: Lawrence Erlbaum Associates.

Kintsch, W. (1988). The role of knowledge in discourse comprehension: A construction-integration model. *Psychological Review, 95,* 163–182.

Kintsch, W. (1993). Information accretion and reduction in text processing: Inferences. *Discourse Processes, 16,* 193–202.

Kintsch, W., Kozminsky, E., Streby, W. J., McKoon, G., & Keenan, J. M. (1975). Comprehension and recall of text as a function of content variables. *Journal of Verbal Learning and Verbal Behavior, 14,* 196–214.

Kintsch, W., & van Dijk, T. A. (1978). Toward a model of text comprehension and production. *Psychological Review, 85,* 363–394.

Kintsch, W., Welsch, D., Schmalhofer, F., & Zimny, S. (1990). Sentence memory: A theoretical analysis. *Journal of Memory and Language, 29,* 133–159.

Kolodner, J.L. (1984). *Retrieval and organizational strategies in conceptual memory: A computer model.* Hillsdale, NJ: Lawrence Erlbaum Associates.

Lehnert, W. G. (1981). Plots units and narrative summarization. *Cognitive Science, 5,* 283–331.

Loftus, G. R., & Mackworth, N. H. (1978). Cognitive determinants of fixation location during picture viewing. *Journal of Experimental Psychology: Human Perception and Performance, 4,* 565–572.

Long, D. L., & Golding, J. M. (1993). Superordinate goal inferences: Are they automatically generated during comprehension? *Discourse Processes, 16,* 55–73.

Long, D. L., Golding, J. M., & Graesser, A. C. (1992). The generation of goal related inferences during narrative comprehension. *Journal of Memory and Language, 5,* 634–647

Long, D. L., Golding, J. M., Graesser, A. C., & Clark, L. F. (1990). Goal, event, and state inferences: An investigation of inference generation during story comprehension. In A. C. Graesser & G. H. Bower (Eds.), *Inferences and text comprehension* (pp. 89–102). New York: Academic Press.

Lorch, R. F., Balota, D. A., & Stamm, E. G. (1986). Locus of inhibition effects in the priming of lexical decisions: Pre- or post-access? *Memory and Cognition, 14,* 95–103.

Magliano, J. P., Baggett, W. B., Johnson, B. K., & Graesser, A. C. (1993). The time course of generating causal antecedent and causal consequence inferences. *Discourse Processes, 16,* 35–53.

Magliano, J. P., & Graesser, A. C. (1991). A three-pronged method for studying inference generation in literary text. *Poetics, 20,* 193–232.

Mandler, J. M. (1984). *Stories, scripts, and scenes: Aspects of schema theory.* Hillsdale, NJ: Lawrence Erlbaum Associates.

McKoon, G., & Ratcliff, R. (1989a). Semantic associations and elaborative inferences. *Journal of Experimental Psychology: Learning, Memory, and Cognition, 15,* 326–338.

McKoon, G., & Ratcliff, R. (1989b). Assessing the occurrence of elaborative inference with recognition: Compatibility checking vs. compound cue theory. *Journal of Memory and Language, 28,* 547–563.

McKoon, G., & Ratcliff, R. (1992). Inference during reading. *Psychological Review, 99,* 440–466.

Miller, G. A., Beckwith, R., Fellbaum, C., Gross, D., Miller, K., & Tengi, R. (1993). *Five papers on Wordnet™* (CSL Rep. No. 43). Cognitive Science Laboratory, Princeton University.

Millis, K. K., Morgan, D., & Graesser, A. C. (1990). The influence of knowledge-based inferences on the reading time of expository text. In A. C. Graesser & G. H. Bower (Eds.), *Inferences and text comprehension* (pp. 197–212). New York: Academic Press.

Morrow, D. G., Bower, G. H., & Greenspan, S. L. (1987). Accessibility and situation models in narrative comprehension. *Journal of Memory and Language, 26,* 165–187.

O'Brien, E. J., Shank, D. M., Myers, J. L., & Rayner, K. (1988). Elaborative inferences during reading: Do they occur on-line? *Journal of Experimental Psychology: Learning, Memory, and Cognition, 14,* 410–420.

Olson, G. M., Duffy, S. A., & Mack, R. L. (1984). Thinking-out loud as a method for studying real-time comprehension processes. In D. E. Kieras & M. A. Just (Eds.), *New methods in the study of immediate processes in comprehension* (pp. 253–286). Hillsdale, NJ: Lawrence Erlbaum Associates.

Potts, G. R., Keenan, J. M., & Golding, J. M. (1988). Assessing the occurrence of elaborative inferences: Lexical decision versus naming. *Journal of Memory and Language, 27*, 399–415.

Reiser, B. J., Black, J. B., & Abelson, R. P. (1985). Knowledge structures in the organization and retrieval of autobiographical memories. *Cognitive Psychology, 17*, 89–137.

Rumelhart, D. E., & Ortony, A. (1977). The representation of knowledge in memory. In R. C. Anderson, R. J. Spiro, & W. E. Montague (Eds.), *Schooling and the acquisition of knowledge* (pp. 99–136). Hillsdale, NJ: Lawrence Erlbaum Associates.

Schank, R. C. (1986). *Explanation patterns: Understanding mechanically and creatively.* Hillsdale, NJ: Lawrence Erlbaum Associates.

Schank, R. C. (1990). *Tell me a story: A new look at real and artificial memory.* New York: Scribner's.

Schank, R. C., & Abelson, R. (1977). *Scripts, plans, goals and understanding: An inquiry into human knowledge structures.* Hillsdale, NJ: Lawrence Erlbaum Associates.

Schmalhofer, F., & Glavanov, D. (1986). Three concepts of understanding a programmer's manual: Verbatim, propositional, and situational representations. *Journal of Memory and Language, 25*, 279–294.

Seifert, C. M., Robertson, S. P., & Black, J. B. (1985). Types of inferences generated during reading. *Journal of Memory and Language, 24*, 405–422.

Sharkey, A. J. C., & Sharkey, N. E. (1992). Weak contextual constraints in text and word priming. *Journal of Memory and Language, 31*, 543–572.

Singer, M. (1988). Inferences in reading. In M. Daneman, G. E. Mackinnon, & T. G. Waller (Eds.), *Reading research: Advances in theory and practice* (pp. 177–219). New York: Academic Press.

Singer, M. (1990). *Psychology of language.* Hillsdale, NJ: Lawrence Erlbaum Associates.

Singer, M., & Ferreira, F. (1983). Inferring consequences in story comprehension. *Journal of Verbal Learning and Verbal Behavior, 22*, 437–448.

Singer, M., Graesser, A. C., & Trabasso, T. (1994). Minimal or global inference during reading. *Journal of Memory and Language, 33*, 421–441.

Singer, M., Hallsdorson, M., Lear, J. C., & Andrusiak, P. (1992). Validation of causal bridging inferences in discourse understanding. *Journal of Memory and Language, 31*, 507–524.

Stein, N. L., & Levine, L. J. (1991). Making sense out of emotion: The representation and use of goal-structured knowledge. In W. Kessen, A. Ortony, & F. I. M. Craik (Eds.), *Memories, thoughts, and emotions: Essays in honor of George Mandler* (pp. 295–322). Hillsdale, NJ: Lawrence Erlbaum Associates.

Suh, S., & Trabasso, T. (1993). Inference during reading: Convergence from discourse analysis, talk-aloud protocols, and recognition priming. *Journal of Memory and Language, 32*, 279–301.

Till, R. E., Mross, E. F., & Kintsch, W. (1988). Time course of priming for associate and inference words in a discourse context. *Memory and Cognition, 16*, 283–298.

Trabasso, T., & Suh, S. Y. (1993). Using talk-aloud protocols to reveal inferences during comprehension of text. *Discourse Processes, 16*, 283–298.

van den Broek, P., Fletcher, C. R., & Risden, K. (1993). Investigations of inferential processes in reading: A theoretical and methodological integration. *Discourse Processes, 16*, 169–180.

van den Broek, P., & Lorch, R. F. (1993). Network representations of causal relations in memory for narrative texts: Evidence from primed recognition. *Discourse Processes, 16*, 75–98.

van Dijk, T. A., & Kintsch, W. (1983). *Strategies of discourse comprehension.* New York: Academic Press.

Whitney, P. (1987). Psychological theories of elaborative inferences: Implications for schema-theoretic views of comprehension. *Reading Research Quarterly, 22*, 299–310.

Zwaan, R. A. (1993). *Aspects of literacy comprehension: A cognitive approach.* Amsterdam: John Benjamins.

Zwaan, R. A., & van Oostendorp, H. (1993). Do readers construct spatial representations in naturalistic story comprehension? *Discourse Processes, 16*, 125–143.

Chapter 8

Activating Knowledge of Fictional Characters' Emotional States

Morton Ann Gernsbacher
University of Wisconsin-Madison

One of Kintsch's most prominent contributions to the understanding of discourse comprehension is his proposal that comprehenders build situational models. Kintsch introduced his theoretical concept of situational models in the following way: "A major feature of our model [of discourse comprehension] is the assumption that discourse understanding involves not only the representation of a textbase in episodic memory, but at the same time, the activation, updating, and other uses of a so-called *situation model* in episodic memory: This is the cognitive representation of the events, actions, persons, and in general the situation, a text is about" (van Dijk & Kintsch, 1983, p. 337).

Kintsch (van Dijk & Kintsch, 1983) argued for the necessity of situational models during discourse comprehension by writing:

> The problem is that a text representation involves not only text elements, but also knowledge elements. How many of these become part of the text representation? In other words, is the text representation the kind of rich, elaborated structure that our intuition as well as our experiments tell us it can be, or is it more text bound? Where do we draw the boundaries? In this book, we have consistently opted for keeping the text representation relatively uncontaminated and unelaborated: Only those inferences become part of it that are necessary to establish coherence at the local or global level. Others have hypothesized much richer text representations including the discourse and its context as well as the internal knowledge brought to bear during interpretation. We propose that these elaborations, except for the ones that are textually necessary as outlined in Chapter 5, are not part of the text representation proper but of a model that the hearer or reader constructs about the

situation denoted by the text. It is this model which supplies and collects all the relevant information for the adequate comprehension of the text. (pp. 336–337)

Indeed, Kintsch proposed that building a situational model is tantamount to successful comprehension. "To understand a text, we have to represent what it is about. If we are unable to imagine a situation in which certain individuals have the properties or relations indicated by the text, we fail to understand the text itself" (van Dijk & Kintsch, 1983, p. 337).

How are these situational models built? According to Kintsch (van Dijk & Kintsch, 1983), one of the critical steps in building a situational model is activating previously represented knowledge:

Using knowledge in discourse comprehension means being able to relate the discourse to some existing knowledge structure, which then provides a situation model of it. The process is one of being reminded of past situations, be they specific episodic or generalized semantic ones. Many of the discourses we interpret are about objects, person, places, or facts we already know from past experience. In memory, these experiences form part of (overlapping) clusters of similar experiences. To the extent that they are episodic, they are, of course, subjective and differ from person to person. Thus, each person has subjective experiential clusters about the town he or she lives in, the house, friends, place of work, and major life events. Similarly, each person shares, to some extent at least, other clusters of experiences about such items as countries, towns, historical events, political events, or well-known people. At the other extreme, as decontextualization sets in, these experiences become entirely general or almost so, such as one's knowledge of arithmetic or chess. (p. 337)

DO READERS ACTIVATE EXPERIENTIAL KNOWLEDGE WHEN COMPREHENDING TEXTS?

Kintsch's proposal that comprehension involves activating previously stored knowledge has been one of the many aspects of his work that has greatly influenced my work (see also Gernsbacher, 1990). The experiments described in this chapter were based on that proposal.

Consider the following narrative:

Joe worked at the local 7-11 store, to get spending money while in school. One night, his best friend, Tom, came in to buy a soda. Joe needed to go back to the storage room for a second. While he was away, Tom noticed the cash register drawer was open. From the open drawer Tom quickly took a ten dollar bill. Later that week, Tom learned that Joe had been fired from the 7-11 store because his cash had been low one night.

What information becomes activated in readers' minds when they read this story? Perhaps readers activate spatial knowledge as suggested by the work of Morrow, Bower, and Greenspan (1989) and Glenberg, Meyer, and Lindem (1987). If readers activate spatial knowledge, then reading the sentence, "While Joe was away, Tom noticed the cash register was open [and] quickly took a ten dollar bill," might stimulate readers to activate knowledge about the typical layout of convenience stores. With that knowledge activated, they might build a mental representation of the 7-11 store such that Tom could not be seen by Joe when Tom was in the storage room and Joe was near the cash register.

Readers might also activate temporal knowledge, as suggested by the work of Anderson, Garrod, and Sanford (1983). If readers activate temporal knowledge, then reading the expression, *Later that week*, might stimulate readers to activate knowledge about the activities that can occur within the period, *1 week*. With that knowledge activated, readers might build a mental time frame for the story that allows other events to occur between the time that Tom took the $10 bill and the time he learned that Joe had been fired. One obvious event is that Joe's boss could have learned of the missing cash.

In Gernsbacher, Goldsmith, and Robertson (1992), we investigated whether readers activate another type of knowledge while comprehending stories. We investigated whether readers activate knowledge about human emotions and use that activated knowledge to build mental representations of fictional characters' emotional states. If so, then reading several sentences in this story might stimulate readers to activate the knowledge of how someone feels when he finds out that his best friend was fired from a job for something the best friend did. In other words, readers might build a mental representation of a fictional character's emotional state. In this case, readers might build a mental representation of *Tom* experiencing the emotional state, *guilt*. In a series of laboratory experiments, we tested this hypothesis.

DO READERS ACTIVATE EMOTIONAL KNOWLEDGE WHEN COMPREHENDING TEXTS?

We began to test the hypothesis that readers activate emotional knowledge when comprehending texts by constructing 24 experimental stories. Each experimental story was intended to stimulate readers to activate knowledge about a particular emotional state. But, importantly, these emotional states were implied without explicit mention of any emotion. The experimental stories described concrete actions, such as Tom going to the 7-11, Joe going to the storage room, Tom taking the $10 bill, and Tom learning that Joe had been fired. But never was there any mention of emotion until a final "target" sentence.

Subjects read the stories sentence by sentence, and unknown to the subjects, the last sentence of each experimental story was a target sentence. Each target sentence contained an emotion word (e.g., *guilt*), as in "It would be weeks before Tom's guilt would subside." We manipulated whether the emotion word in the target sentence matched the emotional state implied in the story, as does *guilt*, or whether the emotion word mismatched. Across three experiments we manipulated the nature of the mismatch.

In our (Gernsbacher et al., 1992) first experiment, the matching and mismatching emotion words were what we called "perceived converses." By this we meant that the matching and mismatching emotion words were opposite along one important dimension, but they were almost identical along other dimensions. The dimension along which they were opposite was their affective valence: One emotion word had a negative affective valence (for example, *guilt*), whereas the other had a positive affective valence (for example, *pride*). The dimensions along which they were almost identical were their intensity; duration; relevance to self versus others; temporal reference to events in the past, present, or future; and so forth (Frijda, 1986). The 12 pairs of converse emotional states were guilt–pride, boredom–curiosity, shyness–confidence, depression–happiness, disgust–admiration, callousness–care, anger–gratitude, sadness–joy, despair–hope, fear–boldness, envy–sympathy, and restlessness–contentment.

For each pair of converse emotional states, we wrote two stories. For one story, one member of the converse emotional states matched while the other member mismatched; for the other story, the opposite was true. For instance, we wrote two stories for the pair, *guilt–pride*. The story for which *guilt* matched and *pride* mismatched was the story about Joe, Tom, and the 7-11. The other story, for which *pride* matched and *guilt* mismatched, was the following:

> Paul had always wanted his brother, Luke, to be good in baseball. So Paul had been coaching Luke after school for almost 2 years. In the beginning, Luke's skills were very rough. But after hours and hours of coaching, Paul could see great improvement. In fact, the improvement had been so great that at the end of the season, at the Little League Awards Banquet, Luke's name was called out to receive the Most Valuable Player Award.

For this story, a target sentence containing a matching emotion word would be, "It would be weeks before Paul's pride would subside," whereas a target sentence with a mismatching emotion word would be, "It would be weeks before Paul's guilt would subside."

To measure whether readers activated knowledge about fictional characters' emotional states, we measured how long subjects needed to read each story's target sentence. We predicted that the target sentences would be read more rapidly when they contained matching emotion words than when they contained mismatching emotion words, because reading the story would activate information corresponding to the emotional state captured by the matching emotion word.

In addition to the 24 experimental emotional stories, each subject read 24 filler stories. The filler stories were written in the same style as the experimental stories, but they were not intended to activate information about any emotional state; they were relatively neutral, for example:

> Today was the day Tyler was going to plant a garden. He put on his work clothes and went out to the shed to get the tools. The ground was all prepared so he began planting right away. It was a small garden, but then he didn't really need a large one. It was large enough to plant a few of his favorite vegetables. Maybe this year he'd plant some flowers, too.

A filler story preceded each experimental story.

The results of this experiment are displayed by the two bars on the left of Fig. 8.1. These data are subjects' mean reading times for the target sentences in the experimental emotional stories. As those two leftmost bars illustrate, subjects read the target sentences considerably more rapidly when they contained an emotion word that matched the emotional state implied in the story as opposed to when they contained an emotion word that mismatched the emotional state implied in the story.

HOW MUCH EMOTIONAL KNOWLEDGE IS ACTIVATED DURING TEXT COMPREHENSION?

In a further experiment, we altered the nature of the mismatching emotion words to discern how much experiential knowledge about emotions is activated during text comprehension. In this experiment, the mismatching emotion words were not converses of the matching emotion words (as they had been in Gernsbacher et al.'s, 1992, first experiment). Rather, in this experiment, the matching and mismatching emotion words were dissimilar along the dimensions that the converses shared; but, as in our first experiment, the matching and mismatching emotion words were opposite in their affective valence. For instance, following the story about Tom and the 7-11 store, a target sentence with a matching emotion word would be *It would be weeks before Tom's guilt would subside*, just as it was in Gernsbacher et al.'s (1992) first experiment. But a target sentence with a mismatching emotion word would be *It would be weeks before Tom's hope would subside*; *hope* (a mismatching emotion word) has the opposite affective valence of *guilt* (the matching emotion word), but *hope* and *guilt* are not converses. In this experiment, the emotional states were paired in the following way: guilt–hope, pride–shyness, envy–joy, sympathy–anger, disgust–gratitude, admiration–callousness, care–restlessness, despair–contentment, happiness–fear, curiosity–sadness, confidence–depression, boredom–boldness.

The results of this experiment are displayed in the two middle bars of Fig. 8.1. As these two bars illustrate, subjects read the target sentences considerably more rapidly when they contained matching as opposed to mismatching emotion words. However, subjects read the mismatching target sentences more rapidly in this experiment than they did in the first experiment. Recall that the difference

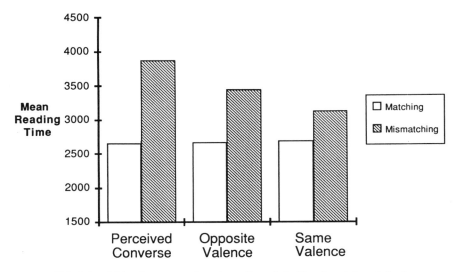

FIG. 8.1.   Subjects' mean reading times (in ms) in Experiment 1 and 2 of Gernsbacher et al. (1992) and in a previously unreported experiment. The leftmost bars illustrate reading times when the matching and mismatching emotion words were "perceived" converses (e.g., *guilt–pride*). The middle bars illustrate reading times when the matching and mismatching emotion words were opposite in affective valence, but not perceived complements (e.g., *guilt–hope*). The rightmost bars illustrate reading times when the matching and mismatching emotion word shared their affective valence (e.g., *guilt–shyness*).

between these two experiments was the nature of the mismatching emotion words: In the first experiment, the mismatching emotion words were the converses of the matching emotion words (for example, *guilt–pride*); in this experiment, the matching and mismatching emotion words were dissimilar along the dimensions that the converses shared, although they were still opposite in affective valence (for example, *guilt–hope*).

In a third experiment (Gernsbacher et al., 1992, Exp. 2), we again altered the nature of the mismatching emotion words. In this experiment, the mismatching emotion words were again not the perceived converses of the matching words. In fact, they had the same affective valence as the matching emotion words, although they were less likely than the matching emotion words. For instance, the mismatching target word for the story about Tom and the 7-11 store, which implied the emotional state *guilt*, was *shyness*. *Shyness* has the same affective valence as *guilt*; however, when someone finds out that his best friend was fired for something he did, a person is less likely to experience *shyness* than *guilt*.

The results of this experiment are displayed in the two rightmost bars of Fig. 8.1. Subjects again read the target sentences more rapidly when they contained matching as opposed to mismatching emotion words, as we found in our other two experiments. However, subjects read the mismatching target sentences more rapidly in this experiment than they did in the other two experiments.

The striking similarity among the three sets of data illustrated in Fig. 8.1 lies in subjects' reading times for the matching target sentences. In each experiment, subjects read the matching target sentences at approximately the same rate, regardless of the nature of the mismatching target sentences. The striking difference among these three sets of data lies in subjects' reading times for the mismatching sentences. The more disparate the mismatching emotion words were to the implied emotional states, the more slowly subjects read the target sentences containing those mismatching emotion words. When the mismatching emotion words were the converses of the implied emotional states, subjects read the target sentences most slowly; when the mismatching emotion words were opposite in affective valence but not converses, subjects read the target sentences less slowly; and when the mismatching emotion words were the same affective valence as the implied emotional states, subjects read the target sentences most rapidly, although not as rapidly as they read target sentences containing matching emotion words.

Gernsbacher et al. (1992) suggested that these data illustrate the role that activation of previously acquired knowledge plays in how readers understand fictional characters' emotional states. The content of the stories stimulated readers to access certain emotional knowledge. In a fourth experiment, we specifically tested the hypothesis that the content of the stories—not the target sentences—activated readers' knowledge of emotional states.

In this experiment (Gernsbacher et al., 1992, Exp. 3), we employed a different laboratory task. We employed a task that some cognitive psychologists argue reflects only what is currently activated in readers' mental representations; it does not reflect how easily a stimulus (such as a target sentence) can be integrated into that representation. The task is simply to pronounce a printed word as rapidly as possible (Balota & Chumbley, 1984; Chumbley & Balota, 1984; Keenan, Golding, Potts, Jennings, & Aman, 1990; Lucas, Tanenhaus, & Carlson, 1990; Seidenberg, Waters, Sanders, & Langer, 1984).

Pronouncing a printed word is considered to be such an easy and relatively automatic task that some researchers assume that subjects do not attempt to integrate the word into their mental representations; presumably, subjects simply pronounce the test word as fast as they can. If most of the test words are unrelated to the stories (and in our experiment, 87.5% were unrelated), subjects are discouraged from interpreting the test words vis-à-vis the ongoing story; they simply view the pronunciation task as an additional (and unrelated) task involved in completing the experiment.

Therefore, subjects in this experiment read the same stories as the subjects in the first three experiments. As in the first two experiments, there was no explicit mention of emotion in the stories. For instance, one story began:

Joe worked at the local 7-11, to get spending money while in school. One night, his best friend, Tom, came in to buy a soda. Joe needed to go back to the storage room for a second. While he was away, Tom noticed the cash register was open. From the open drawer Tom quickly took a ten dollar bill. Later that week, Tom learned that Joe had been fired from the 7-11 because his cash had been low one night.

However, unlike the stories in the first three experiments, each story in this experiment was not followed by a target sentence that contained a matching or mismatching emotion word. Instead, at different points during both the experimental and filler stories, test words appeared on the screen, and the subjects' task was simply to pronounce each test word as rapidly as possible.

In the experimental stories, one of the test words was our target word, and it appeared immediately after subjects read the last line of the story (e.g., after they read *Later that week, Tom learned that Joe had been fired from the 7-11 because his cash had been low one night*). The target word either matched (e.g., *guilt*) or mismatched (e.g., *pride*) the emotional state implied by the story. We found that test words were pronounced reliably more rapidly when they matched as opposed to mismatched the characters' implied emotional states. For example, after subjects read the story about Tom and the 7-11, they pronounced the word *guilt* more rapidly than they pronounced the word *pride*. After they read the story about Paul and his brother's little league banquet, they pronounced the word *pride* more rapidly than they pronounced the word *guilt*. Therefore, this experiment demonstrated the powerful role that knowledge activation plays in readers' understanding of fictional characters' emotional states. In two further experiments, we further demonstrated the role that knowledge activation plays.

In one experiment (Gernsbacher & Robertson, 1992; Exp. 1), we manipulated the number of emotional stories that our subjects read. In our previous experiments, all subjects read 48 total stories. Half (24) of the stories were experimental, emotional stories, and the other half (24) were filler, nonemotional stories. In our more recent experiment (Gernsbacher & Roberston, 1992; Exp. 1), there were two conditions such that in a high-density condition, 36 of the 48 stories were emotional stories, and only 12 were nonemotional, filler stories. In a low-density condition, only 12 of the 48 stories were emotional stories, and 36 were nonemotional, filler stories. The data we analyzed were reading times to the target sentences in a "common" set of 12 emotional stories that occurred in both the high- and low-density conditions. Half the target sentences contained matching emotion words, and half contained mismatching emotion words. The matching and mismatching emotion words were perceived converses.

We predicted that the density manipulation would not affect reading times to the matching target sentences. This is because information about the implied (matching) emotional states would already be highly activated by the content of the stories; therefore, the matching emotional states could not be "helped" by the greater activation of emotional knowledge produced by the higher density of emotional stories. Neither could the activation level of the matching emotional states be "hurt" by the lesser activation of emotional knowledge produced by the lower density of emotional stories.

In contrast, we predicted that the density manipulation would affect reading times to the mismatching target sentences. This is because reading many emotional stories should greatly activate subjects' knowledge about emotional states; if so, then mismatching emotional states should be more activated when subjects read a high density of emotional stories. Therefore, the mismatching sentences should have been read more rapidly in the high-density condition than in the low-density condition (because the mismatching emotional states would be more activated in the high-density condition than in the low-density condition).

The results of this experiment are displayed in Fig. 8.2. The data displayed are subjects' reading times for the common set of matching versus mismatching target sentences. As Fig. 8.2 illustrates, subjects read the target sentences considerably more rapidly when they contained matching as opposed to mismatching emotion words. This was the case in both the high- and low-density condition. As Fig. 8.2 also illustrates, the density manipulation did not affect subjects' reading times for the matching target sentences. In contrast, the density manipulation did affect subjects' reading times for the mismatching target sentences: Mismatching target sentences were read more rapidly in the high-density condition than in the low-density condition. Thus, the more emotion stories read by the subjects, the faster they read the mismatching sentences.

Gernsbacher & Robertson (1992) attributed this high-density effect on the mismatching sentences to knowledge activation rather than sentence integration.

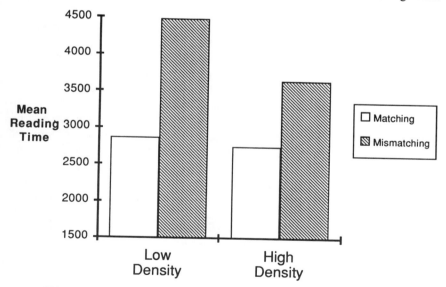

FIG. 8.2. Subjects' mean reading times (in ms) in Gernsbacher and Robertson (1992) Experiment 1. The leftmost bars illustrate subjects' reading times in the low-density condition (25% emotional stories; 75% nonemotional filler stories). The rightmost bars illustrate subjects' reading times in the high-density condition (75% emotional stories; 25% nonemotional filler stories).

The high-density effect manifests knowledge activation rather than the ease with which subjects could integrate the target sentences into their mental representations because the mismatching target sentences and the experimental stories were the same in the high- and low-density conditions; therefore, any difference in reading times must have been produced by factors outside the 12 experimental stories and their 12 target sentences.

We suggested that reading more emotional stories more strongly activates readers' knowledge of emotional states, whereas reading fewer emotional stories less strongly activates readers' knowledge of emotional states. This greater versus lesser activation of emotional knowledge affected subjects' reading times only to the mismatching sentences because information about the implied (matching) emotional states was already highly activated by the content of the stories. However, a counterexplanation for the density effect is that subjects adopted a strategy. In the high-density condition, subjects read more mismatching target sentences. Although subjects also read more matching target sentences in the high-density condition, perhaps the higher incidence of mismatching sentences encouraged subjects to adopt a strategy for dismissing them or reading them less thoroughly.

In a further experiment (Gernsbacher & Robertson, 1992; Exp. 2), we performed a proportion manipulation to investigate this counterexplanation. The logic underlying a proportion manipulation is this: If a certain type of experimental trial occurs rarely, subjects are unlikely to adopt a strategy for that type of trial. But if a type of trial occurs frequently, subjects are likely to adopt a strategy for responding to that type of trial—if the cognitive process tapped by that type of trial is under the subjects' strategic control.

For instance, consider the following experimental task: Subjects see pairs of letter strings (e.g., *bortz–blaugh*). The subjects' task is to decide whether each member of the pair is a word. On some trials, both members are words, and on some of the trials in which both members are words, the two words are semantically related, for example, *bread–butter*. A classic finding is that subjects respond to the second letter string more rapidly when it is a member of a related pair (Meyer & Schvaneveldt, 1971). For example, subjects respond to *butter* more rapidly when it is preceded by *bread* than when it is preceded by *nurse*.

Now, consider the following manipulation: In a low probability condition, only one eighth of the word pairs is related (*bread–butter*; seven-eighths are unrelated (*nurse–butter*). In an equal probability condition, half the word pairs are related, and half are unrelated; and in a high probability condition, the majority of the words are related, and only a small proportion is unrelated.

In each condition, subjects recognize the second word of the pair more rapidly if the pair is related, but the advantage is a function of the proportion of related trials. In the low probability condition, the advantage is smallest; in the high probability condition, the advantage is largest (Tweedy, Lapinsky, & Schvaneveldt, 1977). Presumably, the high proportion of related words encourages subjects to adopt a strategy for capitalizing on the words' relations.

However, subjects do not always adopt a strategy, even when there is a high proportion of a particular type of trial. Subjects only adopt a strategy if they can. For instance, in a *bread–butter* experiment, subjects typically adopt a beneficial strategy when there is a high proportion of related trials. However, they do not adopt a strategy if they are not given enough time to process the first word of the pair; without enough time to process the first word, there is no difference between the low, equal, or high probability conditions (den Heyer, Briand, & Dannenbring, 1983). In other words, there is no effect of the proportion manipulation.

Similarly, a proportion manipulation does not affect how likely it is that subjects will access the less-frequent versus more-frequent meaning of an ambiguous word, for example, the river's edge meaning of the word *bank* versus the monetary meaning. According to Simpson and Burgess (1985), activating the less- versus more-frequent meaning of an ambiguous word is not under subjects' strategic control; therefore, response times are unaffected by the probability manipulation.

To discover whether subjects' reading times for the mismatching sentences in the high-density condition were due to a strategy subjects might have adopted for dismissing or not fully attending to those mismatching sentences, we manipulated the proportion of matching versus mismatching target sentences while holding constant the density of emotional stories. We used the highest possible density of emotional stories—all 36 stories that subjects read were emotional stories.

There were three conditions. In the 75% mismatching condition, the target sentences for 27 stories contained mismatching emotion words, and the target sentences for the remaining 9 stories contained matching emotion words. In the 50% mismatching condition, the target sentences for 18 stories contained matching emotion words, and the target sentences for another 18 stories contained mismatching emotion words. In the 25% mismatching condition, the target sentences for only 9 stories contained mismatching emotion words whereas the target sentences for 27 stories contained matching emotion words.

The data we analyzed were reading times to target sentences in a common set of 18 stories that occurred in all three probability conditions. Half the target sentences contained matching emotion words, and half contained mismatching emotion words. The matching versus mismatching emotion words were perceived converses. If subjects' faster reading times to the mismatching target sentences in the high-density condition manifested a strategy, then the proportion manipulation should have invoked that strategy. That is, subjects should have read the mismatching target sentences most rapidly in the 75% mismatching condition and least rapidly in the 25% mismatching condition. In contrast, if subjects' faster reading times to the mismatching target sentences in the high- versus low-density condition manifested greater knowledge activation, then the proportion manipulation should not have affected subjects' reading times.

The results of this experiment are displayed in Fig. 8.3. In all three probability conditions subjects read the target sentences considerably more rapidly when they contained matching as opposed to mismatching emotion words. However, the proportion manipulation did not affect either the subjects' reading times to the matching target sentences or their reading times to the mismatching target sentences. These data suggest that the effect of the high-density condition on subjects' reading times to the mismatching sentences in our previous experiment was not due to a strategy. Instead, we suggested that in the high-density condition, readers activated more emotional knowledge, and, therefore, they read the mismatching sentences more rapidly.

HOW DO READERS ACQUIRE AND ACTIVATE EXPERIENTIAL KNOWLEDGE?

Together, the experiments reviewed here demonstrate that readers activate previously stored knowledge about emotional states while comprehending narratives. This conclusion fits squarely within the theoretical positions advanced by several leading text comprehension researchers (Fletcher & Bloom, 1988; Graesser & Zwaan, chap. 7, in this vol.; van den Broek & Trabasso, 1986). These researchers

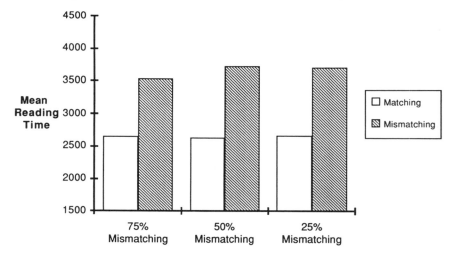

FIG. 8.3. Subjects' mean reading times (in ms) in Gernsbacher and Robertson (1992) Experiment 2. The leftmost bars illustrate subjects' reading times in the condition in which 75% of the stories had target sentences with matching emotion words; the middle bars illustrate subjects' reading times in the condition in which 50% of the stories had target sentences with matching emotion words; the rightmost bars illustrate subjects' reading times in the condition in which 25% of the stories had target sentences with matching emotion words.

propose that the situational models that readers construct contain information about the characters' goals. Thus, when reading the narrative about Paul and his brother Luke, readers' situational models would contain the goal structure of "Paul wants Luke to excel in baseball." Events and their outcomes that are consistent with that goal should therefore lead Paul to experience a positive emotion; events and their outcomes that are inconsistent with that goal would lead Paul to experience a negative emotion.

How is this knowledge about emotional states learned, and how is it activated? Again, my theoretical proposals have been guided by Kintsch, who wrote:

> We assume that during understanding such clusters are retrieved and form the basis for a new model of the situation. Sometimes this model is directly ready for use, sometimes it must be constructed from several partly relevant existing models. . . . Thus, the understander is reminded by the text of some prior experience, and then uses that experience to construct a model of the present situation. (van Dijk & Kintsch, 1983, pp. 337–338)

Kintsch (1988) likened the process by which previously acquired knowledge is activated during discourse comprehension to the process by which a previously learned list of words is retrieved during a recall test. According to Kintsch:

> How people recall relevant knowledge when they read a text is reminiscent of another experimental paradigm that has been studied extensively in psychological laboratories: how people recall lists of words. A widely used explanation for the recall of word lists is based on the generation-recognition principle. Some words are recalled directly, perhaps from a short-term memory buffer, and these words are then used to generate other semantically or contextually related, plausible recall candidates. (p. 179)

We can apply these proposals to describe how readers encode and activate knowledge about emotional states. Presumably, subjects in our experiments had previously encountered experiences (either personally or vicariously, e.g., through literature) that resembled the experiences we wrote about in our stimulus stories. Indeed, we constructed our stimulus stories so that they would be relevant to our undergraduate population of subjects. The stories revolved around typical under-graduate activities, such as going on a date, interviewing for a job, studying for exams, and living in a dorm.

When subjects in our experiments originally encountered experiences (either personally or vicariously) that were similar to those reproduced in our stimulus stories, presumably the subjects themselves or the fictional characters (about whom they were reading or watching in a movie) experienced a resulting emotional state. These emotional states became part of the memory trace. Therefore, reading about similar experiences should have activated those memory traces, and the memory traces included information about the concomitant emotional states. Our experimental task, which required subjects to continue telling each narrative after they read the target sentence, probably provided even more inducement for subjects to recollect their own experiences in order to think about what the fictional character would do next.

The hypothesis that the ability to understand fictional characters' emotional responses is based on exposure to actual or vicarious emotional experiences predicts that the more emotional situations a person encounters, the more memory traces are stored, and, therefore, the more emotional knowledge is available during comprehension. Indeed, developmental studies demonstrate that older children are more adept than younger children at assessing the appropriate emotional state of a fictional character (Harris & Gross, 1988). Surely, individuals must differ in their ability to experience and interpret emotional states; most likely they also differ in their tendency to encode and activate emotional knowledge. If so, Kintsch would predict that individuals would differ in their ability to comprehend fictional descriptions of emotional events, because—according to Kintsch and supported by the research presented here—comprehension requires activating previously acquired knowledge.

ACKNOWLEDGMENTS

The experiments reported in this chapter were conducted with support from NIH Research Career Development Award KO4 NS-01376, Air Force Office of Sponsored Research Grants 89-0258 and 89-0305, and NIH Research Grant RO1 NS-00694. These experiments were published with Rachel R. W. Robertson and H. Hill Goldsmith as co-authors.

REFERENCES

Anderson, A., Garrod, S. C., & Sanford, A. J. (1983). The accessibility of pronominal antecedents as a function of episode shifts in narrative text. *Quarterly Journal of Experimental Psychology, 35A*, 427–440.

Balota, D. A., & Chumbley, J. I. (1984). Are lexical decisions a good measure of lexical access? The role of word frequency in the neglected decision stage. *Journal of Experimental Psychology: Human Perception and Performance, 10*, 340–357.

Chumbley, J. I., & Balota, D. A. (1984). A word's meaning affects the decision in lexical decision. *Memory & Cognition, 12*, 590–606.

Fletcher, C. R., & Bloom, C. P. (1988). Causal reasoning in the comprehension of simple narrative texts. *Journal of Memory and Language, 27*, 236–244.

Frijda, N. (1986). *The emotions.* Cambridge, England: Cambridge University Press.

den Heyer, K., Briand, K., & Dannenbring, G. L. (1983). Strategic factors in a lexical-decision task: Evidence for automatic and attention-driven processes. *Memory & Cognition, 11*, 374–381.

Gernsbacher, M. A. (1990). *Language comprehension as structure building.* Hillsdale, NJ: Lawrence Erlbaum Associates.

Gernsbacher, M. A., Goldsmith, H. H., & Robertson, R. R. W. (1992). Do readers mentally represent characters' emotional states? *Cognition and Emotion, 6*, 89–111.

Gernsbacher, M. A., & Robertson, R. R. W. (1992). Knowledge activation versus sentence mapping when representing fictional characters' emotional states. *Language and Cognitive Processes, 7*, 353–371.

Glenberg, A., Meyer, M., & Lindem, K. (1987). Mental models contribute to foregrounding during text comprehension. *Journal of Memory and Language, 26*, 69–83.

Harris, P. L., & Gross, D. (1988). Children's understanding of real and apparent emotion. In J. W. Astingtio, P. L. Harris, & D. R. Olson (Eds.), *Developing theories of mind* (pp. 295–314). Cambridge, England: Cambridge University Press.

Keenan, J. M., Golding, J. M., Potts, G. R., Jennings, T. M., & Aman, C. J. (1990). Methodological issues in evaluating the occurrence of inferences. In A. C. Graesser & G. H. Bower (Eds.), *The psychology of learning and motivation* (pp. 295–312). New York: Academic Press.

Kintsch, W. (1988). The role of knowledge in discourse comprehension: A construction-integration model. *Psychological Review, 95*, 163–182.

Lucas, M. M., Tanenhaus, M. K., & Carlson, G. N. (1990). Levels of representation in the interpretation of anaphoric reference and instrument inference. *Memory & Cognition, 18*, 611–631.

Meyer, D. E., & Schvaneveldt, R. W. (1971). Facilitation in recognizing pairs of words: Evidence of a dependence between retrieval operations. *Journal of Experimental Psychology, 90*, 227–234.

Morrow, D. G., Bower, G. H., & Greenspan, S. L. (1989). Updating situation models during narrative comprehension. *Journal of Memory and Language, 28*, 292–312.

Seidenberg, M. S., Waters, G. S., Sanders, M., & Langer, P. (1984). Pre- and post-lexical loci of contextual effects on word recognition. *Memory & Cognition, 12*, 315–328.

Simpson, G. B., & Burgess, C. (1985). Activation and selection processes in the recognition of ambiguous words. *Journal of Experimental Psychology: Human Perception and Performance, 11*, 28–39.

Tweedy, J. R., Lapinsky, R. H., & Schvaneveldt, R. W. (1977). Semantic-context effects on word recognition: Influence of varying the proposition of items presented in an appropriate context. *Memory & Cognition, 5*, 84–89.

van den Broek, P. W., & Trabasso, T. (1986). Causal networks versus goal hierarchies in summarizing text. *Discourse Processes, 9*, 1–15.

van Dijk, T., & Kintsch, W. (1983). *Strategies of discourse comprehension.* New York: Academic Press.

Chapter 9

Understanding the Special Mnemonic Characteristics of Fairy Tales

Mark A. McDaniel
University of New Mexico

Doreen Blischak
Purdue University

Gilles O. Einstein
Furman University

This chapter focuses on recall of discourse. Our story starts innocuously enough with the broad orientation described by van Dijk and Kintsch (1983):

> The well-structured, multilevel, coherent textbase that is the result of the comprehension process quite naturally functions as an efficient retrieval system so that just reading or listening to a text assures a respectable level of recall. Of course, this does not mean that it would be impossible to achieve even better recall for discourse as a function of special memory encoding procedures. (p. 364)

In the early 1980s, some of the special memory encoding procedures were those that increased the cognitive effort or difficulty required to encode a stimulus (cf. McDaniel, 1981; Tyler, Hertel, McCallum, & Ellis, 1979). Accordingly, we attempted to produce improvements in text recall (relative to a condition in which the subject just read the text) by implementing several encoding conditions designed to increase the difficulty of encoding the text. In one condition letters were removed from each word in the text and replaced with blanks. Subjects were required to fill in the missing letters while reading. In another condition the sentences in the text were presented in random order, and subjects were required to reorder the sentences to construct a coherent text. The intriguing finding from this research was that there was an interaction between the particular encoding difficulty task used and the kind of text to which it was applied (McDaniel, Einstein, Dunay, & Cobb, 1986). Completing words with deleted letters improved recall for fairy tales but not for descriptive passages, whereas the sentence ordering task significantly enhanced recall for the descriptive passages but not for the fairy tales. Einstein, McDaniel, Owen, and Cote (1990, Exp. 1) replicated this interaction and extended it to more ecologically valid encoding tasks. Specifically, embedded questions significantly improved free recall for the fairy tales but not the descriptive texts (relative to a read-only control), and the reverse occurred for subjects who outlined the text.

These results reveal that it is too simplistic to assume that there is a set of mnemonic encoding procedures that will generally improve recall for discourse. On the contrary, it appears that the unique combination of the particular encoding procedure and the kind of discourse to which that encoding procedure is applied is critical for obtaining improvements in recall. In this chapter, we first review a general framework for understanding and predicting these encoding task by discourse type interactions (in terms of affecting free recall) and present some new data in accord with this framework. In the second part of the chapter, we consider the usefulness of various constructs embedded in the van Dijk and Kintsch (1983) theory for providing more precision to our framework. (To fore-shadow, our current research fails to show that these constructs are useful for understanding the observed encoding by text type interactions.) In the final section we present a number of new possibilities for clarifying the mechanisms that give fairy tales their special mnemonic characteristics.

MATERIAL APPROPRIATE PROCESSING (MAP)

The material appropriate processing framework is detailed in McDaniel and Ein-stein (1989), but a précis is needed here to set the stage for what follows. The starting assumption is that for relatively good text recall, two types of conceptual processing are necessary: proposition-specific and relational processing. Propo-sition-specific processing entails a focus on each individual proposition or idea-unit in the text (see Perfetti & Britt, chap. 2 in this vol.). Relational processing organizes, interrelates, and/or binds together the individual propositions (see Ein-stein, McDaniel, Bowers, & Stevens, 1984, or Hunt & McDaniel, 1993, for more extensive discussion of these types of processing and demonstrations of their involvement in discourse recall; also refer to Graesser & Zwaan, chap. 7, and McKoon & Ratcliff, chap. 6 in this vol.). We further assume that memory en-coding procedures can induce predominantly one kind of processing on the text. For instance, filling in missing letters would appear to produce a focus on the elements (words) comprising each proposition as well as on the local semantic and syntactic information to help identify the fragmented words, that is, propo-sition-specific processing. By contrast, requiring sentence reordering would ap-pear to focus processing on the interrelations among the sentences of the text. These premises are supported by the finding that cued-recall probes designed to assess memory for relational and proposition-specific information are responded to differentially as a function of these encoding conditions. Filling in missing letters produces superior performance on the probes about details contained in individual propositions (relative to a read-only control and the sentence reordering condition), whereas reordering sentences produces the best performance on the relational probes, probes requiring integration of a number of propositions (McDaniel, Hines, Waddill, & Einstein, 1994, Exp. 1).

The next critical assumption is that particular types of text themselves afford different degrees of proposition-specific and relational processing. With this assumption in place, the key aspect of our framework can be stated: Special memory encoding procedures will significantly enhance recall only to the extent that the type of processing encouraged by these encoding procedures does not overlap with the type of processing afforded by the text itself.

The results described at the outset of the chapter can be thus understood. Because fairy tales seem to afford the extraction of organizational or relational information during casual reading, an encoding task that requires relational processing (like sentence reordering or outlining) will produce minimal improvements in fairy tale recall. In contrast, an encoding task that requires proposition-specific processing (like missing letters or appropriately designed embedded questions) will produce more substantial improvements in fairy tale recall. On the other hand, descriptive passages seem to invite processing at the proposition-specific level (perhaps because they do not readily afford the extraction of relational information; cf. Graf & Levy, 1984), so that relational encoding tasks significantly improve recall of these texts but proposition-specific encoding tasks do not (Einstein et al., 1990).

A central concern of this chapter is to investigate more deeply the component(s) of fairy tales (components that apparently are not captured in non-fairy tales) that produce sufficient relational processing during casual reading such that more extensive, controlled relational processing (encouraged by particular encoding procedures) has little or no benefit for free recall. We first, however, illustrate the fruitfulness of the MAP framework by applying it to an analysis of imagery encoding on text recall (see Weaver & Bryant, in press, and Weaver, Bryant, & Burns, chap. 10 in this vol., for an application of MAP to metamemory for text).

Imagery and Text Recall

Van Dijk and Kintsch (1983) further amplified their statement on the mnemonic value of special text encoding procedures (presented at the outset) by continuing, "for instance, it appears plausible that the use of imagery would greatly improve discourse memory" (p. 364). Contrary to this expectation, however, the majority of studies have shown no significant improvements in free recall due to imagery processing (relative to more neutral processing instructions; see Perrig, 1986). Similarly, concrete texts (those assumed to promote imagery) typically are not recalled better than more abstract texts (e.g., Marschark, 1985; Marschark, Warner, Thompson, & Huffman, 1991). A common account of these failures of imagery to improve free recall of discourse is that imagery does produce better encoding of microelements or individual propositions (especially the concrete ones), but free recall is more dependent on thematic encoding or extraction of a coherent macrostructure (cf. Marschark, 1985). On this view, then, imagery should not enhance free recall of discourse.

The MAP framework offers a different analysis. Embracing the point that imagery encoding increases proposition-specific processing, imagery would produce processing that overlaps or is redundant with text that also invites proposition-specific processing. In our work, these texts have been non-fairy tales, so that one would expect to find little or no benefit of imagery encoding for non-fairy tales. Consistent with this expectation, the research on imagery and text recall has used non-fairy tales (passages are typically constructed by the experimenter so that concreteness can be controlled, etc.). The novel prediction of MAP, however, is that imagery will significantly improve free recall for fairy tales. This is because the proposition-specific elaboration produced by imagery will be complementary to the relational processing presumably afforded by fairy tales. Following, we report the first experiment of which we are aware to test this prediction (conducted by Walter Perrig and M. M.).

Perrig and McDaniel Experiment. A relatively obscure German fairy tale (*Sticke aus Sand*, or "Ropes Made Out of Sand") was selected that was similar in length to the non–fairy tale texts used in the Perrig (1986) study (29 sentences long and 134 propositions). Subjects were 22 German-speaking students from the University of Basel, randomly assigned to two encoding groups (11 subjects per group). The instructions for the imagery and understanding encoding groups were those used in Perrig. The tale was presented to subjects in a booklet, with one sentence per page, and the imagery group was instructed that "your task is to read the sentences carefully and to form a visual image of the content of each sentence in your mind. Your task will then be to judge how difficult it was for you to form an image of the sentence content." The understanding group was instructed in similar fashion, except instead of "form a visual image" they were told to "understand." Subjects recorded their judgments on a 1 ("very easy") to 5 ("very difficult") scale. The judgment scale was presented below the sentence on each page. Subjects processed and rated the sentences at their own pace. After processing the tale, the subjects were given a perceptual identification task with some of the stimuli having been embedded in the tale (this was part of another experiment). This task took subjects from 7 to 10 min, after which an unexpected free recall test of the passage was given.

The predicted advantage in free recall for the imagery encoding group was obtained. The imagery group recalled 61 propositions on average and the understanding group recalled 49 propositions, a statistically significant difference [F $(1, 20) = 5.24$]. This is an important finding, because the prevailing research has suggested that imagery encoding (or concreteness) does not improve text recall (e.g., Marschark, 1985; Marschark et al., 1991; except under within-subject manipulations, Ransdell & Fischler, 1989). The present data demonstrate significant imagery effects for a certain type of text, a text type anticipated by MAP to yield imagery effects. Clearly, these results bear replication with other tales and other subject populations. Nevertheless, they reinforce the theme that the mnemonic effects of particular text encoding procedures will depend critically on the type of text to which they are applied.

WHAT MAKES FAIRY TALES IMMUNE
TO MNEMONIC BENEFITS
OF RELATIONAL PROCESSING TASKS

An interesting and central challenge raised by the MAP framework is that of specifying the aspect(s) of certain text types that invite a tendency toward relational or proposition-specific processing. We focus here on fairy tales, and attempt to identify what properties of fairy tales might function to provide sufficient relational processing such that extensive and controlled relational processing (such as that induced by sentence unscrambling or outlining) has little benefit on free recall relative to a brief reading (from 1 to 2 min. for our 14- to 20-sentence tales). This seems an especially salient finding given that one principle confidently embraced by most memory researchers is that relational (i.e., organizational) processing improves free recall. Moreover, the failure to obtain significant improvements in free recall for short fairy tales after a relational processing task (e.g., Einstein et al., 1984, 1990; McDaniel et al., 1986) is not due to the fact that better recall cannot be achieved for these tales. Better free recall for these tales is produced by other kinds of encoding tasks (e.g., those encouraging proposition-specific processing).

There are a number of constructs, all of which are incorporated within the van Dijk and Kintsch (1983) theory, that presumably enable and encourage a well-organized representation for narratives like fairy tales. Indeed one of the major contributions of the van Dijk and Kintsch theory was the specification of the many processes and levels at which text representations are organized. In the last several years, our research has tried to pinpoint which of these organizational processes, if any, may play a role in providing sufficient relational encoding for fairy tales such that they negate the influence of otherwise potent relational processing tasks. We examine in turn the possible role of general knowledge, more specific schemata or scripts, causal structures, and text superstructures.

General Knowledge and Scripts

The role of prior knowledge in the comprehension and memory for text has been well documented in the last two decades. One effect of general or prior knowledge in language appears to be a better organized representation of the text, as well as better organized production of discourse. This influence is revealed in experiments in which the subjects' familiarity of the topic is manipulated. Recall of texts by subjects familiar with the topic appears to be better organized than that of subjects not as familiar with the topic (e.g., Spilich, Vesonder, Chiesi, & Voss, 1979). And, similarly, production of ideas about familiar topics is more organized and better structured than production about unfamiliar topics (Caccamise, 1981).

Perhaps it is the case that fairy tales do not significantly benefit from relational encoding tasks because general knowledge can be used extensively in the comprehension process, thereby conferring sufficient organization. That is, the kinds of actor interactions, motivations, and so forth described in fairy tales are familiar to readers through many encounters with such topics as well as through personal experiences, and, consequently, this information is easily interrelated and organized. In contrast, descriptive passages about avalanches in the Himalayas or icebergs in Antarctica (used in Einstein et al., 1990; McDaniel et al., 1986), for example, are on topics that presumably do not allow instantiation of rich background knowledge, and accordingly benefit from special memory encoding procedures that encourage organizational or relational processing.

McDaniel et al. (1994) attempted to test the aforementioned hypothesis. They reasoned that if the availability of background knowledge plays a key role in whether or not a particular text profits from relational encoding tasks (in terms of increasing recall), then manipulating readers' prior knowledge should influence the degree to which a relational encoding task enhances recall. Following Spilich et al. (1979), McDaniel et al. selected subjects high and low in knowledge about baseball, but matched on general reading ability. Three different texts were constructed (each used in a separate experiment) describing some aspect of a baseball game (a half inning of play, or a scripted narrative of a couple attending a game). For present purposes, consider the two encoding conditions to which the high- and low-knowledge subjects were each assigned: a read-only control and a sentence unscrambling condition. After processing the text, subjects were required to perform free recall.

If extensive background knowledge instantiated in the service of understanding a text precludes the need for additional relational processing, then the sentence unscrambling condition should significantly enhance recall only for the low-knowledge subjects. Contrary to this prediction, in three experiments McDaniel et al. (1994) found consistent and significant improvements in free recall (relative to the control) due to sentence unscrambling for both high- and low-knowledge readers. The standard recall advantage for high- relative to low-knowledge readers was also found in every experiment, so that it is not that the knowledge manipulation was not potent. Thus, availability of general background knowledge to guide the organization and retrieval of a text's content did not eliminate the benefit to free recall of unscrambling randomly ordered sentences. Relatively good recall (as high as 51% for high-knowledge readers) was improved even more when additional relational processing was required by the encoding task.

The implication, then, is that the absence of such effects in fairy tales is not due to whatever background knowledge readers may bring to these tales.

Note that some kinds of background knowledge may be more structured and unified than others. These knowledge packets may take the form of scripts, viewed as unitized, ordered sets of actions that serve as guides during comprehension and as cognitive cueing structures during retrieval of script-based texts (cf. van Dijk & Kintsch, 1983, pp. 307–311). One might argue that the knowledge instantiated by readers when they encounter fairy tales is highly scripted. Perhaps then activation of scripted knowledge serves to sufficiently organize the text representation so that additional relational processing is superfluous. If this is so, then relational encoding tasks should produce minimal mnemonic benefits for scripted passages. This hypothesis does not appear to fare any better than the more general hypothesis regarding the role of general knowledge. In Experiment 3, McDaniel et al. (1994) used a highly scripted passage that contained many events associated with attending a baseball game. Moreover, these events usually occur in a fixed order (e.g., entering the ball park, standing for the National Anthem, and stretching during the seventh inning). For those readers knowledgeable about baseball, presumably a highly structured memory representation of the text would be formed, and a well-articulated retrieval scheme would be available to guide access of the representation. Yet, for high-knowledge subjects, reordering a scrambled version of this passage produced substantial increases in free recall. Having found no evidence that general knowledge, even more particularized scripted knowledge, may be the critical factor in preempting the mnemonic value of relational encoding tasks (at least the sentence unscrambling task), we turn to another candidate.

Causal Structure

One of the primary features of narrative that readers appear to exploit in their comprehension and representation of such texts is the causal relations that connect the actions and events embedded in narratives (perhaps especially folk tales). Such causal relations can include motivation, psychological causation, and physical causation (cf. Trabasso & van den Broek, 1985). On this view, when comprehending a narrative such as a folk tale, readers attempt to extract a sequence of causal links (relations) that connect a text's opening to its outcome. Extraction of a coherent sequence of links allows a causal structure of the text to be formed (cf. Fletcher, Arthur, & Skeate, chap. 11 in this vol.; Fletcher & Bloom, 1988; Fletcher, Hummel, & Marsolek, 1990). Arguably, a representation rich in causal structure (like that presumably extracted for a fairy tale) might obviate the need for additional relational processing encouraged by selected encoding tasks (e.g., sentence unscrambling).

To test the possible role of causal structure in modulating the benefits of relational encoding tasks, McDaniel et al. (1994, Exp. 2) modified their original baseball text into a narrative for which a chain of causally linked idea units connected the opening of the text to its end. The causal relations were designed to reflect general knowledge about the physical and social interpersonal world (rather than baseball per se). For instance, one portion of the text mentioned that it was raining, which caused the bat to become slippery. Consequently, the batter lost his grip on the bat as he swung at the baseball. The bat hit the umpire, causing the umpire to become angry, and so on.

Some subjects read an intact version of the passage, and others were given a randomly ordered version to unscramble. For a causally structured narrative, recall was significantly improved by requiring readers to perform sentence unscrambling. To ascertain whether subjects were in fact perceiving and extracting the causal structure, following Fletcher and Bloom (1988), idea units were classified as part of the causal chain or outside of the causal chain. Paralleling Fletcher and Bloom's findings, in-chain idea units were recalled significantly better than out-of-chain idea units. This pattern was obtained for both encoding conditions, so it appears that subjects in general were sensitive to the causal structure of the passage.

As mentioned previously, McDaniel et al. (1994) also found significant enhancement for free recall due to sentence unscrambling in a script-based passage. Given that scripts typically involve causal sequences, this finding represents another case in which causal structure is not sufficient to eliminate the sentence unscrambling effect. It is also worth noting that for both of these passages, the prior knowledge of the subjects was manipulated (high vs. low baseball knowledge), and the sentence unscrambling benefit did not interact with prior knowledge. Thus, the combination of these several factors (prior knowledge, causal structure, and scripted events) also does not appear to converge on the apparently special feature of fairy tales that precludes the necessity for additional relational processing (as encouraged by sentence unscrambling or outlining). It is interesting to note that Foss and Bower (1986) reported that the representation of a real-world narrative (tale) was less causally structured (in terms of goal hierarchies) than a laboratory narrative. There appears to be something more to the representation of a fairy tale.

Superstructures

Readers are assumed to have knowledge about conventional organizational patterns of particular types of discourse (we label these patterns *superstructures* in keeping with van Dijk & Kintsch, 1983). In the van Dijk and Kintsch model, superstructures (that is, readers' knowledge of conventional text grammars) are assumed to provide additional organization to a text. Narrative superstructures are thought to be well specified (e.g., Stein & Policastro, 1984) and are the most familiar and most easily handled by readers (van Dijk & Kintsch, p. 252). These considerations would suggest that instantiation of a narrative superstructure in the processing of fairy tales may provide so much organizational structure that additional organizational processing is not needed.

Testing the previous hypothesis poses a worthy challenge. Work to date that has tried to illuminate the role of superstructures in story comprehension and memory suffers from unavoidable confounding. Typically, differences in comprehension and memory are examined between stories for which a familiar Western European narrative superstructure applies and stories for which that superstructure does not apply (e.g., Kintsch & Greene, 1978). Better performance is found for the former, but the interpretation is clouded because the stories inevitably differ in other characteristics as well (e.g., temporal coherence and/or causal structure).

McDaniel et al. (1994) tried to circumvent the problems inherent in the standard approach to experimentally investigating the role of superstructures in story memory by adopting the following strategy. They presented exactly the same fairy tale across subjects, but varied the contexts in which the tale was embedded so as to encourage the instantiation of different superstructures. This tale (entitled "The Old Man and His Grandson") was about an old grandfather who was mistreated by his children. The children eventually realized the cruelty of their ways when their own child started imitating the things they had done to the grandfather. In one condition, subjects were simply presented with the tale (in some experiments the subjects were also explicitly told that the passage was a fairy tale). In this condition, presumably the subjects would activate their familiar narrative superstructure in reading the tale. In the other condition, the tale was embedded in an actual newspaper article about elderly abuse, which involved discussion of how the abuse was perpetuated by the older adult's children. The tale was physically inserted in the newspaper article, and this stimulus was in turn embedded in the actual pages of a particular issue of a university paper. In other words, from the subjects' perspective, they were reading an article that appeared in a newspaper. The assumption was that in this context, subjects would be processing the contents of the tale within a newspaper article superstructure (van Dijk, 1980, has identified and described such a superstructure distinctly from that of a story superstructure). For both of these processing contexts, subjects either read the tale intact or had to reorder a scrambled presentation (for the newspaper context, just the fairy tale part of the article was scrambled).

If fairy tales are unaffected by relational encoding tasks because a narrative superstructure (instantiated by readers to assist comprehension) provides a very powerful organizational structure, then a relational task should produce significant improvements in free recall (relative to the read-only control) when the tale is presented in a newspaper context. In this context, a newspaper article superstructure would presumably be instantiated (van Dijk, 1980), a superstructure that is considered to be less well structured than a narrative structure and for which the contents of the tale would perhaps function as Detail (one of the presumed components of the news superstructure). Accordingly, the elements of the tale within a news superstructure should not receive the same degree of structured, relational processing as when those same elements are processed within a narrative superstructure.

In opposition to the just-mentioned prediction, in three experiments McDaniel et al. (1994) found no significant improvement in free recall due to sentence unscrambling for the tale, regardless of whether or not it was presented in the newspaper context. This failure to obtain an effect was probably not a power problem because no effect emerged, even when all three experiments were collapsed into one analysis (with at least 72 subjects per cell). Nor was it the case that the context manipulation was ineffective. Ratings regarding how well the target materials exemplified either a newspaper article or a folk tale were collected from an independent set of 16 subjects. Subjects read and rated six texts from the two genres (three narratives and three newspaper articles) before reading and rating either the target tale (the "Old Man" tale) or the newspaper article with the tale embedded in it. All subjects receiving the target news article rated it as a news article (75% rated it as "very much like a news article," and 25% rated it as "somewhat like a news article"), and all subjects receiving the tale rated it as a tale (25% rated it as "very much like a tale," and 75% as "somewhat like a tale"). Thus, both targets were perceived as intended, and most importantly, the target news article was not thought to be somehow odd. This pattern suggests that the absence of significant improvement in free recall due to a relational processing task (like sentence unscrambling) does not hinge on possible organizational benefits of a story superstructure. Such a conclusion must be cautiously advanced, however. The experiments were able to blend only one particular fairy tale into a newspaper article, so that replicating with other stimulus samples is desirable.

In addition, one could argue that a story superstructure was instantiated during comprehension of the tale, despite the newspaper article context (cf. van Dijk & Kintsch, 1983, p. 252). Though empirically difficult to evaluate, the sentence unscrambling processing data (time and accuracy in unscrambling the passage) provide initial leverage in evaluating this alternative interpretation. Kintsch and his colleagues (Kintsch, Mandel, & Kozminsky, 1977; van Dijk & Kintsch, 1983) suggested that one powerful effect of story superstructures can be observed when subjects are required to process scrambled stories (in their work the stories were scrambled at the paragraph level). The scrambled stories were summarized as well as normal stories, implying that the story superstructure provides an organizational frame that overrides and makes more coherent the actual scrambled text sequence. Extending this finding to the McDaniel et al. (1994) work, one would expect that superstructures would be exploited in reordering the scrambled tale. In the folktale context, because subjects were told that the contents were a folk tale, the familiar and appropriate story structure could be immediately instantiated. These subjects should thus be able to use the superstructure straightaway to help reorganize the scrambled elements. By contrast, in the newspaper context it is implausible that upon encountering a portion of scrambled text within an actual newspaper article, subjects would immediately know to activate their familiar and well-structured story superstructure. Admittedly, these subjects might eventually realize that a story superstructure was more appropriate than a news article superstructure. But, even so, it should have taken these subjects longer to unscramble the passage and perhaps with less accuracy (relative to the normal ordering) than the subjects in the folk tale context. Contrary to the expectations just sketched, unscrambling time and accuracy consistently did not significantly differ as a function of the context in which the tale was presented. This result appears to support recent challenges to the psychological reality of superstructures in the comprehension process (e.g., Johnson-Laird, 1983; Weaver & Dickinson, 1982).

To summarize at this point, the available work does not implicate prior general knowledge, more specific script-based knowledge, causal structure, or superstructures (at least as currently operationalized) as being sufficient to account for why some fairy tales are resistant to recall benefits from relational (organizational) encoding tasks. These findings perhaps underscore van Dijk's (1980) statement that "some of the properties of stories can only be understood only if we assume that storytelling has important cognitive and emotional functions" (p. 110) (many others hold a similar view, e.g., Bruner, 1990). In the final part of this chapter, we explore some approaches to this puzzle that are more resonant with possible cognitive and emotional functions of fairy tales.

Affective Comprehension of Literary Narratives

Miall (1989) proposed that comprehension of literary narratives (such as short stories) is controlled by affect, with the emotional reactions of the reader playing a determining role in the cognitive processing (e.g., memory) of the narrative. A key idea is that self-referentially based emotions especially determine cognitive functions (e. g., attention, memory). For example, one such self-referential effect is that the readers identify with or share the concerns of the main character. In addition, the reader's self-concept and current concerns may be activated and projected onto the interpretation of the narrative. This approach is richer than can be conveyed here, but for present purposes the important point is that verbal material judged in relation to the self is typically better recalled than when the material is processed under a semantic encoding task (Rogers, Kuiper, & Kirker, 1977). It may be then that the self-referent encoding activated by affective processes supports special organizational processing of a literary narrative not found in expository prose or in laboratory-constructed narratives (like those used in McDaniel et al., 1994).

Brewer and Lichtenstein's (1982) structural-affect theory of stories similarly suggests that an essential feature of real-world stories is that they produce affective responses in the reader. Burke, Heuer, and Reisberg (1992) further reported that emotionally arousing parts of a story produce better memory for plot-relevant information embedded in those parts of the story (echoing Miall, 1989, their interpretation was that emotional events are thought about in more personal terms). Extending from this theoretical and empirical work, one hypothesis purports that the emotionally arousing material generally assumed to be included (if not a central feature) in fairy tales, produces processing that provides a mnemonic advantage, perhaps obviating the need for additional relational processing.

McDaniel and Blischak Experiment. As an initial attempt to gain some information on the fruitfulness of the previous hypothesis, we explored the possible mnemonic effects (with regard to free recall) of emotional arousal in folk narratives (tales). Our experimental approach was based on Brewer and Lichtenstein's (1982) framework, which has linked emotional arousal to the surprise elicited by a story. Further, in this framework emotional arousal is related to the entertainment value of the text. Because literary text (e.g., folk narratives) is written for entertainment purposes, such texts are assumed to employ surprise as one technique to produce emotional arousal and entertainment (cf. Brewer & Ohtsuka, 1988). Accordingly, we reasoned that folk narratives would produce a reasonable level of surprise (hence emotional arousal), and we selected three tales ("Caps for Sale," "The Old Man and his Grandson," and "The Wolf and the Seven Kids") of approximately the same length (49–51 propositions). We changed each tale's ending to make them more mundane and/or more expected (less surprising). In changing the endings, care was taken not to alter the length and not to reduce the degree of causal structure. That is, the surprise manipulation involved modification of real-world folk narratives to diminish their surprise value while trying to maintain their structural, causal, and thematic coherence.

If surprise and the emotional reaction presumed to accompany surprise do produce mnemonic benefits to relatively short literary texts like folk narratives, then the original narratives should be better recalled than the altered narratives. Of course, this finding is predicated on successfully manipulating surprise. As a manipulation check, subjects were required to rate the extent to which they found the events surprising in each of four segments of each text. The ratings task and the memory data were collected concurrently in the following design (due to practical difficulties with combining both objectives surprise ratings for the "Old Man" tale were not obtained).

Fifty-two subjects were instructed that they would be reading and providing ratings for several short passages. The target passage was presented first (the one for which recall would be required, though subjects were not informed of this). This passage was either the original or modified version of "Caps for Sale," "The Wolf and Seven Kids," or "The Old Man and his Grandson" (16 subjects were randomly assigned "Caps for Sale," 24 were assigned "The Wolf and Seven Kids," and 12 were assigned "The Old Man and his Grandson," with half of each given the original and half given the modified version). Subjects read the passage at their own pace. Upon completing the passage, subjects answered two questions (one question asked if subjects had ever read the story before and the second asked how good an example of a story was the passage). Then subjects were presented with either the original or modified version of the second narrative (i.e., if "Caps for Sale" was presented first, then "The Wolf and Seven Kids" was presented second, and vice versa; when "Old Man" was the first passage, for reasons unimportant here, "Caps" always followed). This second narrative provided the data for the manipulation check. For this second narrative, subjects were told they would be providing ratings after every few sentences of the passage.

For present purposes, the rating of primary importance was subjects' responses to the question: "In the portion just read, to what extent did you feel surprised by any information or events in the passage?" Subjects responded on a 7-point Likert-type scale with anchor points "1—not surprised," "4—somewhat surprised," and "7—very surprised." This rating question was presented after approximately each quarter of the passage, with the first three presentations of the question occurring for contents that were unchanged across versions (the sentences were exactly the same in the original and modified versions). The last presentation of the question occurred after the entire passage was read and was directed at the passage in general. After completing the ratings on the second passage, all subjects were required to recall the first passage as completely as they could.

First, the surprise ratings collected from the second narrative were analyzed (the ratings taken after the "Old Man" narrative were excluded because otherwise too much weight is given to "Caps"). This analysis showed that for the surprise question directed at the entire narrative, the original narratives were rated as significantly more surprising ($M = 4.7$) than the altered narratives ($M = 2.8$). As would be expected, for the first three surprise ratings (for which the original and altered narratives were identical), there were no significant differences between the original and altered versions. The surprise ratings, then, indicated that the modified versions of the original narratives had the intended effect of reducing the surprise value of the passage (at least for "Caps" and "Wolf").

The recall protocols were scored in terms of proportion of propositions recalled (there were between 49 and 51 propositions for all passages). Despite a nominal difference in recall across the two versions of the narratives (.57 for the original and .53 for the modified), there was no statistical difference in recall for the two versions. We further analyzed recall in terms of propositions that were common to both versions (primarily the first three-quarters of the passage), and propositions that differed across versions (the proportion of propositions that were common across versions ranged from .74 to .88; thus proportion of different propositions ranged from .26 to .12). This analysis revealed a significant interaction such that recall of the original version was approximately equivalent to that of the modified version only for the propositions common to both versions (.54 and .52, respectively). For the propositions that had been altered to influence surprise, there were significantly more recalled from the original than from the modified versions (.70 and .55, respectively). Thus, for these short narratives it appears that the degree of surprise, and by extension emotional arousal, could have affected the level of recall, albeit in a limited fashion. Of course, most of the content of the modified version was still a naturalistic literary text, and accordingly would have elements to trigger emotional reactions, interest, and so forth (cf. Graesser & Kreuz, 1993). Thus, it is possible that memory effects due to affective components would have been more encompassing if modifications to the tale had not been so limited.

More extensive changes pose potentially serious methodological problems, however. The tales were modified as little as possible because the more extensive the changes, the more likely that other dimensions on which the changed material differs might also mediate any recall differences. Unfortunately, even interpretation of the present pattern of results is clouded because of possible confounds due to item selection effects as just mentioned. Also, it may be that the mnemonic effects of the surprise manipulation were as much due to the text's predictability per se as to any affective reaction. O'Brien and Myers (1985) showed that an unpredictable target word leads to better recall of information preceding that target than does a predictable target word. Their interpretation of this finding was that unpredictable concepts produce more reprocessing or elaboration of the passage in order to integrate those concepts. Evaluation of these possibilities awaits further work, work in which affective responses are more directly ascertained. But to the extent that affective responses were responsible for the present recall patterns, this study offers preliminary encouragement to the idea that affective components of literary text like folk tales may somehow contribute to the kinds of recall patterns that have been the focus of this chapter.

Reconstructive Retrieval from a Core

McDaniel and Blischak's findings suggest an alternative approach (or at least a complementary approach) to explaining the absence of effects of relational processing tasks on fairy tales. Another way to view their obtained interaction is that for the modified passages the resolution of the tales (the last part of the tale) was not recalled significantly better than the initial parts of the tale (.55 vs. .52, respectively). In contrast, for the original tales, the resolution was recalled extremely well (.70 of the time) and better than the other parts of the narrative (.54). It seems that folk tales could have a highly memorable core, and perhaps this memorable core serves as the foundation for reconstructing or retrieving the remainder of the story. The idea here is that there is a core around which the events of the tale cohere, the core being the marker for why the tale is entertaining, interesting, or worth retelling. For example, in "Caps for Sale" the part about the man throwing his hat on the ground (the part changed to produce the modified version) was remembered by every subject. In the "Old Man" tale, the most well recalled segment is about a young boy pretending to make a trough for his mom and dad to eat out of when they become old (like the grandfather). These parts of the stories are the resolution or solution to the challenge facing the protagonist, and standard story grammars would expect them to be well recalled.

But we are proposing more than this. We maintain that folk tales are worth retelling because they are entertaining (in accord with Brewer & Lichtenstein, 1982), not just because they offer solution(s) to the problems arising in our sociocultural context (cf. Bruner, 1990). Perhaps part of the entertainment value has to do with the clever, ironic, and/or interesting way in which the solution is reached (as opposed to laboratory narratives, e.g., see Trabasso & Suh, 1993, which conform to formal analyses of narrative in terms of containing goals and causal links related in a hierarchical superstructure but are not especially entertaining in our opinion; see Waddill, 1992, for data suggesting different representational properties of real-world vs. laboratory tales). Stories that have endured (like "The Old Man and His Grandson," "The Wolf and the Seven Kids," and "Caps for Sale") most likely are those that are also entertaining. Comprehension of these tales, then, is probably more than just building a textbase and a situation model; comprehension probably also entails appreciation of the components (irony, cleverness, and so on) that make the tale entertaining.

The central point is that in retelling (i.e., recalling) the tale, capturing the irony, cleverness, or whatever makes it interesting places constraints on the sequence and contents. Not just any sequence of events will do: The sequence has to be such that the solution is somehow special for that chain of events. If the recaller does not rebuild the event chain appropriately, then the characteristic of the tale that makes it worth retelling (the irony, cleverness, humor, or the "impossible logic" as Bruner, 1990, termed it) is not captured. It is perhaps these constraints that provide sufficient relational information that recall after a casual reading is as good as recall after substantial relational processing induced by extra encoding tasks.

Inferencing Difficulty

Paula Waddill (personal communication, May 1993) has suggested that at least certain fairy tales do not profit from additional relational encoding because a moderate amount of inferencing and elaboration is required to complete comprehension (Waddill extended McDaniel et al.'s, 1986, finding of no recall effects of relational processing tasks to another tale, "The Ant and the Snake.") For example, in the "Old Man and Grandson" tale, after the young boy makes a trough for his parents to eat out of when they become old, tears come to the parents eyes and they end the grandfather's banishment to the corner, where he has been eating out of a wooden bowl. In order to establish relational (in this case causal) links between these events, the reader must infer that the boy's actions made his parents realize the cruelty of their behavior toward the grandfather. The reader must further infer that the realization caused the parents to feel sorrow, which in turn motivated the events explicitly described in the text (tears and allowing the grandfather at the table for meals). Additional elaborations might occur as well concerning the possible insightfulness/intuitiveness of the boy relative to his parents.

Such inferencing and elaboration may create better-remembered linkages than if this information were explicitly stated. This conjecture is in line with research on causal inferencing. Such inferencing involving explanatory processes—for example, retrieval of prior text—or activation of other knowledge in long-term memory to provide reasons for the information encountered, has been found to account for a significant portion of variance in long-term recall of narratives (Trabasso & Suh, 1993). Further, and perhaps more related to present concerns, Keenan, Baillet, and Brown (1984; see also Myers, Shinjo, & Duffy, 1987) reported an inverted U-shaped relation between the difficulty of establishing causal reference and memory for that part of the text (which is also, perhaps not co-incidentally, the relationship Weaver & Bryant, in press, report between difficulty and metamemory for text). Causal relations that are easily or directly established are not recalled as well as causal links that are moderately related or difficult to form. But as the difficulty of forming the causal link increases, then memory for that information again declines relative to the moderate difficulty level.

The Keenan et al. (1984) study was conducted with two sentence passages. Perhaps a similar functional association between the difficulty of establishing causal relatedness and memory extends to more complex discourse. If so, then this suggests a possible account of the mnemonic effects of relational processing tasks on different text types. For texts in which the action/event relations are explicit (like the texts constructed in McDaniel et al., 1994, that had a clearly explicated causal and/or script-based sequence) and for texts in which the information is difficult to relate together and required inferences may not even be drawn due to an absence of background knowledge (like the descriptive texts in Einstein et al., 1990, about avalanches in the Himalayas or ice flows in the Arctic), memory for relational information (information that links the elements or propositions of the text together) is not as good as it potentially could be. Accordingly, encoding tasks that require relational processing serve to boost memory of relational information, and as a result increase free recall for the text. On the other hand, texts in which the relational links are moderately difficult to form—perhaps just enough to make one stop and think (like the tales used in Einstein et al.)—result in good memory for these relational links. (Parenthetically, it is interesting that jokes that are most successful [i.e., elicit humor] may be those that require an intermediate amount of comprehension time. Those that are quickly understood or those that require some time for comprehension are viewed as less funny [Wyer & Collins, 1992].) Thus, encoding tasks that require relational processing are unnecessary.

Note that this account is not incompatible with the "reconstruction from a core" notion outlined earlier. It may be that the core enables reconstruction of the other events in the text because a moderate amount of inferencing/elaboration was required to relate it to those other events. Recent evidence suggests another possible link; even easy to moderately challenging inferences that are needed to establish causal coherence may not be drawn for descriptive/technical text (Noordman, Vonk, & Kempff, 1992). It may be that the entertainment aspect of tales (irony, cleverness, etc.) in part encourages readers to engage in the effort to draw inferences and generate elaborations.

The ideas presented in this last section go well beyond the available data. We intend them as speculative, and as guidance for further inquiry. Our hope is that this chapter provides a first step toward illuminating important characteristics of narrative tales that appear not to be captured by existing constructs of narrative comprehension and that obviate the need for additional relational processing. Whatever these special characteristics are (affective processes, an especially salient core or punch line, appropriate levels of inferencing difficulty), they need not be restricted to folk tales. The idea is that expository text may be rewritten so as to capture the mnemonic characteristics of narratives. In as much as students are notoriously poor at using effective mnemonic strategies (Stein, Bransford, Franks, Owings, Vye, & McGraw, 1982), then creating texts that invite relational processing has exciting and important educational implications.

ACKNOWLEDGMENTS

Preparation of this chapter was supported in part by NIA Grant AG05627 to Mark McDaniel.

REFERENCES

Brewer, W. F., & Lichenstein, E. H. (1982). Stories are to entertain: A structural-affect theory of stories. *Journal of Pragmatics, 6*, 475–486.

Brewer, W. F., & Ohtsuka, K. (1988). Story structure, characterization, just world organization, and reader affect in American and Hungarian short stories. *Poetics, 17*, 395–415.

Bruner, J. (1980). *Acts of meaning*. Cambridge, MA: Harvard University Press.

Burke, A., Heuer, F., & Reisberg, D. (1992). Remembering emotional events. *Memory and Cognition, 20*, 277–290.

Caccamise, D. J. (1981). *Cognitive processes in writing*. Unpublished doctoral dissertation, University of Colorado.

Einstein, G. O., McDaniel, M. A., Bowers, C. A., & Stevens, D. T. (1984). Memory for prose: The influence of relational and proposition-specific processing. *Journal of Experimental Psychology: Learning, Memory, and Cognition, 10*, 133–143.

Einstein, G. O., McDaniel, M. A., Owen, P. D., & Cote, N. C. (1990). Encoding and recall of texts: The importance of material appropriate processing. *Journal of Memory and Language, 29*, 566–581.

Fletcher, C. R., & Bloom, C. P. (1988). Causal reasoning in the comprehension of simple narrative texts. *Journal of Memory and Language, 27*, 235–244.

Fletcher, C. R., Hummel, J. E., & Marsolek, C. J. (1990). Causality and the allocation of attention during comprehension. *Journal of Experimental Psychology: Learning, Memory, and Cognition, 16*, 233–240.

Foss, C. C., & Bower, G. H. (1986). Understanding actions in relation to goals. In N. E. Sharkey (Ed.), *Advances in cognitive science* (Vol. 1, pp. 94–124). New York: Wiley.

Graesser, A. C., & Kreuz, R. J. (1993). A theory of inference generation during text comprehension. *Discourse Processes, 16*, 145–160.

Graf, P., & Levy, B. A. (1984). Reading and remembering: Conceptual and perceptual processing involved in reading related passages. *Journal of Verbal Learning and Verbal Behavior, 23*, 405–424.

Hunt, R. R., & McDaniel, M. A. (1993). The enigma of organization and distinctiveness. *Journal of Memory and Language, 32*, 421–445.

Johnson-Laird, P. N. (1983) *Mental models: Toward a cognitive science of language, inferences, and consciousness.* Cambridge, MA: Harvard University Press.

Keenan, J. M., Baillet, S. D., & Brown, P. (1984). The effects of causal cohesion on comprehension and memory. *Journal of Verbal Learning and Verbal Behavior, 23*, 115–126.

Kintsch, W., & Greene, E. (1978). The role of culture-specific schemata in the comprehension and recall of stories. *Discourse Processes, 1*, 1–13.

Kintsch, W., Mandel, T. S., & Kozminsky, E. (1977). Summarizing scrambled stories. *Memory and Cognition, 5*, 547–552.

Marschark, M. (1985). Imagery and organization in the recall of prose. *Journal of Memory and Language, 24*, 734–745.

Marschark, M., Warner, H., Thompson, R., & Huffman, C. (1991). Concreteness, imagery and memory for prose. In R. H. Logie & M. Denis (Eds.), *Mental images in human cognition* (pp. 193–207). Amsterdam: North-Holland.

McDaniel, M. A. (1981). Syntactic complexity and elaborative processing. *Memory and Cognition, 9*, 487–495.

McDaniel, M. A., & Einstein, G. O. (1989). Material appropriate processing: A contextualistic approach to reading and studying strategies. *Educational Psychology Review, 1*, 113–145.

McDaniel, M. A., Einstein, G. O., Dunay, P. K., & Cobb, R. E. (1986). Encoding difficulty and memory: Toward a unifying theory. *Journal of Memory and Language, 25*, 645–656.

McDaniel, M. A., Hines, R. J., Waddill, P. J., & Einstein, G. O. (1994). What makes folk tales unique: Content familiarity, causal structure, scripts, or superstructures? *Journal of Experimental Psychology: Learning, Memory, and Cognition, 20*, 169–184.

Miall, D. S. (1989). Beyond the schema given: Affective comprehension of literary narratives. *Cognition and Emotion, 3*, 55–78.

Myers, J. L., Shinjo, M., & Duffy S. A. (1987). Degree of causal relatedness and memory. *Journal of Memory and Language, 26*, 453–465.

Noordman, L. G. N., Vonk, W., & Kempff, H. J. (1992). Causal inferences during the reading of expository text. *Journal of Memory and Language, 31*, 573–590.

O'Brien, E. J., & Myers, J. L. (1985). When comprehension difficulty improves memory for text. *Journal of Experimental Psychology: Learning, Memory, and Cognition, 11*, 12–21.

Perrig, W. J. (1986). Imagery and the thematic storage of prose. In D. G. Russell, D. F. Marks, & J. T. E. Richardson (Eds.), *Imagery Two* (pp. 77–82). Dunedin, New Zealand: Human Performance Associates.

Ransdell, S. E., & Fischler, I. (1989). Effects of concreteness and task context on recall of prose among bilingual and monolingual speakers. *Journal of Memory and Language, 28*, 278–291.

Rogers, T. B., Kuiper, N. A., & Kirker, W. S. (1977). Self-reference and the encoding of personal information. *Journal of Personality and Social Psychology, 35*, 677–688.

Spilich, G. J., Vesonder, G. T., Chiesi, H. L., & Voss, J. F. (1979). Text processing of domain-related information for individuals with high and low domain knowledge. *Journal of Verbal Learning and Verbal Behavior, 28*, 275–290.

Stein, B. S., Bransford, J. D., Franks, J. J., Owings, R.A., Vye, N. J., & McGraw, W. (1982). Differences in the precision of self-generated elaborations. *Journal of Experimental Psychology: General, 3*, 399–405.

Stein, N. L., & Policastro, M. (1984). The concept of a story: A comparison between childrens' and teacher's viewpoints. In H. Mandl, N. L. Stein, & T. Trabasso (Eds.), *Learning and comprehension of text* (pp. 113–155). Hillsdale, NJ: Lawrence Erlbaum Associates.

Trabasso, T., & van den Broek, P. (1985). Causal thinking and the representation of narrative events. *Journal of Memory and Language, 24*, 612–630.

Trabasso, T., & Suh, S. (1993). Understanding text: Achieving explanatory coherence through on-line inferences and mental operations in working memory. *Discourse Processes, 16*, 3–34.

Tyler, S. W., Hertel, P. T., McCallum, M. C., & Ellis, H. C. (1979). Cognitive effort and memory. *Journal of Experimental Psychology: Human Learning and Memory, 5*, 607–617.

van Dijk, T. A. (1980). *Macrostructures: An interdisciplinary study of global structures in discourse, interaction, and cognition.* Hillsdale, NJ: Lawrence Erlbaum Associates.

van Dijk, T. A., & Kintsch, W. (1983). *Strategies of discourse comprehension.* New York: Academic Press.

Waddill, P. J. (1992). *The mental representation of narrative: All stories are not created equal.* Unpublished doctoral dissertation, Purdue University, West Lafayette, IN.

Weaver, C. A., III, & Bryant, D. S. (in press). Metamemory for text: The role of text type and text difficulty. *Memory and Cognition.*

Weaver, P. A., & Dickinson, D. K. (1982). Scratching below the surface structure: Exploring the usefulness of story grammars. *Discourse Processes, 5*, 225–243.

Wyer, R. S., Jr., & Collins, J. E., II (1992). A theory of humor elicitation. *Psychological Review, 99*, 663–688.

Chapter 10

Comprehension Monitoring: Extensions of the Kintsch and van Dijk Model

Charles A. Weaver, III
Deborah S. Bryant
Kevin D. Burns
Baylor University

Because this volume is a tribute to Walter Kintsch, I open this chapter with an anecdote. When I first became interested in the topic of comprehension monitoring, I was a fourth-year graduate student searching for a novel dissertation topic. I had already done some situation model work with mental maps (Weaver & Kintsch, 1987), and some preliminary work with algebra word problems (later published, with a tremendous amount of revision; Weaver & Kintsch, 1992). Neither of these captured my imagination, though. While skimming though journals one day, I happened upon the work of Glenberg and Epstein (1985), and decided that this was a puzzle worth exploring. It seemed to me so intuitively obvious that readers were able to monitor their reading, yet here was abundant evidence suggesting that they could not. I read everything I could on the topic, and finally approached Kintsch about it, as a possible topic: Why can't readers better monitor their reading behavior? Did it have something to do with the level at which they were asking the questions? Could the Kintsch model be applied here?

Walter read my proposal, and sat, silently, for what seemed like 20 min (in reality, it was no more than a few seconds). He nodded, and said, "I suppose *someone* might find this interesting." However, he agreed to let me pursue it (one of Walter's greatest strengths as a mentor is to allow his collaborators and students the freedom to pursue what they deem valuable). The results of this (Weaver, 1990) and other work by Maki (Maki & Berry, 1984; Maki & Swett, 1987) gave the field of comprehension monitoring a second wind, and recent years have showed a renewed interest in the topic (Maki, Foley, Kajer, Thompson & Willert, 1990; Maki & Serra, 1992; Walczyk & Hall, 1989a; Weaver, 1990;

Weaver & Bryant, in press). Even Walter himself now admits to the importance of the topic (I return to that later).

HISTORY OF RESEARCH
IN COMPREHENSION MONITORING

The work in comprehension monitoring (also called "calibration of comprehension" [Glenberg & Epstein, 1985, 1987; Glenberg, Sanocki, Epstein, & Morris, 1987], or "metamemory for text" [Maki & Berry, 1984; Maki & Serra, 1992; Maki & Swett, 1987]) was initiated in the early 1980s. Investigators in the developmental literature proceeded to some degree independently of those with skilled readers (see Baker & Brown, 1984, for a review of the developmental literature. See also Walcyzk & Hall, 1989b, for a recent work). Essentially, in this type of research, we allow subjects to read a passage, and then we ask them to make predictions about their future performance on a comprehension test. By correlating predicted and actual performance, we can determine how well readers are able to monitor their comprehension.

The first phase of research with skilled readers was initiated by Art Glenberg and his colleagues at the University of Wisconsin in the early 1980s (Glenberg & Epstein, 1985, 1987; Glenberg, Wilkinson, & Epstein, 1982). This roughly 5-year research program culminated in what appeared to be the definitive conclusion of Glenberg et al. (1987): Readers were able to monitor their comprehension only under highly constrained circumstances, and even then they were able to do so only marginally (gamma correlations were never higher than .20, for example; readers were above chance with their predictions, but just barely). This characterizes what I consider to be the first phase of research, the "readers cannot monitor their comprehension" stage.

Weaver (1990) suggested that part of the problem may lie in how we ask the readers what they know. Specifically, adding additional items to the comprehension test increased our ability to detect comprehension monitoring. Asking a subject four questions over a passage instead of just one resulted in higher correlations between predicted and actual performance. This makes sense. Comprehension is seldom all or none, so the better we can discriminate the level of comprehension (by asking more questions about the topic), the better we should be able to assess comprehension monitoring.

Ruth Maki and her colleagues (Maki, et al., 1990; Maki & Serra, 1992) independently came to the same conclusion. By manipulating certain critical factors, we were able show modest, but *nonzero*, correlations between predicted and actual performance.

We characterize this as the "readers can calibrate, but not very well" phase. During this second phase, we consistently found effects showing readers could monitor their comprehension, but that they could not do it very well. Such a finding could result from several causes. First, of course, it might simply be that readers cannot monitor as well as intuition suggests. This certainly would not be the first time that intuition was incorrect. Alternatively, it might simply result from us not knowing the appropriate techniques for measuring comprehension monitoring. For example, Maki consistently observed higher correlations when she asked subjects to assess "how poorly" they are going to do on a test, rather than "how well" they expect to do. Still, we thought these small correlations underestimated the true ability of readers to monitor their comprehension.

During the next few years, there were several important influences on our work on comprehension monitoring. First was Britton's work (Britton & Gulgoz, 1991; Gulgoz, 1989) on principled text revision. We took advantage of the work he and his colleagues had performed in revision of texts, and used their materials in many of our studies.

In addition, McDaniel and Einstein (McDaniel, Einstein, Dunay & Cobb, 1986; McDaniel, Einstein, & Lollis, 1988) were working on the puzzling question of why increasing cognitive effort sometimes improved memory for text, but other times it did not (see McDaniel, Blischak, & Einstein, chap. 9 in this vol.). They resolved this by developing their notion of material appropriate processing (MAP). Essentially, the MAP framework says that processing manipulations will enhance memory for text only to the extent that such processing adds to the processing already induced by the text itself. For example, they considered narrative texts to naturally induce relational processing; readers of narration will process the global thematic parts of the text, but will not necessarily attend to the details. Therefore, processing that enhances processing of the thematic information (such as outlining) will have no effect on memory. However, processing that encourages attention to details, such as answering detail-oriented adjunct questions, will add to the memory for the text.

Expository texts, by contrast, induce detail-oriented processing. In order to increase memory for these texts, processing tasks should induce thematic processing. In a series of studies, McDaniel and Einstein (Einstein, McDaniel, Owen, & Coté, 1990) showed this to be the case.

The work described here is a compilation of the theoretical work of Kintsch and van Dijk (Kintsch & van Dijk, 1978; van Dijk & Kintsch, 1983), the research on principled text revision by Britton and colleagues (Britton & Gulgoz, 1991), and the MAP framework of McDaniel and Einstein (Einstein et al., 1990). Hopefully, by the end of the chapter, it will be obvious that we have entered the third phase in the comprehension monitoring literature, that is, the "oh, so those are the important variables!" phase.

FACTORS INFLUENCING COMPREHENSION MONITORING

We view calibration as being dependent on at least three different kinds of variables:

1. *Subject variables*, which examine how the individual characteristics of readers might affect comprehension monitoring in certain ways (such as impulsivity; see Walcyzk & Hall, 1989b);

2. *Processing variables*, which examine calibration across different kinds of comprehension tasks (i. e., recall, recognition, inference performance, and summary ability). These tasks may be induced by the materials themselves (see Einstein et al., 1990; Maki & Serra, 1992; McDaniel et al., 1986), or they may be induced by explicit instructions.

3. *Stimulus variables*, which explore the differences in readers' abilities to monitor different types of texts, such as those that have been improved through readability analyses or revisions. This third group is particularly important, because this is the only set of variables under the direct control of the writer. For example, the writer may not be able to change the characteristics of the readers, but the writer *can* change the nature of the texts.

Throughout the years there has been a considerable amount of research into writing texts to improve their readability, but virtually no one has looked at how text revision can influence readers' metamemory for texts.

BURNS (1993) EXPERIMENT 1

The first set of experiments are based on Burns (1993). He examined the ability of readers to monitor a passage from an Air Force textbook that had been revised in several ways. The original text was roughly 1,000 words long, detailing the success and failure of the air bombing "Operation Rolling Thunder" offensive in the Vietnam war (Greene, 1985). One revision, the *principled version*, was performed along the lines of the Kintsch and van Dijk (1978) framework, along with the given new strategy of Clark and Haviland (1977) (see Britton & Gulgoz, 1991, for a full description). Another revision, the *heuristic version*, was performed by an expert in text revision (Bruce Britton), and was designed to make the text as understandable as possible. A third revision, the *readability version*, was constructed, which increased the objective readability of the passage to match that of the heuristic version. Essentially, this text had shorter sentences and more frequently used words. This revision was necessary, because in the process of producing the heuristic revision, the objective readability score of it was lowered (that is, they were made objectively easier to read, primarily by using more frequent words for less frequent words, and by shortening sentences). The original text had a grade level equivalent of about 13.5 years, as measured by the Flesch–Kincaid Index, while the heuristic revision had grade levels of about 12 (the principled version was also at 13.5).

All our subjects were recruited from the Baylor University Psychology Subject Pool, and virtually all were between the ages of 18–23. Occasionally, subjects had to be dropped from the analyses when they produced no variance in their confidence ratings or in their comprehension performance. We ended up with a total of either 30 or 31 subjects in each condition.

Each subject was tested individually, and the texts were presented on an IBM-compatible monitor. In Experiment 1, we excluded the principled version from our stimulus materials. Therefore, subjects read one of the three versions of the text (original, heuristic, or readability). The texts were broken into five different sections, each approximately 200 words long. Subjects were allowed to read at their own pace, and after each of the five text sections, subjects were asked to predict how well they thought they would do on a series of multiple-choice questions over the section they had just read, using a 1–6 confidence scale (6 being the highest). When they had read all the text sections, they were asked 30 multiple-choice questions developed by Britton and Gulgoz (1991). The questions were designed to tap information from only one section.

Results and Discussion of Burns (1993) Experiment 1

We measured three dependent variables associated with comprehension: reading time, confidence ratings, and performance on the multiple-choice questions. Furthermore, by correlating the last two variables, we were able to measure their comprehension monitoring ability.

The revisions of the original text had their intended effect on the comprehension measures. Readers spent 10% less time reading the heuristic version (500 ms/word vs. 450 ms/word). They rated their level of comprehension higher for the heuristic revision (4.57 vs. 3.97) and they performed better on the multiple-choice test (56% vs. 46%). On multiple-choice performance, those who read the readability version performed somewhere between the two other groups. These results are shown in Fig. 10.1.

Our real interest, though, was in comprehension monitoring ability. Again, the heuristic version was superior. We used the gamma correlation here, because it is most appropriate for the type of data we have (see Nelson, 1984, for a discussion). In our studies, readers of the original and readability versions produced correlations that were not statistically different from zero. However, readers of the heuristic version displayed gammas of .37, which were not only different from zero, but also were as high as any currently reported in the literature. The gamma correlations are shown in Fig. 10.2.

Our early work, then, looked promising. We had found that under some conditions, readers were able to monitor their comprehension. Specifically, we found that the more understandable the text, the higher the correlation between predicted and actual performance. As it will turn out, we were partly right.

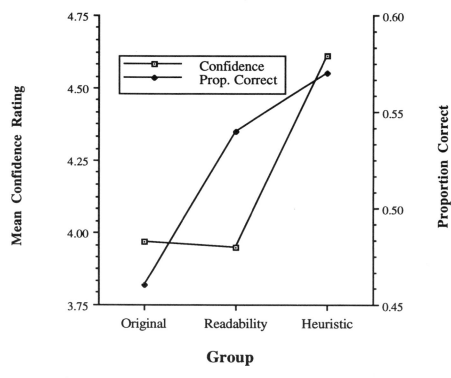

FIG. 10.1.   Confidence ratings and proportion correct in Burns (1993, Experiment 1).

BURNS (1993) EXPERIMENT 2

In the second experiment, we wished to test whether the improvements seen with the heuristically revised text would hold when the text was revised in a different manner. Basically, we wanted to see whether improvements guided by the Kintsch and van Dijk (1978) model would produce a text that would also be easy to monitor. We followed Britton and Gulgoz (1991), and called this the principled version. One hundred-forty subjects were recruited from the same subject pool, and were assigned to one of the four text conditions. The procedures were identical to those used in Experiment 1.

Results and Discussion of Burns (1993) Experiment 2

In most respects, we confirmed the findings of Experiment 1. We found that the reading times for the heuristic and principled text were faster (380 msec/word and 401 msec/word, respectively) than the original version (480 msec/word). The performance on the multiple choice comprehension test was also slightly better

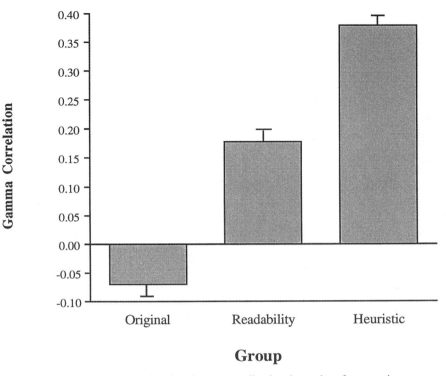

FIG. 10.2.   Gamma correlations between predicted and actual performance in Burns (1993, Experiment 1).

for those two groups (57%) than the original (52%), though the effect was not as large.[1] With the confidence ratings, though, we found confidence associated with the heuristic version to be higher than the other three. These results are summarized in Fig. 10.3.

We were also a bit surprised at the outcome of the comprehension monitoring measures. We expected the heuristic version to once again be well monitored, but we thought the principled version would be as well; it wasn't. The correlation between predicted and actual performance for the principled version was only .18, which was not statistically different from zero. Furthermore, the gamma correlation for the readability version was as high as that for the heuristic version (both were about .30; see Fig. 10.4)! Frankly, we were stumped.

One of the problems that has plagued the comprehension monitoring research is the elusiveness of uniformly replicable findings. That's not to say that those nonzero findings are Type I errors, but informal discussions with others who do similar research indicate that they have the same problem—usually a given pro-

---

[1]The two results are not directly comparable, though, because the tests were not identical.

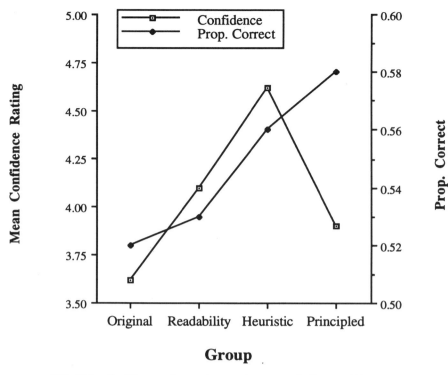

FIG. 10.3. Confidence ratings and proportion correct in Burns (1993, Experiment 2).

cedure or stimulus produces a significant result. Sometimes, inexplicably, it does not. We thought we had hit such a point in our research.

At the same time Burns was doing this research, Bryant was completing her thesis. She had been tackling a more theoretical question. What kind of existing comprehension frameworks could be imported into the comprehension monitoring domain? The greatest weakness in the this area had been the lack of a theoretical basis. We were producing empirical demonstrations of nonzero correlations, but had no real mechanisms to explain it. Initially, Glenberg et al. (1987) favored a "domain familiarity" hypothesis, which suggested that readers are basing their judgments on what they already know about a topic, rather than what they learned in the given passage. Though this has found some support (i.e., Maki & Serra, 1992), it does not explain all the findings.

Maki (Maki et al., 1990) later proposed a cognitive effort hypothesis: Making reading "less automatic" should produce greater attention to detail, and thus should result in better comprehension monitoring. Though she has some evidence supporting this notion, it is clearly inconsistent with the findings we just reported: We found that revised text were easier to read (as shown by faster reading rates),

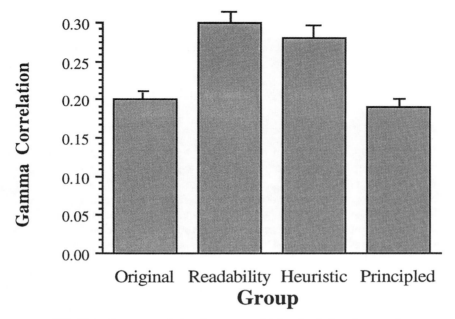

FIG. 10.4. Gamma correlations between predicted and actual performance in Burns (1993, Experiment 2).

easier to comprehend (performance on the tests were higher), and that subjects were aware these were easier texts (they gave them higher confidence ratings, and those confidence ratings were more accurate). Other work (Weaver & Burns, 1990) also showed that making texts difficult—in this case by making topic macrostatements either explicitly stated or leaving them for the reader to infer— did not improve calibration.

Weaver and Bryant (in press; see also Weaver & Bryant, 1992) adopted the material appropriate processing framework of McDaniel and Einstein (Einstein et al., 1990; see also chap. 10 in this vol.). We did this for several reasons. First of all, with one exception (Maki & Swett, 1987), all the work on adults' comprehension monitoring used expository text. And no study had ever compared monitoring of narrative and expository texts. Perhaps this might be a clue as to why the literature was so spotty.

There are some important differences in the way we approached this experiment and the way McDaniel and Einstein approached theirs. First of all, we consistently use multiple texts, so that we can obtain a correlation for each subject. McDaniel and Einstein typically used but one, which precludes any metamemory judgment done within subjects. In addition, we used a multiple-choice recognition test, rather than a free recall test used by McDaniel and Einstein. They hinted that their findings might not extend to tasks other than recall, because recognition tests are somewhat less sensitive to weaknesses in a text's coherence. Finally, we varied the level of difficulty of our texts, realizing the confounding that existed between text style and level of readability.

WEAVER AND BRYANT (1994) EXPERIMENT 1

Subjects, Materials, and Procedures

We recruited 98 students from the same Baylor University subject pool, and assigned them to one of two text conditions. Following Einstein et al. (1990), we chose fairy tales for our four narrative texts (taken from Manheim, 1977[2]). For our expository texts we chose four entries from encyclopedia-type sources. The narratives averaged about 775 words each, the expositions slightly more than 500. Each of these texts was broken into four sections for presentation, and each section was presented on an IBM-compatible computer. Subjects could proceed at their own pace.

For each text we constructed 16, 4-alternative multiple-choice questions. Four questions came from each of the four text sections, and were constructed so that 2 of the questions tapped relational information, and 2 tapped interitem information. Subjects were shown all four texts, in random order. Following the fourth section of each text, subjects were asked to predict how well they thought they would do on a subsequent comprehension task, using the same 1–6 scale as in the previous experiments. After all texts had been read and ratings made, subjects answered the questions. The order of the questions was randomized, with the constraint that all 16 questions from a given text were presented as a block. The procedure took less than an hour.

Results and Discussion

Our dependent measures of interest here are confidence ratings and performance on the recognition text. They are shown in Table 10.1. Also, we computed each subjects' correlation between rated performance and actual performance.

Subjects consistently performed better on the questions from the narrative text. However, we had made no effort to equate item difficulty, so we do not make any strong judgments concerning those. However, the possible interaction we thought we might observe—readers of narration doing better on relational tasks, readers of exposition doing better on interitem tasks—did not materialize. Initially, then, we found little support for the MAP framework with respect to recognition.[3] Subjects also consistently rated the narratives easier to read, by a considerable margin.

---

[2]Stimulus materials for all these studies are available upon request.

[3]Note, however, that we did not include a processing manipulation. We get to that later.

TABLE 10.1
Recognition and Confidence (SEM) as a Function of Passage Type and Test
Question Type in Weaver and Bryant (in Press) Experiment 1

| Recognition | Test Question Type | | |
	Relational	Interitem	Overall
Narrative	.65 (.02)	.64 (.03)	.64 (.03)
(conf = 4.8)			
Expository	.45 (.03)	.39 (.03)	.41 (.03)
(conf = 3.6)			

*Reliably different from zero, $p < .05$.

However, the gamma correlations between predicted and actual performance produced a very MAP-like effect, shown in Fig. 10.5. Neither group did consistently poorer when comparing recognition performance of relational and interitem tasks. However, readers of narration were better able to monitor their performance on relational questions, and readers of expositions better monitored their interitem performance.

This makes perfect sense. When reading narratives, readers' attention is naturally focused toward narrative information. The reverse would be true of readers of expository texts, whose attention is directed toward gleaning details. As a result, they will better monitor their understanding of those concepts.

However, when looking over our results, and comparing them to the work described earlier regarding revision and readability, something else struck

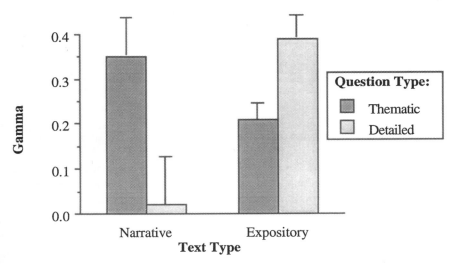

FIG. 10.5. Gamma correlations between predicted and actual performance for relational and interitem questions in Weaver and Bryant (1994, Experiment 1).

TABLE 10.2
Recognition and Confidence (SEM) as a Function of Readability and Test
Question Type in Weaver and Bryant (in Press) Experiment 2

| Recognition | Test Question Type | | |
	Relational	Interitem	Overall
Easy	.68 (.02)	.53 (.03)	.61 (.03)
(conf = 4.7)			
Standard	.50 (.03)	.48 (.03)	.49 (.03)
(conf = 4.2)			
Difficult	.46 (.03)	.46 (.03)	.46 (.03)
(conf = 3.8)			

us.[4] All of the narrative texts we had used were fairy tales intended for children. Despite their sometimes bizarre content, they were all highly readable, by standard indices like the Flesch Index (Flesch, 1951). Though these readability measures have faults (see Davidson & Green, 1988, for a discussion of some of these problems), they can prove helpful in crudely classifying texts. That is, a text that has a grade level of 12 may or may not be more difficult than one at level 11, but it certainly is more difficult than one that grades out at level 8.

WEAVER AND BRYANT (1994) EXPERIMENT 2

For this experiment, we constructed a whole new set of stimuli. We found both narratives and expositions that fit into one of three reading levels: easy (grade level below 8), standard (grade level around 12, the level where we believe our readers to be), and difficult (grade level about 16). Each reader read 4 passages from the same difficulty level, 2 narratives and 2 expositions. Thus, reading level was varied between subjects, with about 30 subjects in each condition. All other procedures were identical to those described previously, with the recognition text again consisting of 16 questions.

Recognition performance followed the expected pattern. Readers of the easy texts scored the highest (61%), followed by the standard (49%), followed by the difficult (41%). A similar linear trend was seen in the confidence ratings: easy passages were rated the highest (4.7), followed by standard (4.2), then difficult (3.8). The second set of findings is especially impressive given that text difficulty was manipulated between subjects. These are shown in Table 10.2.

---

[4]We are grateful to Tom Hanks in Baylor's English Department for pointing this out to us.

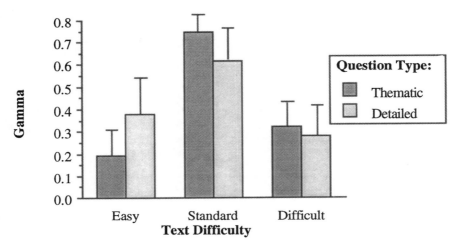

FIG. 10.6. Gamma correlations between predicted and actual performance as a function of text difficulty, in Weaver and Bryant (1994, Experiment 2).

However, the correlations between predicted and actual performance did not follow a linear trend. Rather, they displayed an inverted-U shape function, as shown in Fig. 10.6. Despite having performance and confidence ratings lower than readers of the easy text, their predictions were by far the most accurate.

The magnitude of the gamma correlations here are *qualitatively* unlike anything previously reported in the comprehension monitoring area. In fact, this is as high as many other areas of metamemory (for example, Leonesio & Nelson, 1990, or Lovelace, 1984). It appears we had entered Phase 3, which I referred to earlier as the, "Oh! So those are the important variables!" phase.

Whenever a researcher gets as startling a result as we found here, the first inclination is to try to replicate. As I have already mentioned, comprehension monitoring experiments have been notoriously difficult in this respect. We ran one final experiment, which combined elements of Weaver and Bryant (1992) Experiment 2 and included a processing task, following the work of McDaniel and Einstein (adjunct questions during reading, focusing attention on either global or thematic information). We replicated the inverted U-shape function perfectly (and the correlations were at least as high as we just reported). These findings are shown in Fig. 10.7. We failed to find any effect of our adjunct question manipulation, however. Thus, we can draw two conclusions: First, adjusting the texts for appropriate levels of readability will indeed produce large correlations between predicted and actual performance. Second, we are only somewhat sure of saying that MAP effects extend to comprehension monitoring (see also Bryant, 1992, for a more in-depth discussion of this second issue, as well as a comparison of recognition and recall).

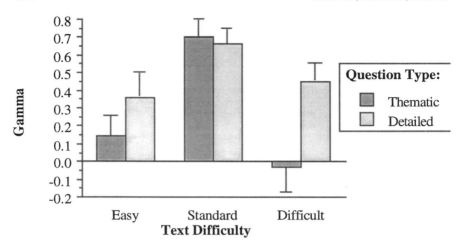

FIG. 10.7.   Gamma correlations between predicted and actual performance as a function of text difficulty, in Weaver and Bryant (1994, Experiment 3).

CONCLUSIONS

We now feel that readers can and do monitor their comprehension accurately under some circumstances. For many of us in the field, we have been hesitant to say that in the past. It seems that part of the problem has been with the nature of the stimuli. Earlier research (Weaver, 1990) demonstrated that the type and number of questions used is important. Maki also showed that multiple alternative questions are more sensitive than two-item tests. In the present set of studies, we have shown that the texts themselves can substantially affect the observed levels of calibration.

We have assumed (correctly, we think) that our readers are reading at about a grade 12 level. All of our subjects were taken from Baylor's Psychology Subject Pool, which is comprised primarily of freshmen and sophomores taking Introductory Psychology. However, we did not administer reading batteries that would allow us to make an even stronger conclusion.

Comprehension, then, depends a great deal on the ability to monitor that comprehension. Part of what it means to say, "this person is reading at a grade X level," is saying, "this person can accurately monitor their comprehension with texts written at that grade level."

It is interesting to speculate about the potential developmental trends that might be observed. For example, readers in the sixth grade should show the same inverted U pattern, but their peak should be with level 6 texts. When comparing children of the same chronological age, we would expect advanced readers to demonstrate a different peak than poor readers. Indeed, comprehension monitoring might be a very sensitive "leading indicator" of reading ability. Perhaps ability to monitor texts at a certain level indicates that readers have "mastered" that level of text, and are ready to proceed to more difficult texts.

The present results also help resolve one of the paradoxes of this literature. We have all relied heavily on the materials originally developed by Glenberg and Epstein (1985). These are good, short, informative expository texts. However, a systematic investigation of the texts reveal what now must be deemed a real problem. The average readability of these texts is about a Grade 16 level, which, according to our results, would preclude most readers' accurate monitoring. Texts at a more reasonable grade level (or the same texts with a group of highly skilled readers) would produce more positive results.

What is the source of this metacognitive ability? Again, this is pure speculation, but it seems likely that it is mediated by available working memory resources. As the basic reading processes become more efficient, and therefore consume less working memory space, this space is freed up for activities such as comprehension monitoring. In fact, such an hypothesis could explain the sometimes contradictory findings on cognitive effort and increased comprehension monitoring. Maki and Serra (1992) showed that making reading less automatic improved comprehension monitoring, but that has not always been the case. Were they using easier texts, making reading less automatic might well improve comprehension. However, as the texts become more difficult, dividing attention might impair comprehension monitoring.

The relationship between working memory demands and comprehension monitoring is likely to be a fertile area of investigation, just as the relationship between comprehension and working memory has been. Under some divided attention tasks, comprehension monitoring might be unimpaired (or even improved!). Under other conditions (say, with more difficult texts), comprehension monitoring is likely to be impaired when attention is divided.

The metamemory function used in text comprehension is strikingly similar to the "graeculi" mentioned in Schönpflug (see chapter 14 in this vol.). In his system, the graeculi are aware of how memory works, and when called on, perform the appropriate actions. These graeculi know the contents of memory, and are aware of which processes need to be utilized for a given task. This is perfectly analogous to the functions served by our comprehension monitoring mechanisms. Perhaps a more clever title for this chapter would be "the 'graeculi' of text comprehension."

I started this chapter with an anecdote about Kintsch saying that "*someone* might find this interesting." Well, it turns out someone did—Walter himself. Otero and Kintsch (1992) recently used the Kintsch (1988) construction-integration model to predict certain readers' inabilities to monitor their comprehension. By simulating where these readers go wrong, they were able to predict what kinds of comprehension monitoring failures they would show. Given this example, monitoring of readers' levels of comprehension is likely to become interesting to even more people in the future.

REFERENCES

Baker, L., & Brown, A. L. (1984). Metacognitive skills and reading. In R. Barr, M. L. Kamil, & P. Mosenthal (Eds.), *The handbook of reading research*, (pp. 230–245). New York: Longman.

Britton, B. K., & Gulgoz, S. (1991). Using Kintsch's computational model to improve instructional text: Effects of repairing inference calls on recall and cognitive structures. *Journal of Educational Psychology, 83*, 329–345.

Bryant, D. S.(1992). *Metamemory for written materials: Re-evaluating the Material Appropriate Processing framework.* Unpublished master's thesis. Baylor University, Waco, TX.

Burns, K. D. (1993). *The role of test and stimulus variables in comprehension and comprehension monitoring.* Unpublished master's thesis. Baylor University, Waco, TX.

Clark, H. H., & Haviland, S. E. (1977). Comprehension and the given-new contract. In R. O. Freedle, (Ed.), *Discourse Production and Comprehension* (pp. 1–40). Norwood, NJ: Ablex.

Davidson, A., & Green, G. M. (Eds.). (1988). *Linguistic complexity and text comprehension: Readability issues reconsidered.* Hillsdale, NJ: Lawrence Erlbaum Associates.

Einstein, G. O., McDaniel, M. A., Owen, P. D., & Coté, N. C. (1990). Encoding and recall of texts: The importance of material appropriate processing. *Journal of Memory and Language, 29*, 566–581.

Flesch, R. (1951). *How to test readability.* New York: Harper & Brothers.

Glenberg, A. M., & Epstein, W. (1985). Calibration of comprehension. *Journal of Experimental Psychology: Learning, Memory, and Cognition, 11*, 702–718.

Glenberg, A. M., & Epstein, W. (1987). Inexpert calibration of comprehension. *Memory and Cognition, 15*, 84–93.

Glenberg, A. M., Sanocki, T., Epstein, W., & Morris, C. (1987). Enhancing calibration of comprehension. *Journal of Experimental Psychology: General, 116*, 119–136.

Glenberg, A. M., Wilkinson, A. C., & Epstein, W. (1982). The illusion of knowing: Failure in the self-assessment of comprehension. *Memory and Cognition, 10*, 597–602.

Greene, M. P. (1985). *U. S. air power: Key to deterrence.* Maxwell Air Force Base.

Gulgoz, S. (1989). *Revising text to improve learning: Methods based on text processing models, expertise and readability formulas.* Unpublished doctoral dissertation, University of Georgia.

Kintsch, W. (1988). The use of knowledge in discourse processing: A construction-integration model. *Psychological Review, 95*, 163–182.

Kintsch, W., & van Dijk, T. A. (1978). Towards a model of text comprehension and production. *Psychological Review, 85*, 363–394.

Leonesio, R. J., & Nelson, T. O. (1990). Do different metamemory judgments tap the same underlying aspects of memory? *Journal of Experimental Psychology: Learning, Memory, and Cognition, 16*, 464–470.

Lovelace, E. A. (1984). Metamemory: Monitoring future recallability during study. *Journal of Experimental Psychology: Learning, Memory, and Cognition, 10*, 756–766.

Maki, R. H., & Berry, S. L. (1984). Metacomprehension of text material. *Journal of Experimental Psychology: Learning, Memory, and Cognition, 10*, 663–679.

Maki, R. H., & Serra, M. (1992). The basis of test predictions for text material. *Journal of Experimental Psychology: Learning, Memory, and Cognition, 18*, 116–126.

Maki, R. H., & Swett, M. (1987). Metamemory for narrative texts. *Memory and Cognition, 15*, 72–83.

Maki, R. H., Foley, J. M., Kajer, W. K., Thompson, R. C., & Willert, M. G. (1990). Increased processing enhances calibration of comprehension. *Journal of Experimental Psychology: Learning, Memory, and Cognition, 16*, 609–616.

Manheim, R. (Ed.). (1977). *Grimms' tales for young and old.* Garden City, NY: Doubleday.

McDaniel, M. A., Einstein, G. O., Dunay, P. K., & Cobb, R. E. (1986). Encoding difficulty and memory: Toward a unifying theory. *Journal of Memory and Language, 25*, 645–656.

McDaniel, M. A., Einstein, G. O., & Lollis, T. (1988). Qualitative and quantitative considerations in encoding difficulty effects. *Memory and Cognition, 16*, 8–14.

Nelson, T. O. (1984). A comparison of current measures of the accuracy of feeling-of-knowing predictions. *Psychological Bulletin, 95*, 109–133.

Nelson, T. O., & Narens, L. (1990). Metamemory: A theoretical framework and new findings. *The Psychology of Learning and Motivation, 26*, 125–173.

Otero, J., & Kintsch, W. (1992). Failures to detect contradictions in a text: What readers believe versus what they know. *Psychological Science, 3*, 229–235.

van Dijk, T. A., & Kintsch, W. (1983). *Strategies of discourse comprehension.* San Diego, CA: Academic Press.

Walcyzk, J. J., & Hall, V. C. (1989a). Effects of examples of embedded questions on the accuracy of comprehension self-assessments. *Journal of Educational Psychology, 81*, 435–437.

Walcyzk, J. J., & Hall, V. C. (1989b). Is failure to monitor comprehension an instance of cognitive impulsivity? *Journal of Educational Psychology, 81*, 294–298.

Weaver, C. A., III. (1990). Constraining factors in calibration of comprehension. *Journal of Experimental Psychology: Learning, Memory, and Cognition, 16*, 214–222.

Weaver, C. A., III, & Bryant, D. S. (1992). *Metamemory for text: Extensions of the Material Appropriate Processing Framework.* Poster presented at the 33rd annual meeting of the Psychonomic Society, St. Louis.

Weaver, C. A., III, & Bryant, D. S. (in press). Metamemory for text: The role of text type and text difficulty. *Memory and Cognition.*

Weaver, C. A., III, & Burns, K. D. (1990). *The effects of text revision on comprehension and comprehension monitoring.* Paper presented at 31st Meeting of the Psychonomic Society, New Orleans.

Weaver, C. A., III, & Kintsch, W. (1987). Reconstructions in the recall of prose. *Text, 7*, 165–180.

Weaver, C. A., III, & Kintsch, W. (1992). Enhancing students' comprehension of the conceptual structure of algebra word problems. *Journal of Educational Psychology, 84*, 419–428.

Chapter 11

Top-Down Effects in a Bottom-Up Model of Narrative Comprehension and Recall

Charles R. Fletcher
Erik J. Arthur
Robert C. Skeate
University of Minnesota

To understand any discourse, a reader must construct an accurate mental representation of both the states and events that it describes, and the relations among those states and events. This task is complicated by the fact that a great many types of relations can exist among the elements of a discourse (e.g., causal, spatial, logical, and set-theoretical). It is further complicated by our inability, as readers, to quickly and reliably recognize some categories of relations (i.e., logical relations). These observations may explain why, relative to most genres of discourse, narratives are understood quickly and easily. Narrative events are related to one another primarily by means of easily recognized causal and enabling relations (see, e.g., Black & Bower, 1980; Fletcher & Bloom, 1988; Graesser, 1981; Lehnert, 1978; Mandler & Johnson, 1977; O'Brien & Myers, 1987; Rumelhart, 1977; Schank, 1975; Stein & Glenn, 1979; Trabasso & Sperry, 1985; van den Broek, 1990). Consider, as an example, the simple narrative shown in Table 11.1. To understand this story, a reader must construct a mental representation of 17 distinct states and events, together with 23 causal and enabling relations, as shown in Fig. 11.1 (see Trabasso, van den Broek, & Suh, 1989).

Narrowing the possible categories of relations that can occur between two states or events does not, however, trivialize the process of understanding a narrative. There are 272 potential causal connections among the states and events in Table 11.1 (17 potential antecedents × 16 potential consequences). Research on human memory clearly suggests it is impossible for a reader to hold more than a few of these states and events in working memory at any one time (e.g., Baddeley, 1986; Miller, 1956; Simon, 1974), and that a causal connection cannot

TABLE 11.1
"Fishing with Hand Grenades"

No.	State/Event	Category	Level
1. As the German army retreated across the Austrian Alps,	Setting	1
2. some of the soldiers deserted	Event	1
3. and left their weapons behind.	Event	1
4. This allowed young Walter to start a collection of hand grenades.	Outcome	1
5. At first, simply having the grenades was enough to keep him happy.	Reaction	1
6. But in time the novelty wore off	Reaction	1
7. and Walter started looking for interesting things to do with his grenades.	Goal	1
8. He decided to go fishing.	Goal	2
9. He stood in the middle of a creek	Action	2
10. and tossed a live grenade up-stream.	Action	2
11. When it exploded	Outcome	2
12. a lot of fish were stunned	Outcome	2
13. and floated to the surface of the water.	Outcome	2
14. As the current carried them by	Outcome	2
15. Walter tried to scoop them up.	Action	2
16. Unfortunately, the creek was much too fast	Setting	2
17. and he didn't actually catch any fish.	Outcome	2

be encoded unless its antecedent and consequence are simultaneously active in working memory (e.g., McClelland & Rumelhart, 1985; Raaijmakers & Shiffrin, 1980, 1981). A major hurdle for any theory of narrative comprehension is to explain how the richly interconnected representation illustrated by Fig. 11.1 is constructed within the known limits of the human information-processing system. This chapter describes two very different solutions to this problem and explores the possibility of combining them.

TOP-DOWN MODELS

In a pioneering series of experiments, Bartlett (1932) asked English college students to retell an American Indian folk tale called "The War of the Ghosts." He observed a consistent pattern of enhancements, distortions, and deletions that became more pronounced with repeated retellings or longer retention intervals.

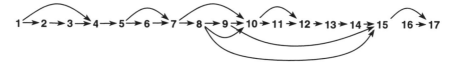

FIG. 11.1.   The causal structure of "Fishing with Hand Grenades." An arrow from Event 1 to Event 2 indicates that 1 causes or enables 2.

He concluded that understanding, telling, and retelling a story are guided by culturally specific expectations that he called "schemata." He supported this claim by showing that subjects accurately reproduced those parts of "The War of the Ghosts" that are consistent with the European story schema, while distorting or forgetting those parts that are not.

During the 1970s, schemata became one of the core constructs of cognitive psychology and artificial intelligence. Schema-based theories were proposed for a variety of tasks, including object recognition, problem solving, and language comprehension (see, e.g., Rumelhart, 1980). In the domain of story understanding, two different types of schemata were proposed: *story grammars* and *scripts*. Of these, story grammars are closer in spirit to Bartlett's schemata. They represent our expectations about the elements of a typical story, along with the causal and enabling relationships among those elements. Scripts, by contrast, represent our expectations about the elements of certain highly stereotyped situations, together with the causal and enabling relationships among those elements. During comprehension, story grammars and scripts serve similar functions. As each state and event in a story is read, it is bound to one of the expected elements of the schema. Because the schema already includes a representation of how its elements are related to one another, the fundamental problem of narrative comprehension is neatly solved. Working memory is never required to hold more than one state or event at a time, so long as it also holds a pointer to the appropriate schema in semantic memory.

Scripts

Scripts are usually thought of as static knowledge structures that capture our expectations about common, everyday activities such as eating in a restaurant, visiting a doctor's office, or going on a fishing trip (Bower, Black, & Turner, 1979; Schank & Abelson, 1977). The elements of a script include roles and props to which information from a text can be bound, but the heart of each script is a set of entry conditions that enable a series of causally related scenes that in turn cause a set of results. As an example, Schank and Abelson (1977) argued that the restaurant script includes: roles such as "customer," "waiter," and "cashier"; props such as "food," "menu," and "check"; the entry conditions "customer has food" and "customer is hungry"; scenes that describe in detail the activities involved in entering a restaurant, ordering a meal, eating a meal, and exiting a restaurant; and the results "customer is full" and "customer has less money." When a discourse describes a typical evening at a restaurant, all the reader has to do is associate information from the text with the appropriate elements of the restaurant script. The script itself provides a complete, prefabricated representation of all of the states and events in the discourse (even those that are not explicitly mentioned) along with the causal and enabling relations that bind them together.

Story Grammars

Fables, children's stories, and other simple narratives have their own highly predictable structure. In Western European and American cultures, such stories begin with one or more setting statements that introduce a protagonist and establish the spatial and temporal context of the story. These enable an initiating event that evokes a reaction in the protagonist. This reaction causes the protagonist to formulate a goal. In the simplest stories, the goal motivates a sequence of intentional actions that eventually lead to some outcome (e.g., protagonists achieve their goal). In more complex stories, the sequence of actions is interrupted, causing the protagonist to pursue one or more subgoals before the final outcome is reached. In story grammars (e.g., Mandler & Johnson, 1977; Rumelhart, 1977; Stein & Glenn, 1979; Thorndyke, 1977), knowledge of this structure is captured by a set of rewrite rules similar in form to the phrase structure rules of transformational-generative grammar (Chomsky, 1957). These rules decompose a story into smaller and smaller constituents. Consider as an example, the following rules:

STORY→SETTING enable EPISODE(S)
EPISODE→BEGINNING cause DEVELOPMENT cause ENDING
DEVELOPMENT→REACTION cause GOAL cause ACTION(S) cause OUTCOME

The first rule decomposes a story into a setting, which enables one or more episodes. The second rule, in turn, breaks each episode down into a beginning, which causes a development, which causes an ending. The final rule decomposes the development into a reaction, which causes a goal, which causes one or more actions, which cause an outcome. The endpoint for this process is a sequence of categories into which the states and events of a story can be inserted. The categories themselves vary slightly from one story grammar to another, but typically include settings, events, reactions, goals, actions, and outcomes, as illustrated by Table 11.1. During comprehension, the rules of a story grammar serve two functions. They allow readers to anticipate the category of the next state or event and they automatically encode the causal and enabling relationships that tie together the parts of a story.

Empirical Support for Top-Down Models

Historically, free recall data have provided a major source of empirical support for top-down, schema-based models of narrative understanding. One of the clearest examples is found in the story grammar literature. Various authors have noted that some story grammar categories (e.g., goals and their outcomes) play a more central role than others (e.g., minor setting statements). The more central categories tend to be obligatory rather than optional, tend to lie on a direct causal path that links a narrative's opening to its final outcome, and tend to be more richly interconnected to other story elements. An obvious prediction, therefore, is that story grammar categories will vary in memorability, with more central categories recalled better than less central categories. This prediction has been confirmed repeatedly (e.g., Mandler & Johnson, 1977; Omanson, 1982; Stein & Glenn, 1979) and is usually viewed as a major source of support for story grammars.

Story grammars also allow readers to parse a story into episodes, where each episode revolves around a single goal. In some stories the episodes follow one another sequentially. But in most stories the episodes are hierarchically organized. This occurs when satisfying the goal that motivates a subordinate episode is a necessary or sufficient condition for satisfying the goal that motivates its superordinate episode. Consider again the simple story in Table 11.1. Here the protagonist goes fishing with hand grenades (the subordinate goal) in order to do something interesting with his hand grenades (the superordinate goal). Many researchers have found that this hierarchical structure has a major impact on the free recall of narrative texts (e.g., Black & Bower, 1980; Goldman & Varnhagen, 1986; Rumelhart, 1977; Thorndyke, 1977). States and events at higher levels of the hierarchy are almost always recalled better than those at lower levels. Once again, this finding is typically seen as strong support for story grammars.

Both story grammars and scripts encode the temporal order of narrative events. As a result, if comprehension is a top-down, schema-driven process, readers should have little or no problem recalling the elements of a story in the proper order. In an early test of this claim, Mandler and Johnson (1977) showed that when the structure of a text deviates from subjects' expectations (as captured by a story grammar), inversions in the order of free recall become more frequent. In a particularly strong test of the same hypothesis, Bower, Black, and Turner (1979) presented subjects with script-based stories in which the order of events was randomized. In a later free recall task, they found a systematic tendency for events to "drift" away from the scrambled order in which they were presented, and toward the canonical order prescribed by the appropriate script. Similar results have been reported by Thorndyke (1975) for non-script-based narratives.

A BOTTOM-UP ALTERNATIVE

Despite their success, schema-based models of narrative comprehension are not without their limitations. Many authors have observed that schemata are too rigid to account for the full range of human performance (e.g., Kintsch & Mannes, 1987; Rumelhart, Smolensky, McClelland, & Hinton, 1986; Schank, 1982). Consider, for example, the "Fishing with Hand Grenades" story in Table 11.1. If the information in this story were forced into a fishing trip script, readers would probably infer that the protagonist placed hooks into the hand grenades which were then swallowed by the fish. Other scholars (Rumelhart, 1980) have noted that culturally specific schemata can only be acquired through repeated exposure to, and comprehension of, highly similar situations and/or stories. Both of these observations suggest the need for a more general model of the comprehension process.

The Van Dijk and Kintsch Framework

In 1983 van Dijk and Kintsch (see also Kintsch & van Dijk, 1978) proposed a bottom-up alternative to schema-based models of discourse comprehension. To accommodate the limited capacity of working memory, this approach assumes that comprehension occurs in cycles, one sentence at a time. During each cycle, processing proceeds as follows:

1. The sentence is parsed into individual propositions (Perfetti & Britt, chap. 2 in this vol.).
2. The propositions from each clause are mapped into a single state or event.
3. The relationships among the states and events are encoded.
4. If a completely interconnected network of states and events cannot be constructed, long-term memory is searched for information from earlier in the discourse that preserves the coherence of the representation.
5. A single state or event is selected for reprocessing during the next cycle.
6. Everything except the selected state or event is purged from working memory.

Selecting the state or event that remains active at the conclusion of each cycle is a strategic process that varies from one genre of discourse to another. An effective strategy must maximize the likelihood that a selected state or event will be semantically related to the following sentence, thereby minimizing the need for time-consuming searches of long-term memory.

The Current-State Selection Strategy

In order to apply van Dijk and Kintsch's approach to narrative discourse, Fletcher and Bloom (1988) examined several candidate selection strategies. They found that the need for long-term memory searches is minimized by a strategy that always selects the most recent state or event with causal antecedents, but no consequences, among the other states and events in working memory. This strategy, which they call the *current-state strategy*, always focuses a reader's attention on the end of the causal path through a text. It is illustrated by Fig. 11.2 which shows the contents of working memory as each sentence of "Fishing with Hand

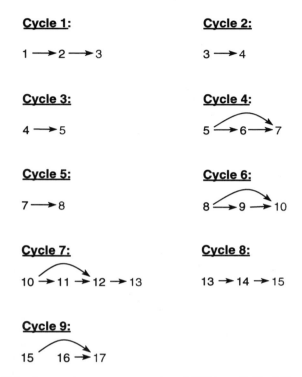

FIG. 11.2. Sentence-by-sentence processing of "Fishing with Hand Grenades."
The event that remains in working memory at the conclusion of each processing
cycle, as predicted by the current-state selection strategy, is highlighted.

Grenades" is processed. It is worth noting that the current-state strategy permits
this entire story to be processed with no long-term memory searches. It is also
worth noting that without such searches, 4 of the 23 causal connections shown
in Fig. 11.1 will be overlooked because their antecedents and consequents never
co-occur in working memory.

To test the psychological validity of the Current-state strategy, Fletcher, Hummel and Marsolek (1990) constructed a set of short narrative texts that ended
with a critical sentence, followed by either a causal antecedent or a causal consequence of that critical sentence:

Critical Sentence: As she was mixing the cake batter, her sister came home
and told Kate that the oven was broken.

Antecedent: Her sister had tried to use the oven earlier but discovered that it
would not heat up.

Consequence: Since she had the cake batter all ready, she thought that she
would use the neighbor's oven.

If the current-state strategy is correct, then the critical sentence should remain in working memory after an antecedent sentence is read, but should only be available from long-term memory when the critical sentence is followed by a causal consequence. Fletcher et al. (1990) were able to verify this prediction by showing that the antecedent condition results in faster and more accurate recognition of probe words from the critical sentence (e.g., "told"), faster reading times for continuation sentences causally related to the critical sentence (e.g., "From the parlor, Kate's mother heard voices in the kitchen."), and a higher percentage of subject-generated continuations that are causally related to the critical sentence.

Implementation in SAM

Fletcher, van den Broek, and Arthur (in press) implemented a formal, computational model of narrative comprehension and recall by combining van Dijk and Kintsch's (1983) framework and the current-state selection strategy with Raaijmakers and Shiffrin's (1980, 1981) search of associative memory (SAM) model of retrieval from long-term memory. The Fletcher et al. model has two components: a *comprehension* component and a *retrieval* component. The comprehension component takes as input a list of propositions that make up a narrative, the locations of clause and sentence boundaries within the proposition list, and a list of causal connections among the clauses. Its output is a network of propositions in which each connection is assigned a strength. This output (which Raaijmakers & Shiffrin called a "retrieval structure") is generated by the following procedure:

1. Propositions are added to working memory one at a time.

2. As each proposition is added, associative connections are created in long-term memory between it and all other propositions in working memory.

3. The strength of each connection is controlled by a series of numerical parameters. One parameter strengthens the connection between propositions from the same clause, a second between propositions from causally related clauses, and a third between propositions that share a referent. A fourth strength parameter applies to all pairs of propositions that co-occur in working memory.

4. Whenever a sentence boundary is reached, the current-state strategy is used to identify the propositions from the most recent clause with antecedents, but no consequences, in working memory. The associative connections among these propositions are strengthened while all other propositions are purged from working memory.

5. The process stops when all of the propositions have been processed.

In the retrieval structure that results from this process, the most strongly associated propositions are those from the same clause. The next strongest associations are those between propositions from causally related clauses. One important element of van Dijk and Kintsch's (1983) outline is not implemented in this model—the long-term memory searches that follow any break in the coherence of the representation. As a result, this model represents an extreme version of the "minimalist" reader proposed by McKoon and Ratcliff (1992, chap. 6 in this vol.).

The retrieval component of the model takes as input the retrieval structure created by the comprehension component and produces an ordered list of recalled propositions as output. Here is how it works:

1. The model begins by using two "special" propositions as retrieval cues. One of these propositions represents the title of the text, the other the context in which the text was studied.

2. Retrieval cues are used to repeatedly search long-term memory (as described by Raaijmakers & Shiffrin, 1980, 1981). Each search has two possible outcomes. Either a new proposition is recalled or a "retrieval failure" occurs. The probability of recalling a particular proposition increases as the strength of its associations to *all* of the cues increases.

3. Each time a new proposition is recalled, it is added to the list of recalled propositions.

4. Each time a retrieval failure occurs, the values of two variables are incremented. One variable keeps track of the number of failures that have occurred with the current set of retrieval cues (local failures). The other keeps a running count of all retrieval failures (global failures).

5. When the number of local failures exceeds the value of a model parameter, a new set of retrieval cues is selected. Whenever possible, the model uses the current-state strategy to choose retrieval cues. That is, it selects the propositions corresponding to the causally last clause on the list of recalled propositions. If this strategy fails because the model has reached a causal dead-end, it "backs up" by selecting the propositions corresponding to the most immediate causal antecedent of its current cues.

6. The model stops when the number of global retrieval failures exceeds the value of yet another model parameter.

Using these procedures, the model simulates the recall of a narrative text by attempting to reconstruct a causal path that connects its opening to its final outcome.

INITIAL EVIDENCE

To test their model, Fletcher et al. (in press) asked 24 college students to read and recall four short narrative texts. They then calculated the free recall probability for each proposition. For each text, they found the set of numerical parameters that maximize the correlation between the subjects' free recall probabilities, and those observed in the model during 100 simulation runs. They found that the model can account for 37% of the variance in the subjects' free recall data. They also found that, for any pair of recalled propositions, the probability that the model recalls them in the correct (input) order is .73, midway between the .99 observed in subjects' free recall protocols and the chance level of .50.

To what extent is this model's success due to an ability to mimic the psychological processes involved in understanding a narrative, and to what extent does it depend on an ability to mimic the free recall process? To answer this question, Fletcher et al. (in press) performed two computational experiments. In the first experiment, they replaced the current-state strategy in the comprehension component of the model with a random selection process. This dramatically diminished the model's ability to predict which propositions are recalled, but had a minimal impact on its ability to predict the order of free recall. In the second experiment, they restored the current-state strategy to the comprehension component of the model but replaced the strategy for selecting new retrieval cues during free recall with a random process. These changes had very little impact on the model's ability to predict which propositions are recalled, but significantly reduced its ability to recall propositions in the correct order. Taken together, these results suggest that comprehension processes determine what we remember about a narrative, retrieval processes determine the order in which we remember it, and the Fletcher et al. model correctly captures elements of both.

"TOP-DOWN" EFFECTS IN A BOTTOM-UP MODEL?

Despite the limitations of schema-based models of narrative comprehension and the initial success of Fletcher, van den Broek, and Arthur's model, it is certainly the case that mature readers have expectations about the structure of both stories and situations. It seems unlikely that these expectations play no role in the comprehension or recall of narrative discourse. As a result, we have begun to explore the possibility of combining the two approaches. As a first step in that direction, we ask the following question: If knowledge of story grammars and scripts were somehow added to the Fletcher et al. model, how would its performance improve?

Story Grammar Categories and Hierarchical Position

One possible answer to this question is that schemata would allow the model to provide a better description of what readers remember from a narrative by duplicating the effects of story grammar categories and goal hierarchies. To explore this possibility we reanalyzed the free recall data reported by Fletcher et al. (in press). First we sorted each state or event into one of the following story grammar

TABLE 11.2
Rank Order of Story Grammar Categories in Free Recall

Category	Model	Subjects
Outcome	5	1
Goal	1	2
Event	2	3.5
Action	4	3.5
Reaction	3	5
Setting	6	6

Note. Lower numbers indicate better recall.

categories: setting, event, goal, action, outcome, or reaction. Then we calculated the free recall probabilities for propositions from each category (see Table 11.2). The subjects' data are fairly typical. Goals and their outcomes are recalled best, whereas minor setting statements are recalled worst. The model's performance deviates from this pattern in one major respect. Outcomes are recalled quite poorly.

Next we examined each proposition's free recall probability as a function of its location in the goal hierarchy. The results, shown in Fig. 11.3, are somewhat surprising. The model exhibits a typical, robust levels effect. Propositions from the highest level of the goal hierarchy are recalled best, whereas those from the lowest level are recalled worst. By contrast, the effect of hierarchical position is greatly diminished in the subjects' data.

As a final step, we performed a series of multiple regression analyses. The results reveal that whereas the model, by itself, can account for 37% of the variance in subjects' free recall data, story grammar categories and hierarchical position together account for only 4%. Moreover, when the model's predictions are combined with story grammar categories and hierarchical position, they account for 38% of the variance, an increase of just 1% over the model alone. These results suggest that adding top-down, schema-based processes to the model would have very little impact on its ability to predict the pattern of free recall observed in this particular set of stories.

Reordering in Recall of Scrambled Stories

It is also conceivable that schema-based processes would improve the model's ability to recall propositions in their input order. To examine this possibility, we asked 10 volunteers to read and recall two short narrative texts. The order of the sentences in these texts was randomized so that, on average, only 50% of the proposition pairs were presented in their original order. Subjects were instructed to recall each text exactly as it was presented. Using procedures recommended by Bovair and Kieras (1985) and Turner and Greene (1978), we determined

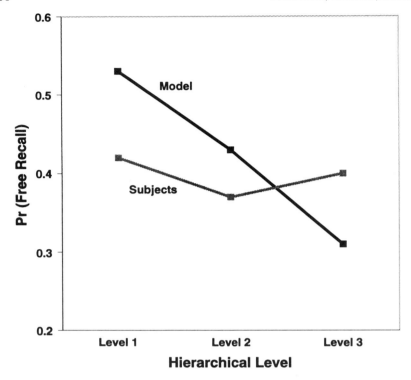

FIG. 11.3. Free recall probability as a function of hierarchical level for subjects and for the model.

which propositions were recalled by each subject. The results were used to calculate the free recall probability for each proposition.

Next we fit the Fletcher, van den Broek, and Arthur model to these data by finding the parameter values for each text that maximize the correlation between the free recall probabilities observed in our subjects, and those predicted by the model during 100 simulation runs. The details of this model-fitting procedure are described elsewhere (Fletcher et al., in press). We found that the model can account for 38% of the variance in subjects' free recall data. Thus, the model's ability to predict which propositions subjects will recall is almost exactly as good for scrambled narratives as it is for narratives presented in their normal order.

Lastly, we investigated the order of free recall. Using the optimal parameters for each text, we calculated the probability that any pair of propositions recalled by the model will be recalled in their original, unscrambled order. The results, shown in Fig. 11.4, reveal that the model's performance of .60 is reliably greater than the chance level of .50, but reliably less than the .73 observed in our subjects' free recall protocols. Taken together with the earlier finding (Fletcher et al., in press) that the model's ability to recall normally ordered narratives in the correct

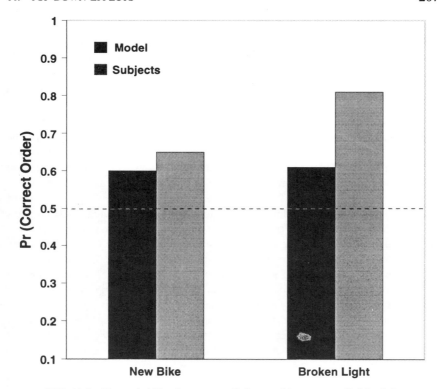

FIG. 11.4. The probability that two recalled propositions are recalled in their canonical order for two scrambled stories ("New Bike" and "Broken Light"). Chance performance is indicated by the dashed horizontal line.

sequence falls far short of human performance (.73 versus .99), this result suggests considerable room for improvement. Whether this improvement can be achieved by adding schema-based, top-down processing to the model remains to be seen, but intuition suggests that the possibility is well worth pursuing.

FUTURE DIRECTIONS

How might schema-based processes be incorporated into the model developed by Fletcher et al. (in press)? A number of possibilities are suggested by the discourse comprehension literature. One option is to replace (or supplement) the current-state strategy with a schema-based selection process (Kintsch & Greeno, 1985; van Dijk & Kintsch, 1983). Another is to add schema-based macrorules that create a concise summary of the retrieval structure as it is created (Kintsch & van Dijk, 1978; van Dijk, 1980). Unfortunately, the research reported here suggests that these approaches will not markedly improve the model's performance. Both would affect the encoding rather than the retrieval of a discourse, and encoding processes seem to have relatively little impact on the order in which narrative events are recalled. Because it appears that the order of free recall is the major area in which schemata could improve the model's performance, our efforts to incorporate schema-based processes are now focused on the retrieval process.

Yekovich and Thorndyke (1981) argued that when readers recall a story they use their knowledge of narrative structure to search long-term memory for the type of state or event (setting, goal, etc.) that should occur next. This suggestion can be implemented in the Fletcher et al. model as follows: During comprehension associative connections are encoded between each proposition and its story grammar category. Then, during free recall, the model "anticipates" the category of the next event (using transition probabilities) and uses that category as an additional retrieval cue. This option is currently under investigation in our laboratory.

A final option that we are exploring requires replacing the SAM architecture with Kintsch's (1988) construction-integration architecture. With this modification, each time the model searches long-term memory several propositions are recalled in parallel. Then activation and inhibition spread among the propositions in working memory until only a subset of the newly retrieved propositions remain. The expectations captured by story grammars and scripts can then be incorporated into the model in the form of constraints that guide the flow of activation and inhibition. For example, because goals are often followed by actions, and seldom followed by setting statements, activation would flow from goals to actions, whereas inhibition would flow from goals to settings. This modification should improve the model's ability to recall a story in the proper order.

ACKNOWLEDGMENTS

This research was supported in part by the Center for Research in Learning, Perception, and Cognition at the University of Minnesota. We are grateful to Paul van den Broek and the other members of the Minnesota Text Comprehension Research Group for their many helpful and encouraging suggestions.

REFERENCES

Baddeley, A. D. (1986). *Working memory*. New York: Oxford University Press.
Bartlett, F. C. (1932). *Remembering*. Cambridge, England: Cambridge University Press.
Black, J. B., & Bower, G. H. (1980). Story understanding as problem solving. *Poetics, 9,* 223–250.
Bovair, S., & Kieras, D. E. (1985). A guide to propositional analysis for research on technical prose. In B. K. Britton & J. B. Black (Eds.), *Understanding expository text* (pp. 315–362). Hillsdale, NJ: Lawrence Erlbaum Associates.

Bower, G. H., Black, J. B., & Turner, T. J. (1979). Scripts in memory for text. *Cognitive Psychology, 11*, 177–220.

Chomsky, N. (1957). *Syntactic structures*. The Hague: Mouton.

Fletcher, C. R., & Bloom, C. P. (1988). Causal reasoning in the comprehension of simple narrative texts. *Journal of Memory and Language, 27*, 235–244.

Fletcher, C. R., Hummel, J. E., & Marsolek, C. J. (1990). Causality and the allocation of attention during comprehension. *Journal of Experimental Psychology: Learning, Memory, and Cognition, 16*, 233–240.

Fletcher, C. R., van den Broek, P., & Arthur, E. (in press). A model of narrative comprehension and recall. In B. K. Britton & A. C. Graesser (Eds.), *Models of understanding text*. Hillsdale, NJ: Lawrence Erlbaum Associates.

Goldman, S. R., & Varnhagen, C. K. (1986). Memory for embedded and sequential story structures. *Journal of Memory and Language, 25*, 401–418.

Graesser, A. C. (1981). *Prose comprehension beyond the word*. New York: Springer-Verlag.

Kintsch, W. (1988). The role of knowledge in discourse comprehension: A construction-integration model. *Psychological Review, 95*, 163–182.

Kintsch, W., & Greeno, J. G. (1985). Understanding and solving arithmetic word problems. *Psychological Review, 92*, 109–129.

Kintsch, W., & Mannes, S. M. (1987). Generating scripts from memory. In E. van der Meer & J. Hoffmann (Eds.), *Knowledge aided information processing* (pp. 61–80). North-Holland: Elsevier Science.

Kintsch, W., & van Dijk, T. A. (1978). Toward a model of text comprehension and production. *Psychological Review, 85*, 363–394.

Lehnert, W. G. (1978). *The process of question answering*. Hillsdale, NJ: Lawrence Erlbaum Associates.

Mandler, J. M., & Johnson, N. S. (1977). Remembrance of things parsed: Story structure and recall. *Cognitive Psychology, 9*, 111–151.

McClelland, J. L., & Rumelhart, D. E. (1985). Distributed memory and the representation of general and specific information. *Journal of Experimental Psychology: General, 114*, 159–188.

McKoon, G., & Ratcliff, R. (1992). Inference during reading. *Psychological Review, 99*, 440–466.

Miller, G. A. (1956). The magical number seven, plus or minus two: Some limits on our capacity for processing information. *Psychological Review, 63*, 81–97.

O'Brien, E. J., & Myers, J. L. (1987). The role of causal connections in the retrieval of text. *Memory and Cognition, 15*, 419–427.

Omanson, R. C. (1982). The relation between centrality and story category variation. *Journal of Verbal Learning and Verbal Behavior, 21*, 326–337.

Raaijmakers, J. G. W., & Shiffrin, R. M. (1980). SAM: A theory of probabilistic search of associative memory. In G. H. Bower (Ed.), *The psychology of learning and motivation* (Vol. 14, pp. 207–262). New York: Academic Press.

Raaijmakers, J. G. W., & Shiffrin, R. M. (1981). Search of associative memory. *Psychological Review, 88*, 93–134.

Rumelhart, D. E. (1977). Understanding and summarizing brief stories. In D. LaBerge & S. J. Samuels (Eds.), *Basic processes in reading: Perception and comprehension* (pp. 265–304). Hillsdale, NJ: Lawrence Erlbaum Associates.

Rumelhart, D. E. (1980). Schemata: The Building blocks of cognition. In R. J. Spiro, B. C. Bruce, & W. F. Brewer (Eds.), *Theoretical issues in reading comprehension: Perspectives from cognitive psychology, linguistics, artificial intelligence, and education* (pp. 33–58). Hillsdale, NJ: Lawrence Erlbaum Associates.

Rumelhart, D. E., Smolensky, P., McClelland, J. L., & Hinton, G. E. (1986). Schemata and sequential thought Processes in PDP models. In J. L. McClelland, D. E. Rumelhart, & the PDP Research Group (Eds.), *Parallel distributed processing: Explorations in the microstructure of cognition: Volume 2. Psychological and biological models* (pp. 7–57). Cambridge, MA: MIT Press.

Schank, R. (1975). The structure of episodes in memory. In D. G. Bobrow & A. M. Collins (Eds.), *Representation and understanding: Studies in cognitive science* (pp. 237–272). New York: Academic Press.

Schank, R. (1982). *Dynamic memory.* New York: Cambridge University Press.

Schank, R., & Abelson, R. (1977). *Scripts, plans, goals and understanding: An inquiry into human knowledge structures.* Hillsdale, NJ: Lawrence Erlbaum Associates.

Simon, H. A. (1974). How big is a chunk? *Science, 183,* 482–488.

Stein, N. L. & Glenn, C. G. (1979). An analysis of story comprehension in elementary school children. In R. O. Freedle (Ed.), *New directions in discourse processing* (Vol. 2, pp. 53–120). Hillsdale, NJ: Lawrence Erlbaum Associates.

Thorndyke, P. W. (1975). *Cognitive structures in human story comprehension and memory* (Doctoral dissertation, Department of Psychology, Stanford University) (Tech. Rep. No. P–5513). Santa Monica, CA: The Rand Corporation.

Thorndyke, P. W. (1977). Cognitive structures in comprehension and memory of narrative discourse. *Cognitive Psychology, 9,* 77–110.

Trabasso, T., & Sperry, L. L. (1985). Causal relatedness and importance of story events. *Journal of Memory and Language, 24,* 595–611.

Trabasso, T., van den Broek, P., & Suh, S. Y. (1989). Logical necessity and transitivity of causal relations in stories. *Discourse Processes, 12,* 1–25.

Turner, A., & Greene, E. (1978). Construction and use of a propositional text base. *JSAS catalogue of selected documents in psychology.* (Ms. No. 1713)

van den Broek, P. (1990). The causal inference maker: Towards a process model of inference generation in text comprehension. In D. Balota, G. Flores d'Arcais, & K. Rayner (Eds.), *Comprehension processes in reading* (pp. 423–445). Hillsdale, NJ: Lawrence Erlbaum Associates.

van Dijk, T. A. (1980). *Macrostructures: An interdisciplinary study of global structures in discourse, interaction, and cognition.* Hillsdale, NJ: Lawrence Erlbaum Associates.

van Dijk, T. A., & Kintsch, W. (1983). *Strategies of discourse comprehension.* New York: Academic Press.

Yekovich, F. R., & Thorndyke, P. W. (1981). An evaluation of alternative functional models of narrative schemata. *Journal of Verbal Learning and Verbal Behavior, 20,* 454–469.

Chapter 12

Simulating Recall and Recognition by Using Kintsch's Construction-Integration Model

Isabelle Tapiero
Université Lyon 2

Guy Denhière
Université de Paris

The current conceptions of text comprehension assume a multilevel representation of the text and of its content (Kintsch, 1988). The same textual elements occur in different relational networks: surface structure, syntactic structure, local semantic structure (the microstructure), the global semantic structure (the macrostructure), and the mental model (Johnson-Laird, 1983) or the activated situation model (van Dijk & Kintsch, 1983).

If we refer to the classical cognitivist framework, to proceed through the different levels requires a system of mapping rules (see Kintsch & van Dijk, 1978) that allows the construction of a macrostructure resulting in the expression of the summary of a text (van Dijk, 1980). If we adopt a connectionist conceptualization, the higher level structures emerge, partly in an automatic manner and, partly, in a controlled manner from subordinate structures (see Kintsch, Welsch, Schmalhofer, & Zimny, 1990; Smolensky, 1988, 1992).

Whichever processing we assume—strictly controlled either by schemas stored in long-term memory (Schank, 1982), or by textual data (Kintsch et al., 1990)—the results obtained lead to consider the following issues:

1. The prior knowledge of the reader/listener directs the elaboration of the representation at these different levels (Baudet & Denhière, 1991; Jhean-Larose, 1991; Tardieu, Ehrlich, & Gyselinck, 1992).

2. Forgetting decreases from the surface structure, through the micro- and the macrostructure, to the situation model (Mullet, 1991; Tapiero, 1992).

3. The information retrieved from memory, in an automatic and controlled manner (Baudet, 1988; Walker & Kintsch, 1985), and produced in response to the task requirements, varies as a direct function of its relative importance in the text (Denhière, 1988; Denhière & Le Ny, 1980).

4. The final representation, product of the actual processings and of the activated knowledge structures, is integrated into the prior knowledge of the reader/listener (Denhière & Baudet, 1992).

The goal of this chapter, therefore, is then to study the contribution of these different levels to the elaboration of the final representation, assuming that, all things being equal, the characteristics of the microstructure influence the elaboration or the emergence of the macrostructure and of the situation model and the elaboration of the macrostructure is necessary to account for the reader's representation. We chose the construction-integration model proposed by Kintsch in 1988 to investigate this problem. Briefly summarized, this model, in contrast with expectation-based models of comprehension, is strictly bottom-up and does not use prestored schemata or "smart" rules for controlling the process of comprehension. According to this model, reading a text also leads to the activation of the "correct" representations to the activation of nonrelevant, redundant, and even contradictory information, which will be, during a second phase, deactivated by a relaxation connectionist process. We tested this model of cognitive architecture with two tasks: immediate free recall following the reading of stories with children and recognition following the reading of an expository text with adults and we examined how the simulations fit the experimental data. We motivated the choice of these two tasks by the fact that the resulting processes for both tasks show the evidence of the contribution of the different levels in the elaboration of the reader's representation. The way the construction-integration model works fits well with our view of how the reader performs this elaboration.

THE EXTENDED USE OF THE
CONSTRUCTION-INTEGRATION MODEL
IN AN IMMEDIATE FREE RECALL TASK

The aim of this work was to extend the use of the construction-integration model by comparing different simulations on the performances of 7-year-old children on immediate free recall task. We first contrast three different classes of hypotheses concerning the emergence of the coherence of the representation of the microstructure: the causal coherence, the referential coherence, and the coherence by the activity of minimal predication. Then, for each type of microstructure, we contrast two hypotheses concerning the elaboration of the relevant macrostructure: the sequence of events (van Dijk, 1977) and the intentional system (Denhière & Baudet, 1992). We show that the elaboration of the macrostructure is necessary to account for the reader's construction of a coherent representation. Finally, we tested three different sizes of short-term memory buffer, each size referring to a hypothesis concerning the step-by-step elaboration of the text representation, and we studied two different values of weights between the propositions in the network.

THE ELABORATION
OF A COHERENT REPRESENTATION

According to the authors who emphasize the causal coherence (Baudet & Cordier, 1992; Black & Bower, 1980; Trabasso, 1991; van den Broek & Trabasso, 1985), reading a text leads to the construction of a causal path or a causal network (van den Broek & Lorch, 1993), which relates the propositions participating in the initial and final states of the story. It is assumed that for the construction of a coherent representation, the propositions, so-called events and actions that belong to the causal path, are more important than those located on the dead ends (see Fletcher & Bloom, 1988).

For the authors who emphasize referential coherence by argument overlap (Kintsch, 1974; Kintsch & van Dijk, 1978), coherence is established by the arguments that different propositions share in common. A hierarchy of relative importance of the propositions constitutes the first step of the elaboration of the macrostructure.

According to the authors who emphasize referential coherence by the activity of minimal predication (Denhière, 1984; Le Ny, 1979; Tapiero, 1992), and in contrast with referential coherence, the fact that propositions shared arguments in common do not necessarily lead to the inheritance of a link.

One way to contrast these three hypotheses—that is, causal coherence versus referential coherence versus coherence by activity of minimal predication—is to examine, for the elaboration of the microstructure, the semantic nature of the propositions in the stories (states, properties, events, or actions) and for the elaboration of the macrostructure, their relative importance, measured by a task of judgments of importance provided by adults.

Indeed, according to the causal coherence view, this is the number of propositions denoting events and actions that determine the facility with which the causal path can be established and then the coherence. We can then postulate that the number of these propositions will determine the probability of propositional recall.

According to the referential coherence, this is the number of arguments shared by the propositions that determines the establishment of the coherence and the hierarchy of importance, independently of the semantic nature of the propositions. Here, we assume the number of important propositions will determine the probability of propositional recall rather than their semantic nature.

According to the coherence by the activity of minimal predication and as for the referential coherence, it is the number of important propositions that determines the probability of propositional recall rather than their semantic nature. Thus, the only difference between this type of coherence and the referential coherence will consist in the fact that for the simulations performed, we removed from the network the links automatically generated by the procedure of argument overlap (Kintsch, 1988).

The work described here first examines the effects of the semantic nature of the propositions and of their relative importance in the recall of stories by 7-year-old children. Then a set of simulations on the microstructure and on the conjunction of the micro- and macrostructure is presented to finally contrast the experimental results with the activation values obtained in the simulations.

EXPERIMENT

Methods, Materials, and Procedure

Four stories respectively titled "Giant on a Cliff," "Giant in the Forest," "Bear Cub," and "Truck" were identical on a maximum of dimensions (see Table 12.1): the surface structure (number of characters, words, and sentences), the syntactic structure (same degree of complexity), the local semantic structure (number of propositions, $n = 66$; and different arguments, $n = 12$), the narrative superstructure (only one episode), and the internal structure (similar story grammar categories). The content of the four stories is presented in the Appendix 12.1. (The translation of English from the French, although not exact, provides a close approximation.)

These four stories were different in terms of their local semantic structure. They varied in the semantic nature of the propositions they contained—that is, the number of stative predications (properties and states: 23 and 24 vs. 15 and 12) versus the number of state modifications (actions and events: 16 and 15 vs. 27 and 28). They also varied in the number of propositions judged important by adults: 20 and 33 versus 23 and 33 (see Table 12.2).

Fifty-two 7-year-old children were randomly divided into two groups, differing in the type of stories they read. The first group, G1, read texts with the same

TABLE 12.1
Characteristics of the Four Stories

Narrative	Characters	Words	Sentences	Propos.	Arg.
"Giant on a Cliff"	632	117	10	66	12
"Giant in the Forest"	619	117	12	65	11
"Truck"	646	116	11	68	13
"Bear Cub"	620	113	10	68	13

Note. Propos. = Propositions, Arg. = Arguments.

TABLE 12.2
The Semantic Characteristics of the Four Stories

Narrative	Properties & States	Actions & Events	Imp. Propositions
"Giant on the Cliff"	23	16	20
"Giant in the Forest"	24	15	33
"Truck"	15	27	23
"Bear Cub"	12	28	33

Note. Imp. = Important.

main character "Gargantua": "Giant on the Cliff" and "Giant in the Forest." The second group, G2, read the texts "Truck" and "Bear Cub," which were unrelated. The two stories with the same character ("Giant on the Cliff" and "Giant in the Forest") were in a previous experiment (see Denhière & Larget, 1989) set into only one story with two episodes. The results showed a big discrepancy in the number of propositions recalled for these two episodes (with better performances of recall for the episode "Giant in the Forest"). The goal of the experiment reported here is to investigate if the same superiority effect is observed using two separate stories, despite their numerous similarities.

Children were tested individually out of their classroom. Each child participated in immediate free recall task of two different stories with one week delay between them, each story requiring two readings, each one followed by a recall. We analyzed the number of propositions recalled using Kintsch's propositional analysis (1988) by distinguishing the concepts from the propositions with concepts noted as propositions, and by distinguishing the propositions referring to stative predications (state and properties) and state modifications (events and actions).

The Simulations

The simulations carried out are derived from the construction-integration model (Kintsch, 1988; Kintsch et al., 1990).[1] For each story, simulations of comprehension processes were performed to test different hypotheses about the elaboration of the microstructure and of its conjunction with the macrostructure. Fig. 12.1 presents a schematic description of the different simulations performed.

For the microstructure, three types of local semantic coherence were simulated: co-referential coherence by argument(s) overlap, activity of minimal predication, and causal coherence.

Co-referential Coherence. The first type of establishment of coherence we used, *co-referential coherence*, was proposed by Kintsch (1974) and consists of the overlap of argument(s) shared by propositions in the text. In its most general

---

[1]We are indebted to Walter Kintsch, who permitted us to use the CI program.

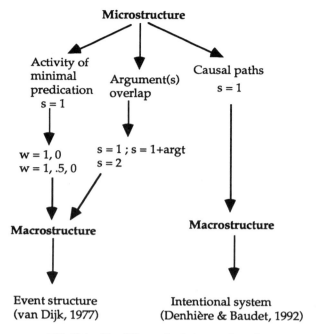

FIG. 12.1.   The different simulations performed.

form, this model predicts that two propositions are related if they share at least one argument in common.

Activity of Minimal Predication.   The second type of coherence, *activity of minimal predication*, is based on the psychological activity of predication as it is described in Le Ny (1979). In general, this activity consists in the successive adding of new information to old information. As we only used narrative texts, the successive operations of predication are done by using propositions that essentially denote properties and states for a limited number of characters and state modifications initiated and controlled or not by these characters as a function of the goal they want to achieve. In contrast to co-referential coherence, the propositions that share an argument in common do not necessarily inherit a link.

Next is an illustration of the difference between these two types of coherence for a sentence belonging to the narratives "Giant in the Cliff" and "Giant in the Forest": "The giant helped poor people."

"The giant helped poor people" → "TO HELP (Giant, (POOR) People)"

According to Kintsch's propositional analysis (1988), we parsed this sentence into four propositions (two propositions referring to the concepts and two propositions referring to the relations between concepts).

P1   Giant
P2   People
P3   TO HELP (P1,P2)
P4   POOR (P2)

According to the criterion of "Activity of minimal predication":

P1 IS RELATED TO P2 via P3 and
P2 IS RELATED TO P4

The following graphic representation presents the relations between the propositions:

P1——P3——P2——P4

According to the criterion of "Argument overlap":

P1 IS RELATED TO P2 via P3 and
P2 IS RELATED TO P4
PLUS P3 IS RELATED TO P4 (argument P2 shared)

Compared to the criterion of "activity of minimal predication," for the criterion of argument(s) overlap, a new relation is added between P3 and P4 as they share the same argument P2.

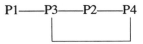

Temporocausal Coherence.   Last, but not least, we used the works of Trabasso (1991) and of Baudet and Denhière (1991) to relate the textbase propositions to establish a temporocausal path, relating the final situation to the initial one described by the narrative (see Fletcher & Bloom, 1988; Kintsch, 1991).

For illustrating the temporocausal coherence, we present three sentences of the story "Giant in the Forest." "The giant saw a poor old woman. She gathered dead wood. He decided to help her." The way we parsed the propositions follows Kintsch's propositional analysis (1988).

Sentence 1:
P1 Giant
P2 Woman
P3 TOSEE [P1,P2]
P4 POOR [P2]
P5 OLD [P2]

Sentence 2:
P6 Wood
P7 TOGATHER [P2,P6]
P8 DEAD [P6]

Sentence 3:
P9 TOHELP [P1,P2]
P10 TODECIDE [P1,P9]
P11 CAUSAL PATH 1: TEMPORAL LINK: DOING [P3, P7]
P12 CAUSAL PATH 2: GOAL: [P9,P10]
P13 CAUSAL PATH 3: GOAL: [P11,P12]

In Sentence 3, "He decided to help her," the causal coherence is represented by adding three propositions in the textbase (P11, P12, P13), which account for the temporocausal path. The graphic representation of these three sentences is presented in Fig. 12.2 with the propositions referring to the causal paths necessary to construct the coherence in bold:

The Variation of the Short-Term Memory Buffer
and the Weights Between the Propositions in the Network

The Referential Coherence. For each cycle (roughly corresponding to one sentence), we tested three sizes of short-term memory buffer: $s = 1$, $s = 1+$ argument, and $s = 2$. We did not use highest values of s because of the relatively small size of the sentences (or cycles) in the stories. The correlations obtained between the simulations performed and the recall were quite low and we did not observe any difference between $s = 1$ and $s = 1+$ argument (respectively .39 and .37). The correlations were the lowest for $s = 2$ (.24).

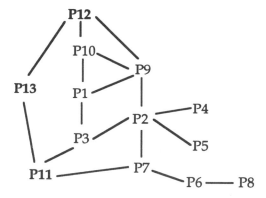

FIG. 12.2.   Coherence graph of the causal representation (P refers to propositions and concepts).

The Coherence by Activity of Minimal Predication.   We chose two values for the weights between the propositions: $w = (1, 0)$:1 for a direct relation between two propositions, and 0 for other relations; and $w = (1, .5, 0)$:1 for a direct relation between two propositions, .5 for a relation between two propositions via a third one, and 0 for other relations. The correlations between the two types of weights and the recall did not show any difference (.47).

Types of Macrostructure Used

In addition to the original Kintsch's model, we added to each type of micro-structure simulated the simulation of the relevant macrostructure; two types of macrostructure were used: The first type, proposed by van Dijk (1977), corresponds to the decomposition of a story into a structure of events. It has been used with the microstructure referring to the co-referential coherence and the activity of minimal predication. The second type is the intentional structure, which is the linear causal relations hierarchized in goal–subgoal relations (Denhière & Baudet, 1992). It has been used with the microstructure referring to the temporocausal coherence.

We do not conceive of the macrostructure as a prestored structure in the reader's long-term memory but rather as an emergent structure of the microproc-essing of the narratives (see Rumelhart, Smolensky, McClelland, & Hinton, 1986, pp. 7–58; Smolensky, 1988). According to this hypothesis, the macropropositions assumed to represent the simulated macrostructure are added progressively to the microstructure depending on their likelihood of emergence, that is, they are not added as a whole, at the beginning of the simulation of the microstructure.

Taking into account the fact that the number of propositions judged as im-portant in the four narratives varies from 20 to 33, we limit the number of macropropositions added to the microstructure to 20. This limitation of 20 macro-propositions added to the simulation of the microstructure holds for the two types of macrostructure simulated: event structure and intentional system. To control the relevance of the simulation of the macrostructure as a structure of event, we tried to determine if, whatever the type of macropropositions added to the mi-crostructure, the correlations between the simulations and the recall tended to be increased mechanically. In that purpose, we made a simulation by adding 20 propositions that did not belong to the propositions judged as important by adults.

EXPERIMENTAL RESULTS

The main relevant result is that the number of propositions recalled is significantly higher for the stories with a greater number of propositions judged important by adults ("Giant in the Forest" and "Bear Cub") whichever the number of propo-sitions denoting actions and events.

Comparison of the Experimental Results and the Simulations

The activation values obtained for each one of the simulations performed are not described in detail here (for more details, see Tapiero, 1992). This chapter focuses on the correlations calculated between the activation values obtained to the different simulations and the experimental data. The correlations values presented on Table 12.3 correspond to the average of the first and the second recall.

Concerning the type of microstructure simulated, the correlations show that for two out of the four stories ("Giant on the Cliff" and "Truck") the correlations between the simulations and recall are higher for the coherence by the activity of minimal predication than for the two other types of coherence, whereas for the two other stories ("Giant in the Forest" and "Bear Cub") the correlations for the activity of minimal predication and the causal path are almost identical but are higher than those for argument(s) that overlap.

When the simulation of the macrostructure is added to the simulation of the microstructure, the correlations with recall increase on average by 16 points. If we look at the type of macrostructure added (structure of events vs. intentional structure) we notice that at the exception of the story "Truck," the adding of the macrostructure as a structure of events leads to higher correlations than the adding of the macrostructure as intentional structure.

Finally, if we compare the correlations obtained to the macrostructure as a structure of events for the two types of local coherence (the activity of minimal predication and the argument(s) overlap), we notice that for "Giant on the Cliff" and "Bear Cub" we do not observe any difference, but for "Giant in the Forest" and for "Truck" the correlations obtained to the macrostructure show a greater

TABLE 12.3
Correlations Between the Experimental Data and the Activation Values
Obtained in the Simulations of the Microstructure and of the
Conjunction Micro- and Macrostructure

Microstructure	Activity of Predication	Argument(s) Overlap	Causal Path
"Giant on the Cliff"	.45 **	.37 **	.34 **
"Giant in the Forest"	.48 **	.33 **	.47 **
"Truck"	.63 **	.40 **	.34 **
"Bear Cub"	.29 *	.24	.30 *
Macrostructure	Structure of events		Intentional structure
"Giant on the Cliff"	.61 **	.52 **	.47 **
"Giant in the Forest"	.63 **	.57 **	.53 **
"Truck"	.62 **	.62 **	.71 **
"Bear Cub"	.56 **	.54	.35 **

Note. Micro = Microstructure; Micro & Macro = Macrostructure added to the microstructure. Significance level: $n = 60$, $r = .25$, $p < .05$ (*); $r = .31$, $p < .01$ (**).

increase when added to the coherence defined as argument(s) overlap than when added to the activity of minimal predication.

The most important finding of the comparison of the three different values of short-term memory buffer results in the inferiority in the correlations values obtained with $s = 2$ compared with those obtained with the two other values of s. We can postulate that the main problem concerns more the nature of the propositions stored in the short-term memory buffer and to their capacity to ensure the relation with the forthcoming information than the size of the buffer. Furthermore, the fact that we do not observe any difference in the correlations for $s = 1$ and $s = 1 +$ argument indicates that the model functions in an identical way in both cases and activates the same set of propositions.

We do not have any interpretation about the lack of difference between the two values of weights, we only suggest that these differences are too small to be noticed by the model.

Recognition Task

The goal of this second experiment was to study the recognition of an expository text by adults and to extend the construction-integration model proposed by Kintsch (1988; Kintsch et al., 1990) to the simulation of the recognition of six types of statements.

Reading and understanding a text imply for a subject to construct different levels of representation: the surface structure, the syntactic structure, the local and global semantic structure (the micro- and macrostructure), and the situation model. Related to these levels, we constructed six types of statements to be recognized: verbatim (verb), syntactic surface variation (ssv), close semantic variation (paraphrase: csv), inference (inf), distant semantic variation dealing with the situation model referring to the text (mdsv), distant semantic variation dealing with an other situation model than the one referring to the text (odsv). We suppose these different statements to be recognized will inform us on the mnemonic traces associated to the representation of these different levels and on the differential forgetting of these traces related to these levels (Kintsch et al., 1990).

EXPERIMENT 2

Methods, Materials, and Procedure

Four groups of 26 psychology students read a text, "Manatee." This text was composed of an introduction (3 sentences), a first topic on "Breathing" (10 sentences), a second topic on "Reproduction" (10 sentences), and a conclusion (3 sentences). The recognition task only dealt with the topic "Reproduction." As an illustration, we present 2 out of the 10 sentences dealing with the "Reproduction of the Manatee." The text about the topic "Reproduction" is presented in Appendix 12.2.[2]

> The manatee female has a single pair of mammary glands attached to the chest.
>
> The reproduction period for a manatee lasts from April to August.

For each text sentence, 2*6 types of statements to be recognized have been derived, each type referring to a specific level of representation: verbatim (VERB), which means identical to a text statement; surface syntactic variation (SSV), which consists of a modification of the location of a clause of a text statement; close semantic variation or paraphrase (CSV): which is a statement with an identical semantic structure but a different surface structure (words) than the text statement; inference (INF), which is never mentioned in the text but has to be inferred from it; and two types of distant semantic variations, one dealing with the same situation model as the one described in the text and one dealing with another situation model (respectively, MDSV and ODSV). The statements to be recognized are presented in Appendix 12.2. As an example, the statement "From April to August lasts for a manatee the reproduction period" refers to the surface syntactic variation issued from the text statement "The reproduction period for a manatee lasts from April to August."

Experimental Results

Correct Responses.   The performances of the subjects are the highest for the verbatim, the inferences, and the distant semantic variations, and are the lowest for the surface variations (see Fig. 12.3). The hierarchy obtained is : ODSV > MDSV > VERB > INF > SSV > CSV.

The Recognition Times.   A reverse pattern than that for the correct responses is obtained for the response times. The results show a superiority of the recognition times for the inferences compared to the other statements to be recognized (see Fig. 12.4). It seems quite difficult for the subjects to quickly respond to the inferences and we can then make the assumption that the readers have constructed these inferences either during reading or during the retrieval process. On the contrary, the distant semantic variation shows the lowest times and indicates that the readers have elaborated an accurate model of the situation described by the text. The hierarchy obtained is: INF > SSV = CSV ≥ MDSV > ODSV.

If we relate the results obtained to the response times with those obtained to the correct responses, we notice that even though the response times for the

---

[2]As the experimentation has been performed in France, the text about the topic "Reproduction" and the statements to be recognized have been translated in English and are only an approximation of what the subjects read.

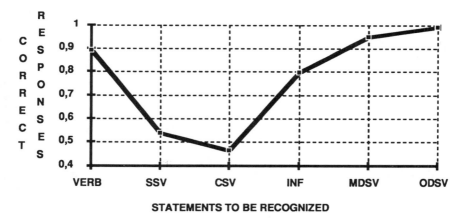

FIG. 12.3. Correct responses of the different statements to be recognized. VERB = verbatim; SSV = syntactic surface variation; CSV = close semantic variation; INF = inference; MDSV = distant semantic variation referring to the manatee; ODSV = distant semantic variation referring to another animal.

inferences are the highest, the probability of correct responses is quite high. This result suggests the readers are able to correctly reject the inferences but that this task requires more time to process it.

The results described earlier indicate that the readers are in good agreement with the hypothesis of different levels of representation of the information described in a text. The results to the surface variations (SSV & CSV) indicate that the decay of the surface level in the mnemonic traces is faster than for the

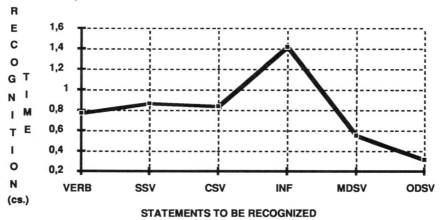

FIG. 12.4. Recognition time (cs) of the different statements to be recognized. VERB = verbatim; SSV = syntactic surface variation; CSV = close semantic variation; INF = inference; MDSV = distant semantic variation referring to the manatee; ODSV = distant semantic variation referring to another animal.

other levels: The readers cannot differentiate what they read in the text with the statements to be recognized even though recognition task has to be performed just after the reading of the text.

The Simulation and Its Principles

In the simulations performed, we compared the activation values of each verbatim issued from the text with its corresponding statement to be recognized. Because we wanted to account for different levels of representation, we introduced in the matrix the level of the local semantic structure (the propositions), the level referring to the surface structure introduced by words (the lexical items), and the surface level corresponding to the order of presentation of words in the sentence. For this purpose, each text statement leading to the construction of a statement to be recognized has been parsed into propositions and concepts at the microlevel and we added in the parsing the nodes corresponding to the lexical items referring to the corresponding propositions plus the nodes that constitute the order of words presentation of the statements. From this parsing, a matrix relating each element of the network described previously has been constructed. The comparison between the statement to be recognized and its corresponding verbatim has been performed by introducing in the matrix of the verbatim only the relevant differences between the verbatim and the statement to be recognized. Two general principles have been applied to the construction of the matrix. We assigned an initial value of 1 for the relations between the propositions and the words, and between the words. And, a value of 2 relates the propositions of the textbase. These weights of 1 and 2 are supposed to account for the differences in the strengths between the mnemonic traces of the surface representation and those of the semantic structure of the text.

As an example, we present the simulation of a statement to be recognized: a surface syntactic variation "From April to August lasts the reproduction period of a manatee," with its verbatim (statement read in the text) "The reproduction period of a manatee lasts from April to August." In this case, the syntactic variation differs from the verbatim statement only by the order of words presentation in the sentence; the semantic textbase is identical. As the verbatim matrix is composed by the propositions (P), the concepts (C), the lexical items (W), the order of words presentation (O1), and the relations between these nodes, to account for the difference between this statement and the syntactic variation we need to construct a new matrix by adding in the old one a node corresponding to the order of presentation of words in the syntactic variation (O2) and to relate this node with the elements with which the statement to be recognized is related. Thus, the new matrix is composed by the propositions (P), the concepts (C), the lexical items (W), the order of words presentation (O1), and the relations between these nodes of the verbatim plus the node corresponding to the new order (O2) and its relations with the elements in the matrix. We chose to relate the two orders of presentation with a value of −3, making the assumption that the activation of one order inhibits the activation of the other. We ran the simulation and obtained for each node in the network an activation value (see Table 12.4). To get the resulting activation value of the statements to be compared (verbatim vs. surface syntactic variation), we just have to add the values of the nodes that compose each statement. Here, the only difference between the verbatim and the syntactic variation statements deals with the node "order of words presentation" and then the activation value of each one of the node "order" is added with its corresponding items (in this case, the items are identical for both statements). To account for the experimental results, the resulting activation value of the statement to be recognized has to be lower than that of the verbatim.

Figure 12.5 presents a graphic representation of the simulation of the surface syntactic variation and of its verbatim.

The same principles are applied for the simulation of the close semantic variation, of the inference, and of the distant semantic variation dealing with the same situation than the one described in the text. The *close semantic variation* or *paraphrase* is supposed to differ from the verbatim statement by the type of lexical items and by the order of presentation of the words. Thus, as for the surface syntactic variation, we added in the matrix of the corresponding verbatim statement the nodes corresponding to the new lexical items and to the new order of words presentation. To account for the differences between the two statements, we assigned a value of −3 to the relation between the verbatim lexical items and the close semantic lexical items and between "Order 1" corresponding to the words presentation order in the verbatim statement and "Order 2" referring to the order in the close semantic variation. If some of the lexical items do not differ from one statement to the other, no new node is added. For the *inference*, the only difference consists in including in the matrix besides the new lexical items and their presentation order, several new

TABLE 12.4
Comparison Between the Activation Values of the Verbatim
and of its Surface Syntactic Variation (SSV)

Label	Identification of the Elements in the Network	Values for the Verbatim Alone	Values for the Verbatim plus SSV
P1: concept	Manatee	2928	2935
P10	REPRODUCTION[P1]	5830	5837
P11	PERIOD OF[P10]	8154	8146
P12: concept	April	5090	5079
P13: concept	August	5090	5079
P14	TO LAST FROM TO [P11, P12, P13]	10000	10000
W2	Manatee	2576	2774
W7	Period	4490	4669
W8	Manatee reproduction	3644	3829
W9	To last from	2818	3017
W10	April to August	4898	5074
O1	Order 1	3776	2435
O2 (SSV)	Order 2		2435
Total/100		592,94	588,74

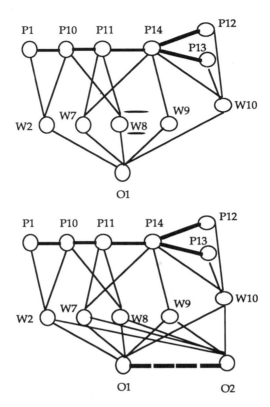

FIG. 12.5. Graphic representation of the simulation of the verbatim statement (upper part of the figure) and of its combination with its surface syntactic variation (lower part of the figure). P refers to propositions and concepts; W refers to the lexical items or words; 0 refers to the order of words presentation with 01 corresponding to the order for the verbatim and 02 corresponding to the order for the surface syntactic variation.

propositions to explain the semantic distance between the inference and the verbatim statement. Finally, as for the inference, the *distant semantic variation* referring to the Manatee, differ from the verbatim statement by the type of lexical items and by the type of propositions.

Comparison of the Experimental Results and the Activation Values

Figure 12.6 presents the experimental and simulation data for the six statements to be recognized.

The hierarchies obtained for the activation values of the simulation of the different types of statements to be recognized (VERB ≤ SSV > CSV > INF >

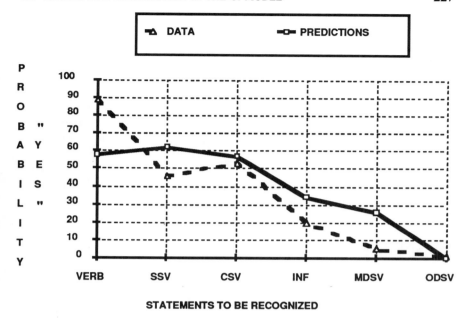

FIG. 12.6. Probability of response "Yes" as a function of the experimental data and the predictions of the model. VERB = verbatim; SSV = syntactic surface variation; CSV = close semantic variation; INF = inference; MDSV = distant semantic variation referring to the same situation model; ODSV = distant semantic variation referring to an other situation model.

MDSV > ODSV) and for the responses "Yes" (VERB > SSV < CSV > INF > MDSV > ODSV) are almost identical. The only difference concerns the activation values obtained to the verbatim.

CONCLUSION

The construction-integration model proposed by Kintsch (1988) permits us to investigate in depth the subjects' representation and the processes they apply in immediate free recall and in recognition tasks, in the study of stories and expository texts with children and adults. We showed that the construction-integration model could account for the different levels of representation the readers construct during a comprehension/memorization task.

The simulations as a function of the type of local coherence introduced (activity of minimal predication, argument(s) overlap, and causal path) led to important variations in the correlations between the activation values and the recall. This result shows that the construction-integration model is very sensitive to the type of structure given as an input.

In our work, we chose to use this model in a qualitative way, but we could make more quantitative predictions. Indeed, the main part of our work consisted in calculating correlations between the simulations performed and the experimental data. One of our next goals is to use this model to predict the processes implied by the subjects in a comprehension/memorization task.

Furthermore, in the work described here, we did not account for the representation of the situation model. A next step is to investigate the representation of this level by introducing the prior knowledge of the readers necessary in order to more accurately study the processes involved in text comprehension.

Finally, we could use the model in a more connectionist way. Although in our work we give as an input the structure to the model, we could imagine this construction part using a more connectionist procedure.

APPENDIX A: RECALL

"Giant on the Cliff"

1. A long time ago, there was a good giant named Gargantua.
2. He was a good giant and he liked to help poor people.
3. One day, seated on a cliff, he soaked his feet in the water to wash them.
4. The sun shone and he was hot.
5. Then, in his two cupped hands, he took some water to refresh himself.
6. But, just as he plunged his hands into the water, a boat came.
7. He grasped it without becoming aware of it.
8. When the giant drank, he swallowed the boat and the masts tickled his throat.
9. He said to himself that he had swallowed a speck of dust.
10. Although the giant was not thirsty anymore, the boat and the sailors have disappeared forever.

"Giant in the Forest"

1. A long time ago, there was a good giant named Gargantua.
2. He was a good giant and he liked to help poor people.
3. One day, he was walking in the forest.
4. He saw a poor old woman.
5. She gathered dead wood.
6. He decided to help her.
7. In a moment, he uprooted some of the most beautiful oaks of the forest.
8. He put them on his shoulder.

9. He went with the old woman to her home.
10. As the road was long, he was very happy to lay his bundle on the wall of the old woman's house.
11. The house collapsed.
12. The poor old woman now has wood to warm herself but no longer has a house to shelter her.

"Truck"

1. The old truck has now reached the trail which leads to the village of the jungle.
2. Suddenly, something comes into sight on the trail: it is a lion.
3. Seated, his head proudly raised, he looks at the truck coming, he does not move.
4. The driver slows down and stops the truck.
5. The seconds pass and seem like hours.
6. The lion gets up and moves in the direction of the truck.
7. The driver, his hands gripping on the wheel, starts at once.
8. The lion moves aside and starts to run alongside the truck, the driver goes as fast as he can.
9. The lion slows down, stops, then turn his back and sits down again majestically.
10. Very pale, the driver slows down.
11. He is not afraid anymore, the danger has past.

"Bear Cub"

1. One day, Winnie the bear cub, was walking in the forest.
2. Tired, he sat down under a big oak and fell asleep.
3. He dreamed about golden honey which fell drop to drop into his mouth.
4. Suddenly, a buzzing sound woke him up.
5. He took his head between his paws.
6. He said to himself that the buzzing should come from bees and that if there were bees, then he could find honey.
7. He started to climb the tree, stopped to breathe, then started again to climb.
8. He had almost reached the top when the branch broke under his weight.
9. He fell down into the middle of a thorn-bush.
10. Half bored, he sat down again under the big oak tree and fell asleep.

APPENDIX B: RECOGNITION

Text "Reproduction"

1. The manatee female has a single pair of mammary glands attached to the chest.
2. The reproduction period for a manatee lasts from April to August.
3. The gestation period for a manatee lasts six months.
4. The mother gives birth in the water to only one young.
5. The mother pushes its youngster to the surface of the water and permits him to breathe.
6. The mother suckles its youngster during eighteen months.
7. The youngster's suckling is done at the surface of the water.
8. At birth, the manatee weighs on average 60 pounds.
9. The skin of the young manatee, pink in color, is bare.
10. The young manatee becomes an adult at the age of three years.

Statements to Be Recognized

1. Verbatim (VERB)

1. The gestation period for a manatee lasts six months.
2. The young manatee becomes an adult at the age of three years.

2. Surface Syntactic Variation (SSV)

1. From April to August, lasts the reproduction period for a manatee.
2. Pink in color, the skin of the young manatee is bare.

3. Close Semantic Variation (CSV)

1. The manatee female gives life to a single youngster in the water.
2. The mean weight of the new born manatee is around 60 pounds.

4. Inference (INF)

1. At birth, the manatee has to be pushed at the surface of the water to breathe.
2. The youngster manatee is feeding by its mother.

5. Manatee Distant Semantic Variation (MDSV)

1. The manatee female has two pairs of mammals attached to the pectoral limbs.
2. The manatee female weans its youngsters one month after the birth.

6. Other Distant Semantic Variation (ODSV)

1. The children enjoy the show of the sea-lion balancing a ball on its nose.
2. Hanged by their legs, upside down, the bat gets out during the night.

REFERENCES

Baudet, S. (1988). Récupération de l'information sémantique en mémoire [Retrieval of semantic information from memory]. [Special issue, Acquisition of knowledge from text and picture]. *European Journal of Psychology of Education, 3*(2), 163–176.

Baudet, S., & Denhière, G. (1991). Mental models and acquisition of knowledge from text: Representation and acquisition of functional systems. In G. Denhière & J. P. Rossi (Eds.), *Text and text processing* (Vol. 79, pp. 155–189). Amsterdam: North Holland.

Baudet, S., & Cordier, F. (1992). Representation of complex actions: A developmental study. *European Bulletin of Cognitive Psychology, 12*, 141–172.

Black, J. B., & Bower, G. H. (1980). Story understanding as problem solving. *Poetics, 2*, 223–250.

Denhière, G. (1984). *Il était une fois. . . . Compréhension et souvenir de récits.* Lille: Presses Universitaires de Lille.

Denhière, G. (1988). Story comprehension and memorization by children: The role of input, conservation, and output processes. In F. Weinert & M. Perlmutter (Eds.), *Memory development: Universal changes and individual differences* (pp. 185–210). Hillsdale, NJ: Lawrence Erlbaum Associates.

Denhière, G., & Baudet, S. (1992). *Lecture, compréhension de texte et science cognitive.* Paris: Presses Universitaires de France.

Denhière, G., & Larget, E. (1989). Etude du rappel de récit: Influence de l'âge, de la structure des épisodes, de leur ordre de présentation, et du délai temporel entre la présentation et le rappel. *Questions de Logopédie, 21*, 31–66.

Denhière, G., & Le Ny, J. F. (1980). Relative importance of meaningful units in comprehension and recall of narratives by children and adults. *Poetics, 9*, 147–161.

Fletcher, C. R., & Bloom, C. P. (1988). Causal reasoning in the comprehension of simple narrative texts. *Journal of Memory and Language, 27*, 235–244.

Jhean-Larose, S. (1991). L'apprentissage d'un système fonctionnel complexe. *Psychologie Française, 36*, 167–176.

Johnson-Laird, P. N. (1983). *Mental models.* Cambridge, MA: Harvard University Press.

Kintsch, W. (1974). *The representation of meaning in memory.* Hillsdale, NJ: Lawrence Erlbaum Associates.

Kintsch, W. (1988). The role of knowledge in discourse comprehension: A construction-integration model. *Psychological Review, 95*, 163–182.

Kintsch, W. (1991). How readers construct situation models for stories: The role of syntactic cues and causal inferences. In A. F. Healy, S. M. Kosslyn, & R. M. Shiffrin (Eds.), *From learning processes to cognitive processes: Essays in honor of William K. Estes* (Vol. 2, pp. 261–278). Hillsdale, NJ: Lawrence Erlbaum Associates.

Kintsch, W., & van Dijk, T. A. (1978). Toward a model of text comprehension and production. *Psychological Review, 85*, 363–394.

Kintsch, W., Welsch, D., Schmalhofer, F., & Zimny, S. (1990). Sentence memory: A theoretical analysis. *Journal of Memory and Language, 27*, 133–159.

Le Ny, J. F. (1979). *La sémantique psychologique.* Paris: Presses Universitaires de France.

Mullet, V. (1991). L'activation et la mise à jour d'un modèle de situation: Etude par le rappel et la reconnaissance [Activation and updating of a situation model: Investigation by a recall and a recognition task]. Unpublished master's thesis, Universités de Paris V et Paris VIII.

Rumelhart, D. E., Smolensky, P., McClelland, J.L., & Hinton, G. E. (1986). Schemata and sequential thought processes in PDP models. In J. L. McClelland, D. E. Rumelhart, & the PDP Research Group, *Parallel distributed processing: Explorations in the microstructure of the cognition* (Vol. 2, pp. 7–58). Cambridge: MIT Press.

Schank, R. C. (1982). *Dynamic memory.* New York: Cambridge University Press.

Smolensky, P. (1988). On the proper treatment of connectionism. *Behavioral and Brain Sciences, 11*, 1–75.

Smolensky, P. (1992). IA connexionniste, IA symbolique et cerveau. In D. A. Andler (Ed.), *Introduction aux sciences cognitives* (pp. 77–109). Paris: Gallimard, Collection Folio/essais.

Tapiero, I. (1992). *Traitement cognitif du texte narratif et expositif et connexionnisme: Expérimentations et simulations* [Cognitive processing of story and expository text and connectionism: Experimentations and simulations]. Unpublished doctoral dissertation, Université de Paris 8.

Tardieu, H., Ehrlich, M. F., & Gyselinck, V. (1992). Levels of representation and domain-specific knowledge in comprehension of scientific texts. *Language and Cognitive Processes, 7*(3/4), 335–351.

Trabasso, T. (1991). The development of coherence in narratives by understanding intentional action. In G. Denhière & J. P. Rossi (Eds.), *Text and text processing* (Vol. 79, pp. 297–317). Amsterdam: North Holland.

van den Broek, P. W., & Trabasso, T. (1985). Causal thinking and the representation of narratives events. *Journal of Memory and Language, 24*, 612–630.

van den Broek, P. W., & Lorch, R. F., Jr. (1993). Network representations of causal relations in memory for narrative texts: Evidence for primed recognition. *Discourse Processes, 16*, 75–98.

van Dijk, T. A. (1977). *Text and context.* London: Longman.

van Dijk, T. A. (1980). *Macrostructures.* Hillsdale, NJ: Lawrence Erlbaum Associates.

van Dijk, T. A., & Kintsch, W. (1983). *Strategies of discourse comprehension.* New York: Academic Press.

Walker, W. H., & Kintsch, W. (1985). Automatic and strategic aspects of knowledge retrieval. *Cognitive Science, 9*, 261–283.

Chapter 13

Priming of Inference Concepts in the Construction-Integration Model

Janice M. Keenan
University of Denver

Tracy M. Jennings
IBM, Santa Teresa Lab

"The price that has to be paid for promiscuity is not very high." This sounds like a quote from Madonna that is basically wrong—the price to be paid for promiscuity these days can be quite high with AIDS as a possible consequence. But in fact, this is a quote from Kintsch (1988, p. 180) regarding his Construction-Integration model. The Construction-Integration model posits that as the words of a text are formed into concepts and propositions, they each activate a set of neighboring associations. It is a context-free process of activation; so, material that is irrelevant, and perhaps inconsistent with the meaning of a text, can be activated. In short, the result is a network of promiscuous associations. This is what Kintsch was referring to when he used the term *promiscuity*. When he said, "the price to be paid for promiscuity is not very high," he was referring to the fact that the integration process that needs to work on this promiscuous network to rid it of inconsistencies and irrelevancies is a small price to pay for the flexibility and power of such a system.

The purpose of this chapter is to consider the role that this promiscuous network plays in inferencing. Specifically, we will examine the extent to which results previously interpreted as evidence for instrument inferences can be attributed instead to this low-level process of neighbor activation. In short, we will argue that the price to be paid for promiscuity can be quite high—mistaken claims for inferences—if one ignores the role promiscuity plays in activating inference concepts.

WORD-BASED AND TEXT-BASED PRIMING
IN THE CONSTRUCTION-INTEGRATION MODEL

According to the Construction-Integration model, there are two ways in which a concept that is not explicit in a discourse can become activated: word-based priming and text-based priming. As soon as a word in a text is perceived, it immediately activates its whole associative neighborhood in a context-independent way. Activating a concept in this way is referred to as *word-based priming*. So, for example, reading the word *bug* would activate its insect associates, its espionage associates, and its computer associates, regardless of the meaning of the sentence. As time passes, text-level processes come into play. These processes can inhibit concepts activated by word-based priming that are inappropriate to the meaning of the text, sustain the activation of meaning-appropriate concepts, and activate new concepts such as inferences. When a concept is activated by these text-level processes, it is referred to as *text-based priming*. So, if the sentence containing *bug* was about insects, text-level processes would eventually inhibit the espionage and computer associates of *bug*, sustain the insect meaning of *bug*, and activate related text-appropriate information, perhaps the fact that birds eat insects.

As the preceding discussion shows, word-based priming and text-based priming differ in their time of onset. Word-based priming has a rapid onset; text-based priming has a relatively slower onset. That is because word-based priming is based on construction, whereas text-based priming is the result of integration. Evidence to support this aspect of the Construction-Integration model derives from studies of ambiguous words, like *bug*. These studies show that all meanings of an ambiguous word are activated immediately; but after 250 ms, only the meaning of the word that fits the meaning of the text is still activated (Kintsch & Mross, 1985; Swinney, 1979). The fact that inappropriate meanings are initially activated suggests that it takes some time for the text to exert its influence; in other words, it shows that text-based priming has a slower onset.

Word-based priming and text-based priming are thought to also differ in how easily they are disrupted. Word-based priming is said to be easily disrupted because in studies of priming using word lists, one intervening item is sufficient to eliminate any priming effects (Foss, 1982; Gough, Alford, & Holley-Wilcox, 1981; Meyer, Schvaneveldt, & Ruddy, 1972). Text-based priming, on the other hand, is said to be sustained over several unrelated words, dissipating only when there is a change in topic (Sharkey & Mitchell, 1985).

Word-based priming is not only easily disrupted, it is also thought to dissipate quickly (Sharkey & Sharkey, 1992). This conclusion is derived from studies of ambiguous words where it is shown that the inappropriate meanings activated through word-based priming are no longer activated after 250 ms (Kintsch & Mross, 1985; Swinney, 1979).

Distinguishing Word-Based Priming from Inferencing

In recent years, it has become clear that the interplay of word-based priming and text-based priming is important to interpreting the results of inference experiments that assess the activation level of inference concepts through recognition, lexical decision, or naming (Keenan, Golding, Potts, Jennings, & Aman, 1990). To illustrate, consider the text, "Bobby pounded the boards together with nails." To see if subjects who read this sentence inferred that a hammer was the instrument of the action, the activation level of *hammer* is assessed after reading this sentence versus after reading a sentence in which *hammer* would not be a possible inference, for example, "Bobby stuck the boards together with glue."

The problem with this method of assessing inferences is that inferencing is not the only way in which the inference concept can be activated. It may also be activated by virtue of reading words that are semantically related to it—in this case, *pounded, boards*, and *nails*. In other words, it may be activated by word-based priming.

In recent years, researchers have recognized that word-based priming might be a problem in assessing the occurrence of inferences, leading to conclusions that inferences are drawn when in fact the inference concept may have only been activated through word-based priming. As a result, studies using activation measures of inferencing now often try to control for word-based priming (e.g., McKoon & Ratcliff, 1986; Potts, Keenan, & Golding, 1988). This is done by constructing a control version for each text that contains all of the words in the inference version that are related to the inference concept, but arranged in such a way so as not to induce the inference.

Constructing word-based priming controls is difficult. To illustrate, consider this example from Potts et al. (1988) that was concerned with inferences about the consequences of events. Here is the *Inference* version:

No longer able to control his anger, the husband threw the delicate porcelain vase against the wall. He had been feeling angry for weeks, but had refused to seek help.

The inference was that the vase broke. In order to construct a Control version that controlled for word-based priming, we needed to get all the words related to the breaking scenario into the text without implying anything about breakage. Here is the *Control* version:

In one final attempt to win *the delicate porcelain vase*, the *angry husband threw* the ball at the bowling pins that stood *against the wall*. He had never won anything, and was determined not to miss this time.

As this example illustrates, it taxes one's creative juices to come up with these word-based priming controls. The prospect of having to do this for longer texts raises the question of whether word-based priming controls are really necessary.

In order to know whether it is necessary to construct word-based priming controls, we need to know how long word-based priming lasts. Does it last long enough to contaminate activation measures of inferencing? Or does it dissipate quickly as the ambiguous word studies would lead us to believe?

Duration of Word-Based Priming

The data on the duration of word-based priming using ambiguous words in discourse are plentiful and consistent (e.g., Kintsch & Mross, 1985; Seidenberg, Tanenhaus, Leiman, & Bienkowski, 1982; Swinney, 1979; Tanenhaus, Leiman, & Seidenberg, 1979). They suggest that the duration of word-based priming is approximately 250 ms. There is, however, reason to question whether estimates of the duration of word-based priming derived from these studies would apply to nonambiguous words.

When words are represented in a distributed network, as in the Construction-Integration model, it seems like the type of connections between words would play an important role in determining the duration of word-based priming. Specifically, if a word had strong inhibitory connections, we would expect those inhibitory connections to quickly shut down whatever excitatory activation was coming from other connections. Consequently, the duration of word-based priming should be shorter for words with strong inhibitory connections.

Kintsch (1988) proposed that the alternative meanings of an ambiguous word are connected to each other by inhibitory links with the highest possible weightings. So, for example, the insect meaning of the word *bug* would be connected to the spy meaning of *bug* with a weighting of -1. With such a strong inhibitory link, it would not take the integration process very long to deactivate the word-based activation of the inappropriate meaning. However, if a concept lacks such strong inhibitory input and has mainly positive connections, like the connection between *hammer* and *nail*, then it could remain active for a while based purely on its connections to the words in the text, not because of any inference about it as the instrument of the action. In other words, there are theoretical reasons to expect that word-based priming could persist longer than the 250 ms estimate derived from studies using ambiguous words if the words of the text are not ambiguous.

Unfortunately, the data on the duration of word-based priming using nonambiguous words in a discourse context are scarce and inconsistent. Foss (1982) compared the duration of word-based priming in lists and discourse. He found that priming effects on a lexical decision task were quite short-lived in a list context, but rather long-lived in a discourse context. Specifically, he found as much priming after 12 intervening words in a discourse context as after only 1.5 intervening words in a list context. If word-based priming is this long-lived in a discourse context, then it could be a serious contaminant of activation measures of inferencing.

Sharkey and Sharkey (1992), on the other hand, found no priming effects in a discourse with a lexical decision task; yet they did find them in a list. There are, however, some methodological problems with this study. First, their experiment that found no word-based priming also had no other significant effects, suggesting a possible problem of statistical power. Moreover, the critical comparison between intact sentences and scrambled versions was between experiments.

Finally, Carrol and Slowiaczek (1986) found effects of word-based priming in discourse like Foss (1982); but, unlike Foss, they found that the effects were short-lived, dissipating by the end of a clause. They used a gaze duration methodology with sentences that contained related words like *king* and *queen*. They manipulated whether the two words occurred in the same clause or a different clause of the same sentence, while maintaining the same number of intervening words. They found that *king* primed *queen* only when they occurred in the same clause. These results suggest that any effect of word-based priming should dissipate at the end of a sentence and thus not influence test words presented after the sentence.

It is hard to know how to reconcile these discrepant results. One possibility is the difference in methodologies—lexical decision versus gaze duration. Another possibility is the strength of the connections between the particular associates used. Regardless, it is clear at this point that more research is needed to determine whether there can be word-based priming effects in discourse that are of sufficient potency and duration to contaminate activation measures of inferencing. The purpose of the research reported in this chapter is to help clarify this situation.

The Role of Word-Based Priming in Instrument Inference Research

Previous studies of inferences have used either one or the other, but not both, of the following types of controls. They either used No Inference Control versions that were not controlled for word-based priming (e.g., McKoon & Ratcliff, 1981) or they used No Inference Control versions that were controlled for word-based priming (e.g., McKoon & Ratcliff, 1986; Potts et al., 1988). For simplicity, we refer to these as the *Control* version and the *Word-Based Priming Control* version (WBP Control). Table 13.1 gives examples of each.

In the present studies, we used both types of controls in the same experiment. This allowed us to compare performance across the controls and thereby answer two questions. The first question was whether there was any word-based priming occurring. If there is word-based priming, then latencies to recognize the inference concept should be faster after a WBP Control version than after the Control version. The second question was whether any inference or text-based priming was occurring. If there is activation of the inference concept from inferencing in addition to that provided by word-based priming, then latencies to the inference target should be faster following the Inference version than the WBP Control.

TABLE 13.1
Sample Paragraph

Initial Text
Bobby got a saw, hammer, screwdriver, and square from his toolbox. He had already selected an oak tree as the site for the birdhouse. He had drawn a detailed blue-print and measured carefully. He marked the boards and cut them out.

Final Sentence Version	
Inference	Then Bobby pounded the boards together with nails.
Control	Then Bobby stuck the boards together with glue.
Word-Based Priming Control	He pounded his fist on the boards when he saw that he had no nails.

Note. The Inference and Control versions are from McKoon & Ratcliff (1981); the WBP control was designed for the present experiments.

The example paragraph in Table 13.1 is taken from McKoon and Ratcliff's (1981) study of instrument inferences. All of the paragraphs used in our studies were adapted from McKoon and Ratcliff's materials. The major modification we made was to construct WBP Controls for each of their paragraphs. The reason we chose McKoon and Ratcliff's study as a domain in which to examine the question of word-based priming is because the literature on instrument inferences is so divided on whether or not these inferences are drawn during reading. McKoon and Ratcliff's study is one of the few studies using activation measures that found evidence for subjects making instrument inferences. We wondered, however, to what extent their evidence was really evidence for inferences as opposed to evidence for word-based priming. As Table 13.1 shows, there is a large difference in the potential for word-based priming between their Inference and Control versions. The Inference version contains words highly related to the target word, *hammer*—namely, *pound* and *nails*—whereas the Control version does not. So, a secondary goal of this research was to provide further evidence on the question of the occurrence of instrument inferences.

McKoon and Ratcliff (1981) used a recognition task to assess activation of the instrument inferences. Elsewhere we have argued that recognition measures do not allow one to determine whether the inference was drawn during reading or at the time of test, and consequently, are not the measure of choice in inference research (Keenan, Potts, Golding, & Jennings, 1990). Despite our earlier admonitions, we used recognition in the present experiments. We did this because we wanted to replicate McKoon and Ratcliff's procedure as closely as possible so that we could assess the degree to which word-based priming was affecting their results. But because we did use recognition, any evidence for inferences above and beyond word-based priming should not be attributed to inferences occurring during reading; they could also have occurred at the time of the recognition test.

EXPERIMENT 1

This experiment extended McKoon and Ratcliff's (1981) Experiment 1 on instrument inferences by adding WBP Controls. The goal was to determine whether the activation of instrument inference concepts observed by McKoon and Ratcliff was due to inferencing, word-based priming, or both. A more complete description of this experiment and the following one can be found in Jennings (1993).

The materials consisted of 39 of McKoon and Ratcliff's (1981) original 40 paragraphs. As illustrated by the example in Table 13.1, each paragraph consisted of five sentences. The first sentence always mentioned the target instrument, so the correct response on the recognition test was always *Yes*. The middle three sentences elaborated the topic, but did not mention the instrument. The final sentence had three possible versions: the Inference version, the Word-Based Priming Control (WBP Control), and the Control.

Sixty-three filler paragraphs were included. They differed in length from the experimental paragraphs so that the subject saw a variety of paragraph lengths and thus was discouraged from trying to anticipate when the target would be tested. The fillers were also designed to keep subjects from detecting the fact that the targets for the experimental paragraphs were always instruments, and they also provided the targets to which the correct response on the recognition test was *NO*.

Subjects read each paragraph one sentence at a time on a video monitor. After reading the final sentence of a paragraph, there was a 250 ms delay. Then a line of asterisks appeared on the screen directly above a test word. Subjects indicated whether the target word had appeared in the previous paragraph by pressing either a "Yes" or "No" key. A comprehension test occurred after every six paragraphs. It consisted of a test sentence from each of the preceding six paragraphs to which the subject had to respond "True" or "False."

Recognition latencies for the target instrument are presented in Table 13.2 as a function of version of the final sentence. The first thing to note is that we replicated McKoon and Ratcliff's (1981) finding that latencies to recognize the target instrument were significantly faster following the Inference version than the Control versions. However, we also found that latencies to the target following WBP Controls were also significantly faster than those following the Controls, suggesting that much of the facilitation coming from the Inference versions was due to word-based priming.

Is there an effect of inferencing above and beyond that provided by word-based priming? Latencies to recognize the target were faster following Inference versions than WBP Controls, but the difference was not significant in the subjects analysis and only marginally significant in the item analysis. The error data are also presented in Table 13.2. They follow the same pattern as the latency data, with Inference versions showing the fewest errors, followed by the WBP Controls, and then the Controls.

TABLE 13.2
Mean Recognition Latencies (ms) and Error Percentages for Experiment 1

Version	Recognition Latency	Errors
Inference	905	9
WBP Control	923	12
Control	949	13

It is interesting to note that subjects in our study made far fewer errors than in McKoon and Ratcliff's (1981) study. Error rates in McKoon and Ratcliff's study were 30% for Inference versions and 24% for Controls, compared to 9% and 13% in our study. This suggests that the marginal effect of inferencing observed here cannot be due to subjects not reading as carefully as in McKoon and Ratcliff's study.

The goal of this study was to determine whether the activation of instrument inference concepts observed by McKoon and Ratcliff (1981) was due to inferencing, word-based priming, or both. Because we found that inference concepts could be recognized almost as fast following the WBP Controls as following the Inference versions, and because WBP Controls did not imply the instrument but just used the same related words, we conclude that much of the activation of inference concepts in these experiments is due to word-based priming.

Our results leave open the question of whether there is also an effect of inferencing. That is because even though recognition latencies following Inference versions were faster than those following WBP Controls, the difference was, at best, only marginally significant. If there really was no effect of inferencing here, that would make these results consistent with other studies showing that instrument inferences are not drawn (e.g., Dosher & Corbett, 1982).

The results we obtained are consistent with the predictions we derived from the Construction-Integration model for the duration of word-based priming for nonambiguous words. Specifically, we found that word-based priming can persist beyond 250 ms. Furthermore, it can persist beyond the boundaries of a sentence. Our results suggest, therefore, that researchers wishing to test the effects of inferencing apart from the effects of word-based priming need to incorporate WBP controls in their studies. The purpose of the next experiment was to provide further evidence on this question.

EXPERIMENT 2

McKoon and Ratcliff (1981) hypothesized that if the instrument in the first sentence was described in such a way that it could not possibly be used as the instrument of the action in the final sentence, then the instrument concept would not be inferred when reading the final sentence. So for the example in Table

13.1, if the hammer was described as broken in the first sentence, then in reading the final sentence that *Bobby pounded the boards together with nails*, subjects should not infer that Bobby used a hammer because the hammer is broken. The logic is similar to that used by Glenberg, Meyer, and Lindem (1987), where if the character takes off the sweatshirt, it is no longer available in the mental model. Similarly, if the hammer is described as broken, it is no longer available in the mental model. If *hammer* is not available and therefore not inferred, then recognition times for *hammer* should be the same after the Inference version as after the Control version. In fact, that is exactly what McKoon and Ratcliff found in their Experiment 5.

The finding of no difference between Inference and Control versions suggests that they eliminated not only the inference effect but also the effect of word-based priming. After all, if word-based priming is operating, then latencies to recognize *hammer* should be faster following the Inference version than the Control version, regardless of whether an inference is drawn, because the Inference version has more words that are related to *hammer* that can activate it. However, McKoon and Ratcliff used a delayed recognition test requiring subjects to read two unrelated paragraphs before taking the recognition test; so the inference concept would not be expected to still be activated, either by word-based or text-based priming, when a paragraph intervenes like this.

The question we addressed in Experiment 2 is what would happen with an immediate test involving these materials. As in Experiment 1, we included the Controls originally used by McKoon and Ratcliff and the WBP Controls that we constructed. We assumed that the word-based priming effects observed in Experiment 1 would obtain again in this experiment; consequently, we expected recognition to be faster following WBP Controls than following Controls.

The Inference versions in this experiment differed from those used in Experiment 1 in that the first sentence precluded the target concept from being the instrument of the action in the final sentence. So, the first sentence in Table 13.1 was revised to read: "Bobby opened his toolbox and pulled out a mallet, a hammer which had been broken earlier that week, and a screwdriver." Note these versions always included an alternative instrument (e.g., mallet) to make the final sentence comprehensible ("Bobby was able to pound the boards with the mallet"). Because the first sentence precluded the use of the target, we did not expect to see any effect of inferring the target in this experiment, only an effect of word-based priming.

The results are presented in Table 13.3. As predicted, we found virtually no difference in recognition times between the Inference and WBP Controls. This suggests that the first sentence was successful in preventing the inference. It should be recognized, however, that having the inferencing effect go away in this experiment may not be all that impressive, because the results of Experiment 1 showed that the effect of inferencing was not that much beyond the activation provided by word-based priming alone.

TABLE 13.3
Mean Recognition Latencies (ms) and Error Percentages for Experiment 2

Version	Recognition Latency	Errors
Inference	831	10
WBP Control	833	7
Control	845	11

More importantly, we again found support for the persistence of word-based priming. Targets were recognized significantly more accurately following WBP Controls than normal Controls. They were also recognized faster following WBP Controls than Controls, but this difference failed to reach significance. The results of this experiment, therefore, support the conclusions of Experiment 1: Simply reading a sentence with words related to the instrument target is sufficient to facilitate recognition of the target, even when it occurs after the end of the sentence and after 250 ms.

CONCLUSIONS

The main question addressed by these experiments was whether word-based priming is of sufficient duration to contaminate activation measures of inferencing. Our discussion of word-based priming in the context of the Construction-Integration model suggested it certainly could. Recognizing this possibility, recent investigations of inferencing have gone to considerable trouble constructing control versions of texts that control for word-based priming (e.g., McKoon & Ratcliff, 1986; Potts, Keenan, & Golding, 1988). Because it is difficult to construct word-based priming controls, especially for texts longer than a single sentence, we set out to determine if such controls are necessary. The results of our experiments suggest they are. In both experiments we found clear evidence for word-based priming: inference concepts were responded to faster and more accurately following Word-Based Priming Controls than normal Controls. If we had not included the WBP Controls, it would have been easy to misattribute the difference in latencies between Inference and Control versions as due to inferencing. With both controls included in this study, it is clear that much of the effect that gets interpreted as inferencing is merely due to word-based priming. Maybe that is why evidence for the occurrence of instrument inferences has been so inconsistent; the evidence may reflect differences in word-based priming.

One might question whether it really is important to distinguish word-based priming from text-based priming, if as in the Construction-Integration model, word-based priming is the first step toward text-based priming. But the difference between them is more than just different points along a continuum of processing. It is basically the difference between labeled and unlabeled associations; in other words, the difference between knowing *that* concepts go together versus knowing *how* they go together. It is the difference between knowing that *pound* and *hammer* are associates versus knowing that *hammer* is an instrument that can be used to *pound* and not the other way around.

These are important differences if you are modeling the knowledge structures underlying comprehension. In fact, it is precisely this difference that allows us to account for the fairly common comprehension failure known as the Moses illusion (Erikson & Mattson, 1981; Reder & Cleeremans, 1990). The Moses illusion refers to the finding that when subjects are asked, "How many animals of each type did Moses take upon the ark?", they frequently respond "two," even though they know that it was Noah, not Moses, who had the ark. This finding suggests that subjects respond to questions on the basis of word-based consistencies—Moses fits with ark because of their association with the Old Testament—before higher level processes can provide a knowledge or reality check.

The difference between word-based processes and text-based processes is likely to also be important in understanding individual differences in comprehension. For example, poor comprehenders may be thought of as operating more at a word-based level because they lack either the knowledge or the skill to do text-level integration processes. In this regard, it is interesting to note that patients with right-hemisphere damage seem to have intact word-based priming skills, as evidenced by word association tasks, but clear deficits in inferencing and appreciation of textual coherence (Bihrle, Brownell, Powelson, & Gardner, 1986; Brownell, Potter, Bihrle, & Gardner, 1986).

In sum, we believe that there are many situations in language research where it is important to distinguish between concepts activated by the construction phase of the Construction-Integration model and concepts activated by the integration phase. We have demonstrated the importance of the distinction for inference research. And we have shown that only by incorporating WBP Controls into the design of the study can one determine whether an inference concept got activated merely by word-based priming or if text-based priming contributed as well.

REFERENCES

Bihrle, A. M., Brownell, H. H., Powelson, J. A., & Gardner, H. (1986). Inference deficits in right-brain damaged patients. *Brain and Language, 27*, 310–321.

Brownell, H. H., Potter, H. H., Bihrle, A. M., & Gardner, H. (1986). Comprehension of humorous and nonhumorous materials by left and right brain-damaged patients. *Brain and Cognition, 5*, 399–411.

Carrol, P., & Slowiaczek, M. L. (1986). Constraints on semantic priming in reading: A fixation time analysis. *Memory and Cognition, 14*, 509–522.

Dosher, B. A., & Corbett, A. T. (1982). Instrument inferences and verbs schemata. *Memory and Cognition, 10*, 531–539.

Erikson, T. A., & Mattson, M. E. (1981). From words to meaning: A semantic illusion. *Journal of Verbal Learning and Verbal Behavior, 20*, 540–552.

Foss, D. J. (1982). A discourse on semantic priming. *Cognitive Psychology, 14*, 590–607.

Glenberg, A. M., Meyer, M., & Lindem, K. (1987). Mental models contribute to foregrounding during text comprehension. *Journal of Memory and Language, 26*, 69–83.

Gough, P. B., Alford, J. A., & Holley-Wilcox, P. (1981). Words and contexts. In O. Tzeng & H. Singer (Eds.), *Perception of print: Reading research in experimental psychology.* Hillsdale, NJ: Lawrence Erlbaum Associates.

Jennings, T. M. (1993). *The role of word-based priming in instrument inference research.* Unpublished doctoral dissertation, University of Denver.

Keenan, J. M., Golding, J. M., Potts, G. R., Jennings, T. M., & Aman, C. J. (1990). Methodological issues in evaluating the occurrence of inferences. In A. Graesser & G. Bower (Eds.), *Inferences and text comprehension* (pp. 295–312). New York: Academic Press.

Keenan, J. M., Potts, G. R., Golding, J. M., & Jennings, T. M. (1990). Which elaborative inferences are drawn during reading?: A question of methodologies. In D. Balota, G. Flores d'Arcais, & K. Rayner (Eds.), *Comprehension processes in reading* (pp. 377–402). Hillsdale, NJ: Lawrence Erlbaum Associates.

Kintsch, W. (1988). The role of knowledge in discourse comprehension: A construction-integration model. *Psychological Review, 95*, 163–182.

Kintsch, W., & Mross, E. F. (1985). Context effects in word identification. *Journal of Memory and Language, 24*, 336–349.

McKoon, G., & Ratcliff, R. (1981). The comprehension processes and memory structures involved in instrumental inference. *Journal of Verbal Learning and Verbal Behavior, 20*, 671–682.

McKoon, G., & Ratcliff, R. (1986). Inferences about predictable events. *Journal of Experimental Psychology: Learning, Memory, and Cognition, 12*, 82–91.

Meyer, D., Schvaneveldt, R., & Ruddy, M. (1972, November). *Activation of lexical memory.* Paper presented at the meeting of the Psychonomic Society, St. Louis, MO.

Potts, G. R., Keenan, J. M., & Golding, J. M. (1988). Assessing the occurrence of elaborative inferences: Lexical decision versus naming. *Journal of Memory and Language, 27*, 399–415.

Reder, L. M., & Cleeremans, A. (1990). The role of partial matches in comprehension: The Moses illusion revisited. In A. Graesser & G. Bower (Eds.), *Inferences and text comprehension* (pp. 233–258). New York: Academic Press.

Seidenberg, M. S., Tanenhaus, M. K., Leiman, J. M., & Bienkowski, M. (1982). Automatic access of the meaning of ambiguous words in context: Some limitations of knowledge-based processing. *Cognitive Psychology, 14*, 489–537.

Sharkey, N. E., & Mitchell, D. C. (1985). Word recognition in a functional context: The use of scripts in reading. *Journal of Memory and Language, 24*, 253–270.

Sharkey, A. J., & Sharkey, N. E. (1992). Weak contextual constraints in text and word priming. *Journal of Memory and Language, 31*, 543–572.

Swinney, D. A. (1979). Lexical access during sentence comprehension: (Re)consideration of context effects. *Journal of Verbal Learning and Verbal Behavior, 18*, 645–659.

Tanenhaus, M. K., Leiman, J. M., & Seidenberg, M. S. (1979). Evidence for multiple stages in the processing of ambiguous words in syntactic contexts. *Journal of Verbal Learning and Verbal Behavior, 18*, 427–440.

Chapter 14

Memory and its *Graeculi*: Metamemory and Control in Extended Memory Systems

Wolfgang Schönpflug
Klaus Berthold Esser
Freie Universität Berlin

Graeculi (singular *Graeculus*, "little Greek") were Roman slaves of Greek descent. They were intellectually trained and also acquired memory skills. *Graeculi* served Roman politicians and lawyers by memorizing names, family relations, military rank, private property, and technical information, and prompted their masters during court sessions, political debates, and other social events (Grimal, 1986). Today, friends, spouses, secretaries, consultants, and so forth take over the *Graeculus*' role when they prompt another person, and become available for answering questions. In addition, technical devices such as tapes or prints serve the tasks of preserving and supplying information. Given an advanced cultural setting, human memory is supplemented with social and technical extensions. This should be considered in psychological research. From a biological perspective, individual memory functions can be studied without taking extensions into account. From an ecological perspective, individual memory should be analyzed as a component of an extended system that also comprises social and technical supports. The latter perspective is taken in this chapter.

Thus, *Graeculi* is used as metaphor for social and technical memory support systems. The association of memory and *Graeculi* is regarded as an extended memory system (Fig. 14.1). The metaphor implies a master–slave relation, with the master being the controlling agent. Then concerning memory functioning, the ideal master (a) knows the *Graeculus*' memory, including its capacity, its encoding specificities, its retrieval conditions; (b) initiates transfer of information to the *Graeculus* within the limits of (a); (c) memorizes (b); and (d) initiates prompts of the *Graeculus* within the limits of (a) and (c).

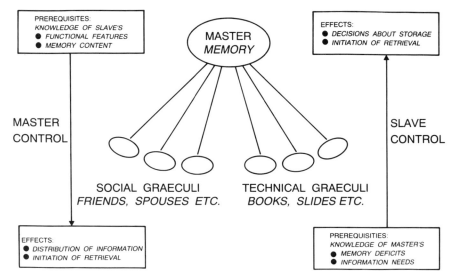

FIG. 14.1. *Graeculus* model of an extended memory system. Individual memory in the position of a master is served by social and technical aids in the position of sophisticated slaves. Both master and slaves may operate as controlling agents. The master as controlling agent distributes information to be stored at different locations, and initiates retrieval from these locations; for that purpose, the master must remember the allocation of information and the conditions of storage and retrieval at different locations. Sophisticated slaves as controlling agents decide themselves about their storage and retrieval; for that purpose, they must remember the master's memory deficits and monitor the master's information needs.

However, given the high social and educational status of Roman *Graeculi*, a *Graeculus* may equally serve as a controlling agent. Then concerning memory functioning, the ideal slave (a) monitors the master's needs and intentions, (b) knows the master's memory deficits, (c) acquires knowledge to compensate for (b) according to (a), and (d) prompts the master according to (c) and (a).

Hierarchical models are quite familiar in cognitive psychology (cf. Hampson & Morris, 1990), and extended memory systems have been designed before (e.g., Jones, 1986). The model presented here specifies the hierarchical aspects of extended memory systems. As a new feature the present model is more flexible regarding the distribution of control within extended memory systems. Effectively operating within such a system requires knowledge about the system. As outlined earlier, agents of control have to enter into their memory internal and external capacities and deficits, allocation of information, retrieval conditions, and so forth. Such knowledge can be subsumed under the now well-established concept of metamemory. *Metamemory* has been defined as knowledge of an individual's own memory, of memory tasks, and strategies of memorizing and recollection. In the context of individual memory performance, it was demonstrated that persons are able to predict the quality of their recall (e.g., Leonesio & Nelson, 1990), and to evaluate the effect of study time invested (Nelson & Leonesio, 1988); depending on their estimated probability of success, persons seem to regulate their efforts of recollection (Light, 1991). Similar effects have also been observed with memory supports. Dobbs and Rule (1987) reported adequate predictions of the efficiency of memory aids, and Schneider and Sodian (1988) of retrieval cues. Thus, when research proceeds from the individual memory to socially and technically extended memory systems, the concept of metamemory should equally extend to comprise knowledge about memory support and the interactions within these systems (Muthig & Schönpflug, 1981).

STORING IN AND RETRIEVING FROM
AN EXTERNAL STORE: TASK ANALYSIS
AND THREE KINTSCHIAN PROBLEMS

For a more elaborated treatment, a specific task will be analyzed: reproducing a text with the support of a data bank. A data bank is a now popular equivalent to a classical *Graeculus*. Given a technical support system and the present standards of commercial data banks, the control in the extended memory system studied is heavily shifted toward the user. Most obviously, an efficient user represents and considers the capacity and functional features of the data bank, whereas present commercial data banks neither represent the user's deficits nor react to these deficits. It is exclusively the user who has to initiate storage in and retrieval from the data bank in order to match the retrieved materials to personal needs and intentions (Schönpflug, 1986). In sum, the paradigm investigated here relates to the master-controlled version of the *Graeculus* model.

Figure 14.2 illustrates the steps required for reproducing a written text when a data bank is available for support (external storage and retrieval). For comparison, Fig. 14.2 also indicates the steps required when no data bank is available, and reproduction can only be accomplished by memorizing (internal storage and retrieval). In the latter case, individuals (a) read the text, (b) enter it into their internal memory, (c) retrieve the text after a retention period, (d) and write it down or otherwise reproduce the text. They may, but it is debatable whether they need to, memorize any of these steps, or construct a metamemory.

When a data bank is used the number of steps increases. Individuals (a) read the text, (e) identify locations of and within the data bank by means of an address, (f) transfer the text to the location (e), (g) enter into their internal memory the text as transferred (f), and (h) enter into their internal memory the associated address (e). (i) After the retention period, the individuals recall the availability of the text in the external store according to (g), (j) recall the associated external address according to (e), (k) enter to the data bank the address as recalled in (j). (l) When then the data bank displays the text, they read the text and (d) write it down or otherwise

INTERNAL
STORAGE

EXTERNAL
STORAGE

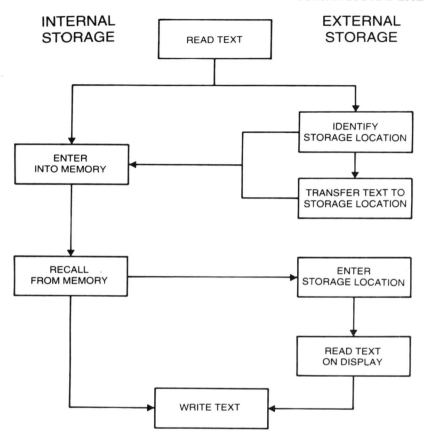

FIG. 14.2. Analysis of a text reproduction task. Two strategies are separated: (a) Memorizing and free recall, (b) transfer to and retrieval from a data bank.

reproduce it. In order to be able to retrieve from a standard data bank, users have to memorize the availability of the text in an external store (g) and the location of the externally stored materials (h). Obviously, the control of the data bank sets specific demands for the memory of the user, or rather requires the construction of a metamemory.

In this process of external storage, three problems arise that can be approached in terms of Kintschian theorizing: The internal representation of externally stored texts, the generation of addresses for representing external storage locations, and the internal control of external retrieval. The first problem results from the apparent paradox that an external text must be internally represented in order to enable the user to initiate retrieval. Particularly, if users must recall a text before external retrieval, why should they bother with the time-consuming operations of external retrieval? The paradox can be resolved by the assumption that the internal representation may be more parsimonious than the external, but still functional to initiate and control external retrieval. A strategy to generate such reduced internal representations is to apply macro-operators as W. Kintsch (1976), W. Kintsch and van Dijk (1978), and E. Kintsch (1990) demonstrated in their analyses of summarizing. Generating and memorizing a macrostructure of a text, and storing this text in full length and detail externally may be an economical option. The option is economical if the load on memory is reduced or the limits of memory capacity are overcome, and the benefits of external retrieval exceeds the operational costs (Schönpflug, 1986).

Similarly, the activation of macro-operators and macrostructures may support the generation of addresses and their association to texts. As a special feature, addresses for texts may be content descriptive (e.g., a coherent text about traveling to Europe may be stored under the address "Europe" as contrasted to location descriptive addresses such as "section 5" or random addresses such as "GW3P"). If content descriptive addresses match the texts they are more easily recalled to serve for external retrieval. Among the processes determining the match of texts and addresses are summarizing procedures (Schönpflug, 1988). Given a reduced internal representation, the initiation of external retrieval resembles the process of asking questions (Graesser & Black, 1985). But what are the internal cues for external retrieval? Apparently, the internal representation must provide empty slots to be filled or global concepts to be elaborated (e.g., "Helsinki is a capital," "what country is Helsinki a capital of?"). Elaboration is also among the processes emphasized in Kintsch's work (W. Kintsch & van Dijk, 1978). Beyond internal elaborations, interactions with external information stores may supplement and differentiate what is initially recalled. This interaction is based on metamemory, as defined earlier, especially on the recollection of information stores and the distribution of materials over stores.

Metamemory builds up during a longer period of time. Therefore, individuals not only remember external storage from a recent task, but also accumulate more extended knowledge about externally stored information. Accumulated knowledge about externally available information should be recognized as another type of situation model. Van Dijk and Kintsch (1983) defined situation models as knowledge structures that base comprehension and recall. Whereas studies of situation models until now have only treated target knowledge, we propose also to consider source knowledge as contents of situation models. The distinction between target and source knowledge is valuable for the analysis of metamemory. Most generally defined, source knowledge implies the representation of the context in which an information was obtained (e.g., "during the last cognitive science meeting") as contrasted to the information conveyed in this context (e.g., "a verification of the construction-integration model") (Schacter, Hrabluk, & McLachlan, 1984). More specifically, a source has been defined as a person or a document, from which a content has been obtained (Hanley & Collins, 1989). As related to extended memory systems, a source is defined as storage location and the operational features for encoding and retrieval at this location. Then, source knowledge can be contrasted to target knowledge, that is, knowledge of the information transferred to, available at, or retrieved from different storage locations (Schönpflug, 1988).

Apparently, source knowledge relates to metamemory as target knowledge relates to memory. With this distinction in mind, different situation models should be envisaged. Some situation models support comprehension and recall of target knowledge (e.g., "Mahler's symphonies," "oriental rugs"), others of source knowledge (e.g., "biographies of famous composers are compiled under their names in encyclopedias, but the variety of oriental rugs is poorly documented in standard encyclopedias"). Situation models being components of metamemory may account for a substantial portion of the processes involved in retrieval from an external information store.

TEXT HIERARCHIES AND MEMORY SAVINGS: AN EXPERIMENTAL PARADIGM

The hypothesis that external information storage leads to reduced internal representations was confirmed in an earlier experiment. Individuals save time for memorizing and recall less if they have the option to store texts in a data bank for later recall (Schönpflug & Esser, 1991). This was demonstrated in an experiment on text acquisition and reproduction. Three conditions were compared in the experiment: One group had a data bank at its disposal during the acquisition period, and was permitted to transfer the texts to the data bank; for each text a separate address had to be entered. The persons in this group were instructed that they were also permitted to use the data bank during the reproduction period; entering the correct address would display the text. However, contrary to the instruction, the persons in this group were not permitted to use the data bank during reproduction, but were restricted to free recall. (In order to maintain motivation, this was explained as simulating a realistic situation where a device is broken or lost.)

The recall scores of the first group served as estimates of text memory if support from a data bank is available. These scores were compared with the performance of another group that had no data bank at its disposal from the beginning. As the former group exhibited significantly lower recall than the latter, the reduction was interpreted as due to saving. A third experimental group should also be mentioned. This group was permitted to use a data bank during both acquisition and reproduction. This third group scored highest, so we concluded that the interaction with the data bank efficiently compensated for reduced memorizing as observed in the first group, and reduced recall can be explained by strategic selection rather than by generalized deterioration of performance.

When memory saving is an efficient option with external support available, the question arises as to how persons select what they enter into their memory and what they transfer to an external store. Based on Kintsch's reasoning outlined earlier, we tried to specify this question by applying the notion of a text hierarchy. We assumed that given the option of external storage, hierarchically low propositions should be stored externally; high propositions should be memorized and serve as retrieval cues for the externally stored low propositions.

To test this assumption, a new experiment was conducted that compared free recall after memorizing with and without a data bank. Six texts about Chinese history were presented for acquisition and reproduction. The texts consisted of a title and four sentences; each sentence consisted of 10 propositions. Two of the texts were hierarchically organized. A hierarchical organization was constructed according to a technique reported by E. Kintsch (1990): The first sentence explicated the title and introduced a focus on a Concept A. Sentence 2 explicated Concept A and introduced another focus on a Concept B. Sentence 3 explicated Concept B and introduced a focus on a Concept C. Finally, Sentence 4 explicated Concept C. For example, title and Sentences 1 and 2 from a hierarchical text read: "The Mandschu-dynasty. (1) During the Mandschu-dynasty . . . the prevailing tolerance is exhibited by the rulers treatment of foreign religions. (2) Various religions, and especially the Jesuit missionaries were welcomed at the courts of the . . . aristocracy." Formally, a coherence graph (W. Kintsch & van Dijk, 1978) was constructed, and propositions were classified as belonging to one of four levels, or rather four groups of levels within that graph.

Two other texts were nonhierarchical. Nonhierarchical texts were composed of propositions that formed a coherence graph with only one level as compared to the hierarchical texts. The four sentences in these texts related to the title, but there was no repetition of concepts in consecutive sentences. For example, the title and the following sentences in a nonhierarchical text read: "The Mongolians in China. (1) When the Mongolians under Dschingis-Khan invaded China, they succeeded to conquer the region of Hsia Hsia. . . . (2) Under Kublai-Khan . . . the Mongolians conquered entire China . . . and moved the capital to Peking." Two additional texts were constructed without regard for their propositional structure.

The six texts were successively exposed on a visual display. The four hierarchical and nonhierarchical texts appeared on Positions 2–5; their sequence varied randomly over individuals. In addition to these critical texts, we placed the two remaining texts as buffers on Positions 1 and 6.

Twenty-four students from various fields participated in the experiment. One half (Group 1) was randomly assigned to a condition where they were instructed to memorize the six texts to prepare themselves for a quiz. Another half (Group 2) received the same instruction. In addition, they were permitted to mark two sentences on the display for transfer to a file. They expected access to the file during the quiz. However, contrary to their expectation, retrieval from the file was not possible, and their answers in the quiz were restricted to free recall. The following quiz consisted of 20 questions. Sixteen questions were related to the four critical texts, one question to each sentence. The four additional questions related to the two buffer texts. The questions could be answered with a word concept.

According to the previous reasoning, we predicted more frequent transfer but lower recall for propositions low in the text hierarchy. We assumed that propositions high in the hierarchy would more likely be memorized to provide the cue for external retrieval. The nonhierarchical texts were introduced to control for sequence effects between consecutive sentences.

RESULTS FROM THE EXPERIMENT
ON THE INTERACTION OF TEXT HIERARCHY
AND EXTERNAL STORAGE

The results of the experiment on external storage and recall of different text levels were in line with our predictions. Scores for estimating the probability of filing a sentence were available from Group 2 (Fig. 14.3). The probability was highest for the first sentence, and gradually declined for the following sentences if the sentences were on the same level. If organized hierarchically, the third and fourth sentence constituting the lower text levels were more frequently transferred to the external file. The probability scores for external storage were submitted to an analysis of variance (ANOVA) with text hierarchy and sentence position as independent factors. The analysis yielded high significance for the interaction between text hierarchy and position of sentence in the text.

Sentences more frequently stored externally were less frequently recalled. To examine recall, the scores from Group 1 and Group 2 were compared (Fig. 14.4). Recall of hierarchical texts decreased from higher to lower levels, and the gradient was more pronounced after learning with a data bank available. The recall data were submitted to an ANOVA with text hierarchy, sentence position, and availability of a data as independent factors. From this analysis the triple interaction between text hierarchy, sentence position, and availability of a data bank was most relevant.

CONCLUSIONS: FUNCTIONS OF ACTIVE MEMORY
IN AN EXTENDED MEMORY SYSTEM

The experiments reported here should illustrate the case of memory as the controlling agent in an extended memory system. As the agent controlling external supports, human memory (a) internally represents the information stores available, and their specific encoding and retrieval conditions; (b) distributes information to be preserved over different stores according to (a); (c) extracts information transferred to different external stores according to (b); (d) preserves

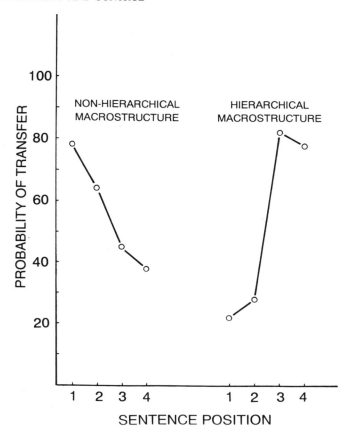

FIG. 14.3. Transfer of sentences from a text to a data bank, separated by type of text (hierarchical vs. nonhierarchical) and position of sentence in the text.

extracted information and the external allocation of full information according to (c); (e) initiates and coordinates retrieval from different external stores according to (d); and (f) connects free recall and information retrieved from external stores according to (e). Components (a) and (d) should further be considered in the conceptualization of metamemory. (See Weaver, Bryant, & Burns, chap. 10 in this volume, for a discussion of some of the aspects of metamemory applied to text comprehension.)

We appeal to enforce psychological research on extended memory systems. Apparently, human memory shares the fate of vision and hearing, of muscular strength and motor skills: Their biological evolution advances slower than their amplification and supplementation by external supports. It is even debatable whether biological functions still continue to evolve over generations or rather degrade due to the current organizational and technical progress. Our approach

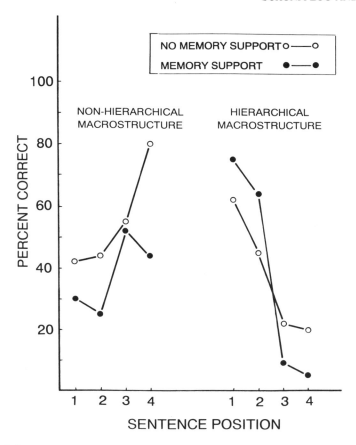

FIG. 14.4. Free recall of concepts from texts, separated by type of text (hierarchical vs. nonhierarchical), position of sentence to which the concept belonged, and availability of a data bank during acquisition.

is less skeptical regarding the role of human memory. Many functions of human memory may be taken over by external stores. Yet, external stores should rather extend than replace human memory capacity. External storage techniques should be a challenge for the development of memory rather than a cause for degeneration. We believe that humans could delegate memory tasks to external, especially technical extensions, and gain efficiency if devoting their internal memory capacity and developing their memory skills for better control of more extended memory systems. Such a shift from personal memorizing and remembering to the organization of an extended memory system should also have an impact on the construction of psychological models of memory. New models should put more emphasis on metamemory.

REFERENCES

Dobbs, A. R., & Rule, B. G. (1987). Prospective memory and self-reports of memory abilities in older adults. *Canadian Journal of Psychology, 41,* 209–222.

Graesser, A. C., & Black, J. B. (1985). *The psychology of questions.* Hillsdale, NJ: Lawrence Erlbaum Associates.

Grimal, P. (1986). *Cicéron.* Paris: Arthème Fayard.

Hampson, P. J., & Morris, P. E. (1990). Imagery, consciousness, and cognitive control: The BOSS model reviewed. In P. J. Hampson, D. F. Marks, & J. T. E. Richardson (Eds.), *Imagery* (pp. 78–102). London: Routledge.

Hanley, G. L., & Collins, V. L. (1989). Metamemory judgments and the origin and content of course information: Comparing text and lecture materials. *Journal of Educational Psychology, 81,* 3–8.

Jones, W. P. (1986). On the applied use of human memory models: The memory extender personal filing system. *International Journal of Man–Machine Studies, 25,* 191–228.

Kintsch, E. (1990). Macroprocesses and microprocesses in the development of summarization skills. *Cognition and Instruction, 7,* 161–195.

Kintsch, W. (1976). Memory for prose. In Ch. N. Cofer (Ed.), *The structure of human memory* (pp. 90–113). San Francisco: Freeman.

Kintsch, W., & van Dijk, T. A. (1978). Toward a model of text comprehension and production. *Psychological Review, 85,* 363–394.

Leonesio, R. J., & Nelson, T. O. (1990). Do different memory judgments tap the same underlying aspects of memory? *Journal of Experimental Psychology: Learning, Memory and Cognition, 16,* 464–470.

Light, L. L. (1991). Memory and aging: Four hypotheses in search of data. *Annual Review of Psychology, 42,* 333–376.

Muthig, K. P., & Schönpflug, W. (1981). Externe Speicher und rekonstruktives Verhalten [External storage and reconstructive behavior]. In W. Michaelis (Ed.), *Bericht über den 32. Kongreß der Deutschen Gesellschaft für Psychologie in Zürich 1980* (Vol. 1, pp. 225–229). Göttingen: Hogrefe.

Nelson, T. O., & Leonesio, R. J. (1988). Allocation of self-paced study time and the "labor-in-vain" effect. *Journal of Experimental Psychology: Learning, Memory and Cognition, 14,* 676–686.

Schacter, D. L., Harbluk, J. L., & McLachlan, D. R. (1984). Retrieval without recollection: An experimental analysis of source amnesia. *Journal of Verbal Learning and Verbal Behavior, 23,* 593–611.

Schneider, W., & Sodian, B. (1988). Metamemory-memory behavior relationships in young children: Evidence from a memory-for-location task. *Journal of Experimental Child Psychology, 45,* 209–233.

Schönpflug, W. (1986). The trade-off between internal and external information storage. *Journal of Memory and Language, 25,* 657–675.

Schönpflug, W. (1988). Retrieving texts from an external store: The effects of an explanatory context and of semantic fit between text and address. *Psychological Research, 50,* 19–27.

Schönpflug, W., & Esser, K. B. (1991). Das Lernen von Texten bei tatsächlicher und vermeintlicher externer Speicherung [Learning of texts and the availability of external storage devices]. *Zeitschrift für Psychologie* (Suppl. 11), 260–267.

van Dijk, T. A., & Kintsch, W. (1983). *Strategies of discourse comprehension.* New York: Academic Press.

Chapter 15

The Acquisition of Knowledge from Text and Example Situations: An Extension to the Construction-Integration Model

Franz Schmalhofer
DFKI, Universität Kaiserslautern

THE ACQUISITION OF KNOWLEDGE FROM TEXT AND EXAMPLE SITUATIONS

Recent research on the acquisition of knowledge has suggested that texts should not contain any examples because they may distract the reader from deeply processing the text (LeFevre & Dixon, 1986). On the other hand, it is a generally held belief that good learning materials should consist of general descriptions in the form of text as well as concrete examples. This chapter first discusses the research on learning from text and examples and presents an integrated computational model of such learning. It then reports two experiments in which the information given in the text stood in a more natural relation to the examples than in the experiments of LeFevre and Dixon. The experimental results are discussed in terms of the extended construction-integration model that describes knowledge acquisition from text and examples in a unified way.

Learning from Text

Current theories of text processing assume that comprehension processes combine the explicit statements from the study material (i.e., the text) with the prior knowledge of the reader (Kintsch, 1988; Singer, Andrusiak, Reisdorf, & Black, 1992). This is accomplished by two types of inferences: automatic inferences and strategic inferences.

Automatic inferences establish coherent representations of concurrently processed parts of the text. These inferences rely on the knowledge of the reader that is quickly and easily available (McKoon & Ratcliff, 1992). This processing produces a *textbase* that is a veridical representation of the meaning of the text and its structure (Kintsch & van Dijk, 1978; Miller & Kintsch, 1980). A textbase is thus closely coupled to the text itself.

When learning from text, a reader may pursue specific learning goals. These learning goals, in addition, yield *strategic inferences* (Trabasso & van den Broek, 1985) that may construct a separate knowledge representation. Such knowledge representations that are not so closely tied to the text itself, but instead reflect the structure of the domain about which knowledge is to be acquired have been termed *situation models* (van Dijk & Kintsch, 1983). It has been shown that in text comprehension situation models are indeed constructed and updated (Fletcher & Chrysler, 1990; Morrow, Bower, & Greenspan, 1989; Morrow, Greenspan, & Bower, 1987; Perrig & Kintsch, 1985). Situation models are constructed in such a way so that they are well suited for solving the anticipated tasks (Schmalhofer & Glavanov, 1986). Unlike the formation of a textbase, the construction of a (appropriate) situation model may require some significant amount of prior domain knowledge (Kintsch, Welsch, Schmalhofer, & Zimny, 1990).

Learning from Examples

Learning from examples has recently become a quite active topic of research. Thereby, the importance of examples for acquiring knowledge in various domains, such as computer programing, mathematics, and physics, has been convincingly demonstrated. Anderson, Farrell, and Sauers (1984) and Pirolli and Anderson (1985) found that in learning to program in LISP, subjects with no prior computer experience relied on concrete examples (i.e., LISP programs) and made very little use of written instructions. From a few similar LISP examples, subjects extracted a so-called *template*. A template is some intermediate knowledge representation that reflects the structural relations among the various surface features of an example. Analogical reasoning may thus be employed to solve a related problem on the basis of a template. Anderson et al. (1984) described, how a subject used such a template to solve a programing task that was somehow related to a previously studied example.

Lewis (1988) investigated how computer-naive subjects understand example sequences of user actions and computer events. His results showed that subjects employed commonsense knowledge. For instance, temporal relationships were analyzed to conjecture a causal relationship between an action and an event. With such commonsense knowledge, the subjects induced rather abstract hypotheses about causal relationships and identities between separately referenced objects. Quintessential hypotheses were thus formed rather than templates. Such hypotheses may be seen as part of a coherent causal structure (Waldmann, Holyoak, & Fratianne, 1993) in a situation model. The self-explanation effect (Chi, Bassok, Lewis, Reimann, & Glaser, 1989; van Lehn, Jones, & Chi, 1992) also demonstrated the significance of a learner's prior knowledge for acquiring deep knowledge from examples.

Learning from examples is believed to be very effective because it requires the learner to actively engage in constructing knowledge rather than simply storing presented information (Black, Carroll, & McGuigan, 1987; Carroll, Mack, Lewis, Grischkowsky, & Robertson, 1985). It may be even more effective when the examples are self-generated rather than being supplied by a teacher (see Schmalhofer & Kühn, 1988). Self-generated examples arise in learning by exploration, in which a learner generates some action in an environment that subsequently yields a specific reaction from the environment. A learner's input to a LISP system together with the corresponding response from the LISP system can be seen as a self-generated example and learning by exploration consists of a sequence of such self-generated examples. Schmalhofer and Kühn (1988) found that subjects with prior domain knowledge were better in writing simple computer programs when they had learned by exploration than when they learned from a teacher-supplied sequence of examples. This difference between the two learning materials was not observed for the subjects who did not have prior domain knowledge.

Learning from Text and Examples

Knowledge can obviously be acquired from text, examples, and a combination of text and examples. Texts will only play an important role for acquiring knowledge if the readers engage in strategic inferences and construct a situation model. This may, however, require some prior domain knowledge that is not easily accessible or not even available at all. The studies on learning from examples show that practically useful knowledge can be acquired with or without prior domain knowledge. When the appropriate prior knowledge is available, a reader may certainly construct a situation model. Without prior knowledge, a reader may still build practically useful templates as an intermediate knowledge representation. It would thus appear that in comparison to examples texts are relatively unimportant for learners without prior domain knowledge. Alternatively, it could be expected, that learners without specific domain knowledge would employ some common-sense knowledge and construct at least some partial situation model. The experimental results of Lewis (1988) show that, in combination with examples, commonsense knowledge can indeed be applied to form a situation model.

In a sequence of six experiments, LeFevre and Dixon (1986) have compared the relative efficacy of the two learning materials. They had subjects study a text together with an example. Although the subjects were led to believe that text and example would provide consistent information, the text actually described one procedure and the example demonstrated another clearly distinct procedure. After the subjects had read these conflicting materials, they were asked to perform the procedure that had supposedly been presented in the learning material. Several control measures indicated that the subjects did not notice that the information from the text was in conflict with the information provided by the examples. Because most subjects consistently used the information from the examples and disregarded the text, LeFevre and Dixon concluded that learners would process a text only superficially when other sources of information, such as examples, are available.

Example-Dominance Hypothesis

In order to interpret LeFevre and Dixon's results in terms of current theories of text processing, it may be assumed that in learning from text and examples, learners do not perform strategic inferencing when reading the text: Only automatic inferencing is performed (McKoon & Ratcliff, 1992) and only a textbase is formed. From the examples, on the other hand, a template base and a (partial) situation model are constructed. However, no attempts are made to integrate the textbase with the situation model or template base. The textbase, on the one hand, and the template base and situation model, on the other hand, exist in memory completely independent of one another. When the subjects are subsequently tested, they will either retrieve information from the textbase or utilize the template base and situation model. Test performance that relies on the template base and the situation model therefore does not depend on the studied text, and test performance that relies on the textbase does not depend on the studied examples. Consequently, subjects would not even notice when text and examples contradict each other. Such a result has been observed in LeFevre and Dixon's experiments.

This explanation rests on three assumptions: the encoding of a text is independent of the encoding of examples, there is only a shallow processing of the text, and examples may be understood at a deeper level. The examples are viewed as the most important part of the instruction materials, so the combination of the three assumptions is termed the *example-dominance hypothesis*. LeFevre and Dixon (1986) concluded from their experiments, in support of this hypothesis, that their results would paradoxically recommend against the use of examples in texts: Because readers are inclined to process a text only shallowly when examples are present, examples would prevent a deep level understanding of the text, thus making the text completely useless for acquiring new domain knowledge (LeFevre & Dixon, 1986, p. 29). A quite different hypothesis is obtained from the KIWi model, which was designed as an extension of Kintsch's construction-integration model in order to integratively explain the acquisition of knowledge from text and example situations. Such example situations are frequently also referred to as cases (Redmond, 1989; Seifert, 1989).

THE KIWi MODEL

An overview of the representational and processing assumptions of the KIWi model is given in Fig. 15.1.[1] As shown in Fig. 15.1, a learner's prior knowledge

---

[1]KIWi stands for *Konstruktion und Integration von Wissen* (construction and integration of knowledge).

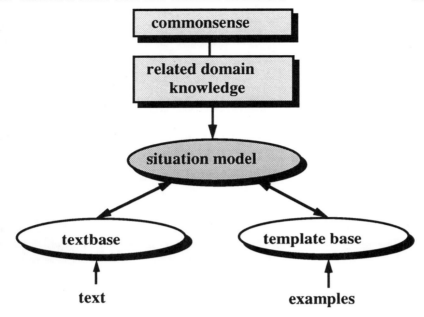

FIG. 15.1. Representational and processing assumptions of the KIWi model.

is assumed to consist of commonsense knowledge and related domain knowledge. Different learners may vary with respect to their prior knowledge. Three knowledge representations are distinguished: the situation model, the textbase, and the template base.

Knowledge Representation

A *situation model* represents the structures and possible transitions of some real-world domain (van Dijk & Kintsch, 1983). A completely and correctly constructed situation model can be understood as an abstract model of the domain as well as the actions that can be performed in the domain. Situation models may, however, sometimes be incomplete and/or contain incorrect hypotheses, which must be revised one or several times before the correct hypotheses are found. When a situation model is constructed, other knowledge (i.e., a textbase or a template base) is built en route to the construction of the situation model.

The *textbase*, which is formed when a learner studies a text, represents the structure and the meaning of the text (Kintsch, 1974). A textbase is built with *propositions*. Propositions are the basic meaning units of texts. A textbase has a micro- and a macrostructure that reflect the local and global coherence of the text, respectively.

A *template base* consists of typical patterns of the domain, which may be indexed by knowledge units from the situation model. Such patterns or templates can be generalized from specific examples (Anderson et al., 1984). This generalization is performed by using information from the situation model or commonsense and heuristic knowledge. Because such patterns conform to the general rules in the situation model, they may also be deduced from the knowledge of the situation model.[2]

During the construction of a situation model, three logical types of knowledge are distinguished in the computer simulation of the KIWi model. The first type of knowledge comprises the rules and facts that are assumed to be true and are thus not modified when new knowledge is acquired. Furthermore, the new knowledge is acquired in such a way that it is consistent with these knowledge units. The second type of knowledge consists of the hypotheses that are currently held by the learner and are modified when additional information becomes available. The hypotheses can have different degrees of confidence that reflect their modifiability. Hypotheses with a high degree of confidence are only modified when the amount of contradicting information is overwhelming. The third type of knowledge encompasses the heuristics that generate or modify hypotheses.

Learning from Text

In the KIWi model, the text studied is assumed to consist of a number of statements that provide the learner with true information about the domain. As a rational analysis has shown (Schmalhofer, Kühn, & Boschert, 1994), simply storing the text statements would be completely inadequate with respect to the learning goal. An isolated piece of information could neither be remembered nor utilized to solve a future task, thus the new information must be integrated into existing knowledge structures. This integration is performed by first comparing the studied statement to the existing knowledge. The comparison shows whether the statement tells something the learner already knows (redundant statement), whether it contradicts the current knowledge of the learner (contradicting statement), or whether it provides new information (new statement). This distinction, which is essential for adequately integrating the provided knowledge, is made by a limited number of inference steps and with a limited number of knowledge units, which are selected by a spreading activation mechanism (Kintsch, 1988).

Redundant statements are only added to the situation model if they enhance the explicitness of the situation model (i.e., if a long inference chain would otherwise be needed to derive them). A statement that is redundant with respect to some hypothesis replaces the respective hypothesis. No further processing is required of redundant statements in order to achieve an optimal integration.

For contradicting statements, the contradiction with the situation model is resolved. The possibility of maintaining a hypothesis despite an existing contra-

---

[2]Examples of the three types of knowledge representations (textbase, template base, situation model) have been presented in Schmalhofer, Boschert, and Kühn, (1990).

diction has not yet been considered or implemented in the KIWi model (see, however, Otero & Kintsch, 1992). If the statement contradicts information of a type known, the learning process is interrupted and a question is asked (Graesser & McMahen, 1993). If the statement contradicts a hypothesis, three different cases must be distinguished:

1. If the contradicting statement is more general than the hypothesis, the hypothesis is substituted by the statement, and any inferences derived from the hypothesis are generalized accordingly.

2. If the contradicting statement is more specific, the hypothesis is too general. The overgeneralized hypothesis is consequently replaced by the contradicting statement. The statements that have been derived from the overgeneralized hypothesis are specialized accordingly.

3. If the statement contradicts a hypothesis without being more general or more specific, the hypothesis is replaced by the contradicting statement, and any information derived from the hypothesis is withdrawn from the situation model.

New statements (i.e., statements that are neither redundant nor contradicting) become part of the situation model. The coherence of the new statement to the situation model is established by deriving inferences from the new statement and the knowledge base. When generating inferences, the knowledge is searched from specific to more general domains. Superordinate domains, such as programing and commonsense, may thus also be used in constructing the situation model. Through the application of commonsense knowledge, it can be explained that under certain circumstances even novices may succeed in forming a partial situation model. By storing inferences in the situation model, its explicitness is increased. Because it is assumed that there is a cost associated with each inference being performed, the inferencing process should stop when the expected utility of the additional inference is exceeded by the cost of its generation. In the current computer simulation of the KIWi model, these considerations are accounted for by performing only a fixed number of inferences for each new statement. A more technical account of the learning processes from text, examples, and by exploration has been presented by Bergmann, Boschert, and Schmalhofer (1992); Schmalhofer and Kühn (1991); and Schmalhofer, Bergmann, Boschert, and Thoben (1993).

Learning from Examples

For learning from examples, the rational analysis showed that the specific information contained in the examples must be generalized in order to be applicable to a larger variety of tasks. For an optimal and efficient integration of an example, it must again be determined whether the example contains redundant, contradicting, or new information.

Although redundant examples do not contain any novel information, they may still be used to explicate knowledge that is currently only implicitly contained in the situation model. The examples are known to be actual interactions in the world, so contradicting examples provide evidence that one or several hypotheses of the situation model are incorrect. Consequently, commonsense heuristics are employed to modify or even replace hypotheses so that the example can be explained. In addition, the inferences derived on the basis of the old hypotheses are appropriately modified or excluded.

For new examples, the heuristic rules from the commonsense knowledge are employed to generate hypotheses so that the example input is mentally evaluated into the observed example result. These hypotheses thus fill the gaps in the situation model and represent the new knowledge that was acquired from the example, the situation model, and commonsense heuristics. The mental evaluation, including the generated hypotheses, provides an explanation of how the specific example input is transformed into the example result. A template is constructed from the obtained explanation. The template is then added to the template base and the respective hypothesis is added to the situation model.

Learning by Exploration

In learning by exploration, the learners themselves must instigate the learning process by starting an interaction with some environment. Whereas most efficient learning can take place when both general and specific questions may be asked, learning by exploration only yields answers to specific questions. In order to generate a question, the situation model is searched for some insufficiently tested hypothesis. Insufficiently tested hypotheses are identified by low confidence values and by the lack of tested alternative hypotheses. From the selected hypothesis, a question is then generated by a sequence of forward and backward inferences. The number of inferencing steps required depends on the explicitness of the situation model. If templates are available, they are utilized for generating a question, and hence only a small number of inferences have to be performed. The generated question is then asked to the environment, and an answer is obtained. The question and the answer to the question constitute an example from which knowledge can be acquired, as in learning from examples.

Learning From Text That Is Followed by Examples

In the previous descriptions of the three learning methods, it was emphasized that the acquisition of knowledge depends on the currently existing knowledge. Because the application of a combination of learning methods can be seen as applying a particular learning method given some existing knowledge, it can easily be determined what knowledge will be acquired from a text and succeeding examples (that may be either presented by the experimenter or generated by the learner). If examples are studied after text (i.e., all the relevant statements have been told), then these statements can be employed to construct templates from the presented examples. Through the previously derived inferences, a considerably shorter explanation is obtained. Studying and inferencing from text thus facilitates the explication of knowledge from subsequent examples.

Knowledge Utilization

In the KIWi model there is a close relation between the acquisition and the utilization of knowledge. On the one hand, learning always involves the utilization of the existing knowledge, and, on the other hand, the inferences made during learning are also used for solving new tasks.

One form of knowledge utilization is the solution of verification tasks. In order to verify a given sentence or example, the system can simply perform the first step as in learning from text or examples (i.e., determine whether the item to be verified is redundant, contradicting, or new with respect to the current knowledge). In these three cases, the answers of the system should be "Yes," "No," and "Don't know," respectively. If the third answer is not acceptable, the system employs heuristics for generating plausible hypotheses from which either a "Yes" or "No" answer can be derived. This procedure corresponds to the generation of hypotheses when trying to explain a new example.

The time needed to answer a verification task will depend on the number of inference steps required for its derivation. In particular, very short latencies should be observed for those sentences that can be verified with the textbase alone and for those examples that match or contradict a template in the template base. In a similar way, experimental predictions can be derived for the performance in synthetic tasks, such as the construction of computer programs (e.g., Doane, McNamara, Kintsch, Polson, & Clawson, 1992; Mannes & Kintsch, 1991).

Integrated Knowledge Acquisition Hypothesis

Given that in real life examples are frequently presented together with text and both materials play an important role for acquiring new knowledge, something appears to be fundamentally wrong with LeFevre and Dixon's recommendations. Although the use of contradictory information allowed LeFevre and Dixon to decide which material dominated the other, it must be noted that such learning materials are quite unnatural. Rather than presenting conflicting or competing information, text and examples should provide consistent and supplementary information. It is therefore questionable whether or not the *example-dominance hypothesis* would also hold for more natural learning materials in which text and examples are consistent and supplement each other.

An alternative to the example dominance hypotheses is the *integrated knowledge acquisition hypothesis*. This hypothesis is derived from the KIWi model, which has been implemented as a computer simulation (Bergmann et al., 1992; Schmalhofer & Kühn, 1991). According to this hypothesis, subjects may very well perform strategic inferencing when studying a text. Next to the textbase, the learners will therefore also construct a more or less complete situation model. The completeness of the situation model depends on the information provided by the text and the learner's prior domain knowledge. When studying subsequent examples, the partially constructed situation model can assist in forming a template base. The (partial) situation model may simultaneously be augmented by abstract hypotheses, which are obtained by interpreting the studied examples in terms of the situation model. In the situation model, the knowledge acquired from the text is thus integrated with the information provided by the examples.

How much new knowledge can or needs to be acquired from the examples depends on the completeness of the information provided by the text. When the text contains sufficient information, the presented examples can be completely explained with the knowledge acquired from the text (Mitchell, Keller, & Kedar-Cabelli, 1986). When some information is deleted from the text, questions are generated (Graesser & McMahen, 1993) and commonsense is used to extract the requested situation knowledge from the examples. When no text is presented, only the examples are available from which a (partial) situation model can be constructed by commonsense considerations (Lewis, 1988). For test tasks that query the text, the text representations and the situation model are utilized (Schmalhofer & Glavanov, 1986). For test tasks that are oriented toward the examples, the situation model is utilized together with the template base. According to the integrated knowledge acquisition hypothesis, the test performance in different tasks would thus depend on the studied examples as well as the amount of text information that had been presented.

Experimental Predictions

Two experiments were performed in which the example-dominance hypothesis could be compared to the integrated knowledge acquisition hypothesis in a more natural learning situation. In both experiments, the amount of text information about a concept of the programing language LISP was systematically manipulated. In three experimental conditions (complete-text, partial-text, and no-text conditions), a LISP function was completely described in the text, partially described in the text, or no text at all was presented. Under all three conditions more knowledge about the same LISP function could then be acquired from examples. Whereas in Experiment 1 an identical sequence of examples was presented to all subjects, in Experiment 2 the subjects learned by exploration; therefore all subjects generated their own sequence of examples. Because learning from examples is believed to be particularly effective when the examples are self-generated, proponents of the example-dominance hypothesis would expect this hypothesis to hold in particular for learning by exploration.

Although the subjects did not have any prior knowledge about programing, they had pertinent commonsense knowledge that they might use to build (at least partial) situation models. In both experiments the subjects' acquired knowledge was tested by sentence and example verification tasks. As a baseline control, a LISP function that had not been presented during the study phase was also tested with a corresponding set of sentences and examples. In order to avoid possible problems in interpreting the experimental results due to trade-offs between the speed and the accuracy of the responses in the different experimental conditions, speed-accuracy trade-off functions were collected with a tapping procedure (Wickelgren, Corbett, & Dosher, 1980). The subjects had to indicate their confidence for every response in this procedure. By pressing one of two buttons, the subjects expressed their current belief about the correctness of the presented item (sentence or example). In addition, they had to press the button for a variable length of time so that the duration of the button press would indicate their confidence.

The following predictions are derived from the two competing hypotheses for the sentence verification tasks of both experiments. The example-dominance hypothesis assumes that independent structures are formed when studying text (textbase) and examples (template base and situation model). The test sentences are only compared to the textbase, so the knowledge acquired from examples would not have any effect on the performance in the sentence verification task. The complete-text condition would consequently yield more correct answers than the partial-text condition, which would in turn yield more correct answers than the no-text condition. Because the textbase remains isolated from the information acquired from the examples, the no-text condition is predicted to perform at the level of the baseline control. The integrated knowledge acquisition hypothesis, on the other hand, assumes that textbase, situation model, and template base form one integrated structure with three representations. For verifying sentences, the textbase and the situation model can be used. The knowledge acquired from examples will thus also assist in verifying sentences. The no-text condition is therefore predicted to perform clearly better than the baseline control.

The following predictions are derived for the example verification tasks of both experiments. The example-dominance hypothesis assumes that the test examples are only compared to the template base and the situation model without utilizing any text information. When there are no differences in the examples studied, subjects should perform equally well in the complete-text condition, the partial-text condition, and the no-text condition. The performance in these conditions should, however, be clearly better than in the baseline control condition. The integrated knowledge acquisition hypothesis, on the other hand, assumes that the text information is used for a better understanding of the examples. The knowledge acquired from text will thus also assist in verifying examples and, therefore, the more text that has been presented, the better the performance in the example verification tasks.

EXPERIMENT 1

Method

A 3 × 3 × 3 Greco-Latin square design was used to counterbalance the experimental manipulation—that is, the complete-text, partial-text, and no-text conditions with the specific LISP functions (i.e., FIRST, EQUAL, LIST)—and the order in which these functions were studied. In this within-subjects design, a subject thus learned one function from a complete text with examples, another function from a partial text with examples, and a third function from examples alone. A fourth function (i.e., REST) was only tested but never studied.

Subjects. Fifty-four University of Colorado students, who did not have any prior knowledge about computer programing, completed the experiment successfully. An additional six subjects failed to pass a criterion test task six times in a row (administered after the first learning phase) and the experiment was terminated without recording any further data.

Materials. The learning materials consisted of the learning materials, which were prerequisite for understanding the experimental learning materials, and the experimental learning materials, in which three specific LISP functions were explained (FIRST, EQUAL, LIST).

The prerequisite learning materials consisted of 16 paragraphs with two to four sentences per paragraph. The introduction consisted of a motivating paragraph. The main topics were how a user interacts with the LISP system; data representations (atoms and lists) in LISP; the evaluation of terms in LISP; and how functions are defined, namely that a function is defined by three specifications: the number of arguments, the type of argument, and the input–output relation. In the last paragraph the presented material was summarized.

The prerequisite learning material consisted of text with some examples and was sufficient for adequately understanding the specific LISP functions to be learned from the experimental learning materials. This sufficiency was demonstrated by running the KIWi model on a formalization of the learning materials: With the content sentences from the prerequisite learning materials, the KIWi model could construct a situational representation of a specific LISP function from the complete description of the function (text) as well as from the sequence of examples used as part of the experimental learning materials. In a previous experiment, Schmalhofer, Boschert, and Kühn (1990) showed that text and examples that were constructed according to this sufficiency criterion did indeed yield an equivalent situation model when the learners were provided with long study phases.

The experimental learning materials described three specific LISP functions. For each function the materials consisted of an introductory sentence together

TABLE 15.1
Learning Materials for the Function FIRST

Now we will introduce the function FIRST.
* The function FIRST is used to select an s-expression from a list.
# The function FIRST requires exactly one argument.
# The argument of the function FIRST must be a list.
* The function FIRST returns the first s-expression of the given argument.

The following examples illustrate how the function FIRST is to be used. The inputs to the LISP system are shown on the left side and the results returned by the system are shown on the right side on the same line after an arrow.

(FIRST '(A B C D))	$\rightarrow$	A
(FIRST '(H (L (P Y))))	$\rightarrow$	H
(FIRST '((Z Q T) (J)))	$\rightarrow$	(Z Q T)
(FIRST '((M E) (I R)))	$\rightarrow$	(M E)

with zero, two, or four content sentences (depending on the experimental condition) followed by two transition sentences and four specific examples. The examples provided as much information as was needed, so that when given unlimited processing resources, the KIWi model would construct a correct representation of the situation model under all three experimental conditions. The learning material for the function FIRST in the complete-text condition is shown in Table 15.1. In the partial-text condition the same material was used, except that the sentences marked with a * were missing. In the no-text condition the sentences marked with # were missing.

The test materials consisted of 24 test sentences and 16 examples. For each of four LISP functions (FIRST, EQUAL, LIST, and REST), 6 test sentences were constructed. The 6 sentences of a function consisted of 3 correct and 3 incorrect test sentences addressing the number of arguments, the type of argument, and the input–output relation of the function. The correct sentences were taken directly from the experimental learning material.[3] The incorrect sentences were obtained by exchanging corresponding properties between different functions.

There were 4 test examples for each function. The 2 correct examples were directly taken from the learning material. Two incorrect examples were constructed by employing an argument specification or an input–output relation from a different function or function combination. The test materials for the function FIRST are shown in Table 15.2.

Procedure. The experiment was run on two IBM-PC/AT personal computers, to which a box with three buttons and a sound generator were connected. Headphones were used for presenting the response signals in the sentence and example

---

[3]Because the function REST was used for the baseline control, the text and the examples for the function REST were not used as learning material.

TABLE 15.2
Test Materials for the Function FIRST

Correct	Incorrect
Sentences	
The function FIRST requires exactly one argument.	The function FIRST can be given any number of arguments.
The argument of the function FIRST must be a list.	The argument to the function FIRST can be an atom and/or a list.
The function FIRST returns the first s-expression of the given argument.	The function FIRST returns a list of all the s-expressions which were given as arguments.
Examples	
(FIRST '((Z Q T) (J))) → (Z Q T)	(FIRST '(Z Q T) '(J)) → (Z Q T)
(FIRST '((M E) (I R))) → (M E)	(FIRST '((M E) (I R))) → M

verification tasks. In a practice session with unrelated materials, the subjects were first trained to study learning materials on the computer screen and to respond according to the requirements of the tapping speed-accuracy trade-off method in the verification tasks.

In the first learning phase, the subjects acquired basic knowledge about data representations (atoms and lists) in LISP, the evaluation of terms in LISP, and how functions are defined. The subjects were instructed to study all learning materials as if they were preparing for an exam in one of their classes. The learning materials were shown in a window on the screen. Unlike the second learning phase, the subjects could move freely here between the paragraphs using the buttons of the button box. However, they could only study one paragraph at a time. The subjects were free to study the material as long as they wanted. The first learning phase was repeated until a subject correctly solved 80% of the items on a following test task or had failed this test six times in a row, in which case the experiment was terminated.

In the second learning phase, the subjects learned about the three specific LISP functions: FIRST, LIST, and EQUAL. Every subject had to learn each function and was presented with exactly one complete text followed by examples, one partial text followed by examples, and one set of examples unaccompanied by text. The sentences and examples were presented one at a time. After they had finished reading an item (i.e., a sentence or an example), they pushed a button and the next item was shown. Reading times were recorded for each sentence and for each example.

In the test phase, which followed the second learning phase, the subjects had to perform the sentence and the example verification tasks. The 24 test sentences were presented individually followed by the 16 examples, all in random order. In order to obtain information about the time course of knowledge utilization and in order to control possible trade-off effects of response time and response accuracy, a tapping speed accuracy trade-off paradigm was used (Wickelgren et al., 1980): The subjects had to give six responses to each sentence or example. The subjects made the first response .75 sec before the test sentence or the test example was presented on the screen. Here, the subjects could only guess, but for the following responses they had increasingly more time to fully process the test item. The following five responses were probed by response signals (tones) that occurred 2 sec apart. The last response signal differed from the previous ones in tone, indicating that there was no time pressure for the final response. For each button press, the subjects were asked to indicate the confidence in their decision by the duration of the button press, with short durations indicating low confidence and long durations indicating high confidence.

Results

A reading times analysis of the individual sentences and examples showed that there was no difference among the three experimental conditions and the reading times decreased from the first to the last presented LISP function. Similar position effects were also found in the analysis of the sentence and example verification tasks. For instance, in the sentence verification tasks differences among the three experimental conditions were more clearly visible for the first than for the last studied LISP function. For the third LISP function, subjects may thus have utilized analogies (Anderson et al., 1984; Novick & Holyoak, 1991) to the previous LISP functions, and thereby improved their performance. Such effects are, however, not suited for differentiating between the example-dominance and integrated knowledge acquisition hypotheses. Because the counterbalancing scheme was only used to control the effects of the specific LISP functions and their position in the learning material, these particular effects need not be reported in any detail.

Sentence Verification. The speed-accuracy trade-off functions of Fig. 15.2 show the relative frequencies of correct responses for the different processing times in the sentence verification task. All the following results were significant. The available processing time and the amount of learning material (complete-text, partial-text, no-text conditions and baseline control) studied affected the correctness of a response. There was also an interaction. At the asymptote of the speed-accuracy trade-off function (i.e., the subjects' responses, which occurred approximately 11 sec after the presentation of the sentence), the test sentences were verified better in the complete-text condition than in the partial-text condition. The partial-text condition was better than the no-text condition, which in turn was better than the baseline control, where no learning material at all had been presented. Correct knowledge was generally acquired from the three types of learning materials (complete-text, partial-text, no-text conditions). For the baseline control, where subjects had not received any learning materials at all, they

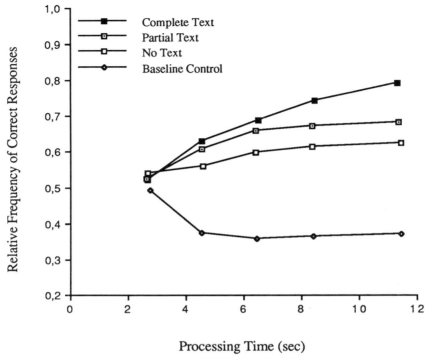

FIG. 15.2.   Relative frequency of correct responses for the pooled test sentences as a function of different amounts of learning materials and at different processing times.

did not respond at chance but made frequently incorrect inferences when they were tested.

The duration of the subjects' button presses, which indicated the confidence in the specific response, were scaled according to the procedure proposed by Wickelgren et al. (1980). This scaling procedure yields confidence ratings that range between 1 and 9. The confidence ratings for the responses are shown in Fig. 15.3. Amount of learning materials and the available processing time also significantly influenced the subjects' confidence in their responses. In addition, there was a significant interaction effect. When no learning material was studied (baseline control), the subjects' confidence was lower than when only examples were presented (no-text condition). The subjects' confidence was about equal for all three experimental conditions.

Depending on the experimental condition, a test sentence may have been explicitly presented or had to be inferred from the examples in combination with the basic LISP knowledge. In order to analyze which inferences were made in the different experimental conditions, the two sentences addressing the input–output relation of a LISP function (explicitly presented only in the complete-text

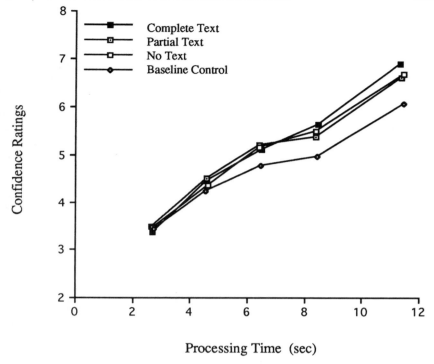

FIG. 15.3. Average confidence ratings in a response for the pooled test sentences as a function of different amounts of learning materials and at different processing times.

condition) and the two sentences addressing the argument specification of a LISP function (explicitly presented in the complete- and partial-text conditions) were separately analyzed.

The results for the input–output sentences are shown in Fig. 15.4. Again, the correctness of a response increased with the amount of learning materials and the available processing time and there was also an interaction effect. For the subjects' responses, which occurred approximately 11 sec after the presentation of the sentences, the no-text condition performed better than the baseline control and there was no significant difference among the three experimental conditions. For the no-text and partial-text conditions, subjects thus correctly inferred the input–output relation from the studied examples. In the complete-text condition, where the input–output relation had been explicitly stated, the input–output test sentences were correctly verified more often, although this difference did not turn out to be statistically significant. Where no learning materials were presented, the subjects performed at about chance level.

The results for the sentences addressing the argument specifications, shown in Fig. 15.5, indicate once more that the amount of the studied learning material

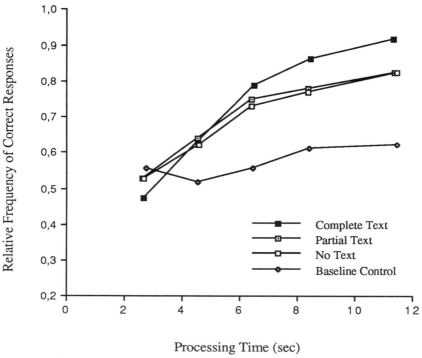

FIG. 15.4.   Relative frequency of correct responses for the input–output sentences as a function of different amounts of learning materials and at different processing times.

affected the correctness of a response. Whereas the available processing time was not significant, there was a significant interaction effect. This is explained by the baseline control yielding mostly incorrect answers and the three experimental conditions yielding mostly correct answers. For the subjects' last responses, there was no significant difference between the complete-text condition and the partial-text condition. The partial-text condition was better than the no-text condition, which in turn was clearly better than the baseline control. In summary, in the complete-text and partial-text conditions, where the argument specifications had been explicitly stated, the particular test sentences were correctly verified about equally well. In the no-text condition, the subjects performed about at chance level. In general, the analysis of the confidence ratings for the different sentence types yielded the same results that had already been obtained from the analysis of the pooled test sentences.

Example Verification.   Figure 15.6 shows the relative frequencies of correct responses for the different processing times in the example verification task. The available processing time and the amount of learning material affected the cor-

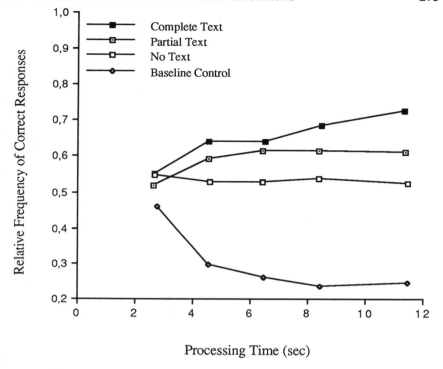

FIG. 15.5. Relative frequency of correct responses for the argument specification sentences as a function of different amounts of learning materials and at different processing times.

rectness of a response, and there was no significant interaction. The complete-text condition performed better than the partial-text condition for the two responses in the processing interval between 6 and 10 sec. The no-text condition performed better than the baseline control for the response given about 6 sec after the presentation of the example. The information acquired from text thus also affected the performance in the verification of the example tasks.

Discussion

In general, the example-dominance hypothesis is supported by results showing that the performance in the sentence verification task depends only on the studied text and the performance in the example verification task depends only on the studied examples. The integrated knowledge acquisition hypothesis, on the other hand, is supported by results showing that the performance in the sentence verification task also depends on the studied examples and the performance in the example verification task also depends on the studied sentences.

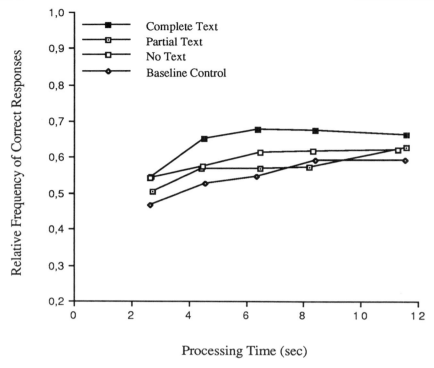

FIG. 15.6. Relative frequency of correct responses for the pooled test examples as a function of different amounts of learning materials and at different processing times.

The analysis of the sentence verification tasks showed the following response patterns: Statements explicitly presented in a condition could be better verified than test sentences that had to be inferred. This result shows that the text had at least been superficially processed and does not discriminate between the two competing hypotheses. In addition, test sentences not explicitly presented in the text were better inferred when examples had been presented than when only the general background knowledge had been acquired. Actually, with the presented examples, such test sentences were quite often correctly inferred. For instance, there were approximately 80% versus 60% correct responses for the input–output sentences. For the argument specifications, there was a difference of approximately 25% between the two conditions. Information acquired from examples was thus utilized for verifying the test sentences. This result contradicts the independence assumption of the example-dominance hypothesis and supports the integrated knowledge acquisition hypothesis.

The analysis of the example verification tasks showed that the amount of text information influenced the overall performance in the example verification task. This result contradicts the assumption that texts would be encoded only superficially and that examples would be the most important part of the learning material. Some text information was obviously integrated with the information from examples. These results thus contradict the example-dominance hypothesis and supports the integrated knowledge acquisition hypothesis.

The amount of text information differentially influenced the verification of examples at different processing times, thus it is of particular interest to analyze differences in the time course. With complete-text information, the verification performance improved faster in early stages of the processing than when the text had been only partially presented. The integration of the complete-text information with the examples may have yielded a consistent structure that facilitated the utilization of the knowledge for verifying examples. Because of the missing information, some incorrect inferences may have been drawn in the partial-text condition. And because of the possible interference effects, the examples could not be verified as easily. The no-text condition may have simply relied on the template base, which is particularly useful for verifying examples, thereby avoiding an interference effect and performing at least as well as the partial-text condition. The relatively good performance of the baseline control may be explained by learning from analogy in combination with the various sentences presented in the preceding sentence verification task. The analysis of the subjects' confidence ratings finally showed that the confidence in a response did not depend on whether the utilized knowledge had been acquired from text or examples.

EXPERIMENT 2

This experiment was identical to Experiment 1 except that instead of learning from the examples supplied by the experimenter, subjects now learned by exploration and could thus generate their own examples. They could become more actively involved in following their individual learning strategies and generate as many examples as they perceived to be necessary for acquiring the respective target knowledge.

Method

Subjects. The same subject pool was used as in Experiment 1. Fifty-four students, who did not have any prior programing knowledge, successfully completed the experiment. No data were recorded for the additional seven subjects who had failed to pass the criterion test task six times in a row.

Apparatus. The experiment was performed on the same equipment as Experiment 1. For the learning by exploration phase, a LISP learning environment was used (Schmalhofer, Kühn, Charron, & Messamer, 1990). This learning environment is based on a reduced LISP interpreter, which was written in TURBO

PASCAL. It can handle the functions LIST, FIRST, REST, and EQUAL, as well as any combination of these functions and the various list structures.

In the exploration phase, one sample input of the specific LISP function was presented (see Table 15.3). The subject could then generate several inputs to the LISP system. In order to avoid unnecessary typing errors, only characters valid in LISP and lines with balanced parentheses were accepted as inputs. The generated input was then evaluated by the LISP interpreter and either the result of the evaluation or an error message was displayed. The generated examples were recorded for later analyses.

Results

The examples generated by a subject during the exploration of a specific LISP function were classified into four different categories. This categorization relied on whether an example was syntactically correct (positive example) or incorrect (negative example), and whether the subject had previously generated a similarly structured example (redundant) or not (new examples). The category into which a specific example would fall thus depended on its position in the exploration episode of a specific function. The four categories were defined as follows: positive new examples provided new information about the specific LISP function, for example, (FIRST '(A B)) and (FIRST (FIRST '((A B) C))); positive redundant examples had an identical structure to a previously generated positive example, for example, (FIRST '(BOB SUE)); negative new examples are syntactically incorrect examples that had not been previously generated, for example, (FIRST 'A B); and negative redundant examples are structurally identical to a previous negative example. In Fig. 15.7, the results of this analysis are shown for the three experimental conditions. A 3×4 analysis of variance (ANOVA) with the factors amount of text information and type of generated example showed no significant difference of the amount of text information. The numbers of generated examples differed for the four categories.

The sentence and example verification tasks yielded the same pattern of results as in Experiment 1, with the exception that some of the effects did not become statistically significant: The interaction effect was not significant for either the input–output sentences or the argument specification sentences. For the example verification task, the amount of text information was not significant, which may,

TABLE 15.3

Instructions for Exploring the Function FIRST

To learn more about the function FIRST you can now generate inputs to the LISP system and observe the returned results.

Select your inputs so that you get as much information as possible about the function FIRST.

Keep generating new inputs as long as you feel you can acquire additional knowledge.

A possible and correct input is (FIRST '(A B C D)).

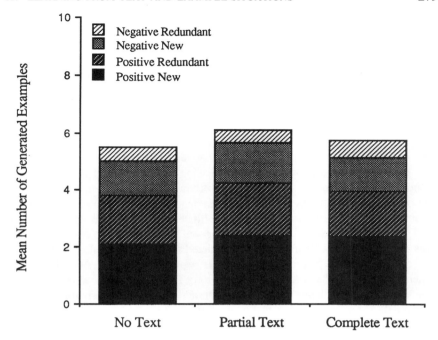

FIG. 15.7. Mean number of four different types of self-generated examples as a function of the amount of text information.

however, be due to the large error variance. Overall, learning from examples (Experiment 1) was at least as effective as learning by exploration (Experiment 2). This can be seen from the sentence (.62 vs. .62 correct answers) as well as the example verification tasks (.63 vs. .58 correct answers).

Discussion

The amount of studied text information did not show any influence on the number or type of examples being generated during the exploration phase. The example verification tasks also did not show any significant effect from the studied text information. These results support the independence assumption of the example-dominance hypothesis. In support of the integrated knowledge acquisition hypothesis, it was found that inferences were derived from the studied examples and utilized in the sentence verification tasks.

Text and example information are apparently more strongly integrated when learning from text and examples (Experiment 1) than when learning from text and by exploration (Experiment 2). Whereas in learning from examples the same examples were studied by all subjects, in learning by exploration subjects could use their own learning strategy to generate an individual sequence of examples. Differences in the learning strategies contributed to the error variance and may have had a larger effect on the test performance than the amount of text information provided to a subject. The relatively large mean-squared-error (MSe) in the analysis of amount of text information in the example verification task (3.96 in Experiment 2 vs. .13 in Experiment 1) supports this conclusion.

CONCLUSIONS

The example-dominance hypothesis assumes an independent processing of text and examples, with only a shallow processing of the text and a deeper understanding of the examples. The integrated knowledge acquisition hypothesis, on the other hand, postulates that information acquired from examples can supplement the text information and that text facilitates the understanding of examples.

The results of the two experiments showed that incomplete text information was supplemented with information extracted from the studied examples. Sentences not explicitly presented in the text were nevertheless correctly verified when examples had been studied. The results of Experiment 1 showed furthermore that examples were better understood when additional text information had been presented. The more text that had been studied, the better the verification of the examples. Although the differences were less clear and statistically not significant, such effects were also hinted at by the results of Experiment 2. This interpretation is further supported by the results of Reder, Charney, and Morgan (1986), who found that the elaboration of texts and the formation of examples play an important role in learning a skill. The result that textual labels can improve the transfer of training examples to novel problems (Catrambone, 1994) also supports the integrated knowledge acquisition hypothesis.

Given the present results, one can no longer simply say that psychological experiments would "recommend against the frequent use of examples in instruction sets" and that "readers are inclined to process written instructions shallowly when other sources of information are available" (LeFevre & Dixon, 1986, p. 29). The present experiments show quite to the contrary, that information from the text was integrated with the information from the examples. Because the subjects did not have any previous programing experience, this claim can even be made for learners with only little prior domain knowledge. Learning materials with text and supplementary examples may therefore be quite effective, particularly for novices.

Under certain circumstances, even the KIWi model will, however, predict that the information encoded from a text may remain isolated from the information encoded from examples. The KIWi model may thus also predict the results observed by LeFevre and Dixon. Therefore, additional research will be required to determine the specific factors that affect a learner's ability to form a situation model and an integrated representation. The KIWi model, which was proposed as an extension to Kintsch's construction-integration model, may be used as a vehicle for addressing this issue.

Some predictions about relevant factors can already be derived. When a text is studied, a reader forms a textbase and possibly, in addition, a situation model. With the situation model, the subsequently presented examples can be understood and explained at a deeper level. When a learner has very limited prior knowledge, only a textbase will be formed and subsequent examples would then indeed be processed independently of the information acquired from the text (notice, that in Fig. 15.1 there is no direct connection between the textbase and the template base). When text and examples are contradictory (as in LeFevre & Dixon's experiments), a straightforward integration becomes impossible and a learner will focus on the learning material that is more directly related to the anticipated test tasks. In the test phase of the experiment, LeFevre and Dixon had their subjects produce the next step to an example (rather than reproduce the studied text), thus the examples and constructed templates (rather than the text and the textbase) were more directly related to the test task.

When a text reproduction or text summarization task would be used as a test task in LeFevre and Dixon's experimental design, the text rather than the examples would become the more influential learning material. It is therefore not true that examples dominate text. Instead, it should be stated that the more pertinent learning material will dominate the less significant learning material. More generally, it can be stated that a learner's knowledge acquisition processes are driven by the goal to solve some future tasks (which are typically ill-defined). The performance in the test tasks will therefore depend on the concordance of this anticipation with the actual tasks. Whereas the textbase and the situation model are used to recognize or verify sentences (Schmalhofer & Glavanov, 1986), the template base and situation model are used to verify examples.

The KIWi model can also be used to derive quite detailed predictions. By entering the presumed knowledge of a learner into the KIWi model and then having the model process the actual learning materials, the knowledge acquired from different learning materials can be predicted for various groups of learners. Different test tasks may subsequently be presented to the model and the model will produce the respective test performance.

ACKNOWLEDGMENTS

This research was supported by grant Schm 648/1 from Deutsche Forschungs-gemeinschaft. The experiments were performed during a visit of the author at the University of Colorado. I would like to express my thanks to Walter Kintsch for his support to conduct this research. Otto Kühn, Paula Messamer, Michael Rohr, and Jörg Thoben helped in designing and running the experiments and analyzing the data. Several anonymous reviewers contributed to the improvement of the exposition of the chapter. Some of the results have been presented at the Thematic Session "Comprehension Processes" at the 25th International Congress of Psychology in Brussels, 1992.

REFERENCES

Anderson, J. R., Farrell, R., & Sauers, R. (1984). Learning to program in LISP. *Cognitive Science, 8*, 87–129.

Bergmann, R., Boschert, St., & Schmalhofer, F. (1992). Das Erlernen einer Programmiersprache: Wissenserwerb aus Texten, Beispielen und komplexen Programmen [The learning of a programming language: The acquisition of knowledge from texts, examples, and complex programs]. In K. Reiss, M. Reiss, & H. Spandl (Eds.), *Maschinelles Lernen: Modellierung von Lernen mit Maschinen* (pp. 204–224). Berlin: Springer-Verlag.

Black, J. B., Carroll, J. M., & McGuigan, S. M. (1987). What kind of minimal instruction manual is the most effective? In *Proceedings of CHI+GI 1987* (pp. 159–162). New York: ACM.

Carroll, J. M., Mack, R. L., Lewis, C. H., Grischkowsky, N. L., & Robertson, S. R. (1985). Exploring exploring a word processor. *Human Computer Interaction, 1*, 283–307.

Catrambone, R. (1994). *The effects of labels in training examples on transfer to novel problems.* Unpublished manuscript, School of Psychology, Georgia Institute of Psychology.

Chi, M. T. H., Bassok, M., Lewis, M. W., Reimann, P., & Glaser, R. (1989). Self-explanations: How students study and use examples in learning to solve problems. *Cognitive Science, 13*, 145–182.

Doane, St. M., McNamara, D. S., Kintsch, W., Polson, P. G., & Clawson, D. M. (1992). Prompt comprehension in UNIX Command Production. *Memory and Cognition, 20*(4), 327–343.

Fletcher, C. R., & Chrysler, S. T. (1990). Surface forms, textbases, and situation models: Recognition memory for three types of textual information. *Discourse Processes, 13*, 175–190.

Graesser, A. C., & McMahen, C. L. (1993). Anomalous information triggers questions when adults solve quantitative problems and comprehend stories. *Journal of Educational Psychology, 85*, 136–151.

Kintsch, W. (1974). *The representation of meaning in memory.* Hillsdale, NJ: Lawrence Erlbaum Associates.

Kintsch, W. (1988). The role of knowledge in discourse comprehension: A construction-integration model. *Psychological Review, 95*, 163–182.

Kintsch, W., & van Dijk, T. A. (1978). Toward a model of text comprehension and production. *Psychological Review, 85*, 363–394.

Kintsch, W., Welsch, D. M., Schmalhofer, F., & Zimny, S. (1990). Sentence memory: A theoretical analysis. *Journal of Memory and Language, 29*, 133–159.

LeFevre, J., & Dixon, P. (1986). Do written instructions need examples? *Cognition and Instruction, 3*, 1–30.

Lewis, C. (1988). Why and how to learn why: Analysis-based generalization of procedures. *Cognitive Science, 12*, 211–256.

Mannes, S. M., & Kintsch, W. (1991). Routine computing tasks: Planning as understanding. *Cognitive Science, 15*, 305–342.

McKoon, G., & Ratcliff, R. (1992). Inference during reading. *Psychological Review, 99*, 440–466.

Miller, J. R., & Kintsch, W. (1980). Readability and recall of short prose passages: A theoretical analysis. *Journal of Experimental Psychology: Human Learning and Memory, 6*, 335–354.

Mitchell, T. M., Keller, R. M., & Kedar-Cabelli, S. T. (1986). Explanation-based generalization: A unifying view. *Machine Learning, 1*, 48–80.

Morrow, D., Bower, G., & Greenspan, S. (1989). Updating situation models during narrative comprehension. *Journal of Memory and Language, 28*, 292–312.

Morrow, D., Greenspan, S., & Bower, G. (1987). Accessibility and situation models in narrative comprehension. *Journal of Memory and Language, 26*, 165–187.

Novick, L. R., & Holyoak, K. J. (1991). Mathematical problem solving by analogy. *Journal of Experimental Psychology: Learning, Memory, and Cognition, 17*, 398–415.

Otero, J., & Kintsch, W. (1992). Failures to detect contradictions in a text: What readers believe versus what they read. *Psychological Science, 3*, 229–235.

Perrig, W., & Kintsch, W. (1985). Propositional and situational representations of text. *Journal of Memory and Language, 24,* 503–518.

Pirolli, P. L., & Anderson, J. R. (1985). The role of learning in the acquisition of recursive programming skills. *Canadian Journal of Psychology,* 39, 240–272.

Reder, L. M., Charney, D. H., & Morgan, K. I. (1986). The role of elaborations in learning a skill from an instructional text. *Memory & Cognition, 14,* 64–78.

Redmond, M. (1989). Learning from others' experience: Creating cases from examples. In R. Bareiss (Ed.), *Proceedings: Case-based reasoning workshop* (pp. 309–312). San Mateo, CA: Morgan Kaufmann.

Schmalhofer, F., Bergmann, R., Boschert, St., & Thoben, J. (1993). Learning program abstractions: Model and empirical validation. In G. Strube & K. F. Wender (Eds.), *The cognitive psychology of knowledge* (pp. 203–231). Amsterdam: North-Holland.

Schmalhofer, F., Boschert, S., & Kühn, O. (1990). Der Aufbau allgemeinen Situationswissens aus Text und Beispielen [The construction of a situation model from text and examples]. *Zeitschrift für Pädagogische Psychologie, 4,* 177–186.

Schmalhofer, F., & Glavanov, D. (1986). Three components of understanding a programmer's manual: Verbatim, propositional, and situational representations. *Journal of Memory and Language, 25,* 279–294.

Schmalhofer, F., & Kühn, O. (1988). Acquiring computer skills by exploration versus demonstration. In *The 10th Annual Conference of the Cognitive Science Society* (pp. 724–730). Hillsdale, NJ: Lawrence Erlbaum Associates.

Schmalhofer, F., & Kühn, O. (1991). The psychological processes of constructing a mental model when learning by being told, from examples and by exploration. In M. J. Tauber & D. Ackermann (Eds.), *Mental models and human-computer interaction* (Vol. 2, pp. 337–360). Amsterdam: North-Holland.

Schmalhofer, F., Kühn, O., & Boschert, St. (1994). The acquisition and utilization of knowledge in beginners and advanced learners. In K. F. Wender, F. Schmalhofer, & H.-D. Boecker (Eds.), *Cognition and computer programming* (pp. 27–61). Norwood, NJ: Ablex.

Schmalhofer, F., Kühn, O., Charron, R., & Messamer, P. (1990). An implementation and empirical evaluation of an exploration environment with different tutoring strategies. *Behavior Research Methods, Instruments, & Computers, 22,* 179–183.

Seifert, C. (1989). Analogy and case-based reasoning. In R. Bareiss (Ed.), *Proceedings: Case-based reasoning workshop* (pp. 125–129). San Mateo, CA: Morgan Kaufmann.

Singer, M., Andrusiak, P., Reisdorf, P., & Black, N. L. (1992). Individual differences in bridging inference processes. *Memory and Cognition, 20,* 539–548.

Trabasso, T., & van den Broek, P. (1985). Causal thinking and the representation of narrative events. *Journal of Memory and Language, 25,* 279–294.

van Dijk, T. A., & Kintsch, W. (1983). *Strategies of discourse comprehension.* San Diego, CA: Academic Press.

VanLehn, K., Jones, R. M., & Chi, M. T. H. (1992). A model of the self-explanation effect. *Journal of the Learning Sciences, 2,* 1–59.

Waldmann, M. R., Holyoak, K. J., & Fratianne, A. (1993, November). *Causal models and the acquisition of category structure.* Paper presented at the 34th Annual Meeting of the Psychonomic Society, Washington, DC.

Wickelgren, W. A., Corbett, A. T., & Dosher, B. A. (1980). Priming and retrieval from short-term memory: A speed accuracy trade-off analysis. *Journal of Verbal Learning and Verbal Behavior, 19,* 387–404.

Chapter 16

The Role of Presentational Structures in Understanding and Solving Mathematical Word Problems

Fritz C. Staub
Kurt Reusser
University of Zurich

Within a theoretical perspective of a cognitive simulation model (Kintsch & Greeno, 1985; Reusser, 1985, 1989b, 1990) we argue that the linguistically cued representation of the situation denoted in a text must be viewed as a crucial step for the successful understanding and solving of word problems. Based on theoretical considerations and empirical data, we suggest that teachers and researchers in mathematics education should become more aware of characteristics of situational and presentational structures of word problems. We suggest further that students would be better helped by focusing attention on characteristics of the episodic situation and problem structure and on how they are presented in the text, rather than on matching linguistic cues or keywords to formal mathematical structures. We conclude that the situational structures to be mathematized are a central source of problem difficulty. Moreover, an analysis of the content-related situational structure of a mathematical word problem makes it possible to examine more precisely the impact of linguistic variations, which may be used to represent specific situational structures. By concentrating on the presentational structure of mathematical word problems, we argue for an integration of different research approaches within a perspective motivated by pedagogical and instructional questions about the purpose and the objectives of using arithmetic word problems in school settings. (For a discussion into similar issues in solving *algebra* word problems, see Weaver & Kintsch, 1992.)

FROM COMPUTATIONAL AND LINGUISTIC FACTORS
TO LOGICO-MATHEMATICAL FACTORS

Early Studies of Computational and Linguistic Factors

Early studies of word problem solving have investigated variables, such as type and number of arithmetic operations, problem length (number of words), order in which numbers are presented in the problem text, syntactical complexity, and cue words (e.g., Jerman, 1973; Jerman & Mirman, 1974; Searle, Lorton, & Suppes, 1974). Even though these studies demonstrate that many different variables may influence the level of difficulty of a particular word problem, they provide a rather inconsistent picture of the variables accounting for the variance in the proportion of correct answers to elementary arithmetic word problems.

In these early studies, the dominant theoretical conceptualization of the processes involved in solving arithmetic word problems was that of a *direct translation* of the linguistic surface structure into an appropriate equation (see Bobrow, 1964, for an early computer model for this kind of theory). A point in case for this conceptualization is the use of terms, such as *verbal cues* and *key words*, which were considered linguistic factors that determine the relative difficulty of verbal arithmetic problems (e.g., Jerman, 1973; Searle et al., 1974). Verbal cues—such as "equal," "altogether," "gained," "left," "lost," or "each"—are assumed to signal specific arithmetic operations. Within this approach verbal cues thus presuppose a straightforward matching of specific terms to corresponding mathematical operations. Obviously, such a direct matching only works for very restricted contexts, because the semantically adequate mathematical meaning of any cue depends on a broad variety of factors contributing to the semantic structure of the problem text and its question. The (mis)conception that underlies the term *verbal cue* may be, in part, the result of an artificial mode of presenting word problems in school settings, which makes use of a specific and limited vocabulary. Indeed, students are very easily misled when using such cue words in tasks where a superficial—that is, a purely local—interpretation of the term leads to a wrong arithmetic operation (Nesher & Teubal, 1975). From a theoretical point of view, a genuine solution of a verbal problem is hardly possible by direct translation of its verbal formulation into the mathematical equation.

Information-Processing Models for One-Step Addition
and Subtraction Word Problems Focusing
on Logico-Mathematical Factors

Over the past dozen years research on understanding and solving arithmetic word problems has been dominated by one very specific problem set for which detailed computational processing models have been constructed. The set of problems referred to are simple one-step addition and subtraction problems that have been constructed within the conceptual framework of three categories of basic semantic structures: *combine, change,* and *compare* structures (Nesher, Greeno, & Riley,

1982; Riley, 1981; Vergnaud, 1982). Such parsimoniously worded problems corresponding to one of these problem types will be referred to as *standard problems*. Examples are shown in Table 16.1.

Combine tasks involve static relationships between sets and ask for a union set or for one of two disjoint subsets. Change problems describe an increase or decrease of some initial state that results in a final state. Compare problems involve comparisons between two static sets, asking either for the difference set or for one of the two sets when the difference set is given. Studies have shown that the overall pattern of relative problem difficulty for these problem types is quite stable (Nesher et al., 1982; Riley & Greeno, 1988). On the average, change problems are the least difficult, compare problems are the most difficult, and combine problems are in between.

Each of the three semantic problem types can be further differentiated, depending on which set corresponds to the identity of the unknown to be determined quantitatively. Within each of the three semantic categories of combine, change, and compare problems, depending, again, on the identity of the unknown, the

TABLE 16.1
Examples of the Standard Problems

Combine Problems

Mary has 3 marbles. Peter has 5 marbles. How many marbles do they have altogether?
Heidi and John have 8 marbles altogether. John has 3 marbles. How many marbles does Heidi have?

Change Problems

Change 1:
Mary had 3 marbles. Then John gave her 5 marbles. How many marbles does Mary have now?
Change 2:
Mary had 6 marbles. Then she gave 4 marbles to John. How many marbles does Mary have now?
Change 3:
Mary had 2 marbles. Then John gave her some marbles. Now Mary has 9 marbles. How many marbles did John give to her?
Change 4:
Mary had 8 marbles. Then she gave some marbles to John. Now Mary has 3 marbles. How many marbles did she give to John?
Change 5:
Mary had some marbles. Then John gave her 3 marbles. Now Mary has 5 marbles. How many marbles did Mary have in the beginning?
Change 6:
Mary had some marbles. Then she gave 2 marbles to John. Now Mary has 6 marbles. How many marbles did she have in the beginning?

Compare Problems

Diana has 5 marbles. Tom has 8 marbles. How many marbles does Tom have more than Diana?
Mary has 9 marbles. She has 4 marbles more than John. How many marbles does John have?

Note. All subtypes are listed only for the category of change problems.

relative difficulty shows rather stable data patterns across several studies. For example, for change problems it has repeatedly been shown that asking for an unknown resulting state (Change 1: after increasing a specific set; Change 2: after decreasing a specific set) are the least difficult problem types. Somewhat more difficult are problems asking for the amount of change or transfer to be determined (Change 3: increasing; Change 4: decreasing). The most difficult are problems with an unknown initial state (Change 5: before increasing; Change 6: before decreasing) (Riley & Greeno, 1988; Riley, Greeno, & Heller, 1983).

Working with parsimoniously worded standard problems within the paradigm of the logico-mathematical categories of combine, change, and compare problems leads to rather consistent data pattern. Several simulation models embodying explicit hypotheses about knowledge structures and processes necessary to solve such standard problems have been worked out in great detail (Briars & Larkin, 1984; Kintsch & Greeno, 1985; Riley & Greeno, 1988; Riley, Greeno, & Heller, 1983) and have provided coherent theoretical explanations.

Most of these models on understanding and solving mathematical word problems, however, deal with the process of mathematization as a process of a more or less direct translation from a textual structure into a logico-mathematical representation. As developmental models (Briars & Larkin, 1984; Riley et al., 1983), they do not deal with language or situation comprehension as sources of word problem difficulty, but rather with the development of *logico-mathematical schemata*.

Only the model of Kintsch and Greeno (1985), whose main objective is to study "the interaction between comprehension and problem solving" (p. 109), includes a thorough analysis of text comprehension processes based on the theory developed by van Dijk and Kintsch (1983). Understanding and solving a word problem is described as a strategic process of constructing a dual representation, including a *propositional textbase* organized around interrelated sets of objects, and an *abstract situation* or *problem model* inferred from the reader's knowledge.

The limitation of the Kintsch and Greeno model, however, lies in an a priori mapping between the propositional structures of the textbase and the set structure of an abstract problem model. The model shows no attempt to explicitly understand the action or situation described by a word problem: The dual representation model jumps directly, in a one-step mathematization process, from the propositional textbase to a set theoretic representation of the problem by applying powerful, cue-word driven arithmetic comprehension strategies.

EFFECTS OF "WORDING" THAT QUESTION
THE VALIDITY OF PROCESS MODELS BASED
ON LOGICO-MATHEMATICAL STRUCTURES

Even though stable data patterns have been replicated for the parsimoniously worded standard problems, there are also intriguing empirical findings generated by using minor variations of the standard problems that do not fit into the pattern of problem difficulty as presented earlier. Some of these are discussed in the following.

Hudson (1983)

In an often-cited study, Hudson had children from nursery school through first grade solve compare problems that asked for the unknown difference set. Subjects were presented with a card depicting two disjoint sets of objects, differing in cardinality by one, two, or three. The drawings on the cards symbolized such entities as children and cookies, or birds and worms. The following are two versions of the verbal formulation of the problem, which—in terms of the classification of Nesher et al. (1982)—did not differ in their underlying logico-semantic structure and the identity of the unknown quantity asked for:

1. The "How Many More" task: In this condition each child was shown one of the drawings with the two sets of objects. As each drawing was presented, the experimenter pointed to the icons on the card and asked for example: "Here are some birds and here are some worms. How many more birds than worms are there?"

2. The "Won't Get" task: Under this condition the wording of the questions was as follows: "Here are some birds and here are some worms. Suppose the birds all race over, and each one tries to get a worm. Will every bird get a worm? How many birds won't get a worm?"

Under Condition 1, children showed poor performance, but they improved dramatically under Condition 2. Hudson interpreted the children's apparent lack of quantitative reasoning when confronted with problem questions following comparative constructions such as "How many ⟨comparative term⟩ . . . than . . . ?" as having to be accounted for by "a linguistic factor." According to Hudson, it is the children's limited comprehension of such linguistic constructions as "How many more . . . than" that leads to misinterpretations and hence to wrong numerical answers.

De Corte, Verschaffel, and De Win (1985)

These authors investigated for a set of six word problems (corresponding to the three basic semantic categories as conceptualized by Riley et al.) how rewording these problems affects their solution. For example, for a Change 5 problem the solutions of the following versions were compared (rewordings shown in italics):

1. Joe won 3 marbles.
   Now he has 5 marbles.
   How many marbles did Joe have in the beginning?

2. *Joe had some marbles.*
   He won 3 *more* marbles.
   Now he has five marbles.
   How many marbles did Joe have in the beginning?

First graders produced only 13% correct responses for problems presented as in Version 1 as compared to 33% correct responses for problems formulated as in Version 2. For second graders corresponding percentages are: 61% for Version 1 as opposed to 79% for Version 2. Explicitly stating the initial state and the direction of change in relation to the initial state proved to be helpful for the children to arrive at an appropriate solution of the task. De Corte et al. (1985, p. 469) gave the following interpretation: "Rewording problems by making the semantic relations more explicit compensates for the less developed semantic schemata and facilitates appropriate bottom-up processing."

Staub and Reusser (1992)

In one of our own studies, 52 first graders (average age 7;11) and 37 third graders (10;0) were presented with a subset of specifically reworded change problems. Out of the six types of change problems the two easiest (Change 1 and Change 2) and the two most difficult (Change 5 and Change 6) problems were chosen. These four problem types correspond to logical combinations of the identity of the unknown quantity (initial state vs. resulting state) by direction of transfer (transfer-in vs. transfer-out). In the following, we list the Change 1 and the Change 6 problems used by Riley and Greeno (1988) followed by an example (in italics) of a reworded version used in our study:

Change 1.   Joe had 3 marbles.
            Then Tom gave him 5 more marbles.
            How many marbles does Joe have now?
            Today Dane got 11 marbles from Susan.
            Yesterday Dane found 5 marbles.
            How many marbles does Dane have now?

Change 6.   Joe had some marbles.
            Then he gave 5 marbles to Tom.
            Now John has three marbles.
            How many marbles did John have in the beginning?
            Peter has 4 apples now.
            Today Peter gave Mary 7 apples.
            How many apples did Peter pick yesterday?

To control material factors such as names, type of objects, numbers, and kind of transfer verbs used, the change problems were each instantiated in different material versions.

TABLE 16.2
Comparison of Proportion of Correct Solutions of Data from Staub and
Reusser (1992) with Data from Riley and Greeno (1988)

	Proportions of Correct Solutions (Without Blocks)			
	Grade 1		Grade 3	
Problem Type	(1)	(2)	(1)	(2)
Change 1	1.00	.63	1.00	.69
Change 2	1.00	.31	1.00	.47
Change 5	.33	.10	.95	.15
Change 6	.39	.32	.90	.30

Note. (1) Data from Riley & Greeno (1988); Grade 1: $n = 18$, Grade 3: $n = 20$. (2) Data from Staub and Reusser (1992); Grade 1: $n = 54$, Grade 3: $n = 37$.

For each of the four problem types the proportion of correct solutions was calculated and compared to the data of Riley and Greeno (1988). Table 16.2 shows that our problems are more difficult. But, regardless of the additional variations in our word problems, we also clearly replicated a strong tendency that has been shown before (e.g., Cummins, Kintsch, Reusser, & Weimer, 1988; Riley & Greeno, 1988; Riley et al., 1983): Problems with an unknown resulting state are easier than problems with an unknown initial state.

However, in our data there is also an interaction between identity of the unknown quantity and direction of transfer, which cannot be accounted for by the cognitive models based on a task analysis that concentrates on the logico-mathematical structure. Problems requiring students to determine a resulting state are easier if it is a transfer-in task (Change 1), as compared to transfer-out tasks (Change 2); when an initial state has to be determined it is the transfer-out tasks (Change 6) that are more likely to be solved.

Stern and Lehrndorfer (1992)

In a study with 45 first graders (average age: 6;10), Stern and Lehrndorfer used compare problems, such as "Peter has 6 crayons. Laura has 4 crayons. How many crayons less does Laura have than Peter?" These problems were better solved if the problem statements followed a description of a situational context referring to a competitive situation that is compatible with the problem question, such as the following: "Peter is Laura's older brother. Because he is older, his bedroom is larger and his toys are more expensive than Laura's. Peter also gets more pocket money than Laura and he has a new bike whereas Laura has Peter's old bike. When Peter does his homework, Laura doodles a little bit." Problem statements following such a situational context were better solved than problems with a preceding incompatible or neutral context description. Stern and Lehrndorfer interpreted these findings as indicating that the difficulties with compare problems are not solely caused by abstract language expressions, such as "How many more . . .", but may also be attributed to a lack of appropriate situational and mathematical knowledge.

The standard problems used by Riley et al. (1983) and others show very little verbal and situational variation. By furthermore acknowledging the empirical effects produced by minor specific changes in wording—without changing the logico-mathematical or basic semantic structure of the problems—it is evident that the theories accounting for the relative difficulty of mathematical word problems may only be valid within a rather narrow task space, whose dimensions have not yet been specified clearly. Children's difficulties in solving mathematical word problems cannot be accounted for solely by a lack of abstract logico-mathematical knowledge.[1] As the results referred to previously demonstrate, (minor) variations in the wording of standard problems may have a significant impact on problem difficulty that cannot be explained by the abstract logico-mathematical knowledge structures.

How does wording relate to abstract logico-mathematical structures? How are we to explain the relevant structural differences that have been captured by such colloquial notions as wording? In what follows, we present a theoretical framework that hopefully will be heuristically fruitful for looking at wording effects from a perspective that will allow the search for logico-mathematical schemata to be integrated with the analysis of situational structure and linguistic surface structure. We think that a theoretical analysis of the notion of wording is necessary not only for further research but also in order to form a coherent picture of what has been learned so far about what makes elementary arithmetic word problems difficult.

A THEORETICAL FRAMEWORK
FOR ANALYZING THE UNDERSTANDING
AND SOLVING OF ARITHMETIC WORD PROBLEMS

Our theorizing is guided by the epistemological intuition that early mathematical learning and thinking are embedded in the development of acting, thinking, language comprehension, and qualitative world knowledge. Children are able, through their experience with everyday acting and problem solving with real objects, to behave in proto-mathematical ways a long time before they enter schooling and master the fine-grained mathematical language.[2] Piaget (1950)

---

[1]Other intriguing findings have been collected by looking at "street math": It has been demonstrated that performance on mathematical problems embedded in real-life contexts was superior to that on school-type word problems and context-free computational problems involving the same numbers and operations (T. N. Carraher, D. W. Carraher, & Schliemann, 1985).

[2]Moreover, accumulating research shows that children have significant implicit understanding of counting, numbers, and sets before they enter formal schooling (Gelman & Greeno, 1989; Resnick, 1989). It has even been shown—by using habituation techniques—that 6- to 8-month-old infants have some sensitivity to numerosity (Starkey, Spelke, & Gelman, 1990). There is evidence that children as young as 3 or 4 years of age have what Resnick (1989) called "implicit protoquantitative reasoning schemas" for interpreting changes as increase or decrease as well as a protoquantitative "part-whole schema."

claimed that mathematical thinking emerges from acting. Mathematical operations are the developmental derivatives of sensorimotor actions, or, as Aebli (1980) put it from his broader cognitive instructional perspective, operations are "abstract actions." Concrete actions, referred to, for example, by the use of action verbs (giving, getting, selling, or losing a set of objects) are seen as bearing an abstract proto-mathematical meaning, a relational core that can be expressed and formalized by abstract mathematical operation schemata (such as adding, subtracting, multiplying, or dividing).

The Psychological Process Model

Extending the work of van Dijk and Kintsch (1983) and Kintsch and Greeno (1985), Reusser (1985, 1989b, 1990) developed a cognitive simulation model of understanding and solving elementary word arithmetic problems called the "Situation Problem Solver" (SPS).[3] The model is based on a decomposition analysis of the language and situation comprehension skills. Its purpose is to model the problem-solving process by emphasizing its language and situation comprehension components.

In SPS the cognitive process of solving mathematical word problems is considered to be a strategic process from text to situation to equation, an elaborative and incremental process of comprehension of the problem situation denoted by the problem text, which is modeled as a stepwise transformation of the initial textual representation of the problem into an equation.

SPS is a rule-based model implemented in LISP. It takes as input elementary addition and subtraction word problems, and "understands" and solves them by means of various types of lexical, syntactic, semantic, and pragmatic (macro)strategies. These strategies are related to four mutually constraining levels of comprehension or problem representation that are constructed (see Fig. 16.1):

1. Text comprehension in SPS refers to the construction of a *textbase* (Kintsch, 1974), a propositional representation of the textual input (see also Perfetti & Britt, chap. 2 in this vol.).

2. Situation comprehension involves the construction of an *episodic situation model*, or mental model, of the situation denoted by the text. This step is achieved through application of comprehension strategies to the textbase, which generate an analysis of the temporal and functional structure of the situations and actions depicted in the problem texts (see also Graesser & Zwaan, chap. 7 in this vol.).[4]

---

[3]So far its implementation is limited to a broad variety of change problems.

[4]With respect to our flexibly worded change problems (transactions of objects between a variable number of co-actors), this means that action-analytic strategies search the problem texts for the initial state, the resulting state, and the direction of transfer. To understand the structure of an action situation in SPS means to figure out the temporal order and the direction of the events: knowing what leads to what in an action sequence.

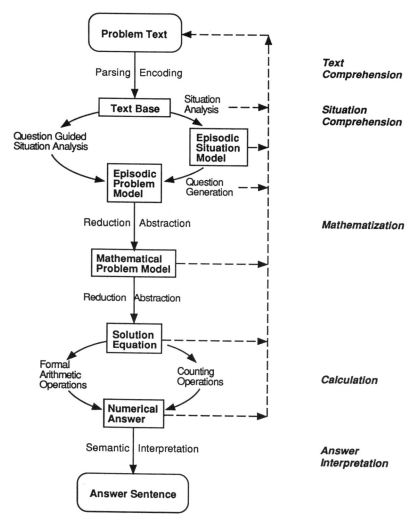

FIG. 16.1. Situation problem solver (SPS): Architecture and macrostrategies (Reusser, 1989b).

3. By constructing the *problem model*, mathematization in a broad sense sets in. A problem model includes all the structural elements and relations of the episodic situation model that are relevant from the point of view of the question to be answered. A meaningful question presupposes that by reflecting on the relevant conceptual and/or causal relations in the episodic situation model the answer can be determined. Such questions are mostly expressed by explicitly

asking for a quantitative answer.[5] By abstracting from situational specificity the problem model arrived at may already be a rather abstract semantic structure.

4. In the fourth phase, the problem model as a structure with a specified quantitative gap is further abstracted and reduced to its abstract mathematical gist, which leads to the *mathematical problem model.* The densest form of representing a structure of mathematical relations underlying a problem model is the numerical solution equation.

Finally, SPS generates an answer sentence referring back to the situation model and giving semantic meaning to the numerical answer.

In SPS the crucial step in the process of mathematization is the creation of a mental model and its reduction to the abstract mathematical gist. An (episodic) situation model, as a model of the real-world action or situation structure denoted by a problem text, can vary a great deal in elaboration and concreteness, and can be processed under very different operative perspectives.[6] In contrast, the problem model implies a quantitative operative perspective. To finally build a mathematical problem model means to see the situation exclusively in the light of a quantitative processing goal. The problem model is a special case of a situation model: It may still be concrete in many ways, but it contains—if it turns out to be suitable for successful mathematization—all the problem-relevant information needed for quantification.[7]

Based on this view of the levels of representation involved in understanding and solving a mathematical word problem for a given specific word problem, we may look for specific structural characteristics of the mental models to be constructed for a successful solution. For example, the following characteristics have to be distinguished:

---

[5]An explicit problem question asking for some numerical entity is only one way to communicate that quantification is to be the processing goal. A mathematical processing perspective can also be communicated by the semantic content of a story without an explicit question. For example, a protagonist expresses a goal that can only be successfully attained by mathematizing certain aspects of the story context (Aebli, Staub, & Ruthemann, 1991). In other words, the pursuit of many goals in everyday life "naturally" leads to mathematical acting, quantification, and calculation. In school settings, the operative perspective of quantification is conveyed to students also—if not mainly—by the situational context in which a task is presented—no matter how (un)meaningful the semantics. Reading a story problem in a mathematics class activates strong expectations about the kind of questions that might be asked by the teacher, or possibly should be asked by the student.

[6]One can think about a story's content in very different ways (aesthetical, motivational, causal, stylistic, etc.).

[7]For the parsimoniously worded "standard problems" it is in fact hardly possible to distinguish between situation and problem models because all the statements referring to the situation model are also part of the problem model. For most traditional math textbooks it is a characteristic feature of arithmetic word problems that situation and problem model overlap almost entirely (see also Aebli et al., 1991).

Situation model: static versus dynamic situation(s), number and type of co-actors involved, direction of transfer(s), and so on.

Problem model: identity of the unknown, "with" versus "without" an explicit action goal whose attainment requires mathematization of the situation.

Mathematical problem model: type of mathematical operation(s), given numerical quantities.

SPS is not a developmental model in the sense of Riley et al. (1983), or of Briars and Larkin (1984). The theoretical power of SPS rests in its implementation of analytic knowledge, allowing the simulation of language and situation comprehension processes while successfully solving a wide range of flexibly worded change problems. The basic psychological and instructional hypothesis associated with the idea of intervening episodic situation and problem models in SPS is that, for most problem solvers, situational understanding based on problem texts is not and, in an instructional context, should not be a superfluous but rather an obligatory outcome. The theoretical and empirical issue is that the logico-mathematical knowledge is merely one (though a very important) constraining factor in arriving at the right mathematical operation. Other important and probably underestimated factors that constrain the understanding and solving of problems are the underlying situations themselves and their linguistic expression or wording. That is, problems differ in the explicitness not only of the (mathematical) problem structure stated, but also in the quality of the problem question present (if at all); in the quality and degree of elaboration, coherence, and completeness of the situation description; in the sequential order of mention of situation elements; and in all kinds of presuppositions (drawing on a variety of world knowledge) implied by the verbal and situational setting.

The Presentational Structure of Arithmetic Word Problems

The facts and events that constitute the "world" referred to in a story text, such as the relations among the events of the story (temporal order, relations of causation, motivation), may be verbally described in many different ways. Following Morgan and Sellner (1980), we used the notion of *presentational structures* to refer to such variations as "the storyteller's choice concerning which points of content to present explicitly and which to leave to the hearer to infer; what order events should be presented in" (p. 185). To recover such structures entails inferring the writer's plan for presenting the story and determining how all the choices involved contribute to reaching the goal that motivates the plan.[8]

---

[8]Morgan and Sellner (1980) not only distinguished between a story's content and its presentational structure, they further spoke of a story's linguistic form, by which they referred to the linguistic elements and relations that make up the means used to express the story. A story's content, presentational structure, and linguistic form are not entirely independent. In discussing questions of linguistic form we refer to them as presentational variations.

The presentational structure of word problems thus refers to the manner in which a specific content is presented by use of specific linguistic means, following (at least implicitly) specific plans that ought to be tuned to the addressees and to the content to be conveyed. This conceptualization of presentational structure analytically presupposes an explication of a word problem's content. Once such a content structure is given, we can ask for possible presentational variations.[9]

By combining the notion of presentational structures with our process model, which distinguishes different levels of comprehension, we hope to gain a clearer view of the multitude of possible structural and presentational variations of mathematical word problems.

In arithmetic word problems, the abstract mathematical structure is of course not explicitly represented in the problem text. Except for the given quantities, the mathematical structure is intentionally hidden; its (re)construction is what constitutes an essential subgoal in order to produce answers to mathematical word problems as used in school settings. A given mathematical structure, posed as an applied mathematical problem, must be situationalized—that is, it must be presented with reference to a specific situational structure. Given that the instructional process aims at specific mathematical structures, then referring to a specific "reality" or situation to be mathematized constitutes the first basic presentational decision. Once a specific situational structure has been specified, one may further ask for possible variations of its presentational structure. For example, in the case of change problems, decisions concerning the presentation of situation and problem models would include text order (e.g., in relation to the "natural" sequence of action); narrative point of view in the episode(s); presence or absence of an explicit question; narrative point of view of the story question; explicitness of relevant relations (necessary inferences); specific lexical constructions referring to an abstract problem model; and manipulative material, pictures, diagrams, and so forth presented with the problem.

The studies using standard addition and subtraction word problems have almost exclusively varied features related to the structure of the problem model (that is, basic semantic structure and identity of the unknown) while limiting presentational variations.

THE EFFECTS OF WORDING REANALYZED

Based on the theoretical framework already presented, we will reanalyze some examples of the reworded standard problems that have been shown to produce effects of wording on solution rates.

We begin by looking more closely at the examples in the Hudson (1983) study. Hudson's more difficult question format, using "More," is indeed quite

---

[9]Such presentational variations in the recall of a given problem text can be used as valuable indicators for diagnosing comprehension (Staub, 1991).

abstract: "Here are some birds and here are some worms. How many more birds than worms are there?" Whereas the problem in the "Won't Get" format, which is also subsumed under the same logico-mathematical structure of the Compare 1 type, is richer in its wording: "Here are some birds and here are some worms. Suppose the birds all race over, and each one tries to get a worm. Will every bird get a worm? . . . How many birds won't get a worm?" Hudson explained the difficulties with the "More" question format to be a matter of linguistic form, in that the children are not able to correctly interpret the meaning of "more" in the question of the problem.

Gelman and Greeno (1989) considered Hudson's result as a demonstration of the effects of wording on children's performance: "It seems that children are able to compare the sets by forming sets with one-to-one correspondence and counting the remainder, when enough linguistic cues are provided" (p. 149). They explained the difficulties of the "More" questions as ignorance of the *principle of linguistic set difference* on the part of the children, that is, the missing linguistic knowledge that quantifiers (e.g., numerals or expressions, such as "some" or "how many") not only denote the cardinality of sets (linguistic cardinality) but may also denote the numerical difference between sets.

This may be a good characterization of the missing knowledge of children who do have difficulty solving the abstractly worded "More" problem. Yet, we think it is also important to ask why the easier "Won't Get" format is successfully solved. The explanation that "enough linguistic cues" are provided, in our view, does not state clearly enough the importance of the underlying situational structure and its presentational structure. The "Won't Get" task refers to a very different situation model. Whereas the question in the "More" task refers to an abstract, static situation, the question in the "Won't Get" format refers to a familiar situation or script that imbues the difference set with real-world meaning. In the "Won't Get" condition, the text is about some familiar action and motivational context (birds racing for worms, people eating cookies, kids picking up bikes). The text sequence follows the natural order of events and the question refers to an aspect of the outcome of the action being described: for example, the cardinality of a set referring to the birds left without any worms. Only the abstract problem model of the "Won't Get" task is the same as in the "More" task. That is, the two problems do not differ with respect to their abstract logico-mathematical structure: In both problem formats it is the difference set that is to be determined. In the "More" task condition the episodic situation model consists of two disjoint sets of entities without any further real-world semantics. The question solely introduces a very abstract relation between the two sets of entities by directly asking for the difference between the cardinalities of the two disjoint sets. Thus, the two task conditions in Hudson's study differ not only in the linguistic form of the question; the two conditions are moreover confounded with differences in the underlying episodic situation models. In terms of Piaget's and Aebli's cognitive developmental framework of mathematical concepts and operations, only the "Won't Get" task makes contact with the everyday proto-mathematical experiences, with familiar action scripts (with underlying motives of their actors and protagonists), or, with the concrete-operational roots in which the understanding of elementary mathematical operations is ultimately grounded—an understanding that gradually evolves long before children enter formal schooling.

As a second example, we again look at a reworded word problem as investigated by De Corte et al. (1985): "Peter and Mary have 8 nuts altogether. Five *of these* nuts belong to Mary. *The rest belong to Peter.* How many nuts does Peter have?"

Compared to its standard version ("Peter and Mary have 8 nuts altogether. Five nuts belong to Mary. How many nuts does Peter have?") the problem, as presented by De Corte et al., has been transformed by adding additional words (in italics). In the previous example, the rewording does not change the underlying situation model, the problem model, or the mathematical structure. It is exclusively the presentational structure of the situation and problem model that is altered by varying the amount of explicitly provided information about relations between elements of the problem model: In addition to the cardinality of two sets, specified by their owners, the relations between these two sets are further explicated. This additional wording is in fact not only helpful, but necessary in order to unambiguously generate the problem model. That is the case unless we assume the reader already has the presupposition that no object can be owned by more than one person at a time, except in an abstract kind of joint ownership referring to the superset of disjoint, privately owned sets (marked by phrases such as "have . . . altogether"). If the relations between the sets of objects are more explicitly and redundantly stated, adequate understanding does not depend as much on understanding single expressions, such as the two different meanings of "have" in the earlier problem text. The more explicit presentational version of the problem is thus less likely to lead to misunderstandings.

Variations in wording of standard problems analyzed by Staub and Reusser (1992) have shown that the following combined variations in presentational structure lead to a dramatic increase in difficulty:

1. The initial state has not been specified as a static state of possession (e.g., "Joe had 3 marbles"). Instead a minor variation in the situational structure was introduced by referring to an action by means of a transfer-in verb (e.g., "Joe collected 3 marbles"; "How many cookies did Tom bake yesterday?"). From this information it has to be inferred, by drawing on general world knowledge about transfer of objects and possession, that the outcome of this action leaves its protagonist as the possessor of the objects involved.[10]

---

[10]This inference corresponds to a special case of an addition problem. An initial state of zero objects of a certain kind is increased by some transfer-in. In this respect, our more complex situation corresponds to a two-step problem with the first operation always corresponding to the trivial operation: $0 + x = x$.

2. The text sequence of problem versions analyzed by Staub and Reusser does not match the *ordo naturalis* of the events as they would occur in the real world. Instead, the following sequences were used: resulting state/transfer/initial state for Change 5 and Change 6 problems, and transfer/initial state/resulting state for Change 1 and Change 2 problems. Our revision consisted of adding the time adverbs "yesterday," "today," and "now," together with appropriate tenses, in order to signal the temporal structure of the episodic elements.

3. In the standard problems the transfer of the objects between two persons is always denoted by the action verb "give" (e.g., "Tom had 8 marbles. Then he gave 5 marbles to Joe."). For problem models depicting a transfer-in, this requires the co-actor to take the position of the grammatical subject: "Tom had 3 marbles. Then Joe gave him 5 marbles." Contrary to this way of linguistically presenting the situation, in Staub and Reusser we used a presentational structure that keeps the protagonist (the subject, whose quantity of objects is of interest) in grammatical subject position. The narrative perspective thus remains constant, which should make it easier to comprehend (cf. Black, Turner, & Bower, 1979; Reusser, 1989a). In order to refer to the same problem model, this manipulation, on the other hand, requires the main transfer verb to be changed to "get"; for example, "Today Dane got 11 marbles from Susan. Yesterday Dane found 5 marbles."

4. In the standard problems, one of the persons involved in the transaction of the objects is pronominalized (for transfer-out problems it is the protagonist, for transfer-in it is the co-actor). This requires a bridging inference in order to connect the pronoun to its referent, a problem we eliminated by repeating the proper names throughout.

We speculate that of all these variations in the presentational structure, the dramatic increase in problem difficulty is mainly caused by the variation in text order (Variation 2), which makes it difficult for children to recover the intended situational structure (see also Ohtsuka & Brewer, 1992).

In Stern and Lehrndorfer (1992), a broad elaboration of the situation model that is compatible with the problem question and hence with the problem model—without any further changes in the presentational structure of the standard problem statements—proved to make the corresponding problem solution easier.

As this brief analysis of a few examples of wording effects demonstrates, the quality of the changes in wording, which have all been shown to affect problem difficulty, are quite diverse in character. The theoretical framework already presented, we think, will make it possible to specify much more clearly what kind of differences in wording are being compared in future studies.

CONCLUSIONS AND EDUCATIONAL SIGNIFICANCE

We first make some comments on theoretical questions and then argue, from an instructional point of view, why we think it is important to look at the presentational structure of mathematical word problems.

Theoretical Questions

The theoretical base of many studies using the standard Riley–Heller–Greeno problems has led to a focus mainly on differences in the underlying logico-mathematical problem structure. Problems with the same underlying logico-mathematical structure are seen as being isomorphic. However, as the empirical evidence shows, there are other factors that easily destroy this kind of problem isomorphism.

Our main focus has been on further characteristics of arithmetic word problems whose impact on problem difficulty has often been called "effects of wording." Within our conceptual framework of a cognitive task analysis, which focuses on the presentational structure of the situation and problem models of arithmetic word problems, we propose to theoretically disentangle the fuzzy colloquial notion of wording. Problem difficulty is analyzed as a complex interaction between semantic content structures (including textbase, situation model and problem model), the underlying mathematical structure, and the surface structures by which these are presented to a reader. There can be no simple theory of problem isomorphs: Problems can be similar (isomorphic) or different with regard to more than one level of structural descriptions. The solving of mathematical word problems is a language and knowledge intensive undertaking and should be seen as a skillful interaction of text comprehension (linguistic knowledge), situation comprehension (world-knowledge), and mathematical comprehension (mathematical knowledge).

Instructional Objectives

Examining the presentational structure of verbal problems is of considerable significance not only for the psychological explanation of the relative difficulty of mathematical word problems, but also for the design of such problems. What we refer to, from a psychological point of view, as presentational structures relates from an instructional point of view to a theory of pedagogical design (see Fig. 16.2). Textbook authors (e.g., in mathematics education) intuitively or consciously draw on knowledge about what makes problems (or texts) difficult and pedagogically valuable when constructing mathematical word problems. Writers are guided by certain intentions in selecting content, presentational structure, and linguistic devices (Clark, 1985). In looking at word problems we should ask the same questions: What do we know about the intentions, reasoning, and strategies of teachers and textbook authors that lead them to select a specific content, to give it a specific presentational structure? What do authors of mathematics textbooks have in mind when they choose or construct a mathematical word problem?

Teachers as well as textbook authors design word problems by drawing primarily on their intuitions about what kind of wording will be appropriate, for

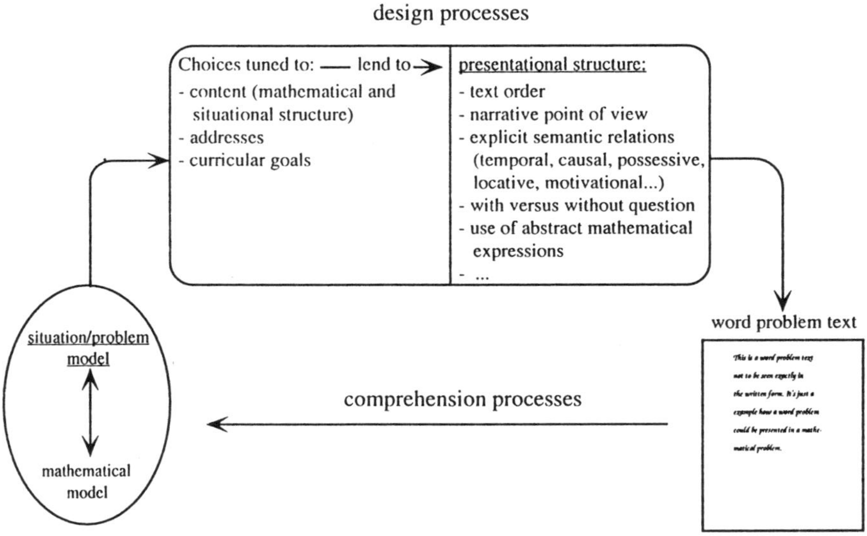

design processes

FIG. 16.2. Analyzing the design of mathematical word problems in terms of content (mathematical structure and situation model) and presentational structure, which both must be adjusted to addressees and curricular goals.

example, what expressions will signal as clearly as possible or with a presumed moderate difficulty the intended arithmetic operation structure.

From an instructional point of view, we need to inquire about the goals, purposes, and plans that are related to the presentational structure of specific word problems. We think that educational psychology can help improve instructional design by contributing to educator's knowledge about how the variation of presentational structures affects both problem difficulty and solution strategies. This instructional knowledge could provide criteria for selecting or generating problem texts whose instructional objectives are to foster students' specific knowledge and skills in comprehending textually presented situations that are to be mathematized. Thus, they contribute to students becoming flexible discourse and problem comprehenders. Because word problems have a clear final processing goal and because a successful solution largely depends on thoroughly understanding the situations denoted in a text, these problems provide excellent opportunities to explicitly apply world knowledge, discourse and language knowledge, as well as arithmetic knowledge.

Word problems should be analyzed with regard to all types of competencies that are required to solve them: language, situation, and mathematical comprehension. Thus, when using word problems in educational settings, the instructional goals should be directed at all these different factors. Word problems are a text type that allows and requires students to bridge the gap between the (textually represented) world of situations and the more abstract conceptual world of mathematics. If mathematics is not only to be taught as a kind of formal game for an elite population, learning to apply mathematical knowledge and principles to real situations ought to be a very important instructional goal.

The objectives being pursued with mathematical word problems should not lie exclusively in the field of mathematics education, but should also include objectives of language education and even content-related topics in science education and the humanities. Word problems should clearly be seen as exercises in applied mathematical thinking, as opportunities for exercising and reflecting on language comprehension skills, and even as opportunities to exercise some general problem-solving skills—such as planning, which is essential for solving complex mathematical story problems (Staub, 1988).

We postulate, from an educational point of view—in parallel with our psychological processing perspective—that the ultimate instructional goal associated with the use of "applied" mathematical problems is to foster and strengthen the relationship or connection between language education, subject matter education, and mathematics education.

ACKNOWLEDGMENTS

We would like to thank Rolf Zwaan for his helpful comments on a draft of this chapter and Eileen Kintsch for her help in editing it. The empirical work presented in this chapter was supported by the Swiss National Science Foundation (Grant No. 10-2052. 86 to Kurt Reusser).

REFERENCES

Aebli, H. (1980). *Denken: Das Ordnen des Tuns: Vol. 1. Kognitive Aspekte der Handlungstheorie* [Thinking: The structuring of action. Cognitive aspects of action theory]. Stuttgart: Klett.

Aebli, H., Staub, F. C., & Ruthemann, U. (1991). Textrechnungen im Mathematikunterricht: Wie und wozu? [Using word problems in mathematics education: How and to what goals?]. *Mathematik Lehren, 44*, 12–17.

Black, J. B., Turner, T. J., & Bower, G. H. (1979). Point of view in narrative comprehension, memory, and production. *Journal of Verbal Learning and Verbal Behavior, 18*, 187–198.

Bobrow, D. G. (1964). *Natural language input for a computer problem solving system.* Unpublished doctoral dissertation, MIT.

Briars, D. J., & Larkin, J. H. (1984). An integrated model of skill in solving elementary word problems. *Cognition and Instruction, 1*, 245–296.

Carraher, T. N., Carraher, D. W., & Schliemann, A. D. (1985). Mathematics in the streets and in schools. *British Journal of Developmental Psychology, 3*, 21–29.

Clark, H. H. (1985). Language use and language users. In G. Lindzey & E. Aronson (Eds.), *Handbook of social psychology: Vol. 2. Special fields and applications* (pp. 179–231). Reading, MA: Addison-Wesley.

Cummins, D., Kintsch, W., Reusser, K., & Weimer, R. (1988). The role of understanding in solving word problems. *Cognitive Psychology, 20*, 405–438.

De Corte, E., Verschaffel, L., & De Win, L. (1985). The influence of rewording verbal problems on children's problem representation and solutions. *Journal of Educational Psychology, 77,* 460–470.

Gelman, R., & Greeno, J. G. (1989). On the nature of competence: Principles for understanding in a domain. In L. B. Resnick (Ed.), *Knowing, learning, and instruction* (pp. 125–187). Hillsdale, NJ: Lawrence Erlbaum Associates.

Hudson, T. (1983). Correspondences and numerical differences between disjoint sets. *Child Development, 54,* 84–90.

Jerman, M. E. (1973). Problem length as a structural variable in verbal arithmetic problems. *Educational Studies in Mathematics, 5,* 109–123.

Jerman, M. E., & Mirman, S. (1974). Linguistic and computational variables in problem solving in elementary mathematics. *Educational Studies in Mathematics, 5,* 317–362.

Kintsch, W. (1974). *The representation of meaning in memory.* Hillsdale, NJ: Lawrence Erlbaum Associates.

Kintsch, W., & Greeno, J. G. (1985). Understanding and solving word arithmetic problems. *Psychological Review, 92,* 109–129.

Morgan, J. L., & Sellner, M. B. (1980). Discourse and linguistic theory. In R. J. Spiro, B. C. Bruce, & W. F. Brewer (Eds.), *Theoretical issues in reading comprehension: Perspectives from cognitive psychology, linguistics, artificial intelligence, and education* (pp. 221–239). Hillsdale, NJ: Lawrence Erlbaum Associates.

Nesher, P., & Teubal, E. (1975). Verbal cues as an interfering factor in verbal problem solving. *Educational Studies in Mathematics, 6,* 41–51.

Nesher, P., Greeno, J. G., & Riley, M. S. (1982). The development of semantic categories for addition and subtraction. *Educational Studies in Mathematics, 13,* 373–394.

Othsuka, K., & Brewer, W. F. (1992). Discourse organization in the comprehension of temporal order in narrative texts. *Discourse Processes, 15,* 317–336.

Piaget, J. (1950). *Introduction à l'épistémologie génétique: Vol. 1. La pensée mathématique* [Introduction to genetic epistemology: Vol. 1. Mathematical thinking]. Paris: Presses universitaires de France.

Resnick, L. B. (1989). Developing mathematical knowledge. *American Psychologist, 44,* 162–169.

Reusser, K. (1985). *From situation to equation. On formulation, understanding and solving "situation problems"* (Tech. Rep. No. 143). Boulder, CO: Institute of Cognitive Science.

Reusser, K. (1989a, September). *Textual and situational factors in solving mathematical word problems.* Paper presented at the Third Conference of the European Association for Research on Learning and Instruction, Madrid.

Reusser, K. (1989b). *Vom Text zur Situation zur Gleichung. Kognitive Simulation von Sprachverständnis und Mathematisierung beim Lösen von Textaufgaben* [From text to situation to equation. Cognitive simulation of text comprehension and mathematization in solving word problems]. Habilitationsschrift: Universität Bern.

Reusser, K. (1990). From text to situation to equation: Cognitive simulation of understanding and solving mathematical word problems. In H. Mandl, E. De Corte, N. Bennett, & H. F. Friedrich (Eds.), *Learning and instruction* (Vol. 2, pp. 477–498). Oxford: Pergamon.

Riley, M. S. (1981). *Conceptual and procedural knowledge in development.* Unpublished master's thesis, University of Pittsburgh.

Riley, M. S., & Greeno, J. G. (1988). Developmental analysis of understanding language about quantities and of solving problems. *Cognition and Instruction, 5,* 49–101.

Riley, M. S., Greeno, J. G., & Heller, I. J. (1983). Development of word problem solving ability. In H. P. Ginsburg (Ed.), *Development of mathematical thinking* (pp. 153–196). New York: Academic Press.

Searle, B. W., Lorton, P., & Suppes, P. (1974). Structural variables affecting CAI performance in arithmetic word problems of disadvantaged and deaf students. *Educational Studies in Mathematics, 5,* 371–384.

Staub, F. C. (1988). Das Problemlösen lernen: Vom Problemverstehen zum Planen der Lösung [Learning to solve problems: From problem comprehension to solution planning]. In J. P. Meylan (Ed.), *Lernbereitschaft und Lernfähigkeit zwischen Schule und Beruf* (pp. 81–93). Bonn-Oedekoven: Köllen-Verlag.

Staub, F. C. (1991, August). *On diagnosing comprehension of mathematical word problems: Transformations in recall as indicators of mental models.* Paper presented at the Fourth European Conference for Research on Learning and Instruction, Turku, Finland.

Staub, F. C., & Reusser, K. (1992, April). *The role of presentational factors in understanding and solving mathematical word problems.* Paper presented at the meeting of the American Educational Research Association, San Francisco.

Starkey, P., Spelke, E., & Gelman, R. (1990). Numerical abstraction by human infants. *Cognition, 36,* 97–127.

Stern, E., & Lehrndorfer, A. (1992). The role of situational context in solving word problems. *Cognitive Development, 2,* 259–268.

van Dijk, T. A., & Kintsch, W. (1983). *Strategies of discourse comprehension.* New York: Academic Press.

Vergnaud, G. (1982). A classification of cognitive tasks and operations of thought involved in addition and subtraction problems. In T. P. Carpenter, J. M. Moser, & T. Romberg (Eds.), *Addition and subtraction: A cognitive perspective* (pp. 39–59). Hillsdale, NJ: Lawrence Erlbaum Associates.

Weaver, C. A., III, & Kintsch, W. (1992). Enhancing students' comprehension of the conceptual structure of algebra word problems. *Journal of Educational Psychology, 84,* 419–428.

Chapter 17

Beyond Discourse: Applications of the Construction-Integration Model

Suzanne Mannes
University of Delaware

Stephanie Doane
University of Illinois

Whether going to work in the morning, writing a research paper, or attempting to read electronic mail, planning plays a large role in the course of our lives. The plans resulting from these activities are created in order to satisfy internal goals, as well as in response to external pressures, such as when directions are given to perform some task. In the context of the research presented here, plans are a series of proposed actions designed to achieve a goal (e.g., Miller, Galantner, & Pribram, 1960), that is determined by and dependent on, a reader's comprehension of some set of verbal instructions. The purpose of this chapter is to demonstrate, by describing two research programs that extend the construction-integration model (Kintsch, 1988) to simulate action planning, the generality and utility of Kintsch's theory as a unifying framework in psychology.

Assembling a series of actions that allows one to interact with a computer serves as the domain for the present work, but the procedures used are relevant to understanding action planning in other domains in which a sequence of interdependent components must be arranged to comprise a plan of action. The way the construction-integration model was extended to explain action planning is presented first. This is accomplished through a description of how the construction-integration model and experimental data mutually constrained the development of a computational model of planning called NETWORK (Mannes & Kintsch, 1991). The structure and processes in NETWORK are described as they apply to the simulation of experts planning solutions to routine computing tasks.

Then a model called UNICOM (Doane, Kintsch, & Polson, 1989) is described, which simulates how users at a variety of levels of expertise comprehend instructions to produce complex UNIX[1] commands. The chapter concludes with a discussion of the practical and theoretical implications of the performance of the described systems, some current research, and possibilities for using the construction-integration model to understand how users acquire planning expertise.

EXTENDING THE CONSTRUCTION-INTEGRATION MODEL TO ACCOUNT FOR ACTION PLANNING

The work presented here examines how users comprehend instructions to complete some task, and how they then use this understanding to plan a course of action. When comprehension is successful, the process of producing a plan to satisfy the stated goal is easy and errorless. However, when comprehension fails, in part or in whole, the production of a plan may be difficult, and the plan produced may be cumbersome or erroneous. Much research has focused on the nature of comprehension processes and how the product of such processes can be used to complete cognitive tasks, such as sentence verification (e.g., Kintsch, Welsch, Schmalhofer, & Zimny, 1990). In that research, performance on the cognitive task is used to evaluate or measure comprehension. In such experiments, readers clearly develop a plan for action; they must, for example, plan their response to an instruction.

This is also true for the present research. Here, the processes of comprehending what to do and planning what to do are dynamically interleaved, and each step of the planning process is treated as a direct product of the reader's current state of comprehension. Plan(s) for accomplishing some task are constructed from comprehension of instructions and are highly dependent on the actual instructions given, the current state of the planner's situation, and the degree of completeness of their knowledge at the time the instructions are encountered. It is the production of these plans—with reference to the provided instructions, the current planning situation, and the planner's prior knowledge—that is to be modeled here.

To tie planning directly to the construction-integration model, which in most instances has centered on knowledge of a declarative nature, required an extension: the addition of "plan knowledge" (Mannes & Kintsch, 1988). In the present research, plan knowledge represents the action-based information users have of elementary computer functions. That is, it is their knowledge of the commands that the computer admits as acceptable in certain situations, and the likely actions that the computer will take in response to these commands. The theoretical addition to the model was to allocate nodes in the memory representation to represent knowledge about the complex states of affairs that must prevail before (preconditions), and result from (outcomes), the execution of certain plan steps. In both NETWORK and UNICOM, plan knowledge is described as a set of plan-element propositions that represent simple actions out of which entire plans can be synthesized. Plan elements represent "executable" forms of knowledge

---

[1]UNIX is a registered trademark of AT&T.

about the computer domain and as such are similar in essence to productions in ACT* (Anderson, 1983).

This approach to "planning as understanding" takes full advantage of the construction-integration principles of overlap (i.e., propositions that share a reference to a common concept are likely to be related in memory) and knowledge activation (i.e., propositions that are related are likely to activate one another). Consistent with prior uses of the model, it is assumed that when users comprehend instructions to perform some task, the incoming instructions act to "overlap" with their existing knowledge (including plan knowledge) to activate a subset of information that is useful in accomplishing the given goal. Activation is then spread throughout the knowledge subset to determine what steps will be taken to accomplish the specified task.

It is important to keep in mind that both NETWORK and UNICOM, the models described here, are instantiations of the construction-integration model, and they share the same underlying computational structure and processes (e.g., parameters, weights, etc.). The only difference between them is in the contents of their knowledge bases; NETWORK contains knowledge about routine file manipulation and editing tasks, and UNICOM contains knowledge about producing complex UNIX commands. Thus, the construction-integration model, implemented in the same computational form, has successfully accounted for two unique sets of empirical data.

Two sets of experimental studies (Doane, Pellegrino, & Klatzky, 1990; Mannes & Kintsch, 1988) provide the foundation for the UNICOM and NETWORK models, respectively. In the Mannes and Kintsch study, veteran computer users were asked to provide verbal protocols about performing certain routine computer tasks. These protocols were solicited while the users were at the computer, though the tasks were not actually done, and were coded according to the methods described by Ericsson and Simon (1984). The tasks were so routine in nature that all subjects were able to solve them correctly while providing concurrent protocols. This work is described in detail in Mannes and Kintsch (1988) and Mannes (1989).

In the Doane et al. (1990) study, subjects with varying degrees of computer experience were asked to produce typed protocols, which were essentially complex UNIX commands, in response to written requests to accomplish particular goals. For example, one goal presented to a subject might be to produce the last 10 alphabetically arranged lines of a certain file. Subjects were asked to produce the most efficient legal UNIX commands that they could to accomplish specified tasks. Here, "efficient" means the command requiring the fewest number of keystrokes. In contrast to the routine problems posed to the subjects in the Mannes and Kintsch (1988) study, subjects in this study actually performed them. They ranged in difficulty from individual (i.e., single), frequently used UNIX commands to composite commands requiring the appropriately sequenced concatenation of several actions using pipes and/or other redirection symbols. The following sections describe how the construction-integration model was used to simulate these performance data.

NETWORK: MODELING ROUTINE COMMAND COMPOSITION

Empirical Research Underlying the NETWORK Model

Mannes and Kintsch (1988) asked experienced computer users to give verbal protocols about how they would perform routine file manipulation and editing tasks. Subjects were able to accomplish these tasks effortlessly and correctly. To identify the knowledge necessary for the successful completion of these tasks, the verbal protocols given by the users were first propositionalized according to standard procedures (Bovair & Kieras, 1985) and then subjected to a detailed content analysis (see Mannes & Kintsch, 1991, for the precise methods used to extract the user knowledge from the protocols). This analysis revealed three types of user knowledge: general knowledge about computers (e.g., files exist), knowledge of the tasks to be accomplished (e.g., a goal is to delete a file), and procedural knowledge (e.g., Anderson, 1983) or knowledge about plan elements and the relationships between them (e.g., plan to delete a file, plan to create a file, and the knowledge that the two plans are contradictory). These plan elements are, as their name suggests, the elements out of which plans are created to accomplish specified tasks. The knowledge gleaned from this analysis was used to create the NETWORK knowledge base.

Building NETWORK's Knowledge Base

The first type of knowledge observed in the verbal protocols was propositionalized, and each proposition became a node in the network representation of the computing domain. In this format each proposition is an atomic unit containing a predicate and some number of arguments. For example, the propositionalization of the sentence "Mike edits manuscripts" would appear as (EDIT MIKE MANUSCRIPT). These propositions share links in long-term memory based on a variety of text-based methods of association.

The third type of knowledge, plan knowledge, was also included in NETWORK's long-term memory. Each plan element describes an action that can be taken in the world, and explicitly specifies the conditions under which each action can be taken, as well as the outcome of executing that action. These plan elements are represented in an extended propositional format, each containing three fields: a name, precondition(s), and outcome(s). For example, the plan element to print a file is as follows.

```
name:          (PRINT FILE)
preconditions: (KNOW FILE LOCATION)
outcomes:      (EXIST HARDCOPY FILE)
```

The plan elements that NETWORK uses to produce a plan of action dynamically, as comprehension progresses, are linked to the general, atomic knowledge propositions via standard text-based procedures (see Bovair & Kieras, 1985), and to each other to form a causal chain. Similar to the rationale to include plan-element knowledge in NETWORK's memory, the decision to incorporate information about sequencing plan elements directly into their representation was based on the observations of expert verbal protocol statements. For example, our experts made statements such as "in order to do that I must first locate the file."

Information about preconditions and outcomes is used in deriving the causal chain using backward chaining, a technique common in artificial intelligence planning systems. NETWORK assesses matches between the precondition and outcome fields of plan-element representations, such that any plan element that provides as its outcome a precondition for another plan element receives a positive link from that plan element. Likewise, a plan element that eliminates, as part of its outcome, the precondition for another plan element receives an inhibitory link from that plan element. A simple example of the nature of this causal chaining is shown in Fig. 17.1.

Whereas the text-based links are bidirectional, the causal chain links are not. In Fig. 17.1, a positive link exists from (DELETE FILE) to (FIND FILE) due to the fact that (FIND FILE) provides a necessary precondition for (DELETE FILE). However, an inhibitory link from (FIND FILE) to (DELETE FILE) is also shown because (DELETE FILE), if executed, would eliminate a precondition for (FIND FILE). During integration, this chaining allows for plan elements whose outcomes provide essential preconditions to receive activation from the plan element requiring that outcome, and for plan elements that eliminate essential preconditions to become inhibited. In this respect the causal chaining is consistent in nature with the relationships that exist among declarative propositions. That is, plan elements will support each other if they work toward a similar goal, or support similar hypotheses, and inhibit each other when they have conflicting goals, such as mutually exclusive preconditions and outcomes.

Together, the propositions representing general knowledge about computers, and knowledge of plan elements are related to form the long-term memory for all of the tasks NETWORK can perform. The next section provides a brief overview of the model's structure. This is followed by a specific example showing how NETWORK plans a solution to a routine computing task.

Example NETWORK Simulation

Overview of Model Execution.   This section describes how the NETWORK model, using the long-term memory derived from verbal protocols, produces a sequence of actions to solve a particular task. The task chosen to demonstrate NETWORK's functioning is to print and delete a file, an example of the class

Three plans in their generic (unbound) form.

NAME	(FIND FILE)
PRECONDITION(s)	(AT-LEVEL SYSTEM) (EXIST FILE)
OUTCOME(s)	(KNOW FILE LOCATION)
NAME	(DELETE FILE)
PRECONDITION(s)	(AT-LEVEL SYSTEM) (EXIST FILE) (KNOW FILE LOCATION)
OUTCOME(s)	NOT (EXIST FILE)
NAME	(ENTER SYSTEM)
PRECONDITION(s)	(AT-LEVEL MAIL)
OUTCOME(s)	(AT-LEVEL SYSTEM)

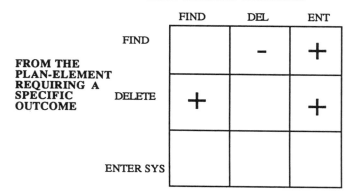

TO THE PLAN-ELEMENT PROVIDING THAT SPECIFIC OUTCOME

FIG. 17.1. A sample of three plan elements are shown in the top panel and the resulting causal chain in matrix form in the bottom panel.

of problems traditionally referred to as "conflicting subgoals" (e.g., Sussman, 1975) and often instantiated as directions to "paint the ladder and paint the ceiling." The potential conflict arises from the fact that solutions to the two subgoals cannot be planned in isolation. In this situation, the planner must recognize that deleting the file will make it unavailable for printing and, thus, though not explicitly told to do so, must sequence plan execution such that the (PRINT FILE) plan element is executed first.

To begin, NETWORK is given the task description in propositional form. This description activates related information in NETWORK's long-term memory, including all of the plan elements. Information other than plan-element information is activated, and thus considered to be residing in working memory, by a probabilistic process. In this process, each proposition in the task description activates a proposition to which it is related in long-term memory with a probability representing the degree of relationship between the task proposition and any given general knowledge proposition residing in long-term memory. Thus, the contents of working memory for any particular task may vary from one solution attempt to another.

The decision to activate long-term knowledge probabilistically was based on both the theoretical foundation of the construction-integration model, as well as on behavioral data. Theoretically, the construction-integration theory assumes that a proposition in the instructions activates some subset of the knowledge to which it is related in long-term memory. Of course, this "task" proposition will be related to propositions in long-term memory to varying degrees and thus, not all propositions have an equal chance of being activated. Those propositions that exhibit stronger relationships with a text proposition will have a greater chance, though not a certainty, of being activated, and propositions remotely related to the text will, some small portion of the time, become active. This type of probabilistic knowledge activation is consistent with behavioral observations. Subjects rarely chose to use less efficient, uncommon methods to solve routine tasks—but this was observed on occasion (Mannes & Kintsch, 1988). This nondeterministic behavior is consistent with the assumption that during different problem solutions, different pools of general computing knowledge are activated.

In contrast to selection of general knowledge, during the solution of any given task all plan elements are available for use in a task solution. That is, the plan elements are activated with probability 1. Again, the empirical data suggest that this is consistent with subject performance. Although they may have chosen different methods for solving routine tasks based on what other general knowledge was activated by the task description, they were always able to produce workable solutions. This suggests that they did have access to all the plan elements (elementary actions) they possessed during plan solution. If plan elements were activated with a probability less than 1, instances where tasks could not be completed should have occurred, however infrequently. This was never the case.

In NETWORK, these plan elements, in their generic form, include things such as (DELETE FILE), (PRINT FILE), (CUT TEXT FILE), and (READ MAIL). When these plan elements are activated in NETWORK's long-term memory and become part of working memory, they become bound to the objects mentioned in the task. For example, if a task description mentions the existence of a particular file called MANUSCRIPT, all the plan elements that deal with knowledge about files in general now become true of the file MANUSCRIPT. This binding process is represented by the inclusion of the file name in the plan elements, for example, (DELETE FILE^MANUSCRIPT).[2] The necessity for this binding process is also supported in the data. Subjects in Mannes and Kintsch (1991) were asked, for example, how they would go about deleting a file. Several subjects asked the experimenter for a file name before they would produce the necessary commands. That is, subjects found it difficult to plan solutions to tasks containing references to generic objects, and we thus equipped NETWORK with the process of binding. In this process, NETWORK searches the task description for instantiations of the generic objects contained in the plan-element propositions. When, for example, a particular file name is found in the task description (e.g., FILE^EGG-PLANT), all the plan elements containing a generic reference to FILE have that generic reference temporarily replaced with the name of the file currently being considered, FILE^EGGPLANT.

After this binding process, NETWORK uses its rules to compute all of the types of relationships between the propositions now residing in working memory, thus producing a task-specific network. The engagement of these rules, which include methods for identifying, for example, instances of argument overlap and causal chaining, constitutes the construction phase of the simulation. This construction results in a network where all the information to be used for the given task has been incorporated. This task-specific network represents the system's understanding of the task to be done, and serves as the input for integration, the second phase of the problem solution in which activation is spread throughout the network.

To integrate activation through the task-specific network, an initial activation vector is created such that all of the propositions in the original task description have equal activation (i.e., they are assigned an activation of $1/n$, where n is the number of propositions in the task description), and the activation values for all of the other knowledge propositions, selected from long-term memory, are set to zero. Activation is allowed to spread through the task network such that propositions related to the current task become strengthened, and the activation values for those apparently unrelated to or inconsistent with the task at hand become weakened.

When activation ceases to flow from the original task description throughout the task-specific network, the system is considered stable, and the most highly activated plan element having all of its preconditions met is allowed to fire. Having its preconditions met requires that all of the propositions contained in a plan element's second field have matching propositions in the current task-specific network. Once a plan element has fired, the task-specific network is reconstructed to incorporate the outcome proposition(s) of that fired plan element. The

---

[2]Note that for tasks that mentioned multiple objects of the same type (e.g., two files), multiple copies of the plan elements were created by NETWORK, one set bound to each unique object. These multiple plan elements afford the model the opportunity to carry out processes on objects irrelevant to the task at hand—a procedure that is observed in human data.

integration phase is then restarted, and when the system stabilizes, another plan element is selected for firing. This (re)construction-integration continues until a task network is constructed in which the original task goal(s) has been satisfied. Thus, each construction-integration cycle contributes one step to the final plan of action that will solve the given task.

Example Task Performance. The following is the original proposition list given to NETWORK at the beginning of the PRINT/DELETE task.

(EXIST FILE^EGGPLANT)
(REQUEST (PRINT FILE^EGGPLANT))
(REQUEST (DELETE FILE^EGGPLANT))

This description probabilistically activates associated information, including some general computing information, and all plan elements (which reside in a generic form) from NETWORK's long-term memory. During this knowledge activation, NETWORK uses knowledge of the task REQUEST to activate an appropriate OUTCOME proposition for the task. Because these are routine tasks, and have probably been solved before, the presence of an appropriate OUTCOME proposition in long-term memory is assumed; however, the implications of a missing OUTCOME are discussed later. The OUTCOME propositions found for the two REQUEST propositions of the PRINT/DELETE task are:

(OUTCOME-OF-REQUEST-PRINT (EXIST HARDCOPY FILE))
(OUTCOME-OF-REQUEST-DELETE (NOT(EXIST FILE)))[3]

A task-specific network can now be constructed using the original and newly activated propositions: task description, related knowledge (including OUT-COME), and plan elements, which become bound to the objects mentioned in the specific task (in this case the file called eggplant) in the manner previously specified. One special form of connectivity comes into play when REQUEST and OUTCOME propositions are encountered by NETWORK in its attempts to link propositions to each other.

When a task REQUEST is encountered, a search for matches between the REQUEST and plan elements' name fields takes place. If a match is found, a positive link is formed from the REQUEST to the plan element(s) with the matching name. Likewise, when a task OUTCOME is considered, it is compared to all plan-element outcome fields and, if a match is found, a link is formed from the OUTCOME to the plan element containing the matching outcome field. If

---

[3]In both the NETWORK and UNICOM models, the REQUEST and OUTCOME statements are redundant for examples shown here. This is not always the case. Both fields are included to give the reader a clear understanding of the features of the model.

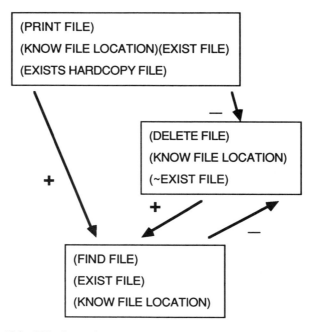

FIG. 17.2. This figure shows how PRINT and DELETE both send positive activation to FIND and how PRINT and FIND both inhibit DELETE as a result of causal chaining.

the match is exact, a positive link is formed. If, on the other hand, a proposition is found in a plan-element outcome field that negates the task OUTCOME, an inhibitory link is formed. Once all methods of determining connectivity for the task-specific network have been completed (i.e., the construction phase for a task step has been accomplished), the integration step is performed.

For the first step of the PRINT/DELETE task, (FIND FILE^EGGPLANT) is the most highly activated plan element with its preconditions met after the network stabilizes. It fires, producing a proposition that specifies that the location of the file called eggplant is now known. Note from the plan elements shown in Fig. 17.2 that this provides a precondition, (KNOW LOCATION FILE^EGGPLANT), for both of the explicit requests. Hence, during the integration phase for the first step of PRINT/DELETE, (FIND FILE^EGGPLANT) received activation from these plan elements, which require its outcome as a precondition.

One last method of determining connectivity between the task-specific network nodes must be explained. In order to prevent the model from repeating its actions, propositions representing the outcomes of plan elements (e.g., [KNOW FILE^EGGPLANT LOCATION]), inhibit the plan elements that produce them. This means that if the outcome of a plan element has already been established, either because it was a part of the original task description or, as in this case, it has become true as the result of a plan element having fired, the plan-element outcome proposition inhibits that plan element from firing again. Here, once the location of the file is known, as produced by the (FIND FILE^EGGPLANT) plan element, (FIND FILE^EGGPLANT) is inhibited by the proposition reflecting the file's location.

Using this method of connectivity, in addition to the others previously described, the PRINT/DELETE network is reconstructed and integration is done once again to select a plan element to fire for the second step of the task. In this step, the plan element to (PRINT FILE^EGGPLANT) is highly active and, as can be seen in Fig. 17.3, the plan element to (DELETE FILE^EGGPLANT) has no activation at all, even though all of its preconditions are present. Although both (PRINT FILE^EGGPLANT) and (DELETE FILE^EGGPLANT) are activated as part of the task description, the inhibition from (PRINT FILE^EGG-PLANT) to (DELETE FILE^EGGPLANT), present due to causal chaining, is stronger than (DELETE FILE^EGGPLANT)'s activation. (PRINT FILE^EGG-PLANT) fires, and its outcome, that there (EXISTS HARDCOPY FILE^EGG-PLANT), is added to the network. Thus, the system has accomplished one of its two goals and is progressing in the proper order. As in the previous step, the newly added proposition representing the plan-element outcome has the ability to inhibit the plan element that produced it. In this case, the plan element to (PRINT FILE^EGGPLANT) is inhibited by the fact that a hard copy already exists. This plays an important role, as can be seen in the results of the next construction-integration cycle.

The third integration step produces a vector of activation values in which the plan element to (DELETE FILE^EGGPLANT) is most active (see Fig. 17.3). This state of affairs came about because of causal chaining and the plan-world inhibition mentioned earlier. In Step 2, the plan element to (PRINT FILE^EGG-PLANT) was very active and as a result had a strong inhibitory effect on the (DELETE FILE^EGGPLANT) plan element via the plan-element causal chaining. After its firing, the plan element to (PRINT FILE^EGGPLANT) becomes inhibited itself and, therefore, no inhibition propagates from its node to the (DELETE FILE^EGGPLANT) node. This allows (DELETE FILE^EGGPLANT) to receive the activation the direct REQUEST provides, and makes it the most active plan element. (DELETE FILE^EGGPLANT) fires and NETWORK has correctly completed the conflicting subgoals task producing a series of steps similar to those produced by experienced users.

In Mannes and Kintsch (1991), subjects produced protocols to six different tasks. The NETWORK simulation was developed based on the protocols for three of these tasks. One test of the simulation then was an assessment of its ability to plan subjectlike series of steps to the other three tasks, and PRINT/DE-LETE was one of these. Another test of the simulation was to give NETWORK instructions for novel tasks for which there were no empirical data, and evaluate the sensibility of its proposed plans. In all cases, the plans that NETWORK

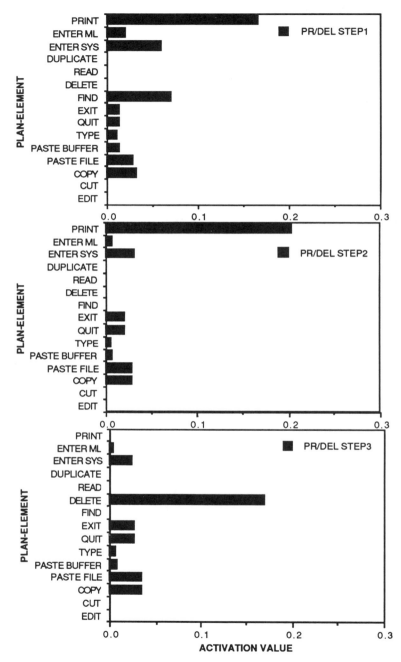

FIG. 17.3. Activation values for some plan elements for the three steps of the PRINT/DELETE task.

proposed were reasonable (i.e., they would accomplish the given task), though perhaps not always the most efficient.

Discussion of NETWORK Simulations

The Role of Theory and Data.   It is important to note that the Mannes and Kintsch (1988) verbal protocol data and the construction-integration model (Kintsch, 1988) mutually constrained each other in the development of NET-WORK. The presence of experimental data made it possible to refer to an objective source when decisions had to be made regarding the implementation of the theory in its computational form, NETWORK. For example, recall that the process of activating general computing knowledge from long-term memory is a probabilistic process. The decision to model it as such was guided by the theory in which the activation of knowledge depends on the current context and the interrelationships among knowledge elements. This decision was in accordance with the experimental data as well. Protocols from our subjects clearly indicated situations in which certain known facts failed to be used in particular task solutions. These instances of "activation failure" were evidenced by statements such as "gee, it never occurred to me, but I know that" and "I just didn't think of it at the time."

Another implementation decision based mutually on theory and data was the causal chaining between plan elements. Whereas most propositions are linked via argument overlap, the plan elements were linked via causal chaining. Expert verbal protocols statements, such as "in order to respond, I first have to get into the mail system," led us to such an implementation decision, just as the subjects' necessity for nongeneric objects prompted us to include the described binding process.

The Influence of Context.   The fact that NETWORK constructs a new task-specific network in the context of each specific problem by activating long-term knowledge in a probabilistic manner allows for simulation of interesting contextually driven phenomena. An example of this can be seen in comparing how NETWORK approaches similar tasks differently depending on the information that has been given. One task, REVISE, is to revise a manuscript and send it to a colleague. Another task, SEND, is to send a copy of a revised manuscript in response to an electronic-mail message asking for it. For REVISE, there is no mention of a mail message to which NETWORK can reply (perhaps the colleague had called in the request using the phone), so it chooses to send the revised manuscript as a file from the system level.

In the SEND task there is a mail message to reply to and, during knowledge activation, NETWORK finds general computing knowledge in long-term memory that states (ISA REPLY-COMMAND SEND-COMMAND), so it chooses to enter mail and reply to the existing message with the file. The plan NETWORK produces for solving the SEND task consists of the following series of commands: (ENTER SYSTEM), (FIND FILE), (EDIT FILE), (CUT PARAGRAPH), (EXIT FILE), (ENTER MAIL), and (REPLY FILE MAIL). Thus, the presence or absence of a seemingly unimportant piece of information, that the request was received via computer mail as opposed to through a phone conversation, encourages NETWORK to produce different solutions. This is a result of the additional weighting that the plan element for replying through mail (REPLY FILE MAIL) gets due to argument overlap with the task description mentioning the mail message and the general knowledge proposition that says that a reply command is a way of sending.

In both the general discussion of NETWORK and the detailed example of the PRINT/DELETE problem, the activation of general knowledge has been mentioned, but because it plays a minimal role in the solution of that task, its role has not been emphasized. In other tasks that NETWORK has solved, such as SEND, the activation of general knowledge makes a difference in the series of steps that is produced. In solution attempts where the proposition (ISA REPLY-COMMAND SEND-COMMAND) had not been activated from long-term memory via the probabilistic knowledge activation process, NETWORK still enters the mail system to send the manuscript, but chooses a SEND command rather than the more efficient REPLY command. (Other illustrations of the role of knowledge in problem solution are presented in Mannes & Kintsch, 1991.) Thus, the solution that NETWORK produces for a given task will depend to some extent on precisely what knowledge is activated at the time. It is not enough to merely possess the requisite knowledge. To be useful it must be activated in response to a task request.

Less than Optimal Performance. Because NETWORK was developed as a simulation of expert performance, the activation in long-term memory of an appropriate OUTCOME for each task is a certainty. Experts would be expected to have encountered so many different tasks that, when presented with a routine task request, they are almost certain to find an appropriate task outcome in long-term memory. The lack of experience on the part of a novice computer user might lead to a failure to find an outcome proposition. In modeling such a user, NETWORK would have to determine plan-element-to-task connectivity based on the REQUEST alone. As a result, no primary connections based on the outcome field of the plan elements would exist between the task description and the plan elements, and less than optimal performance would be expected.

Another way in which the NETWORK simulation of novice computer users might differ from that of the more experienced user is in the strength and nature of the causal chain among plan elements. In another study (Mannes & Hostetter, 1991), novices were asked to provide verbal protocols as they planned solutions to the same routine computing tasks to which the experts had responded in Mannes and Kintsch (1991). These protocols showed that novices often omitted necessary steps in the problem solution, suggesting that either their content knowledge of plan-element preconditions was less than adequate, or they had not developed relationships among plan elements sufficient to form the necessary causal chain. A detailed analysis of these error data, manipulation of the specificity of the plan-element precondition and outcome fields, and manipulation of the parameter value for causal chaining to simulate these data are not yet completed.

The manner in which different levels of expertise could be modeled with NETWORK is purely speculative as no less-than-expert simulations have been attempted. In contrast, different levels of UNIX expertise were successfully modeled using the construction-integration model as implemented in UNICOM. This research is described in the next section.

UNICOM: MODELING COMPLEX COMMAND PRODUCTION

The computational program developed in the NETWORK research provided the foundation for UNICOM, the model that simulates UNIX command production (Doane, Kintsch, Polson, & McNamara, 1991; Doane, McNamara, Kintsch, Polson, & Clawson, 1992). UNICOM contains specific knowledge about the UNIX system, and it is explicitly used to model users at varying levels of expertise by modifications to its long-term memory knowledge base. The goal of this research was to use the construction-integration model to understand the difficulties UNIX users have comprehending instructions and planning actions to produce complex, sequence-dependent UNIX commands. A brief description of the UNIX empirical results used to create the UNICOM knowledge base is given here. This is followed by a description of the UNICOM simulation.

Empirical Research Underlying the UNICOM Model

Doane et al. (1990) examined the development of expertise within the UNIX operating system by asking users to produce the most efficient legal UNIX command that they could to accomplish specified goals (i.e., those with the least number of keystrokes). Goals ranged in difficulty from individual, frequently used UNIX commands to composite commands that accomplished several actions, and had to be sequenced appropriately using pipes or other input–output redirection symbols. Correct production of the composite commands required knowledge not only of individual commands, but also of the input and output concepts, syntax, and information-flow processes required to sequence commands together properly. Tasks involving more elementary commands were designed to include elements that had to be put together to generate a successful composite. For example, the most efficient way to obtain a hardcopy of the files contained in a directory is to combine the elementary commands **ls** (which lists the file names in the current directory) and **lpr** (which prints the contents of a file on the line printer) using a pipe (|) to create the composite command **ls|lpr**. This composite command will first list the file names on the directory, and then "pipe" the output (i.e., the file names) to the line printer.

Another example of a composite task is to "Display the first 10 alphabetically arranged lines of file trash." (The correct production is **sort trash|head**.) A component single would be "Display the alphabetically arranged lines of file trash." (The correct production is **sort trash**.) Thus "single" commands required just one action, and composite commands required several actions that had to be sequenced appropriately using pipes and/or redirection symbols. The composite goals given to the Doane et al. (1990) subjects can be seen as requiring the development of action plans to put familiar elements together in a novel fashion. Thus, it is assumed that subjects were not recalling fixed plans from memory. Rather, they were solving each problem anew by producing action plans online.

The production data indicate that UNIX users differ markedly from one another in performance, according to their history of use with the operating system. One striking aspect of these data was that only the experts could successfully produce the composites, even though the intermediates and novices could perform the other tasks that were designed to assess the component knowledge required to successfully generate a composite (e.g., single commands). That is, some novices could produce the single commands **sort file^trash** and **head file^trash**, and showed knowledge of pipe, but could not chain these together to produce the composite, **sort file^trash|head**.

To understand why less expert subjects had such difficulty developing composite commands, a construction-integration model of their knowledge was developed, and the model was used to simulate comprehension of instructions to produce these commands. The following sections describe how the UNIX knowledge possessed by the novice, intermediate, and expert groups was represented in the UNICOM knowledge base, and how this influenced the simulation outcomes.

Building UNICOM's Knowledge Base

To build a UNICOM knowledge base, all of the general knowledge and plan-element knowledge required to produce the UNIX commands studied was propositionalized in the manner described for NETWORK. As in the NETWORK model, UNICOM is initially given three types of information in propositional form: long-term memory knowledge relevant to the domain (e.g., knowledge of UNIX), knowledge of plan elements, and knowledge of the task description (e.g., "list the first 10 lines of the file named trash"). The following describes each of these types of knowledge as they exist in UNICOM to simulate an expert producing composite UNIX commands. This is followed by a description of how the knowledge base is modified to account for less than expert performance.

Single Commands. The expert model includes knowledge necessary to produce the single commands **cat, cmp, edit, head, lpr, ls, more, nroff, sort, tail,** and **wc.**[4] These are single commands that were later combined into composites in the Doane et al. (1990) study. The command **tail** (which lists the last 10 lines in a file) will be used as an example, and all other single commands are similar in terms of the structure of their singular knowledge prerequisites. Recall that, as for NETWORK, for a single plan element to be executed, it must be activated by being relevant to the task at hand, and the world knowledge and general knowledge that are prerequisites for the plan element to fire must exist in the task-specific network. To execute the plan element for **tail**, the model must have activated general knowledge of the **tail** command, activated knowledge that the **tail** command requires a file argument, knowledge that the file to be processed exists, knowledge that the user is at the system level, and, finally, knowledge of the task to list the last 10 lines in a file. Once the (TAIL) plan element is fired, a proposition representing the existence of a list of the last 10 lines of the relevant file will be added to the world knowledge and the task will be considered done.

Composite Commands. Recall that the production of composite commands requires the sequence-dependent coordination of commands using one or more UNIX input–output redirection symbols (e.g., |, >, etc.). In addition to the knowledge that is necessary for single commands, the model requires five additional pieces of knowledge to successfully plan commands to accomplish composite tasks.

First, the model must have general semantic knowledge about redirection. For example, the model must know that standard input and output exists and that it can be directed. It is interesting to note that this type of information is much more conceptual or abstract than the knowledge required for completing single commands. That is, knowledge about redirection is not attached to a specific command or output. Chi and others (e.g., Chi, Feltovich, & Glaser, 1981) noted that novices have much more difficulty acquiring abstract knowledge than more concrete facts. Similarly, the lack of specificity in certain task instructions posed a problem for even the experts who served as subjects in the Mannes and Kintsch study (1988). Thus, novice UNIX users are expected to have difficulty with this type of knowledge prerequisite.

Second, the model must have general syntactic knowledge about redirection. For example, the model must know that a pipe "|" exists and that it redirects input and output only between commands. It must also know that a filter ">" exists and that it redirects output of commands to files.

---

[4]Note that in the following sections, lowercase bold strings refer to actual UNIX commands (e.g., **tail**) and uppercase, parentheses delimited strings refer to those commands as implemented in UNICOM (e.g., (TAIL)).

Third, the model needs knowledge of the specific redirection properties of each command included in a composite. For example, in order to execute a composite that includes redirecting the output of the command **ls**, the model, in addition to maintaining all of the other types of knowledge, must know that **ls** output can be redirected. This third type of knowledge is critical to understanding the difficulties that people have with UNIX composite production. In UNIX, the redirection properties of different commands are not consistent. As an example, consider the lack of consistency between the redirection properties of the **ls** and **sort** commands. Both the input and output of the **sort** command can be redirected from or to other commands. In contrast, only the output of **ls** can be redirected. If one uses the analogy between the "shape" of the redirection properties of UNIX commands and the shape of puzzle pieces, then different UNIX commands have very different shapes.

There are cognitive consequences to the different shapes of the commands— namely, users cannot assume the redirection properties of a command they are using. Rather, these properties must be memorized and retrieved for each individual command. This may be one source of difficulty for many of the subjects in the Doane et al. (1990) study. The fact that some users could not successfully combine single commands to produce composites, even when they knew the component single commands, suggests that perhaps they could not retrieve the redirection properties of each command.

Fourth, the model must have knowledge of the temporary state of the information flowing between commands. For example, to execute a **sort trash|tail|lpr** command in response to the instruction to "print the last 10 alphabetically arranged lines of file trash on the line printer," the model must select the (SORT) plan element, then keep in memory the result of performing the **sort** (the sorted contents of file trash exist), then select the (TAIL) plan element, then keep in memory the result of executing the **tail** (the last 10 lines of sorted file trash exist), and then select the (LPR) plan element and store the result of executing the **lpr** (a hardcopy of the last 10 lines of sorted file trash exists). The knowledge of information flow is used to sequence the commands properly, and this must take place to achieve the desired result. That is, a reordered composite such as **tail trash|sort|lpr** would result in a very different outcome.

Finally, the model requires plan-element knowledge that represents the ability to produce the redirection symbols, such as pipes and filters. For example, to use a pipe, it must have a plan element to build a pipe command, (BUILD PIPE), and a plan to execute the piped command once it is built, the (USE PIPE) plan element. The precondition fields for the (PIPE) plan elements can be extensive, depending on the single commands that need to be sequenced. For the example composite of **sort file^trash|head**, the (PIPE) plan element will require all of the four types of knowledge already described, including specific input and output knowledge for the **sort** and **head** commands.

Example Expert UNICOM Simulation

Overview of Model Execution. UNICOM simulations have a structure similar to that described for NETWORK. First, UNICOM is given a task description in propositional form that activates related information about UNIX in UNICOM's long-term memory, including all of the plan elements it knows about. Some of the plan elements correspond to single commands (e.g., **sort, head**), and of these, some correspond to commands that are irrelevant to the simulated tasks. Other plan elements allow creation of new plans. These latter plan elements are called "build" plan elements, because they allow UNICOM to build a composite command from the single plan elements. Two of the single plan elements, and one of the build plan elements are shown in abbreviated form in Table 17.1.

Each of UNICOM's plan elements includes three components: a plan name, preconditions, and outcomes. The preconditions are propositions representing the state of the world that must exist for the plan to be executed. The outcomes are propositions that become added to the state of the world if the plan is executed. Once the propositions corresponding to long-term memory, task description, and plan-element knowledge are given to UNICOM, it uses the same associative rules to construct the relationships between the propositions as detailed in previous sections, and creates the task-specific network. This network is UNICOM's representation of the current task, and it provides the input for the integration phase.

The integration phase in UNICOM begins with an initial activation vector with activity $1/n$ for all task description propositions and zeros otherwise. This vector is postmultiplied by the memory matrix until the change in activation between multiplications is small and the system is considered settled. When the system has settled, the most activated plan element whose preconditions are met is allowed to fire and its outcomes are added to the task-specific network. This process is reiterated until the plan element fires whose outcome accomplishes the specified goal, or request.

TABLE 17.1
A Sample of the UNIX Domain Plan Elements

Plan Name	Preconditions	Outcomes
(SORT FL)	(@SYS) (EXIST FL) (KNOW SORT)	(SORT FL)
(DISP 1ST TEN LINES FL)	(@SYS) (EXIST FL) (KNOW HEAD)	(DISP 1ST TEN FL)
(BUILD PIPE)	(KNOW SORT 1ST) (SORT FL)	
	(KNOW HEAD 2ND) (DISP 1ST TEN FL)	
	(KNOW REDIRECT HEAD OUTPUT)	
	(KNOW REDIRECT SORT INPUT)	
	(KNOW REDIRECT SORT OUTPUT)	
	(KNOW REDIRECT HEAD INPUT)	(USE PIPE PLAN)

Single Commands. The expert simulation of comprehending instructions to produce a single command to sort the contents of file1 alphabetically (**sort file1**) is very simple for UNICOM, as it was for the subjects in Doane et al. (1990). The system finds all of the preconditions are met, and the (SORT) plan element is executed immediately.

Composite Commands. The composite problem to produce **sort file1|head** is far more complex, because the task requires that the model go through both a planning phase and a building phase. To explain why the model has two phases, and how it determines when to use them requires discussion of the process that subjects seem to go through in planning a composite. Expert UNIX users from Doane et al. (1990) show reaction time data and protocols, which suggest that they realize there is no single command that will accomplish the specified task, and that they need to chain single commands together to create the desired composite command. Experts take an average of 12 sec to respond initially to requests to produce composite commands. Less expert subjects are much faster to respond (4 sec), and their productions are characterized by misordered and fragmented sequences. These data are consistent with the hypothesis that experts recognize they are being given a complex task, and they spend more time planning their response.

In UNICOM, the expert model first looks to see if there is any single plan element whose outcome will accomplish the specified task. In the case of singles, UNICOM is successful in this search and does not enter into a planning phase. It simply executes the most activated plan element whose preconditions are met, and the task is solved. In contrast, for composites, UNICOM finds no single plan element that will accomplish the goal. When this occurs, the model automatically enters a planning phase where it attempts to chain single plan elements together to comprise a plan for the solution to the task. In the task with single goals, there are no interrelationships between sequences of actions, so the model can immediately generate an action upon determination of the correct plan element. In the case of the composites, it is hypothesized that the appropriate plan elements must be determined and then sequenced correctly using the interrelationships among the preconditions for the various plan elements. Following each integration phase, this planning process adds representations of the individual commands and the order in which they should be executed to the state of the world knowledge.

Figure 17.4 depicts the plan elements considered by UNICOM for the **sort file1|head** task. The relative activation values of the three most highly activated plan elements is indicated on the left side of the figure. The arrows indicate the plan element selected by the model and the flow of execution between construction-integration cycles.

Example Task Performance. The expert model uses all of the types of knowledge detailed earlier to complete a composite command. As an example, the following describes how the model executes the command, **sort file1|head**.

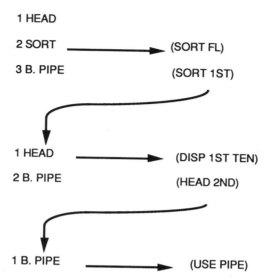

FIG. 17.4. Results of simulating the composite command **sort file1|head**. The build pipe plan is abbreviated as B. PIPE.

The most activated plan element is the goal plan element, which is to take the head of the sorted contents of the file. But to do this, the sorted contents of the file must exist. At this point in the simulation, the preconditions of the (HEAD) plan element have not been satisfied. The second most activated plan element is the (SORT) plan element. This element is fired if the model knows the **sort** command, the file to be sorted exists, and the user is at the system level. These preconditions are met, and the (SORT) plan element is fired. Following its execution, the fact that the sorted contents of the file exist in the world is added to the task-specific network.

Now, the model must chain the results of **sort** to the **head** command using the (BUILD PIPE) plan element. To do this it must possess and activate knowledge that input and output can be redirected, the pipe redirects input and output between commands, the output of **sort** can be redirected to another command, and the destination command, **head**, can take input from another command. Note that if any one of these pieces of information is either missing from long-term memory or fails to be activated during knowledge activation, the (BUILD PIPE) plan element cannot successfully fire. Once the (BUILD PIPE) plan element is fired, its outcome is added to the task-specific network. Finally, the model must select the (HEAD) plan element and store the knowledge that a head on the sorted contents of file exists in the world. At this time, the planning process is complete and the (USE PIPE) plan element is executed.

It is important to note that the representation of the (BUILD PIPE) plan element is more general than it appears in Table 17.1. There, (BUILD PIPE) is shown after it has been bound to the chain of plan elements selected by UNICOM for the specified task. In the beginning of the task, it is generically written as (KNOW PROCESS1) (KNOW OUTCOME PROCESS1); (KNOW PROCESS2) (KNOW OUTCOME PROCESS2); etc. As UNICOM completes construction-integration cycles and planning progresses, each of these processes are bound to (i.e., take on the identity of) specific single plan elements. (This binding is much like NETWORK's binding process in which generic plan elements become bound to the particular objects in the task at hand.) The expert model avoids many pitfalls in the planning phase, such as confusing the order of the plan elements, lacking knowledge of one of the necessary plan elements, or lacking the knowledge of a pipe and how it is used in the context of specific plan elements (i.e., not all single commands can be included on the right side of a pipe).

Recall from the prior discussion that NETWORK solved the REVISE and SEND tasks with different plan elements depending on subtle differences in the task instructions. This is also true for the UNICOM model. Subjects in the Doane et al. (1990) study were asked to produce the most efficient legal UNIX command that they could to accomplish a specified task. They were told to use both pipes and redirection, and that pipes were preferred, because they require use of fewer total keystrokes than other redirection symbols. These directions are translated into the propositions (USE PIPE) and (USE REDIRECTION) and (PREFERRED PIPE) that are included in the task description given to UNICOM for all problems. When asked to produce the command that will list the first 10 alphabetically arranged lines of file1 on the screen, UNICOM has the option of activating a (BUILD REDIRECTION) plan, **sort file1>temp <cr> head temp**, or a (BUILD PIPE) plan, **sort file1|head**, both of which would accomplish the task, one more efficiently than the other. If, in the task instructions, UNICOM is told that pipe use is preferred, the overlap of this instruction with the (BUILD PIPE) plan-element arguments leads to its higher activation relative to the redirection plan. If this part of the instructions is omitted, leaving UNICOM free to use whatever plan it wishes without regard for efficiency, the pipe and redirection options are preferred equally.

Summary of the Expert Simulations.[5]   Producing a composite command for UNICOM requires comprehending an instruction to sequence together many elements within the system. Understanding the instruction in these terms refers to activating and sequencing relevant knowledge in a fashion that will accomplish the specified task. For composites, the sheer number of relevant facts that must be activated above those required for single commands is surprising. Further, the modeling effort suggests that many intervening results must be kept track of while planning a composite, and this must be done in the absence of any guidance from the system. This is exactly what is hypothesized about users as well.

---

[5]In what follows, we summarize the results of the UNICOM expert simulations. The interested reader may find additional detail and data in Doane, Mannes, Kintsch, and Polson (1992).

The Less than Expert UNICOM Simulation

The knowledge base for the simulation of the prototypical expert includes every-thing required to successfully complete all of the tasks. The primary claim is that the major sources of difficulty for novice and intermediate users are the additional knowledge and processing demands placed on them in the context of producing composite commands. The experimental data that led to this claim are summarized later (see Doane, McNamara, Kintsch, Polson, & Clawson, 1992, for details).

The novice and intermediate UNICOM knowledge bases were created by examining the actual novice and intermediate data from Doane et al. (1990). In one portion of that study, users were shown the same composite commands that they had been asked to produce, and were queried as to what each command would do. That is, they were asked to "comprehend," rather than to produce, UNIX commands. A comparison of the comprehension and production perform-ance for each user revealed three main levels of proficiency. The lowest level of proficiency is characterized by a lack of both comprehension and production. In this case, a user can neither understand what a command will do, nor produce the command when asked to do so. The next level of proficiency exists when a user can comprehend, but not produce, a command. For example, a user that can explain what **sort** does, but cannot produce it, must possess factual knowledge that **sort** exists. They may even maintain some general knowledge about its redirection properties, but lack the procedural knowledge, or plan-element knowl-edge, required for its use. The final level of proficiency is possessed by the user that can both produce and comprehend the command. If the user shows this level of proficiency for all commands and redirection symbols, then the user has the equivalent of UNICOM's expert knowledge base.

After examining both the production and comprehension data of the novice and intermediate users in the Doane et al. (1990) study, knowledge bases repre-senting a "typical" novice and intermediate were created, using the rules described earlier (e.g., if novices routinely comprehended **sort** but could not produce the command, their knowledge base was given general knowledge of **sort**, but they did not have the (SORT) plan element).

The detailed knowledge analysis resulting from the novice and intermediate UNICOM simulations (detailed in Doane, Mannes, Kintsch, & Polson, 1992) suggested that less expert users may have trouble because they are lacking in one of the knowledge types specified previously (i.e., general semantic knowledge about redirection, general syntactic knowledge about redirection, I/O syntax knowledge for specific commands, and I/O conceptual knowledge about specific command redirection properties), or are lacking in their ability to sequence the items and keep track of the intermediate results. Again, it is presumed that the latter is a consequence of either knowledge deficits, working memory load prob-lems, or both. Empirical support for these hypotheses was sought.

To provide empirical support for these hypotheses, a "prompting" study was performed where users with varied levels of experience with UNIX were asked to produce composite commands, and then were given help prompts if they failed to produce the correct command (Doane, McNamara, Kintsch, Polson, & Clawson, 1992). The help prompts were designed to assist subjects with both knowledge and process deficits that the UNICOM modeling efforts have suggested are present in less expert users. That is, the help prompts systematically provided them with the four knowledge types (e.g., redirection syntax) mentioned earlier, or assisted them with the process of sequencing the command items and keeping track of the intermediate results (i.e., helping with information-flow-induced memory load). If a user requires information about ordering of commands, then a prompt containing this information should assist their performance. However, if they do not require or cannot use this information, then the prompt should have no impact on their subsequent production.

The results of the prompt study provided support for the knowledge and memory hypotheses originating from the UNICOM simulations (for details see Doane, Mannes, Kintsch, & Polson, 1992). First, experts responded to different prompts than novices. Expert performance was helped by the presentation of abstract information, and they did not need many prompts to produce the correct composite. In contrast, novice and intermediate performance was modified by presenting concrete information about the redirection knowledge and the ordering of commands. That is, the users reacted to the prompts in a manner consistent with the UNICOM analysis.

Discussion of UNICOM Simulations

The main features of the UNIX experimental data concerned performance on different types of problems and performance by users at different levels of expertise. The most salient observation concerning problem types is that single commands make quite different demands on users than do composites. The model presented here gives a good account of these differences: It specifies precisely their locus. Additionally, UNICOM provides an explanation for the differences that have been observed in the ability of novice, intermediate, and expert subjects to produce UNIX commands. Many salient differences between these user populations can be simulated by deleting certain knowledge requirements and processing strategies from the user's repertoire (e.g., Doane, McNamara, Kintsch, Polson, Dungca, & Clawson, 1991).

In summary, the UNICOM simulations suggested that the construction-integration model was effective in representing how UNIX users comprehend instructions to produce complex sequence-dependent plans for action. Using the theory to simulate specific users resulted in further understanding of the knowledge and memory required to comprehend instructions to produce complex commands. It provided a vehicle to characterize the knowledge possessed by users at various stages of expertise.

Note that the knowledge and processes required to chain UNIX elements together are examined in the context of a theory of comprehension that has been used to explain algebra story problem comprehension (Kintsch, 1988), and solution of routine computing tasks (Mannes & Kintsch, 1991). Thus, rather than developing an idiosyncratic knowledge analysis, this research is being performed in the context of a general architecture of cognition.

DISCUSSION

In our work, comprehending an instruction means being able to produce an appropriate plan for action. The modeling and knowledge analyses presented here show how this understanding can be achieved computationally. The analyses were based on the construction-integration theory, which is a general theory of comprehension. At one level, what the simulations achieve is a demonstration that the knowledge and information-processing steps described are indeed sufficient computationally to produce the routine commands and more complex UNIX commands specified by the instructions. At another level, the application of this theory of comprehension to such complex planning tasks effectively demonstrates its breadth.

Work in Progress: Further Planning Extensions

Based on these successes, the construction-integration model is being extended in several directions. For example, the model is being applied to the complex domain of airplane piloting.[6] Specifically, the model is being used to examine what airplane pilots will attend to and what they will find difficult about accomplishing complex sequence-dependent flight maneuvers, such as turning or changing speed, or combinations of such maneuvers. In this context, performing maneuvers refers to the comprehension of task instructions and information displayed in the cockpit, and the resulting association of this information with piloting knowledge in order to develop a plan of action. The focus of the analysis is not so much on understanding the information per se, but on the way the cockpit information activates piloting knowledge, how this activation dictates what displays and controls they will attend to, and how it leads to the development of action plans to accomplish a specified maneuver.

An expert model is currently being developed that contains all of the knowledge required to successfully perform critical maneuvers. The knowledge contained in the expert model is being obtained from manuals, from watching expert pilots, from examining expert pilot data, and from talking with instructional

---

[6]The pilot project is funded in part by a grant from ONR Grant #N00014-93-1-0253 awarded jointly to the second author and to Art Kramer, Chris Wickens, and Gavan Lintern at the University of Illinois.

pilots. While building the expert model, it is being validated by comparing the model's performance to that of expert pilots. The goal of this research is to determine what aspects of cockpit information are difficult for pilots at particular levels of expertise to comprehend, both for single and combination flight maneuvers. Once the expert model is developed, the manner in which pilots at different levels of expertise accomplish the same maneuvers will be simulated. To do this, knowledge will be systematically deleted from the expert knowledge base, using an overlay method common in student modeling (see, e.g., VanLehn, 1988), and used in previous research with UNICOM.

Future Directions

Critical to all of the described applications is the notion of learning. For both UNICOM and NETWORK, the initial knowledge base was derived from expert behavior. To model users at less-than-expert levels of performance, UNICOM's knowledge base was lesioned. Neither research program has yet addressed the manner in which these knowledge bases might develop. That is, questions remain as to how experts get to be experts in the first place, and what distinguishes different types of expertise. Hatano and Inagaki (1986; Holyoak, 1991) suggested that experts can be classified as being either routine and adaptive. In their terms, routine experts can solve familiar problems with accuracy, but they do not fare well when asked to perform novel tasks. In contrast, adaptive experts can solve novel problems using new procedures derived from their expert knowledge. Given our neglect of this aspect to date, a future program of research will investigate ways in which the principles of overlap and spread of activation in the construction-integration theory can be used to develop a model of learning. The premise is that if individuals' ability to attend to and comprehend incoming information is dependent on the overlap of their knowledge with incoming instructions, this may also be a factor in their ability to remember and incorporate this knowledge for future use.

One approach in progress extends the model to account for how individual users learn from help instructions while using the UNIX system. The data from the UNIX "prompt" study (Doane, McNamara, Kintsch, Polson, & Clawson, 1992) serve as the basis for this extension. In this work, one goal is to determine if the model "attends" to the same instructions that users do, as indicated by the activation of both plan and general knowledge. Another goal is to determine how many and what parts of the help prompts will be carried over to later problems as a function of their activation in the model (i.e., when does "prompt knowledge" enter long-term memory?). If the model indeed matches subject performance, this will have important implications for development of help systems and for the extension of the model in general. Specifically, it will suggest that the construction-integration theory can be used effectively to model the background knowledge of a user, based on performance, and then use the overlap between their knowledge and incoming instructions to "predict" when, and to what, they will attend.

Another approach in progress is to introduce sets of incoming instructions and outgoing actions as "cases" into long-term memory. Cases would be the system's analog to episodic memory and would represent memory of a particular problem-solving experience. As such, they might merely consist of some memory for a request that was posed, and the plan elements that were used to achieve it. The use of these prepackaged solutions in the planning process is distinct from the way in which NETWORK and UNICOM currently perform by producing new solutions each time a task is solved.

Long-term memory knowledge of previous successful task solutions can serve two purposes. First, an "expert" might simply use such knowledge to solve a familiar, routine task. For example, after producing a plan to DELETE an unlocated file named tomato, there might be a case proposition in memory such as

[OLD-TASK
     (REQUEST DELETE FILE^TOMATO)
     (PLAN {FIND FILE^TOMATO} {DELETE FILE^TOMATO})]

Reliance on such cases for solution performance would produce routine expertise, and presumably the same solution would be produced for a given task every time it is solved.

More interesting is the application of cases to novel situations where an appropriate outcome or case for a request cannot be found in long-term memory. In this situation, other cases, or episodic memories, might be selected from long-term memory based on argument overlap or similarity between the request of the current task and that of one in memory. Thus, when a novel task was encountered, a planner would fail to find the exact outcome required for the task, but still might find information about the solution to a related task and could apply the previous solution to the current situation. This would oftentimes prove to be a successful strategy; however, this same strategy could produce a serious side effect. To the extent that case selection is based on superficial similarities between the current task and the cases in memory, things such as file names and directory contents would be used as a measure of the similarity between the current task and known cases.

In order to be useful in solution, these cases would have to be appropriately modified. With appropriate methods for modifying a case, adaptive expertise similar to that observed when solutions are planned online, would presumably be observed. If the cases were not subject to modification, the planner could instead be tricked into producing a series of plan elements that would not accomplish the current task, although it would be performed on the appropriate object(s). This less than expert behavior would closely mimic phenomena observed in other types of problem-solving situations. It has been well established that, for example, expert and novice physicists categorize physics problems by concentrating on very different aspects of the problem (e.g., Chi, Glaser, & Rees, 1982). Experts use information regarding the underlying structure of the problem to be solved while novices use superficial information on which to base their plan of action. Similarly, when students of a variety of levels of mathematical expertise are asked to sort algebra word problems into groups, those with more experience sort problems based on the procedures required for their solution whereas the less expert students sort the problems based on, for example, the type of objects mentioned in the problem (e.g., Silver, 1981). The less experienced subjects can be "tricked" into sorting a rate/time/distance problem into the same group as a mixture problem if both mentioned, for example, planes and trains.

In addition to the possibility of using episodic memories in both their original and modified forms to solve tasks, this type of knowledge could be used to develop more accurate derivations of the relationships among plan elements. At this time, plan-element links are derived on the basis of the causal chain only. Experience with solving tasks could serve the role of increasing the strength between plan elements that tend to co-occur repeatedly. That is, rather than setting these links through methods independent of the problem-solving history of the system, they could be learned. As the system becomes more and more experienced, different subsets of plan elements would tend to become more strongly linked to each other, perhaps producing a type of "knowledge encapsulation" observed in experts in other fields (e.g., Schmidt & Boshuizen, 1993).

Clearly, the fruitful applications of the construction-integration model are many. Though it was developed as such, it is clearly not a model of the processes involved in text comprehension alone. Rather, it is a theory about the ways in which prior knowledge interacts with a current context to influence the course of human cognition. Regardless of the specific task being performed in our daily lives, if it involves comprehension and planning, the construction-integration model provides a unitary framework in which these processes can be modeled and understood.

REFERENCES

Anderson, J. R. (1983). *The architecture of cognition.* Cambridge, MA: Harvard University Press.

Bovair, S., & Kieras, D. E. (1985). A guide to propositional analysis for research on technical prose. In B. K. Britton & J. B. Black (Eds.), *Understanding expository text* (pp. 315–362). Hillsdale, NJ: Lawrence Erlbaum Associates.

Chi, M. T. H., Feltovich, P. J., & Glaser, R. (1981). Categorization and representation of physics problems by experts and novices. *Cognitive Science, 5,* 121–152.

Chi, M. T. H., Glaser, R., & Rees, E. (1982). Expertise in problem solving. In R. J. Sternberg (Ed.), *Advances in the psychology of human intelligence* (Vol. 1, pp. 7–75). Hillsdale, NJ: Lawrence Erlbaum Associates.

Doane, S. M., Kintsch, W., & Polson, P. (1989). Action planning: Producing UNIX commands. In *Proceedings of the Eleventh Annual Conference of the Cognitive Science Society* (pp. 458–465). Hillsdale, NJ: Lawrence Erlbaum Associates.

Doane, S. M., Kintsch, W., Polson, P. G., & McNamara, D. S. (1991). *Producing UNIX commands: What experts must know* (Tech. Rep. No. UIUC-BI-CS-91-20). Urbana, IL: Beckman Institute Cognitive Science (Learning Series).

Doane, S. M., Mannes, S. M., Kintsch, W., & Polson, P. G. (1992). Modeling user command production: A comprehension-based approach. *User Modeling and User Adapted Interaction, 2*(3), 249–285.

Doane, S. M., McNamara, D. S., Kintsch, W., Polson, P. G., & Clawson, D. M. (1992). Prompt comprehension in UNIX command production. *Memory & Cognition, 20*(4), 327–343.

Doane, S. M., McNamara, D. S., Kintsch, W., Polson, P. G., Dungca, R. G., & Clawson, D. M. (1991). Action planning: The role of prompts in UNIX command production. In *Proceedings of the 13th Annual Meeting of the Cognitive Science Society* (pp. 682–687). Hillsdale, NJ: Lawrence Erlbaum Associates.

Doane, S. M., Pellegrino, J. W., & Klatzky, R. L. (1990). Expertise in a computer operating system: Conceptualization and performance. *Human-Computer Interaction, 5*, 267–304.

Ericsson, K. A., & Simon, H. A. (1984). *Protocol analysis: Verbal reports as data.* Cambridge, MA: MIT Press.

Hatano, G., & Inagaki, K. (1986). Two courses of expertise. In H. Stevenson, H. Azuma, & K. Hakuta (Eds.), *Child development and education in Japan* (pp. 262–272). San Francisco: W. H. Freeman.

Holyoak, K. J. (1991). Symbolic connectionism: Toward third-generation theories of expertise. In K. A. Ericsson & J. Smith (Eds.), *Toward a general theory of expertise: Prospects and limits* (pp. 301–335). Cambridge, MA: MIT Press.

Kintsch, W. (1988). The role of knowledge in discourse comprehension: A construction-integration model. *Psychological Review, 95*, 163–182.

Kintsch, W., Welsch, D., Schmalhofer, F., & Zimny, S. (1990). Sentence memory: A theoretical analysis. *Journal of Memory & Language, 29*, 133–159.

Mannes, S. M. (1989). *Problem-solving as text comprehension: A unitary approach.* Unpublished doctoral dissertation, University of Colorado, Boulder.

Mannes, S., & Hostetter, D. (1991). *How do novices differ from experts?* Unpublished manuscript.

Mannes, S. M., & Kintsch, W. (1988). Action planning: Routine computing tasks. In A. A. Turner (Ed.), *Mental models and user centered design* (Tech. Rep. No. 88-9). Boulder, CO: Institute of Cognitive Science, University of Colorado.

Mannes, S. M., & Kintsch, W. (1991). Routine computing tasks: Planning as understanding. *Cognitive Science, 15*(3), 305–342.

Miller, G. A., Galantner, E., & Pribram, K. H. (1960). *Plans and the structure of behavior.* New York: Holt, Rinehart & Winston.

Schmidt, H. G., & Boshuizen, H. P. A. (1993). On the origin of intermediate effects in clinical case recall. *Memory & Cognition, 21*, 338–351.

Silver, E. A. (1981). Recall of mathematical problem information: Solving related problems. *Journal for Research in Mathematics Education, 12*, 54–64.

Sussman, G. J. (1975). *A computer model of skill acquisition.* New York: American Elsevier.

Van Lehn, K. (1988). Student modeling. In M. C. Polson & J. J. Richardson (Eds.), *Intelligent tutoring systems* (pp. 55–78). Hillsdale, NJ: Lawrence Erlbaum Associates.

Chapter 18

CAPping the Construction-Integration Model of Discourse Comprehension

Susan R. Goldman
Sashank Varma
Vanderbilt University

The Construction-Integration (CI) model (e.g., Kintsch, 1988, 1992) utilizes a fixed-capacity working memory buffer. Our work extends the CI model by giving it a dynamic, capacity-constrained working memory system. At the same time, our work extends the work of Just, Carpenter, and their colleagues on single sentence processing in a capacity-constrained working memory system (e.g., Just & Carpenter, 1992; McDonald, Just, & Carpenter, 1992) by examining connected discourse processing. The first section of the chapter briefly reviews the CI model in order to provide a context for the contrast with the capacity-constrained models. We then compare the results of CI and capacity-constrained CI (3CI) simulations and examine their predictive ability for behavioral recall of text passages.

CONSTRUCTION-INTEGRATION MODEL

The CI model (e.g., W. Kintsch, 1988, 1992) is a simulation that models how text representations are constructed, understood, and integrated with the reader's knowledge. During the construction phase a semantic networklike coherence matrix is created in which input propositions define the nodes and the links between nodes are created on the basis of argument overlap and propositional embedding. All propositions and their links are given initial activation (usually 1 unit). The representation is "fine-tuned" through an integration process that uses a connectionist algorithm. Integration operates until the network "settles," that is, until changes in the activation vectors resulting from successive cycles are less than some criterion.

The final activations or strengths in working memory predict various memory phenomena (e.g., W. Kintsch, 1988, 1992; W. Kintsch & Welsch, 1991; W. Kintsch, Welsch, Schmalhofer, & Zimny, 1990). In addition, the final activation values can be used to compute strength in long-term memory and these long-term memory activations have been found to satisfactorily predict behavioral recall data (e.g., W. Kintsch, 1992; E. Kintsch, McNamara, Songer, & W. Kintsch, 1992).

A central assumption of the CI model (W. Kintsch, 1988) is that only those things that reside in working memory simultaneously can be connected. Typically, the propositions constituting a single sentence are input in a cycle. If the sentence is not the first sentence of a passage, some input from the previous cycle is "carried over," and processed along with the new input. The number of propositions carried over is given by parameter s, and the s most highly activated propositions are held over. The parameter s depends on assumptions about a fixed-capacity buffer. Frequently, buffer size is set at two propositions (e.g., W. Kintsch, 1988; W. Kintsch & van Dijk, 1978) but other values are possible (e.g., Tapiero & Denhière, chap. 12 in this vol.). Propositions not held over are transferred to long-term storage and are retrievable through reinstatement searches.

CAPACITY-CONSTRAINED
WORKING MEMORY MODEL

The capacity-constrained system we are working with is the Collaborative Activation-based Production System (CAPS) developed by Just and Carpenter (1992). The CAPS architecture is actually a language for writing cognitive simulations. It embodies a few important architectural assumptions such as parallel processing and threshold-based recognition of the condition side of productions. The rationale for these assumptions is provided in Just and Carpenter (1982). Subsequently, Just and Carpenter (1992) expanded the assumption base to include mechanisms for incorporating a limited-capacity memory system. In the present context we highlight those assumptions most relevant to understanding how the architecture is used to model discourse processing. One unique feature of CAPS is that condition sides of productions can exist at levels of activation rather than as present or absent. For an element to match a production, it must be consistent in form and have an activation greater than some threshold. The most common action of a matched production is to direct activation from one element to another. A processing cycle consists of matching all productions against working memory and firing all instantiations in parallel.

A second important architectural assumption is that there exists an activation limit on working memory, sometimes referred to as the "cap." The total amount of activation available for working memory elements is capped. When fired productions request more activation than is available, the "cap" has been reached. The requests and the activation currently assigned to working memory elements are scaled back an amount proportionate to their activation relative to other working memory elements. Because productions iteratively fire until their goals are met, processing at the "cap" results in an overall system slowdown and the graceful loss of working memory elements that are not participating in processing. When elements fall below a minimum level, they are no longer functional in working memory and cannot connect with new information.

ADVANTAGES OF CAPACITY-CONSTRAINED CONSTRUCTION-INTEGRATION (3CI)

There are several potential advantages of embedding CI in a CAPS environment. First is the manner in which propositions are "held over" for further processing. The CAPS architecture permits greater latitude in assumptions about how previously processed propositions are dealt with. Whereas in CI, a fixed buffer of size s in conjunction with final activation values on each processing cycle determine which propositions are held over, the process operates more dynamically in 3CI. In 3CI, working memory functioning determines not only which propositions remain active for the next input cycle but also how many. On some input cycles all previous propositions might remain active; on others, only one or two might remain active.

Second, the dynamic working memory model of 3CI provides a great deal of flexibility in dealing with how prior knowledge is activated and interacts with the input from a passage being read. For example, we are beginning to experiment with different schemes for allocating processing capacity to the information coming in for the first time as opposed to prior knowledge. Differential activation for prior knowledge can be accomplished in CI but the activation value must be specified for each proposition. The 3CI architecture enables processing "biases" to be built into its operation by partitioning the allocation of working memory activation (e.g., 75% to new information; 25% to old). The effect of such differential activation could be applied to a single passage so that emphasis would be placed on the current sentence over previously processed sentences from the same passage. Differential activation could also be applied to information activated from longer term semantic memory so that information from the passage currently being read was emphasized over background knowledge.

Third, we ultimately want to build into our simulations the capability to read strategically. A symbolic architecture of some kind is necessary to accomplish this. Using the CAPS architecture we have already built REREADER, a text processing model that rereads based on a relatively simple coherence evaluation criterion (Goldman, Varma, & Ortega, 1992). This effort has demonstrated to us that the CAPS architecture supports the operation of a nondeterministic, strategic model. Expansions and elaborations of our initial model are planned within the CAPS architecture. We return to a discussion of this issue of strategic reading in the concluding section of this chapter.

COMPARISON OF THE OPERATION OF CI AND 3CI

The remainder of the chapter discusses three simulation models: CI with the fixed buffer s, and two different instantiations of CI in the CAPS architecture. The two versions of 3CI rely on the constrained capacity of the CAPS working memory mechanism to settle activation among propositions. They differ in how they deal with carryover. 3CI-Mimic uses a fixed-buffer, carryover rule just like the CI model. 3CI-Dynamic does not use a fixed buffer; rather, constraints on working memory capacity determine which and how many propositions are carried over. Other similarities and differences among the three simulation models are outlined here.

1. Construction of a semantic network of propositions is based on argument overlap and propositional embedding in all three simulation models. Each proposition acts as a node and is considered to be linked to itself and to other propositions with which it shares arguments, that are embedded in it, or in which it is embedded. All three simulation models share the assumption that propositions must be concurrently active in working memory to be linked. In the CI model, these connections are established in the construction phase and form a coherence matrix. In contrast, there is no distinct construction phase in 3CI-Mimic and 3CI-Dynamic. Instead, the linking rules are embodied in productions and the "coherence matrix" is computed dynamically: The overlap and embedding productions are matched against all propositions in working memory to create the links of the network.

2. In CI, there is an activation vector that is used in the connectionist integration algorithm. In 3CI capacity-constrained working memory replaces the activation vector. Rather than the postmultiplication of CI, the settling process is the firing (in parallel) of the linking productions described earlier. When the distribution of activation is stabilized, that is, there are only small changes in the activations of the nodes and links from iteration to iteration, the system has settled. We used the same "stopping" criterion in the three simulation models: The network was considered settled if the change in activations from one iteration (either one postmultiplication or one round of production firing) to the next was less than .01. When the system has settled, each proposition processed in that cycle has a final activation value for that cycle. A second measure generated by the integration process is the number of iterations to settle. Note that the settling process in CI utilizes a normalization procedure at the end of each processing

cycle such that the final activation values on each cycle are between 0 and 1 (or between −1 and 1 if inhibitory weights are used, which has not been the case in our work). These values are the ones with which the carryover propositions enter the next cycle. This end-of-cycle normalization process is necessary for the CI network to settle. The 3CI models do not require a normalization process at the end of each cycle for the network to settle. The Appendix to this chapter contains additional information regarding the "integration" process.

3. Two propositions may share more than one argument or embedded proposition. In CI, link strength is not incremented for multiple overlaps but link strength in 3CI-Mimic and in 3CI-Dynamic does reflect multiple links.

4. Long-term memory strengths of the nodes and links between propositions are computed according to the procedure outlined by W. Kintsch and Welsch (1991). A second matrix, the long-term memory strength matrix, is constructed from the initial connection matrix formed during the construction phase (see Point 1), and the final activation vector. (Note that these are the normalized final activation values in the CI model.) The effect of this procedure is that the long-term memory strength of a node is the sum of the squares of its final activations over all cycles in which it was active. The long-term memory strength of a link between two nodes is the sum (over all cycles in which both propositions were active) of the product of the connection strength between the propositions on each cycle (found in the connection matrix for that cycle) and the final activations of the propositions on that cycle.

5. Cycle-to-cycle carryover is implemented in the same way in CI and 3CI-Mimic: On each input cycle, the two propositions that were most highly activated when the system had settled are held over for processing with the next input cycle. All other propositions are "cleared out" and do not participate in processing on the next cycle. The 3CI-Dynamic simulation does not use this procedure. Rather, all propositions are held over at their final activation levels. On any particular cycle, some of these fall below threshold for participating in linking. For 3CI models, the final activation levels of the propositional nodes and links vary depending on what the working memory "cap" is set at.

In the work we present here, for all of the simulation models the input consisted of the sentences from the passage "Distance." "Distance" is a descriptive, informational passage. It begins with a paragraph that provides a general definition of distance and then describes two types of distance: absolute and relative. The remainder of the passage provided descriptive information about five types of relative distance, each of which is introduced (Sentences 5, 8, 11, 14, 17) and then elaborated by two sentences. In the passage presented to human subjects, Sentences 1, 4, 8, 11, 14, and 17 were the first sentences of the six paragraphs in the passage.

An input cycle consisted of a single sentence from the text represented as parsed, complex propositions (van Dijk & W. Kintsch, 1983). The propositional input to the simulations discussed here reflected a "pruned" version of the input sentences. The full text of the passage contained 167 atomic propositions. Fully 30% of these were never recalled by any of the subjects. The "pruned" versions of the sentences were generated using two macrorules as heuristics: delete unnecessary details, including many modifiers, and generalization of noun phrases (cf. van Dijk & W. Kintsch, 1983). For example, the input sentence *Distance is simply the space between two points* was "pruned" to *Distance is the space between points*, and represented as a complex proposition. The pruning process, in effect, generates a macropropositional representation for the text. This type of representation corresponds to a "gist" scoring level for behavioral recall data. The majority of sentences generated between 3 and 7 propositions, with a few generating between 10 and 12, to produce a total of 91 input propositions that were processed in 19 cycles. The first two pruned sentences and their propositional input for the first two cycles are provided in Fig. 18.1, along with the network representation.

The simulations were run on Macintosh IIci computers. CI simulation runs were conducted using a program developed in Kintsch's lab (Mross & Roberts, 1992). The 3CI models were implemented in a Common Lisp version of capacity-constrained CAPS (Just & Carpenter, 1992). All propositional nodes and links among them were given initial activations of 1 unit. The 3CI models were run at a "cap" of 20. This value was sufficient to permit processing of a single, average sentence without exceeding capacity. As indicated in the foregoing description, each simulation run generates several measures of interest: number of iterations to settle on each cycle, final activation of each node and link at the conclusion of a cycle, long-term memory node strengths, and long-term memory link strengths. Our discussion here focuses on node strengths, link strengths between propositional nodes in different sentences, and iterations to settle.

The results of the simulations are presented in two parts. In the first section, we compare the models to one another. Following the comparisons of the simulation models we examine their ability to predict behavioral recall and processing data obtained from adults and children.

COMPARISONS OF THE RESULTS
OF THE SIMULATION MODELS

As already indicated, there were certain differences between CI and the CAPS versions of CI in the operation of the integration and settling processes. We first wanted to determine that the two different methods produced similar results; otherwise it might be claimed that any differences between CI and 3CI-Dynamic were due to the integration mechanisms rather than to the more flexible carryover logic enabled by the capacity-constrained working memory model of CAPS. Accordingly, we first compare CI and 3CI-Mimic, the CAPS version of CI that operated with a fixed buffer exactly like Kintsch's CI model. If the comparison of CI and 3CI-Mimic yield negligible differences between the models, we can

Sentence/Cycle 1:

Distance is the space between points.

p1 is[distance,space]
p2 is^between[space,points]

Sentence/Cycle 2:

When measured with a standard unit, the result is called absolute distance and is what persons think of when they think of distance.

p3 measure[someone1,distance,standard^unit]
p4 time[p5,p3]
p5 type^of[distance,absolute]
p6 and[p5,p7]
p7 think[persons,p8]
p8 is^equal[distance,p5]

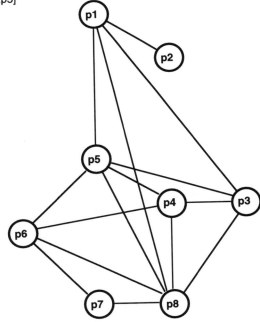

FIG. 18.1. Pruned sentences, propositional input, and network representation for the first two sentences of the "Distance" passage.

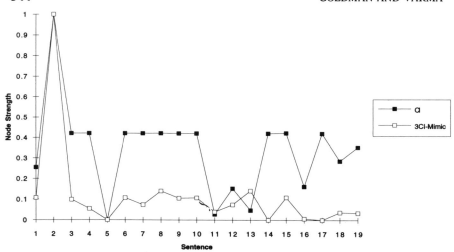

FIG. 18.2.   Comparison of the LTM node strengths, for each sentence, resulting from CI and 3CI-Mimic simulation runs on the "Distance" passage.

compare CI with 3CI-Dynamic and be confident that differences between the models are due to the working memory model rather than to the other differences between the simulations.

CI and 3CI-Mimic

CI and 3CI-Mimic produced long-term memory strength measures that were highly correlated. The node strengths for the main predicates of each complex proposition are shown in Fig. 18.2. (The patterns of results do not differ if the node strength is determined by averaging the node strengths of all of the propositions of the complex proposition.)[1] The overall patterns of node strengths are similar for CI and 3CI-Mimic, although there are some minor deviations around Sentences 13, 14, and the last three sentences of the passage. Although the node strength values for

---

[1]Activation strength measures derived from the models vary widely. As previously noted, in CI the activation measures are normalized during the integration process. In contrast, the CAPS simulations produce strength estimates in the tens for node strength and in the hundreds for link strength between. These absolute differences are not important. What is important is the *pattern* over sentences, so we have normalized all LTM strength measures for each model to range between 0 and 1. The LTM normalization was the only time that the 3CI strengths were normalized. The CI model also normalizes at the end of each cycle, producing less extreme values in the LTM matrices. Hence, normalization of the LTM matrices leads to CI node strengths that, on average, are higher than those of the 3CI models. However, these absolute differences are not important in terms of comparing the patterns of activations among nodes. The link strength measures are not as dramatically affected by the differences in normalization because CI does not form as many links as 3CI. Normalizing the LTM-strength measures does not change the magnitude of the correlations between models or with the behavioral recall data.

CI are generally higher than those for 3CI-Mimic, the strengths of the nodes within each model relative to one another are highly similar. The models are in complete agreement regarding the strongest node: the main predicate of Sentence 3, the sentence that introduces and defines relative distance, the topic of the passage.

The link strengths between propositional nodes are shown in Fig. 18.3 for both models. The general similarity between the two models is obvious, again with some minor variations, for example, Sentences 8 and 16.

The processing measures, number of iterations to settle, were virtually uncorrelated, as illustrated in Fig. 18.4. CI and 3CI-Mimic are similar on only about half the sentences and there is no systematicity to which model took a greater number of iterations to settle. Furthermore, iterations to settle were not correlated with number of words or number of propositions in the input sentence for either model. We were not surprised that this measure differed across the two models because they differ in the algorithm used for settling.

However, it was important that the long-term memory strength measures produced by CI and 3CI-Mimic were highly and significantly correlated. The correlations of the node strength and link strength measures satisfied us that we had a reasonably faithful implementation of CI in the CAPS architecture. Accordingly, we moved on to comparing CI and 3CI-Dynamic.

CI and 3CI-Dynamic

The key difference between the CI model and the 3CI-Dynamic model is in the rule for carrying propositions forward. As described earlier, in CI there is a fixed buffer of size s (set at 2 in these runs) but in 3CI-Dynamic, all propositions

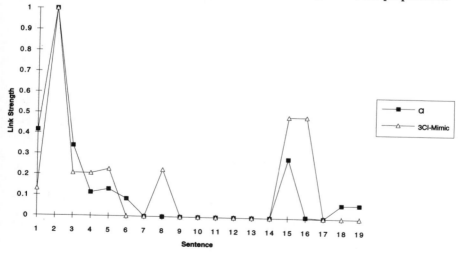

FIG. 18.3. Comparison of the LTM link strengths among sentences, resulting from CI and 3CI-Mimic simulation runs on the "Distance" passage.

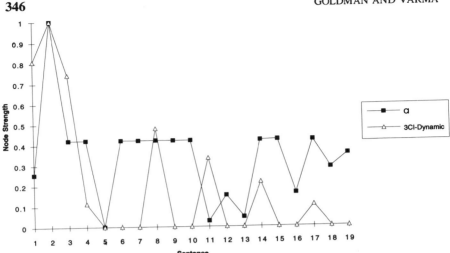

FIG. 18.4. Comparison of the LTM node strengths, for each sentence, resulting from CI and 3CI-Dynamic simulation runs on the "Distance" passage.

retain their final or "end-of-the-cycle" activations when processing begins on the next sentence. New propositions enter working memory with initial activations of 1 unit. Due to capacity constraints, this initialization process may draw activation away from the propositions already in working memory. When a proposition falls below a preset threshold, it is no longer recognized by the system.

The long-term memory strengths generated by CI and 3CI-Dynamic were both significantly correlated, although the link strength correlations were significantly higher than the node strength correlations. Figure 18.4 shows a plot of the node strengths for the two models. There are clearly a number of divergences. It is particularly interesting that these divergences reflect systematic activation peaks for 3CI-Dynamic and these correspond to four sentences that introduced types of relative distance—in other words, the main points of the passage. The CI model does not clearly differentiate these points from their neighbors.

The link strength measures were more highly correlated than the node strengths. However, as Fig. 18.5 shows, there were substantial divergences between the models on each of the main point sentences (i.e., 5, 8, 11, 14, and 17), with 3CI-Dynamic producing greater activation levels for these sentences.

Just as CI and the 3CI-Mimic were uncorrelated on the iterations-to-settle measure, there was no significant correlation on this measure between CI and 3CI-Dynamic. Figure 18.6 shows the iterations to settle for all three models. One interesting aspect of the scatterplots is that the 3CI-Dynamic model shows a much more consistent number of iterations per cycle than does CI or the 3CI-Mimic model. (Dynamic and Mimic were also not correlated on this measure.) The relatively smooth function for 3CI-Dynamic may reflect the situation that incoming sentences are being integrated into more of a global "historical" context

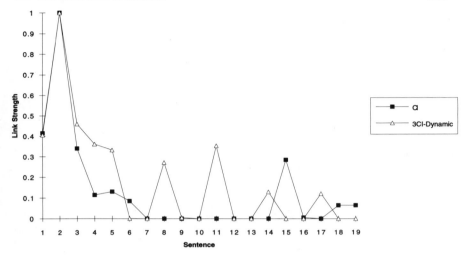

FIG. 18.5. Comparison of the LTM link strengths among sentences, resulting from CI and 3CI-Dynamic simulation runs on the "Distance" passage.

of the passage than tends to be true for CI or 3CI-Mimic, each of which clears out all but the two most active propositions prior to taking in new input. In 3CI-Dynamic, the task with new input is to figure out where new propositions fit into the network active in working memory. This network may be reflecting more of the global structure of the passage. The settling process reflects more of an incremental change in the contents of working memory. In contrast, in CI,

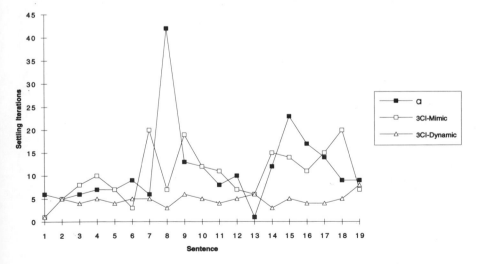

FIG. 18.6. Comparison of the number of iterations needed for the network to settle during simulation runs of the CI, 3CI-Mimic, and 3CI-Dynamic models.

the propositions that are held over are somewhat more susceptible to local conditions. Of course, there are mechanisms to circumvent this. For example, Otero and W. Kintsch (1992) clamped a superordinate proposition so that it would be present on each processing cycle.

Despite the much smaller range in the number of iterations for 3CI-Dynamic as contrasted with CI, there was a significant correlation of iterations in 3CI-Dynamic with number of words ($r = .74$) and number of propositions ($r = .81$) in the input sentence. Recall that there were no such correlations for CI. We speculate that when greater amounts of new information are contained in the input sentence, 3CI-Dynamic takes longer to settle because more of the already active propositions must be scaled back.

To summarize, the 3CI-Dynamic model produced long-term memory propositional node and link strengths that, although correlated with those of the CI model, diverged in interesting ways. In particular, 3CI-Dynamic's divergences from CI corresponded with stronger weighting on the main point nodes of the Distance passage. The 3CI-Dynamic model also produced stronger link strength values for these sentences. These results indicate that allowing propositional carry over to operate dynamically in response to working memory constraints produces a pattern of weights consistent with intuitions about the relative importance of the various sentences in the passage, as well as with a great deal of prior research on main point identification in expository passages (e.g., Kieras, 1980, 1981, 1982; Lorch, 1989; Vipond, 1980).

We want to stress that the 3CI-Dynamic model produced the differentiation without being "told" anything about how to identify main points in a passage and without introducing differential weighting schemes on different propositions. We emphasize this because it is possible to improve CI's differentiation of main points: When we provided the CI simulation with initial activation weights of two units rather than one for the propositions of the main points (e.g., 5, 8, etc.) and clamped those values over the course of processing, the pattern of the resulting node and link weights is much closer to those produced by 3CI-Dynamic. In effect, the capacity-constrained working memory mechanism accomplished on its own what we had to do for the CI model. This seems to be a distinct advantage for the 3CI-Dynamic model.

Comparisons of the simulation models are interesting, but would seem an academic exercise unless we could demonstrate that they have some validity with respect to behavioral data. Indeed, in the next section we consider the ability of CI and 3CI-Dynamic to predict behavioral data.

PREDICTIONS OF BEHAVIORAL RECALL DATA

We turn now to a consideration of the predictive power of CI and 3CI-Dynamic for behavioral recall data. The behavioral data were collected from adults (college students) and from 12- and 13-year-old children. The "Distance" passage was one of several read on a computer using a program that we developed, *Select the Text* (Goldman & Saul, 1990a). With this program, sentences can be exposed one at a time while the others remain masked on the screen. Reading can be done in any order and students can go back and reread sentences at any time. Students knew they could go back and reread. Elsewhere Goldman and Saul (1990b) discussed ways in which the capability to reread in the experimental situation affects some of the reading strategies exhibited, relative to effects related to reading time (e.g., Graesser & Rhia, 1984; Haberlandt & Graesser, 1985).

In two of the adult studies, individuals recalled the passage; in a third, they summarized from memory. In the studies in which children participated, they recalled the passage after reading it. In one of the studies with children, they read from a booklet and wrote their recall; in the other, they read from the computer and orally recalled. Recall was scored at the gist, or meaning preserving, level. We also collected processing time data (computed per word per sentence) when students read on the computer.

Predictions of Recall

Propositional node strength and link strength between propositional nodes as derived from the CI and 3CI-Dynamic simulations were used to predict recall (or inclusion in summary) of each of the 19 sentences in the "Distance" passage. The simple correlations of link strength and recall (or summarization) were significant for each model and there was no significant difference between the correlations of the two models. Node strengths from the 3CI-Dynamic simulation were also significantly correlated with recall in four of the five studies and were significantly greater than the correlations of CI node strength with recall. The one exception was the children's oral recall study where both models produced significant correlations with recall. However, within each model, the simple correlations between node strength and link strength were significantly co-linear ($r = .65$ for CI and $r = .87$ for 3CI-Dynamic). Accordingly, we used regression techniques to determine the amount of variance in recall accounted for by the two measures.[2]

The results of the regression analyses are shown in Table 18.1. For the adult recall data, the R^2s for the 3CI-Dynamic model are substantially greater than for CI, accounting for 60% or more of the variance in adults' recall or summarization performance. In five out of the six cases, link strength between propositions was a stronger predictor of recall/summarization. This finding is particularly interesting in light of the data showing that number of connections among statements

---

[2]We used a stepwise regression but did two analyses for each study; in one node strength was entered first and in the other link strength was first. We report the results in terms of the regression in which the total R^2 was the greatest. In none of the cases did the two-measure regression account for a significant amount of additional variance over a single measure regression.

TABLE 18.1
Amount of Variance (R^2) in Distance Passage Recall Data Accounted for by
Node Strength and Link Strength Between Nodes

	CI	3CI-Dynamic
Adult Recall 1		
Node Strength	ns	ns
Link Strength Between	.37**	.61**
Adult Recall 2		
Node Strength	ns	.60**
Link Strength Between	.34**	ns
Adult Summarization		
Node Strength	ns	ns
Link Strength Between	.28*	.65**
Children Oral		
Node Strength	ns	.39**
Link Strength Between	.67**	ns
Children Written		
Node Strength	ns	.60**
Link Strength Between	.54**	ns

*$p < .05$. **$p < .01$.

is a significant and strong predictor of recall and importance judgments (Goldman & Varnhagen, 1986; Trabasso & Sperry, 1985; Trabasso & van den Broek, 1985).

For the children's data the situation is different: CI accounted for more of the variance in the oral recall study; CI and 3CI-Dynamic accounted for about the same amount in the written recall study. When we looked at the children's probabilities of recall for each proposition, we found that they were not recalling the main points as well as the adults. In fact, much of what the children recalled were the familiar and relatively concrete elements of the passage, for example, *walking up hill takes longer than downhill.* These elaborative/detail propositions were not as highly activated in 3CI-Dynamic as the main points. CI made less of a differentiation between elaborative/detail propositions and main point propositions.

Note that the "Distance" passage read by the children is at the 10th-grade reading level. We are going to pursue the ability of the simulation models to predict children's recall of passages more within their reading levels. We expect that the results will look more like the pattern obtained for the adults.

Prediction of Processing Time

We also had processing time data for four of these studies. None of the CI or 3CI-Mimic model measures correlated significantly with processing time per word or sentence. For 3CI-Dynamic, iterations to settle was significantly correlated with processing time per word. However, contrary to what one might expect, these were negative correlations. Because iterations produced by 3CI-Dynamic were also significantly negatively correlated with number of words and number of propositions in the sentence, we used regression analyses to examine all three variables as predictors of processing time. For each of the adult studies, number of words accounted for the most variance in processing time per word: The longer the sentence, the less time per word. Once the effect of number of words had been removed, number of propositions and iterations did not predict significantly more of the variance. We think that behavioral data on adults' processing times are more likely to be predicted by measures that take into account lexical and syntactic processing, which, of course, the present models do not.

In contrast, the results of the multiple regressions on the children's processing times indicated that 3CI-Dynamic's iterations-to-settle accounted for the most variance in processing time, with a simple correlation of −.57. If iterations do indeed reflect the ease (or difficulty) of integrating new propositions into a developing representation of the text, then for the children, this finding indicates that the harder it is to integrate, the less time children spend processing the sentence. Speculatively, for these passages, it may be that if there were no obvious connections, children quickly moved on to the next sentence.

Summary of Predictive Ability of the Models

Overall, the predictive ability of the CI and 3CI-Dynamic models for recall or summarization data is quite encouraging. First, both models yielded measures that correlated with the behavioral data. However, replacing a fixed-size carryover buffer with a capacity-constrained dynamic working memory improved the degree to which the simulation models predicted the behavioral data: 3CI-Dynamic measures accounted for over 60% of the variance in adult recall compared to about 35% for the fixed-buffer model. The points of divergence between CI and 3CI-Dynamic were that the 3CI-Dynamic model weighted "main point" sentences more heavily than did the CI model. For children the two kinds of models performed more evenly, perhaps because the fixed buffer of size two more closely approximates the capacity constraints for younger individuals. It is possible that a lower "cap" would yield a better fit to the children's data.

On the other hand, processing time data were not well predicted. The major predictors of processing time are undoubtedly at language levels much closer to the surface text, that is, lexical and syntactic levels.

FUTURE DIRECTIONS

We are quite encouraged by the fact that we have been able to develop a settling algorithm built within a symbolic architecture with a capacity-constrained working memory that generates long-term memory strengths that are highly correlated with those generated using a postmultiplication and normalization algorithm. A major reason for being encouraged by this is because the CAPS architecture provides a mechanism for dealing with three major but understandable limitations of the current class of CI and 3CI models. First, they operate on parsed propositional input and have no real mechanisms for generating those parses. Second, the models lack knowledge of discourse structure and strategies for monitoring and repairing comprehension when it falters. Finally, there are no mechanisms for dealing with the equilibration of new and old information. These three limitations are providing direction to our further research activity using the CAPS architecture as an environment for modeling text comprehension. We discuss each of these issues in turn and suggest how mechanisms within CAPS might address them.

Parsing Processes

We noted earlier that the failure of the CI and 3CI models to predict processing time was not surprising because the models do not deal with the derivation of the propositional representations constituting the input. Yet, there is evidence that many comprehension problems occur at just these levels. For example, in protocol data that we have collected, about 75% of the problems people report when they read concern problems that occur within a single sentence, including word and phrase meaning and the coordination of them (Goldman, Coté, & Saul, in preparation). The syntactic and semantic strategies for resolving these kinds of problems are fundamental to understanding how propositions are derived. Specifying these strategies remains a daunting task, but given advances in research on syntactic processing (see Perfetti & Britt, chap. 2 in this volume), it is far less daunting than it was 20 years ago. Clearly, the time has come to attempt to deal with the issue of propositional derivation in the context of a complete model of the comprehension process.

The CAPS architecture seems to be ripe for the development of a compre-hension model that deals with lexical, syntactic, and text-level processes. There are already several sentence-level processing models that operate within a CAPS architecture (e.g., Just & Carpenter, 1992; MacDonald et al., 1992). Building on these requires expanding the scope of sentence types that can be processed and developing the translation algorithms that build complex propositions. A major issue that bears investigation is the interaction among resource allocation to processing at the various levels of language and the impact of difficulties at one level on processing at the other levels.

Knowledge of Discourse Structure and Strategies
for Resolving Coherence Problems

The use of argument overlap and propositional embedding as the rules for con-structing coherence matrices is a reasonable start. These rules can be applied based on surface-level comparisons of the propositions constituting a text. The current class of CI and 3CI models are "dumb" in the sense that these rules require little more than pattern matching. However, it is quite clear that additional rules govern coherence, and in some cases may be more important than argument overlap and propositional embedding. For example, working with narrative texts, both W. Kintsch (1992) and Tapiero and Denhière (chap. 12 in this volume) have introduced links based on causal relations. In both cases, improvements in the fit of the CI model were reported. However, the operationalization of rules at this level requires simulation models that have a great deal more "smarts" than the current models. The symbolic architecture of CAPS enables us to begin to build in some of the information necessary for certain of these linking rules to operate plausibly within the simulation model.

It also seems quite reasonable for the simulations to selectively increase some propositional nodes over others based on their functional role in the text. For example, propositional elements important to the episodic structure of a story, such as goals and outcomes, might be more strongly activated than other kinds of information. It is presently possible to make these decisions for the models, as Otero and Kintsch (1992) did and as we did when we clamped the main points at two units in our CI simulation run. However, part of the reason these elements may be recalled well is because the process of identifying them in itself serves an important function in comprehension. Attempting to model any such identification decision-making process may lead to new insights into how such discourse structure knowledge is applied in comprehension and why it is important.

"Smartening up" our models by providing them with knowledge of different discourse structures and the rules that guide coherence within such structures is perhaps even more important in the case of text designed to convey new information. Unlike the narrative where the episodic structure is dominant, informational text can have any number of structures (cf. Anderson & Armbruster, 1984). And the applicability of argument overlap and propositional embedding for determining coherence probably varies depending on the structure. Additional data that we have collected on a sequentially organized passage suggests that this is the case. First, recall that the "Distance" passage has a fairly standard informational structure: a concept is introduced in the beginning of the text and then is differentiated and embellished. In such a passage, the global structure can be built using rules like argument overlap and propositional embedding. In fact, operating only with these two rules, 3CI-Dynamic differentiated the main points from the elaborations quite well.

However, when we looked at the performance of 3CI-Dynamic on the sequentially organized passage about the four-phase development of multinational corporations, its predictive ability decreased substantially: Link strength between propositional nodes significantly predicted recall ($r = .47$), although the amount of variance accounted for was small (22%). Note that neither CI nor 3CI-Mimic generated long-term memory node or link strengths that were predictive of recall. The contrast in the predictive ability of these models on the two different passage structures highlights the importance of building "smarter" models. This "smarter" class of 3CI models needs to be able to take advantage of surface structure cues to discourse structure in order to identify and construct a globally coherent text representation (for further discussion of this point see Goldman & Saul, 1990b).

There is an additional issue with which a "smarter" class of models will need to deal: rereading. We noted earlier that people frequently reread in response to comprehension problems. The current class of CI and 3CI models has no mechanisms for predicting or simulating rereading. How and when to reread rely on monitoring and evaluation strategies that must be part of these models. In an initial effort to use the CAPS architecture to model rereading behavior, we produced REREADER (Goldman et al., 1992). It rereads based on gaps in coherence; coherence is determined with the same linking rules that CI and 3CI use. RE-READER does a moderately good job of simulating the rereading behavior of some adults (Goldman, Varma, Ortega, & Saul, 1992). However, it is also clear that REREADER needs knowledge of additional procedures for determining coherence, global discourse structure, and in differentiating acceptable from unacceptable "breaks" in coherence.

With the 3CI models we have implemented a CAPS production system algorithm for building coherence networks. Although the algorithm currently uses only two kinds of linking productions, it establishes the basis for the next generation of 3CI models. The next generation of models needs additional productions that embody some of the strategies and knowledge that comprehenders report and demonstrate.

Equilibration of Prior Knowledge and Learning

We indicated earlier that one of the potential advantages of embedding CI in CAPS was the flexibility this would provide in dealing with how prior knowledge is accessed and utilized in processing new input. In the CAPS architecture it is possible to partition working memory capacity differentially. This feature of the architecture enables processing biases to be established and provides a working memory responsive to fluctuating needs of the comprehension system.

Although we are just beginning to tackle the prior knowledge issue in detail, we have done some work on a related problem: the tendency for initial propositions in the passage to accrue large amounts of activation making it difficult for new input to survive the settling process. In an effort to overcome this problem, we conducted some simulations of 3CI-Dynamic where we experimented with drastically cutting the amount of resources available to previously processed sentences. Surprisingly, the activation patterns did not change. It turns out that this was due to the fact that propositions remaining in the buffer tend to be very tightly related propositions. This tightly connected set of propositions tends to accrue greater amounts of activation and biases the system toward what is already in the "buffer" whether it is fixed size or dynamic.

Thus, the further into the passage, the harder it is for any new proposition to accrue substantial amounts of activation. Although this relationship may account for frequently observed primacy effects, it has serious implications for incorporating prior knowledge in text processing. Prior knowledge is likely to reflect a tightly connected network of associates. Hence, there is the danger that this prior knowledge will "swamp" the new information. This could create a situation where, regardless of what a text says, updating fails to occur. Such a situation may account for the fact that what people read often fails to affect misconceptions or prior beliefs.

Tackling this problem involves more tuning of the operation of the working memory model, perhaps by introducing executive control strategies such as monitoring and evaluation for purposes of regulating the allocation of capacity to new and old information. Such control strategies are also important to shifting allocational priorities in response to comprehension problems or in the face of particularly difficult sections of text.

To sum up, 3CI-Dynamic, our implementation of the Construction-Integration model as a capacity-constrained CAPS production system, is a good model of some aspects of comprehension. Its main drawback, and one shared with other current CI-class models, is one of scope: No parsing, discourse-level, or strategic processes are modeled. However, within the CAPS architecture it seems eminently feasible to build a new, smarter class of CI models that can incorporate strategic processing and flexible allocation of working memory resources in the service of discourse comprehension and knowledge acquisition.

ACKNOWLEDGMENTS

The research reported in this chapter was supported, in part, by a National Science Foundation Career Development Award to Susan Goldman, NSF 9009320, and in part by the Office of Naval Research Cognitive Science Program, Grant N00014-91-J1769. However, the opinions expressed are those of the authors. Julie Keeton, Julio Ortega, and Elizabeth Saul assisted with the development of the models discussed herein. Thanks are also expressed to Marcel Just and Patricia Carpenter and to Walter Kintsch for providing Goldman with the opportunity to visit their labs and gain experience with their simulation models.

APPENDIX: ALGORITHMS FOR CI, 3CI-MIMIC, AND 3CI-DYNAMIC

This appendix describes the algorithms behind CI, 3CI-Mimic, and 3CI-Dynamic more precisely. The algorithm for CI is adapted from the description in Kintsch and Welsh (1991). 3CI-Mimic and 3CI-Dynamic are CAPS productions systems. Their behavior arises from an iteration between the explicit logic of their productions and the implicit logic of the capacity-constrained working memory of

CAPS. Rather than describing this complex iteration directly, we have converted the resulting behavior and data structures to their matrix algebra equivalents so as to facilitate comparisons between the three simulation models.

The CI Algorithm

CI takes as input the propositions of the text to be read grouped by sentence; these groups are called *cycles*. CI processes the cycles sequentially, applying the following algorithm to the propositions of each one:

1. Propositions: The propositions of the current cycle and any propositions carried over from the prior cycle make up the n participating propositions.

2. Construction phase: An $n \times n$ coherence matrix C is constructed from the n propositions where entry c_{ij} is 1 if propositions p_i and p_j share arguments, if one is embedded in the other, or if $i = j$ and thus the entry represents the self-strength of p_i; $c_{ij} = 0$ otherwise.

3. Integration phase:
   A. An n-element activation vector A_0 is created where entry a_i is the activation of proposition p_i. All entries are assigned initial activations of 1.
   B. The coherence matrix is multiplied by the activation vector A_k, yielding the new activation vector A_{k+1}.
   C. The activation vector A_{k+1} is normalized by dividing each entry by the largest one.
   D. A_{k+1} is compared with A_k and if the sum of the absolute values of the differences between their respective entries exceeds some threshold, then processing continues at step 3B. The threshold we used was .01.
   E. The activation vector A_{k+1} is said to have settled in k iterations.

4. Derivation of long-term memory strengths: The long-term node strength of each proposition p_i is incremented by the product of the square of its final activation (a_{i2}) and its self-strength (c_{ii}). The long-term memory strength of each link between distinct propositions p_i and p_j is incremented by the product of the final activations of the propositions (a_i and a_j) and the strength of the coherence between them (c_{ij}).

5. Carry Over: Carry over the s propositions with the highest final activations for processing with the next cycle of propositions. The parameter s is the size of the fixed-capacity buffer and it was set to 2 in our simulation runs.

The 3CI-Mimic Algorithm

1. Propositions: Same as in CI.
2, 3. Construction and Integration phases:

A. Same as in CI.

B. A $n \times n$ coherence matrix **C** is constructed where entry c_{ij} is the number of times the linking rules argument overlap and propositional embedding apply between propositions p_i and p_j as long as their activations (a_i and a_j in $\mathbf{A}_k$) are greater than some threshold (.1 in our simulations). In addition, if $i = j$ and thus the entry represents the self-strength of proposition p_i; then c_{ij} is 1. Otherwise, c_{ij} is 0. **C** is multiplied by $\mathbf{A}_k$, producing the next activation vector $\mathbf{A}_{k+1}$.

C. If the sum of the entries in $\mathbf{A}_{k+1}$ exceeds the activation capacity, all entries are scaled proportionately such that they sum to the capacity.

D. Same as in CI.

E. Same as in CI.

4. Derivation of long-term memory strengths: Same as in CI.

5. Carry Over: Same as in CI.

The 3CI-Dynamic Algorithm

1. Propositions: Same as in 3CI-Mimic (and CI).

2, 3. Construction and Integration phases:

A. A n-element activation vector $\mathbf{A}_0$ is created where entry a_i is the activation of proposition p_i. Propositions that have been carried over from the previous cycle retain their final activations, while propositions just entering are assigned initial activations of 1.

B. Same as in 3CI-Mimic.

C. Same as in 3CI-Mimic.

D. Same as in 3CI-Mimic (and CI).

E. Same as in 3CI-Mimic (and CI).

4. Derivation of long-term memory strengths: Same as in 3CI-Mimic (and CI).

5. Carry Over: All propositions are carried over at their final activations to be processed in the next cycle.

REFERENCES

Goldman, S. R., Coté, N., & Saul, E. U. (in preparation). *Flexibility in the repair of comprehension.*

Goldman, S. R., & Saul, E. U. (1990a). Applications for tracking reading behavior on the Macintosh. *Behavior Research Methods, Instruments, and Computers, 22*, 526–532.

Goldman, S. R., & Saul, E. U. (1990b). Flexibility in text processing: A strategy competition model. *Learning and Individual Differences, 2*, 181–219.

Goldman, S. R., & Varnhagen, C. K. (1986). Memory for embedded and sequential stories. *Journal of Memory and Language, 25*, 401–418.

Goldman, S. R., Varma, S., & Ortega, J. (1992). *Application of CAPS modeling to strategy competition and flexibility in discourse comprehension.* Final Report to Cognitive Science Program, Office of Naval Research. Nashville, TN: Vanderbilt University.

Goldman, S. R., Varma, S., Ortega, J., & Saul, E. U. (1992, January). *Modeling strategy competition.* Presented at the Third Annual Winter Text Conference, Jackson Hole, WY.

Graesser, A. C., & Rhia, J. R. (1984). An application of multiple regression techniques to sentence reading times. In D. E. Kieras & M. A. Just (Eds.), *New methods in reading comprehension research* (pp. 183–218). Hillsdale, NJ: Lawrence Erlbaum Associates.

Haberlandt, K. F., & Graesser, A. C. (1985). Component processes in text comprehension and some of their interactions. *Journal of Experimental Psychology: General, 114,* 357–374.

Just, M. A., & Carpenter, P. A. (1992). A capacity theory of comprehension: Individual differences in working memory. *Psychological Review, 99,* 122–149.

Kieras, D. E. (1980). Initial mention as a signal to thematic content in technical passages. *Memory and Cognition, 8,* 345–353.

Kieras, D. E. (1981). The role of major referents and sentence topics in the construction of passage macrostructure. *Discourse Processes, 4,* 1–15.

Kieras, D. E. (1982). A model of reader strategy for abstracting main ideas from simple technical prose. *Text, 2,* 47–81.

Kintsch, E., McNamara, D. S., Songer, N., & Kintsch, W. (1992). *Revising the coherence of science texts to improve comprehension and learning 1: Traits of mammals* (Tech. Rep. No. 92-03). Boulder: University of Colorado, Institute of Cognitive Science.

Kintsch, W. (1988). The role of knowledge in discourse comprehension: A construction-integration model. *Psychological Review, 95,* 163–182.

Kintsch, W. (1992). How readers construct situation models for stories: The role of syntactic cues and causal inferences. In A. F. Healy, S. M. Kosslyn, & R. M. Shiffrin (Eds.), *From learning theory to connectionist theory: Essays in honor of William K. Estes* (Vol. 2, pp. 261–278). Hillsdale, NJ: Lawrence Erlbaum Associates.

Kintsch, W., & van Dijk, T. A. (1978). Toward a model of text comprehension and production. *Psychological Review, 85,* 363–394.

Kintsch, W., & Welsch, D. M. (1991). The construction-integration model: A framework for studying memory for text. In W. E. Hockley & S. Lewandowsky (Eds.), *Relating theory and data: Essays on human memory* (pp. 367–385). Hillsdale, NJ: Lawrence Erlbaum Associates.

Kintsch, W., Welsch, D., Schmalhofer, F., & Zimny S. (1990). Sentence memory: A theoretical analysis. *Journal of Memory and Language, 29,* 133–159.

Lorch, Jr., R. F. (1989). Text signaling devices and their effects on reading and memory processes. *Educational psychology review* (Vol. 1, pp. 209–234). New York: Plenum.

MacDonald, M. C., Just, M. A., & Carpenter, P. A. (1992). Working memory constraints on the processing of syntactic ambiguity. *Cognitive Psychology, 24,* 56–98.

Mross, E. F., & Roberts, J. O. (1992). *The construction-integration model: A program and manual* (Tech. Rep. No. ICS 92-14). Boulder, CO: Institute for Cognitive Science, University of Colorado.

Otero, J., & Kintsch, W. (1992). Failures to detect contradictions in a text: What readers believe versus what they read. *Psychological Science, 3,* 229–235.

Trabasso, T., & Sperry, L. (1985). Causal relatedness and importance of story events. *Journal of Memory and Language, 24,* 595–611.

Trabasso, T., & van den Broek, P. W. (1985). Causal thinking and the representation of narrative events. *Journal of Memory and Language, 24,* 612–630.

van Dijk, T., & Kintsch, W. (1983). *Strategies of discourse comprehension.* New York: Academic Press.

Vipond, D. (1980). Micro- and macroprocesses in text comprehension. *Journal of Verbal Learning and Verbal Behavior, 19,* 276–296.

Chapter 19

Construction-Integration
Theory and Clinical Reasoning

José F. Arocha
Vimla L. Patel
McGill University

EXPERTISE AND COMPREHENSION

A great deal of work in the study of expertise has been conducted in the context of problem solving rather than that of comprehension. Despite this, research in knowledge-based domains indicates that some of the more salient features of expertise involve comprehension. The reason for this is that efficient knowledge structures, rather than processes, seem to define expert performance and that many of the failures found in both experts and less-than-experts are accountable in terms of failures of understanding. Medical expertise is one of those areas of research where the importance of comprehension processes has been demonstrated (V. L. Patel & Groen, 1986). Medical problem solving depends on understanding because problem interpretation and analysis in medicine requires the construction of appropriate clusters of long-term memory knowledge that match the current patient presentation.

The concept of schema has been used to explain many of the phenomena of expert problem solving in medicine. A schema is assumed to be a knowledge structure based on experience with the domain of expertise that serves to filter out irrelevant information and acts as a guide to hypothesis generation. This assumes that schemata exist that efficiently index the knowledge necessary for comprehension and problem solving. The need for the notion of schema is made necessary due to the structured nature of expert knowledge. This structure allows experts to exploit their knowledge in a systematic and efficient way.

The early generation of hypotheses by medical experts is taken as an evidence for the existence of schemata. Indeed, the rapidity with which the correct diagnosis is generated is a most striking feature of the behavior of experts. In the case of routine problems, a small set of hypotheses is generated in a forward-directed manner (i.e., when the direction of inferences proceeds from data to hypothesis). This suggests that many of the phenomena of expertise involve the semi-automatic processing of familiar situations, which arises as a consequence of optimal knowledge organization. Backward-directed reasoning (i.e., the direction of the inferences proceeds from hypothesis to data) accounts for anomalies, such as "loose ends," when comprehension breaks down. These anomalies typically occur when pieces of information do not cohere. The question that arises is the extent to which the construction-integration model provides a satisfactory account of how schemata are constructed in the process of understanding.

The construction-integration theory[1] was developed by Kintsch (1988) to account for the process of text comprehension. However, the theory is believed to be of sufficient generality to be applied to various other phenomena. Within the construction-integration theory, comprehension is seen as a cyclical process, involving two phases: a rule-based construction process and a spreading activation process (or integration process). The construction phase involves activation of text concepts and propositions connecting to the text, and a process of elaboration of these concepts by activation of associated concepts from long-term memory (prior knowledge). One important characteristic of the rules used in this phase is that they are "weak"; these rules do not optimally derive from the input, but fire even if they are not relevant to the task at hand. In this way, the construction process produces relevant as well as irrelevant concepts. The process of integration occurs by spreading activation, which generates a situation model by strengthening the activation values of relevant propositions and deactivating those of irrelevant propositions.

This chapter presents a description of how the construction-integration theory can be used to account for the construction of schemata in the process of diagnostic reasoning. First, we give a brief presentation of the construction-integration theory. Next, we present an account of how the theory applies to the medical domain. Lastly, a series of studies we conducted is presented, which serve as evidence for the validity of the construction-integration theory in accounting for the construction of schemata during online diagnostic reasoning.

---

[1]Although the construction-integration theory is customarily presented as a "model," we prefer referring to it as a theory. A theory gives the major elements of the processes it refers to and is couched in more abstract terms (e.g., a theory of comprehension). A model is a specification of a theory accounting for a particular phenomenon or set of phenomena (e.g., a model of comprehension of anaphora). A model consists then of the theory plus a set of subsidiary assumptions and data (Bunge, 1973).

THE CONSTRUCTION-INTEGRATION THEORY

The construction-integration theory is a symbolic connectionist architecture (Holyoak, 1991) developed by Kintsch (1988; Kintsch & Welsch, 1991) to account for the process of text comprehension. The theory derives from previous attempts at modeling using rule-based systems that, despite providing an account of some aspects of comprehension (van Dijk & Kintsch, 1983; Kintsch & Greeno, 1985), fail to account for several important aspects of the process (Kintsch, 1988). The most important failing of which is probably people's performance flexibility in response to contextual variations.

Notwithstanding its origin in text comprehension research, the theory has been used to account for problem solving in various areas, such as word arithmetic problems (Kintsch, 1988), sentence memory (Kintsch, Welsch, Schmalhofer, & Zimny, 1990), planning (Mannes & Kintsch, 1991), and some aspects of human-computer interaction (Doane, McNamara, Kintsch, Polson, & Clawson, 1992). The generality of the theory makes it a good candidate on which to base a general theory of cognition (Newell, 1990). In this context, this chapter presents a first attempt at interpreting medical diagnosis in terms of the construction-integration theory.

The construction process is composed of several steps (Kintsch, 1988): a process of activation of text concepts and propositions corresponding to the text, a process of elaborations of these concepts by the activation of associated concepts in the knowledge base, a process of inference of additional concepts and propositions from the text concepts and the elaborations, and a process of assignment of strength values to all pairs of concepts and propositions. The integration process occurs through spreading activation, which generates a situation model by strengthening the activation values of relevant propositions and deactivating those of irrelevant propositions.

Each cycle of construction-integration roughly corresponds to the processing of a clause or a sentence. Some elements, or propositions, of the sentences are retained in a working memory, to be processed together with the new sentence. This produces overlap among the sentence elements and coherence is obtained via the reprocessing of propositions. The greater the overlap, the higher the activation level of the overlapping elements; hence, the greater coherence with the rest of the elements.

The previous description sketches the basic mechanism involved in comprehension of text. The process is assumed to occur without much effort and its outcome is invariably the situation model for the text, that is, what the text is about. The process underlying text comprehension exhibits a striking resemblance to the process involved in diagnostic reasoning in routine cases. This resemblance makes the construction-integration theory an excellent candidate for a general theory of comprehension. Furthermore, the study of diagnostic problem solving has been highly influenced by text comprehension paradigms.

Modeling Comprehension in Diagnostic Reasoning

Diagnostic problem solving in medicine has been thought to involve a very important comprehension component. Early research by Patel and colleagues (Coughlin, 1986; V. L. Patel, Groen, & Frederiksen, 1986) attempted to provide a bridge between diagnostic problem solving and comprehension research. Comprehension processes are involved in the generation of a diagnosis, a process of categorizing a given presentation of signs and symptoms from a patient. This process is enriched by the diagnostician's activation of general, as well as specific, medical knowledge (V. L. Patel, Groen, & Arocha, 1990).

The approach to expertise in medicine developed by Patel and colleagues (Groen & V. L. Patel, 1988; V. L. Patel & Groen, 1986) is based on the idea that the construction of a clinical case representation is similar to the construction of a text representation. This similarity is predicated on the correspondence of the construction of the textbase and the situation model between both areas of research. In this regard, previous studies (Groen & Jerney, 1987; Groen & V. L. Patel, 1988) have shown that the Kintsch and Greeno's (1985) model of arithmetic word problems could be used as a good first approximation to the understanding of expert and nonexpert problem solving of routine problems.

The model developed by Groen and colleagues, however, have deficiencies, such as the failure to account for two findings of medical problem-solving research; namely, the apparent nonindependence of the textbase and the situation model, and the flexibility with which expert physicians generate correct diagnoses. In fact, the model assumes that the textbase is independent of the situation model. In this regard, the textbase was the propositional form of the information contained in the text, which is reflected in the recall protocols. This independence have received some support from research in medical problem solving. For instance, several studies conducted by Patel and her colleagues (Groen & V. L. Patel, 1988; V. L. Patel, Evans, & Groen, 1989) have shown that recall protocols by experts do not contain statements referring to the disease process, which is what the situation model in medical comprehension refers to. Statements referring to the disease process appear mostly in explanation protocols. The recall protocols, however, seem to be the result of a very selective encoding of the problem. This selectivity can be accounted for by the hypothesis that the situation model serves as a "filter" for irrelevant information. This suggested that the situation model has more influence on the textbase than it was originally assumed (Groen & V. L. Patel, 1988).

The second finding is that expert physicians exhibit a greater sensitivity to contextual information resulting in greater accuracy and flexibility in their problem solving. Thus, the application of the model by Groen and V. L. Patel (1988; Groen & Jerney, 1987) required at least one major modification to explain the fact that experts accounted for case findings, after they have reached the correct diagnosis. This modification takes the form of a flexible mechanism, such as an associative or a probabilistic process, and a coherence mechanism (Groen & V. L. Patel, 1988; V. L. Patel, 1984).

These same limitations were also acknowledged by Kintsch (1988), which resulted in the development of the construction-integration theory. This theory is an improvement on the earlier theory in that it contains two mechanisms to account for the flexibility in performance due to contextual variation: a "weak" rule-based generation process and a flexible associative network.

TOWARD A CONSTRUCTION-INTEGRATION MODEL OF CLINICAL REASONING

A model of diagnostic problem solving based on the construction-integration theory involves an interaction between the textbase and the long-term memory store, from which a situation model is derived through the cyclical process of construction and integration. In the following paragraphs, the components of a model of diagnostic problem solving are presented, using the construction-integration theory as a framework.

Components of a Construction-Integration Model of Diagnostic Reasoning

The construction integration theory applied to diagnostic reasoning has the following components: a propositional textbase, generated from the patient problem (a description of the patient's signs and symptoms); an associative long-term memory containing knowledge of disease classification; and a process of construction-integration, consisting of two phases: an activation phase, in which the textbase propositions activate long term-memory propositions; and an integration phase, in which propositions become either activated or deactivated, resulting in the situation model for the patient (with its corresponding diagnosis).

The Textbase. The textbase is formed by propositions in the case description. An excerpt from a clinical problem is given in Table 19.1 as an example. The propositional analysis technique we use is based on the system developed by Frederiksen (1975). Although this system differs from the one developed by Kintsch (1974; Bovair & Kieras, 1985; Kintsch & van Dijk, 1978), the differences are unimportant for our purposes. The use of propositional analysis allows us to study the selection and organization of information and its relationship to problem representation, schema construction, and hypothesis generation. The result is a detailed semantic description that captures complex relations in the protocols. To achieve this end, the clinical descriptions are first divided into clauses and then represented propositionally (Bovair & Kieras, 1985; Frederiksen, 1975; van Dijk & Kintsch, 1983). Customarily, a recall task is used to investigate the

TABLE 19.1
Propositional Representation of a Segment of a Clinical Case

Proposition Number	Predicate	Arguments
1 A 27-year-old unemployed male was admitted to the emergency room.		
1.1	ADMIT	OBJ: MALE, RSLT: 1.2, = TNS:PAST;
1.2	MALE	LOC: EMERGENCY ROOM;
1.3	MALE	= ATT: UNEMPLOYED;
1.4	MALE	= ATT: 27 YRS. OLD
2 He complained of shaking chills and a fever of 4 days duration.		
2.1	COMPLAIN	PAT: HE, THM: [2.2, 2.3] = TNS = PAST;
2.2	CHILLS	ATT: SHAKING
2.3	FEVER	= DUR: 4 days

Note. The representation is assumed to be a construction of the meaning of the clinical case.

construction of the textbase, whereas an explanation task used to investigate the construction of the situation model.

The Long-Term Memory Base.   In addition to the textbase, which is constructed from observing the patient or the patient description, there is a long-term memory component, which consists of clinical, pathophysiological, procedural, and episodic associations. The long-term memory base can be viewed as consisting of propositions that are organized into a semantic network with weighted links. A the time of retrieval, a connectivity matrix is computed from the strength of the weighted links in long-term memory. The question remains of what the values of these links are. Unlike other applications of the construction-integration theory (Mannes & Kintsch, 1988, 1991), in which there is little or no indication of the associative strength of items in long-term memory, in the case of diagnostic problem solving, disease profiles (as exemplified in medical decision support systems such as QMR) (Miller, Masarie, & Myers, 1986) serve as crude indicators of the strength of the values. These values can be obtained by examining typical patterns of associations between sets of clinical findings, pathophysiological processes, and diagnoses. The clinical findings are known to vary in their associative strength with different diagnoses.

A second question remains as to what the organization of long-term memory is that allows the generation of diverse hypotheses. A basic assumption of the construction-integration model of diagnostic problem solving is that long-term memory is formed by propositions generated as inferences by the diagnostician. These propositions correspond mostly to diagnostic hypotheses activated from long-term memory to account for the data in the clinical case. In the clinical reasoning literature, the term *diagnostic hypothesis* has been used to refer to any ideas, diagnoses, or guesses that label the phenomena observed, or to proposed explanations that guide the investigation of the patient problem (Barrows &

Tamblyn, 1980). These hypotheses can refer to a variety of concepts such as syndromes, specific disease processes, disorders, pathophysiological processes, and anatomic or biochemical disturbances. The criteria for identifying hypotheses are not defined by a set of explicit rules, but are based on the different methods used in the literature (Barrows & Tamblyn, 1980).

In our research, however, we have distinguished different types of hypotheses by postulating that clinical knowledge is organized in terms of a hierarchical representation containing different aspects of medical knowledge (Evans & Gadd, 1989; V. L. Patel, Evans, & Kaufman, 1989). Figure 19.1 presents a schematic representation of the hierarchical organization of knowledge. This hierarchy is formed by the following constructs: (1) The empirium, which is the raw perceptual material available to experts as well as novices and lay people. By itself, the empirium has no actual or potential clinical interpretation; (2) the observations,

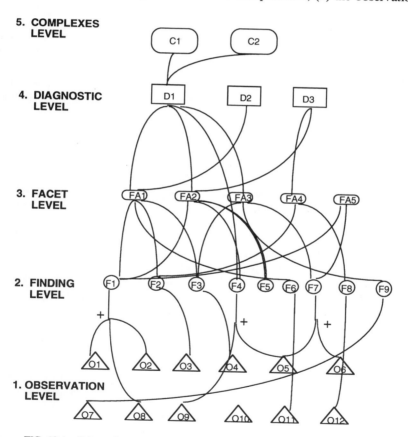

FIG. 19.1. Schematic representation of hierarchical structure of medical knowledge as used for problem solving.

which represent events that have potential clinical interpretation, but are not linked to any particular clinical hypothesis; (3) the findings, which are the basic constructs with clinical significance and are connected to one or several hypotheses; (4) the facets, which are composed of clusters of findings and underlie one or more diagnostic hypotheses; (5) the diagnoses, which are formed by sets of facets, and are the basis for management and treatment; and (6) the complexes. These are constructs involving diagnoses plus information that modify treatment or management in particular ways.

This hierarchy is assumed to represent the full structure of long-term memory (LTM) of medical knowledge required for diagnosis. However, depending on the stimulus material (e.g., verbal case presentations or real patients), the type of case (routine or nonroutine) and the expertise level of the diagnostician one wishes to model (e.g., expert, subexpert, or novice), some of the strata in the hierarchy may be omitted. For instance, in expert diagnostic problem solving of routine cases, we can assume that LTM items are limited to propositions representing knowledge of findings, facets, and diagnoses. Prior research has shown that in such cases, the diagnostic reasoning is mostly bottom up, with most inferences being forward-driven to the diagnosis (V. L. Patel & Groen, 1986).

When the tasks are presented in verbal form, there is already some information encoded as findings. This is analogous to using medical records as stimulus material. In this case, the levels corresponding to empirium and observations are not present, as they are in the case of an actual patient, because the patient description is already clinically interpreted in some way. This does not seem to make much difference in terms of differentiating experts from novices, as the results of V. L. Patel, Evans, and Kaufman (1989) have shown. The hypotheses generated in response to the written patient description correspond, basically, to two kinds: namely, facets and diagnoses. A *facet* is a disease component that summarizes a set of findings and points to one or more diagnoses. There is another kind of information that appears in the hierarchy as complexes, but that in well-known disease processes are part of their disease profile. These are propositions that refer to disease enabling conditions or contextual information that although unspecified, may direct the reasoning process toward a particular diagnosis. Such enabling conditions are exemplified mostly by risk factors and environmental or patient-history factors.

A third question that remains to be answered is what form the schemata that diagnosticians use during problem solving take. The previous model of medical problem solving (Groen & Jerney, 1987; Groen & V. L. Patel, 1988), based on the Kintsch–Greeno theory and its realization as a computer model by Dellarosa (1985), implemented aspects of the knowledge base through the use of an *abnormality schema* (see Table 19.2). An abnormality schema is a knowledge structure corresponding to a facet in the medical knowledge hierarchy described earlier. This abnormality schema contained three slots: an abnormality slot, which consisted of a physiological disorder; an indicator slot, which consisted of a

TABLE 19.2
Structure of an Abnormality Schema

(<schema name>)	(INDICATOR (:<indicator list>))
	(CONSEQUENCE (:<consequence list>))
	(ABNORMALITY (:<abnormality>)))

Note. From Groen and Jerney (1987).

clinical indicator for the abnormality; and a consequence slot, which contained a clinical or physiological consequence of the abnormality. A representation of a clinical case was formed by the interaction of several abnormality schemata.

Using the notion of an abnormality schema, several partial schemata are activated and will account for portions of the case data, at a given point in the subject's processing of the case. These partial schemata are then subjected to an integration process dominated by two kinds of constraints. The first is the propositional overlap between schemata that account for the clinical knowledge, and the other is the causal relationships existing among the schemata and the clinical findings. Although this is still a simple model, the introduction of these two types of constraints remedies the main problems of the previous model (Groen & Jerney, 1987; Groen & V. L. Patel, 1988).

EMPIRICAL RESEARCH ON DIAGNOSTIC TASKS BY EXPERTS AND NOVICES

Having described the construction integration theory as it may be applied to the diagnostic process, we present some experimental results that show the usefulness of the model to account for findings in medical diagnostic problem solving. More specifically, we present evidence for how schemata are built during problem solving.

To this end, we first present some results from the study of experts and subexperts in sequential diagnostic tasks. We show that the construction of schemata involves a process of activation of associations in long-term memory, which change as the clinical case is encoded. Partial schemata that account for aspects of the problem are constructed. Relevant as well as irrelevant associations are produced. Because knowledge organization in the expert is assumed to be hierarchical, activation occurs at a more abstract level than that in less-than-expert subjects. This hypothesis is based on our previous work on medical expertise (V. L. Patel, Groen, & Arocha, 1992) and is also congruent with research by Doane et al. (1992) in which they applied the construction-integration theory to a computing task.

Next, we present some studies of novice problem solving in which it is shown that as novice's experience with clinical medicine increases, they generate a larger set of hypotheses that they later narrow down to fewer and more specific hypotheses. This is presented as evidence of the role that increasingly more sophisticated partial schemata play in the construction of the situation model. This sophistication involves a disadvantage in that a very large number of concepts are activated, negatively affecting performance. This phenomenon, that is, the deterioration of performance of intermediate subjects (those between novices and experts), has been termed the "intermediate effect" (Lesgold, Rubinson, Feltovich, Glaser, Klopfer, & Wang, 1988; V. L. Patel & Groen, 1991; Schmidt, Boshuizen, & Hobus, 1988).

Lastly, we present research results on the online construction of disease schemata in doctor–patient discourse. This process is conceived as a script-building process that has some characteristics of flexibility and adaptability to contextual variations.

Expert–Subexpert Comparison: Schema Construction and the Time Course of Hypothesis Generation

Prior research by Patel and colleagues (V. L. Patel & Groen, 1986; V. L. Patel et al., 1990) has been concerned with the clinical cases presented as a whole. Other research by the same team (Joseph & V. L. Patel, 1990; Patel et al., 1992) has focused on the study of clinical cases presented in sequential format. A sequential problem-solving task is one in which clinical case information is presented in segments; each segment representing some piece of information, such that the gradual construction of a schema can be studied in more detail. This research shows that expert physicians generate initial hypotheses that are mainly facet-type hypotheses. In contrast, subexpert physicians generate specific diagnostic hypotheses. This research also shows the process by which experts generate the corresponding diagnosis by narrowing down the initial set of hypotheses, whereas subexperts generate several hypotheses—but continue generating diagnoses after the correct diagnosis has been generated (Joseph & V. L. Patel, 1990)—or exhibit premature closure (with more than one diagnoses). This shows that, for the expert, the construction process is more focused and the integration process is carried out earlier, after which the diagnostic process is evaluative of the correct diagnosis.

In verbal protocol studies by Joseph and V. L. Patel (1990) and summarized in V. L. Patel, Arocha, and Kaufman (in press), the performance of high-knowledge (HDK) and low-knowledge subjects (LDK) was compared in endocrinology and cardiology cases that were presented sequentially, one sentence at a time. A particular feature characterizing HDK subjects was found. Once they generated all the components necessary for the correct diagnosis (i.e., facet-type hypotheses), they only used the subsequent data to evaluate the hypotheses already generated. The LDK subjects, although able to generate all the necessary components, and hence to interpret correctly the relevant data, failed in evaluating the hypotheses against incoming data. They continued to generate new diagnostic hypotheses or to interpret the new information in terms of new local processes (i.e., explanations of particular findings without generating hypothesis at the diagnostic level).

The analysis of the time course for the production of diagnostic hypotheses focused on differences between HDK and LDK subjects in terms of the relationship between the number of hypotheses generated in the course of presentation of the case description and the time and order of production of accurate diagnostic components (i.e., facets). Figure 19.2 gives the cumulative number of new hypotheses produced with each new segment of information for HDK and LDK subjects in the study by Joseph and V. L. Patel (1990). Each point in the figure represents the total-to-date (for the segment number indicated) of new hypotheses generated. The slope of the lines represents the pattern of hypothesis generation: the larger the slope, the greater the number of new hypotheses generated; zero slope indicates no change, that is, no generation of new hypotheses. The letters *A, B,* and *C* represent the point in time at which the three components necessary for reaching the correct diagnosis were generated. Both HDK and LDK subjects generated all three components between Segments 1 and 10.

There is a clear difference in the patterns of hypotheses generation for the two groups. Before the presentation of Segment 10, the two groups of subjects had generated approximately the same number of hypotheses. After Segment 10, the HDK subjects used the subsequent information to confirm the diagnostic components (i.e., facets) already generated, rather than generating new diagnostic components. LDK subjects, in contrast, continued to generate alternative hypotheses, as reflected in the differences between the two slopes of HDK and LDK subjects from Segments 11 to 25.

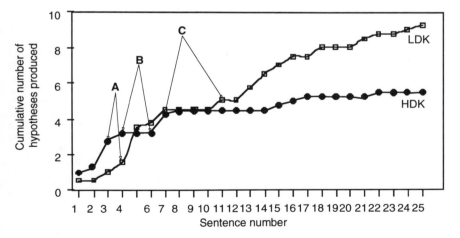

FIG. 19.2. Hypothesis generation over time course of information presented by high domain-knowledge (HDK) and low domain-knowledge (LDK) subjects in an endocrinology case (easier case). A—C generation of diagnostic subcomponents 1 to 3. From Joseph and Patel (1990). Adapted by permission.

The pattern was replicated with a more difficult case. In a study by V. L. Patel, Arocha, and Kaufman (in press), HDK (cardiologists) and LDK (endocrinologists) subjects were compared in a cardiology case, and found that HDK subjects generated the correct hypothesis earlier than the LDK subjects. Also, even after the LDK subjects had generated the correct diagnosis, they kept generating hypotheses, which suggested that their failure was more in the process of integrating the information that they had generated, rather than that of generating, in the first place, the relevant information. This conclusion is supported by the finding that in a recall task for the case, both HDK and LDK subjects were able to recall all the critical information for the case. This result suggested that both groups of subjects could recognize the case, but that only HDK subjects were able to integrate the information in an efficient manner.

There is, however, an important difference in the quality of the diagnoses that HDK and LDK subjects generated. An example of the types of hypotheses generated is presented in Fig. 19.3. The figure presents the initial hypotheses generated at the first segments of the endocrinology case (Joseph & V. L. Patel, 1990). Both subjects, an expert (HDK subject) and a subexpert (LDK subject),

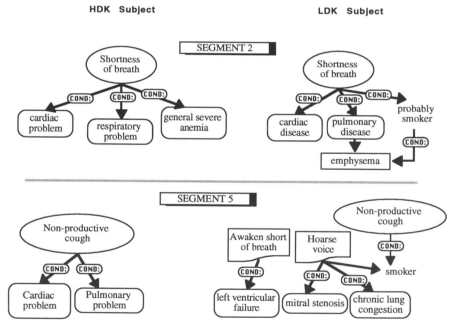

FIG. 19.3. Hypothesis generation by HDK and LDK for segments 2 and 5 of cardiology case. The symbol ⬭ represents the clinical information in the current segment; ▭ represents the hypothesis maintained at the current segment; ▭ represents clinical text information from previous segments; (COND:) represents a conditional relationship.

generated various hypotheses, most of them general (hypotheses that cover several diagnoses). The main difference is that the LDK subject generated specific hypotheses (probably smoker and emphysema) earlier than the HDK subject. In contrast, the HDK subject generated two hypotheses representing classes of similar diagnoses. This pattern is typical of the differences between HDK and LDK in sequential diagnostic problem solving. The same pattern is repeated in subsequent segments, as it is shown in the next segment, in which the LDK subject generates the hypotheses of mitral stenosis (Segment 5). Subsequently, he generates the hypothesis of cor pulmonale (Segment 7). This leads to the generation of several other hypotheses that are more specific than those generated by the HDK subject up to this point (S7). Similar differences to those found between HDK and LDK experts have also been found between novices at different levels of training (Arocha, V. L. Patel, & Y. C. Patel, 1993).

An interpretation consistent with the construction-integration theory suggests that expertise involves the construction of smaller subsets of relevant partial schemata. This process has the benefit that only a small number of activations are generated in the construction phase and that a more efficient integration process takes place. Two consequences can be derived from the results. The first concerns the organization of medical knowledge by experts. Their schemata are organized in a manner that resembles closely the hierarchical structure of medical knowledge hypothesized earlier. This allows them to first activate elements of competing schemata at the facet level before elements at the diagnostic level are activated. As found previously (Doane et al., 1992), experts' knowledge contains abstract concepts that less-than-experts lack. The second consequence is that experts' construction processes consist of the systematic activation of elements of the schemata that are at the same level of the knowledge hierarchy. This is not the case for less-than-expert subjects, who activate elements at different levels of the knowledge hierarchy, which are less discriminative of competing schemata.

Novice Problem Solving: Hypothesis Generation

The second set of research results comes from a study of the process of hypothesis generation by novices. This research, carried out by Arocha et al. (1993; Arocha & V. L. Patel, in press), presented evidence showing that as novices increase their expertise within a domain, they generate more, not fewer, hypotheses for a typical problem. Medical students were given two cases in segments to solve. The first segment was designed to suggest a typical patient problem with subsequent segments contradicting the initial suggestion. The results showed that whereas first-year students generated the suggested diagnosis (the typical one) when presented with the first segment, more experienced students also generated several other diagnoses, some of which were irrelevant to the initial case presentation. This result suggests that the process of construction of case representation involves the use of propositions to generate different hypotheses that are later discarded, once inconsistent information has been encoded. In this way, a case representation that is sensitive to different sources of information is formed.

The novices in this study failed to activate many of the relevant schemata, but failed to integrate the information they had already generated. Although the data suggested increasing accuracy in the activation process, in the sense that the activation resulted in an increasing match between the underlying disease process and the relevancy of the hypotheses, the subjects failed to integrate the diverse hypotheses and the data presented in the case. These results suggest that both aspects of the process of construction-integration play a crucial role in diagnostic reasoning, but that the relative importance of either of the phases may depend on the training level of the subjects. Unlike LDK subjects, whose main distinction consisted in the failure of the to integrate the knowledge activated into a coherent diagnosis, the novices failure seem to be in both phases of the process: failing to activate relevant knowledge and to integrate this knowledge into a single explanation for the case.

This brings us to the phenomenon known as the *intermediate effect*. This refers to the finding indicating a deterioration in performance by intermediate subjects (i.e., those between novices and experts). In a series of studies (V. L. Patel & Groen, 1991; V. L. Patel & Medley-Mark, 1986), in which novices, intermediates, and experts were compared on comprehension tasks, it was found that intermediate subjects recalled and inferred more irrelevant information than either novices or experts. Whereas experts and novices seem to operate on relevant information by making selective inferences, intermediates seem to operate on both high and low relevance knowledge. It is worth noting that this nonmonotonic trend is independent of diagnostic accuracy, because intermediates typically produce more accurate diagnoses than novices, but fewer than experts.

CONSTRUCTION-INTEGRATION
AND DOCTOR–PATIENT DISCOURSE

This section presents a model of medical problem solving and uses the construction-integration theory to account for the comprehension and knowledge acquisition aspects in the model. We view the problem-solving model in the context of heuristically driven problem-solving scripts. Similar to our notion of a schema, a script does not refer to a preformed knowledge structure, but to a structure constructed in the process of problem solving. In a familiar situation, experts use their schemata to understand a problem. A script is called on when there is no schema readily available to evaluate the relevance of the information in a problem. Experts have this ability to organize information such that its application to problem solving is possible and their understanding is reflected in this organization of information.

The application of this general framework in a complex situation involving dialogue during problem solving and knowledge acquisition, such as doctor–

patient interview, can be viewed as follows: The patient presents an initial complaint. In the initial exchange with the patient, the physician uses some global heuristics to decide on the type of problem domain. This leads to a state of knowledge, which we can call Knowledge State 1'. This calls up a heuristic script that "dictates" the nature of the question that should be asked by the physician. The algorithm suggests that if the response is A, then Knowledge State 2' is generated and if the response is B, then Knowledge State 2" is generated. In subsequent question–answer sequences, a general script gets specialized in a specific context (see Fig. 19.4). If Response A is what the physician was expecting, then with this response, the subsequent interaction with the patient will probably be used to confirm the original hypothesis. Response B, in this case, will lead to alternative hypotheses to be evaluated.

The test of successful problem solving is the end state of the process, when the interpretation accounts for all the relevant evidence and supports clinically meaningful explanations. Explanations can be seen as a means of providing valid interpretations. It is only at the end of the problem-solving process that one can account for all the information, and explain the problem solving.

Based on this framework, one can predict that in situations where an expert is familiar with a problem, the initial hypothesis generated using a global script will most likely be an accurate one and the predictions made by the expert on other findings in the case will reflect a prototypical hypothesis. If any errors are made, they are more likely to be those that lead to premature diagnosis, because the prototypical scripts will "dictate" very specific slots a priori and the expert will attempt to fill in these slots, perhaps overlooking other constraints.

When the expert is unfamiliar with the problem, then the heuristic script called up will be very general and will guide data organization, which in turn will lead to a specialized slot in the script. In building such a schema or frame, multiple strategies will have to be used, such as strategies for prediction, elimination, discrimination, and explanation. However, these will be heuristically guided with heavy dependency on the knowledge base.

In an interview situation, there is a dynamic exchange of information and construction of meaning generated from interaction between the interviewer and the person being interviewed. The process of comprehension in a clinical interview situation is intimately related to problem solving (Patel, Evans, & Kaufman, 1989). That study showed a number of phenomena related to expert–novice behavior during the doctor–patient interaction. The characterization of the doctor–patient dialogue is based on initial observations either elicited by the physician or validated by the patient. The dialogue leads to further observations made by the physician, which lead to clusters of observations, which are interpreted as findings. In turn, sets of findings lead to diagnostic components, named facets, and facets to diagnosis (see Fig. 19.1).

In V. L. Patel et al. (1989), a patient suffering from hyperthyroidism with hypokalemic periodic paralysis (an endocrine problem) was interviewed (history

374

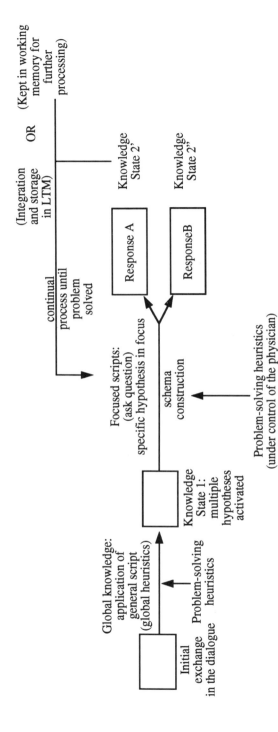

FIG. 19.4. Heuristically driven problem-solving scripts during medical discourse (doctor-patient dialogue).

taking) by six experts, six residents, and six students. The interviews were audio-taped and transcribed for analysis. A typical exchange arising from the analysis of the dialogue between an expert and the patient is shown in Fig. 19.5. The expert used a few initial cues from the patient to generate a useful diagnosis (periodic paralysis associated with hyperthyroidism). Based on this diagnosis, certain predictions are made and subsequent questions are asked to confirm these predictions. The figure shows that the experts made the predictions about palpi-tations, heat intolerance, weight loss, and eating habits, all of which are relevant to the diagnostic component of hypermetabolic state, which is a part of hyper-thyroidism. The questions resulted in positive findings, which were used to con-firm the hypothesis. In order to distinguish between two hypotheses, a specific question that discriminated at the level of patient response was used. The specific hypothesis to be pursued was "Did the patient problem of muscle attacks relate to family history or to other organic disorders?" The negative response from the patient ruled out the family origin.

In contrast, the pattern of results from the resident–patient dialogue was that residents used a continuous search strategy without any resolution of competing information. Figure 19.6 shows that few cues were used to arrive at a diagnostic component (episodic neuromuscular disorder), which was not an accurate or even useful diagnosis. Because it was an inaccurate diagnosis, the predictions based on it served to generate negative findings (negative responses from the patient) during subsequent questioning, which interfered with any resolution of the prob-lem. The negative findings (no weakness in extremities, no tingling or numbness) led to further exploration, which resulted in further inaccurate diagnoses and the cycle repeated itself. This cycle finally resulted in a number of alternative hy-potheses being generated, most of which accounted for unrelated disorders.

In summary, during diagnostic problem solving, experts arrive at the solution very quickly and efficiently when dealing with routine problems. What appears to happen is that small sets of discriminable hypotheses are weakly activated, but only one comes into focus, usually the prototypical one (V. L. Patel, Evans, & Kaufman, 1989). Experts are able to filter out irrelevant information by gen-erating well-formed partial situation models containing highly discriminating features (V. L. Patel & Groen, 1986). Intermediate subjects generate both relevant and irrelevant information (V. L. Patel & Groen, 1991), showing the typical intermediate peak and generating hypotheses with little feature overlap.

Experts work within the problem constraints achieving the correct solution more often than novices, who tend to either undergeneralize or overgeneralize. Experts use rule-out strategies, which enable them to discriminate easily between the competing hypotheses. Less-than-experts do not use their strategies effectively. Experts use backward-directed reasoning to account for "loose ends" in diagnostic explanation tasks. Our results suggest that all subjects seem to use some kind of satisficing heuristic based on coherence criteria (V. L. Patel et al., in press), where coherence is defined as the extent to which every relevant finding is linked to a

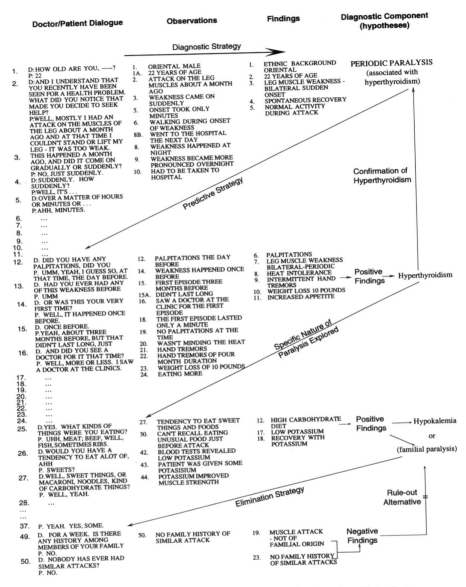

Doctor/Patient Dialogue	Observations	Findings	Diagnostic Component (hypotheses)

Diagnostic Strategy →

1. D:HOW OLD ARE YOU, ----?
P: 22
2. D:AND I UNDERSTAND THAT YOU RECENTLY HAVE BEEN SEEN FOR A HEALTH PROBLEM. WHAT DID YOU NOTICE THAT MADE YOU DECIDE TO SEEK HELP?
P:WELL, MOSTLY I HAD AN ATTACK ON THE MUSCLES OF THE LEG ABOUT A MONTH AGO AND AT THAT TIME I COULDN'T STAND OR LIFT MY LEG - IT WAS TOO WEAK.
3. THIS HAPPENED A MONTH AGO, AND DID IT COME ON GRADUALLY OR SUDDENLY?
P. NO, JUST SUDDENLY.
4. D:SUDDENLY. HOW SUDDENLY?
P:WELL, IT'S . . .
5. D:OVER A MATTER OF HOURS OR MINUTES OR . . .
P:AHH, MINUTES.
6. ...
7. ...
8. ...
9. ...
10. ...
11. ...

1. ORIENTAL MALE
1A. 22 YEARS OF AGE
2. ATTACK ON THE LEG MUSCLES ABOUT A MONTH AGO
3. WEAKNESS CAME ON SUDDENLY
5. ONSET TOOK ONLY MINUTES
6. WALKING DURING ONSET OF WEAKNESS
8B. WENT TO THE HOSPITAL THE NEXT DAY
8. WEAKNESS HAPPENED AT NIGHT
9. WEAKNESS BECAME MORE PRONOUNCED OVERNIGHT
10. HAD TO BE TAKEN TO HOSPITAL

1. ETHNIC BACKGROUND ORIENTAL
2. 22 YEARS OF AGE
3. LEG MUSCLE WEAKNESS - BILATERAL SUDDEN ONSET
4. SPONTANEOUS RECOVERY
5. NORMAL ACTIVITY DURING ATTACK

PERIODIC PARALYSIS
(associated with hyperthyroidism)

Predictive Strategy

Confirmation of Hyperthyroidism

12. D. DID YOU HAVE ANY PALPITATIONS, DID YOU
P. UMM, YEAH, I GUESS SO, AT THAT TIME, THE DAY BEFORE.
13. D. HAD YOU EVER HAD ANY OF THIS WEAKNESS BEFORE
P. UMM
14. D. OR WAS THIS YOUR VERY FIRST TIME?
P. WELL, IT HAPPENED ONCE BEFORE.
15. D. ONCE BEFORE.
P.YEAH, ABOUT THREE MONTHS BEFORE, BUT THAT DIDN'T LAST LONG, JUST
16. D. AND DID YOU SEE A DOCTOR FOR IT THAT TIME?
P. WELL, MORE OR LESS. I SAW A DOCTOR AT THE CLINICS.
17. ...
18. ...
19. ...
20. ...
21. ...
22. ...
23. ...
24. ...

12. PALPITATIONS THE DAY BEFORE
14. WEAKNESS HAPPENED ONCE BEFORE
15. FIRST EPISODE THREE MONTHS BEFORE
15A. DIDN'T LAST LONG
16. SAW A DOCTOR AT THE CLINIC FOR THE FIRST EPISODE
18. THE FIRST EPISODE LASTED ONLY A MINUTE
19. NO PALPITATIONS AT THE TIME
20. WASN'T MINDING THE HEAT
21. HAND TREMORS
22. HAND TREMORS OF FOUR MONTH DURATION
23. WEIGHT LOSS OF 10 POUNDS
24. EATING MORE

6. PALPITATIONS
7. LEG MUSCLE WEAKNESS BILATERAL-PERIODIC
8. HEAT INTOLERANCE
9. INTERMITTENT HAND TREMORS
10. WEIGHT LOSS 10 POUNDS
11. INCREASED APPETITE

Positive Findings → Hyperthyroidism

Specific Nature of Paralysis Explored

25. D.YES. WHAT KINDS OF THINGS WERE YOU EATING?
P. UHH, MEAT; BEEF, WELL, FISH, SOMETIMES RIBS.
26. D. WOULD YOU HAVE A TENDENCY TO EAT ALOT OF, AHH
P. SWEETS?
27. D.WELL, SWEET THINGS, OR MACARONI, NOODLES, KIND OF CARBOHYDRATE THINGS?
P. WELL, YEAH.
28. ...
...
...
37. P. YEAH. YES, SOME.
49. D. FOR A WEEK. IS THERE ANY HISTORY AMONG MEMBERS OF YOUR FAMILY
P. NO.
50. D. NOBODY HAS EVER HAD SIMILAR ATTACKS?
P. NO.

27. TENDENCY TO EAT SWEET THINGS AND FOODS
30. CAN'T RECALL EATING UNUSUAL FOOD JUST BEFORE ATTACK
42. BLOOD TESTS REVEALED LOW POTASSIUM
43. PATIENT WAS GIVEN SOME POTASISIUM
44. POTASSIUM IMPROVED MUSCLE STRENGTH

50. NO FAMILY HISTORY OF SIMILAR ATTACK

12. HIGH CARBOHYDRATE DIET
17. LOW POTASSIUM
18. RECOVERY WITH POTASSIUM

Positive Findings → Hypokalemia
or
(familial paralysis)

Elimination Strategy

Rule-out Alternative

19. MUSCLE ATTACK - NOT OF FAMILIAL ORIGIN
23. NO FAMILY HISTORY OF SIMILAR ATTACKS

Negative Findings

FIG. 19.5. Problem solving process during expert-patient interview. First column designates number of question/answer exchanges in doctor/patient dialogue.

376

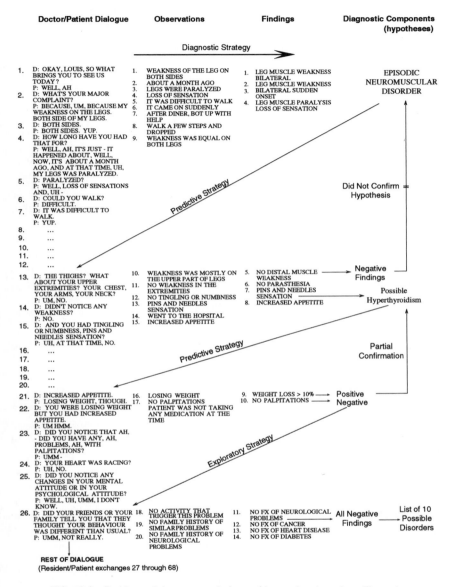

FIG. 19.6. Problem solving process during resident-patient interview. First column designates number of question/answer exchanges in doctor/patient dialogue.

diagnostic hypothesis (in our analysis, it is defined in terms of the connectedness of a semantic network); and the term *satisficing* refers to the use of stop rules based on satisfaction with the pattern of one's reasoning (Simon, 1990).

CONCLUSIONS

We have shown how the construction-integration theory may be used to provide an explanation of some important aspects of expertise in medicine. Differences found in the process of schema construction between experts, subexperts, intermediates, and novices may reflect differences in how knowledge organization and a current case interact. Clinical case comprehension involves the creation of partial schemata that are developed at different levels of the knowledge hierarchy, with more expert subjects generating hypotheses that have a higher degree of overlapping features, increasing their discriminating capability for distinguishing competing hypotheses. This generation process is constrained by their more elaborated and hierarchically organized knowledge bases. This allows experts to solve cases in more effective and systematic ways. Less-than-experts, on the contrary, generate hypotheses that cannot be distinguished on the basis of the presented findings. Their generation process is inefficient, resulting in a failure to integrate their clinical findings in a coherent representation.

In accounting for medical reasoning, comprehension and problem solving are intimately related. Comprehension is needed in order to solve a problem, and also depends on solving the problem. Four cognitive factors can be identified in problem solving in medicine: memory, knowledge, inferences, and strategies. Several difficulties stemming from these factors have to be overcome; among them are memory overload, lack of relevant knowledge, and need to make inferences in the face of many choices. Can the role of these factors be related to the construction-integration theory? We have made an attempt at providing a first approximation to such a question.

We have presented evidence showing the promise of looking at medical reasoning from a perspective, that through the years has shed light on our own research. The construction-integration theory represents a step forward in the direction of a much-needed theory.

The next step in the process of theory construction is to implement a computational model of comprehension during medical reasoning. Another extension is to enrich the model to account for strategic aspects of medical problem solving. This is necessary to account for findings currently outside the scope of the construction-integration theory (cf. Goldman & Varma, chap. 18 in this volume). Some of the more important of these findings are an explanation of comprehension breakdown and the strategies that are effected to solve comprehension impasses; the role of coherence in comprehension; and the relationship between comprehension, problem solving, and decision making to successful action.

ACKNOWLEDGMENTS

The work reported in this chapter was supported in part by a grant from Fonds pour la Formation de Chercheurs et l'Aide à la Recherche (#92-ER1177) to Vimla Patel. We thank David Kaufman and André Kushniruk for their productive discussions of the issues raised in this chapter. Special thanks are due to Suzanne Mannes and Carl Frederiksen for their pertinent comments and suggestions.

We acknowledge Walter Kintsch's leadership in the field of comprehension and discourse processing and, in particular, his influence and contribution to our work over the years on medical comprehension and reasoning.

REFERENCES

Arocha, J. F., & Patel, V. L. (in press). Novice diagnostic reasoning in medicine: Accounting for clinical evidence. *Journal of the Learning Sciences.*

Arocha, J. F., Patel, V. L., & Patel, Y. C. (1993). Hypothesis generation and the coordination of theory and evidence in medical diagnostic reasoning. *Medical Decision Making, 13,* 198–211.

Barrows, H. S., & Tamblyn, R. M. (1980). *Problem-based learning: An approach to medical education.* New York: Springer.

Bovair, S., & Kieras, D. E. (1985). A guide to propositional analysis for research on technical prose. In B. K. Britton & J. B. Black (Eds.), *Understanding expository prose* (pp. 315–362). Hillsdale, NJ: Lawrence Erlbaum Associates.

Bunge, M. (1973). *Method, model, and matter.* Dordrecht, The Netherlands: D. Reidel.

Coughlin, L. D., & Patel, V. L. (1987). Processing of clinical information by physicians and medical students. *Journal of Medical Education, 62,* 818–828.

Dellarosa, D. (1985). A computer simulation of children's arithmetic word problems. *Behavior Research Methods, Instruments, and Computers, 18,* 12–15.

Doane, S. M., McNamara, D. S., Kintsch, W., Polson, P., & Clawson, D. M. (1992). Prompt comprehension in UNIX command production. *Memory and Cognition, 20*(4), 327–343.

Evans, D. A., & Gadd, C. S. (1989). Managing coherence and context in medical problem-solving discourse. In D. A. Evans & V. L. Patel (Eds.), *Cognitive science in medicine: Biomedical modeling* (pp. 211–255). Cambridge, MA: MIT Press.

Frederiksen, C. H. (1975). Representing logical and semantic structure of knowledge acquired from discourse. *Cognitive Psychology, 7,* 371–458.

Groen, G. J., & Jerney, J. P. (1987). From children's arithmetic to medical problem solving: An extension of the Kintsch–Greeno model. *Proceedings of the 9th Annual Conference of the Cognitive Science Society* (pp. 348–354). Hillsdale, NJ: Lawrence Erlbaum Associates.

Groen, G. J., & Patel, V. L. (1988). The relationship between comprehension and reasoning in medical expertise. In M. Chi, R. Glaser, & M. J. Farr (Eds.), *The nature of expertise* (pp. 287–310). Hillsdale, NJ: Lawrence Erlbaum Associates.

Holyoak, K. J. (1991). Symbolic connectionism: Toward third generation theories of expertise. In A. Ericsson & J. Smith (Eds.), *Toward a general theory of expertise: Prospects and limits* (pp. 301–335). New York: Cambridge University Press.

Joseph, G.-M., & Patel, V. L. (1990). Domain knowledge and hypothesis generation in diagnostic reasoning. *Medical Decision Making, 10,* 31–46.

Kintsch, W. (1974). *The representation of meaning in memory.* Hillsdale, NJ: Lawrence Erlbaum Associates.

Kintsch, W. (1988). The role of knowledge in discourse comprehension: A construction-integration model. *Psychological Review, 95*(2), 163–182.

Kintsch, W., & Greeno, J. (1985). Understanding and solving word arithmetic problems. *Psychological Review, 92,* 109–129.

Kintsch, W., & van Dijk, T. A. (1978). Toward a model of text comprehension and production. *Psychological Review, 85,* 363–394.

Kintsch, W., & Welsch, D. W. (1991). The construction-integration model: A framework for studying memory for text. In W. E. Hockley & S. Lewandowsky (Eds.), *Relating theory to data: Essays on human memory in honor of Bennet Murdock* (pp. 367–385). Hillsdale, NJ: Lawrence Erlbaum Associates.

Kintsch, W., Welsch, D., Schmalhofer, F., & Zimny, S. (1990). Sentence memory: A theoretical analysis. *Journal of Memory and Language, 29,* 113–159.

Lesgold, A. M., Rubinson, H., Feltovich, P. J., Glaser, R., Klopfer, D., & Wang, Y. (1988). Expertise in a complex skill: Diagnosing x-ray pictures. In M. T. H. Chi, R. Glaser, & M. J. Farr (Eds.), *The nature of expertise* (pp. 311–342). Hillsdale, NJ: Lawrence Erlbaum Associates.

Mannes, S., & Kintsch, W. (1988). Action planning: Routine computing tasks. *Proceedings of the 10th Annual Conference of the Cognitive Science Society* (pp. 97–101). Hillsdale, NJ: Lawrence Erlbaum Associates.

Mannes, S., & Kintsch, W. (1991). Routine computing tasks: Planning as understanding. *Cognitive Science, 15*(3), 305–342.

Miller, R. A., Masarie, F. A., & Myers, J. D. (1986). "Quick Medical Reference" for diagnostic assistance. *MD Computing, 3,* 34–48.

Newell, A. (1990). *Unified theories of cognition.* Cambridge, MA: Harvard University Press.

Patel, V. L. (1984). *Expert-novice differences in clinical text understanding* (Tech. Rep. No. CME84-CS3). Montreal: McGill University, Centre for Medical Education.

Patel, V. L., Arocha, J. F., & Kaufman, D. K. (in press). Diagnostic reasoning and medical expertise. *The Psychology of Learning and Motivation, 31.*

Patel, V. L., Evans, D. A., & Groen, G. J. (1989). Biomedical knowledge and clinical reasoning. In D. A. Evans & V. L. Patel (Eds.), *Cognitive science in medicine: Biomedical modeling* (pp. 49–108). Cambridge, MA: MIT Press.

Patel, V. L., Evans, D. A., & Kaufman, D. R. (1989). Cognitive framework for doctor–patient interaction. In D. A. Evans & V. L. Patel (Eds.), *Cognitive science in medicine: Biomedical modeling* (pp. 253–308). Cambridge, MA: MIT Press.

Patel, V. L., & Groen, G. J. (1986). Knowledge-based solution strategies in medical reasoning. *Cognitive Science, 10,* 91–116.

Patel, V. L., & Groen, G. J. (1991). The general and specific nature of medical expertise: A critical look. In A. Ericsson & J. Smith (Eds.), *Toward a general theory of expertise: Prospects and limits* (pp. 93–125). New York: Cambridge University Press.

Patel, V. L., Groen, G. J., & Arocha, J. F. (1990). Medical expertise as a function of task difficulty. *Memory and Cognition, 18,* 394–406.

Patel, V. L., Groen, G. J., & Arocha, J. F. (1992, November). *Hypothesis generation as a function of task difficulty.* Paper presented at the 33rd Annual Meeting of the Psychonomic Society, San Francisco, CA.

Patel, V. L., Groen, G. J., & Frederiksen, C. H. (1986). Differences between students and physicians in memory for clinical cases. *Medical Education, 20,* 3–9.

Patel, V. L., Groen, G. J., & Patel, Y. C. (in press). Cognitive aspects of clinical performance: The role of medical expertise. *Medical Education.*

Patel, V. L., & Medley-Mark, V. (1985). Knowledge integration from clinical texts: Use of factual, inferential, and integrative questions. *Research in Medical Education: 1985. Proceedings of the 24th Annual Conference* (pp. 91–96). Association of American Medical Colleges.

Schmidt, H., Boshuizen, H. P. A., & Hobus, P. P. M. (1988). Transitory stages in the development of medical expertise: The "intermediate effect" in clinical case representation studies. *Proceedings of the 10th Annual Conference of the Cognitive Science Society* (pp. 139–145). Hillsdale, NJ: Lawrence Erlbaum Associates.

Simon, H. A. (1990). Invariants of human behavior. *Annual Review of Psychology, 41*, 1–19.

van Dijk, T. A., & Kintsch, W. (Ed.) (1983). *Strategies of discourse comprehension.* New York: Academic Press.

Chapter 20

On Macrostructures, Mental Models, and Other Inventions: A Brief Personal History of the Kintsch–van Dijk Theory

Teun A. van Dijk
University of Amsterdam

It is not my habit to write scholarly articles with the pronoun "I." Instead, rather traditionally, I tend to hide myself and my weaknesses behind the authorial "we." Retracing and evaluating my unique, decade-long (1973–1983) collaboration with Walter Kintsch, however, requires a more personal style, in which the deictic pronoun "I" refers, of course, to me, and "we" to Walter and me.

Well, this is not quite true. Rather than to refer to him and me, as historical persons of flesh and blood (and sweat, no tears), the pronouns should rather be interpreted as my subjective person constructions of him and me in my mental model(s) of our collaborative episode(s). Such subjective representations in my episodic memory are, naturally, partial, one-sided, or otherwise biased, and fraught with social and cognitive imperfections. Which brings me to the nature of mental models, not only of episodes of scholarly cooperation, but also of other forms of discourse. Of all our inventions and fantasies, (situation, event, episodic or, generally, mental) models were for me among the most useful and enduring products of our cooperation on what we called the "strategic" approach to text processing. So, my brief history of our joint efforts pays special attention to these mental constructions, which play such a crucial role in understanding text as well as in other cognitive processes.

However, let me start at the beginning, which is first about me, then about some earlier attempts by others, then about us, and then about what followed.

TEXT GRAMMAR

For me, the beginning was "text grammar," a concept that I now use with some hesitation, if not shame. After all, although it was a good idea, it was a good idea like "democracy"—according to Gandhi—was a good idea: It existed in my theoretical mind, and only some fragments of it were formulated in terms of what pretended to be something like a grammar, for instance in my doctoral dissertation (van Dijk, 1972).

Originally, text grammar for me was a means toward a more lofty end: the account of structures of literature. Starting my academic career as a literary theorist (after a first degree in French language and literature), I soon found out that traditional or even "structuralist" (this was the late 1960s) approaches to literature were hardly explicit, if not impressionistic. With the great linguistic example of the time, Noam Chomsky, descriptive and explanatory adequacy should result from a set of rules, a *grammar*. I knew no persuasive arguments that explain why such grammars should not also be developed for texts as well, although for Chomsky and other syntactically oriented grammarians of the time such an endeavor had little to do with grammar (that is, syntax) as they first defined it. However, the way I saw it was that once we had a more general grammar of texts, the formulation of special rules that would "generate" literary text structures would be a piece of cake. Or, so I thought.

As usual with good ideas, they hardly came alone: Others in (mostly European) linguistics were working on similar ideas, and from then on these fantasies came to be known as *text grammar*, and somewhat later, also in the United States, they were known as *discourse grammar* (see, e.g., De Beaugrande & Dressler, 1981; Longacre, 1983). One crucial argument of the theory of such text or discourse grammars was that structures of sentences in texts influence structures of neighboring sentences. That is, grammar should be relative: Syntactic and especially semantic structures of a sentence need to be described and interpreted relative to those of other sentences in the text. After all, there were no serious reasons why, for instance, a pronoun in a next sentence would require a totally different theoretical account from a pronoun in a next clause of the same sentence. Why sentence-internal pronouns would require description within a grammar, and cross-sentential pronouns would be relegated to a theory of language *use*, or *performance*, made no sense, and would violate the principles of intuition, elegance, simplicity, and parsimoniousness. In other words, sentence boundaries may be syntactically real, but constraints on sentence structures of various kinds do not always stop at that boundary.

This was a fortiori the case for semantics, for which the sentence boundary was even less relevant: One may mean more or less the same thing by uttering one complex sentence or a sequence of sentences. And, more interestingly, some things had to be said in separate sentences, and could not be reduced to a single sentence—for instance, after a change of speech act, perspective, or level of description (as in such pairs as, "It's cold in here. Could you please close the door?" or in, "John was late. In fact, he was always late"). Indeed, many notions that seemed to be relevant for texts were not even discussed in sentence grammars, or only in a rather ad hoc and inelegant way.

One of these notions was that of (semantic) *coherence*: Sequences of clauses, but also sentence sequences, intuitively "hang together." Such coherence seems to be the very core criterion of "textuality." Without coherence, a text would be nothing but an arbitrary sequence of unrelated sentences, much in the same way as a sentence would be merely an arbitrary sequence of words without a grammar. Once we had the basic criteria for this kind of linear, intersentential coherence between sentences (or rather, between propositions, because we are here dealing with semantic objects), we would also have a basic account of the nature of co-reference, textual deixis, and hence of pronominalization and other typical expressions (cohesion devices) that express underlying semantic coherence.

Although these ideas extended the scope of the grammar, they were in fact hardly revolutionary. Indeed, except maybe the notion of coherence per se, virtually all other theoretical instruments were still the same as those of sentential syntax and semantics. Obviously, this would not do. Sentences in a sequence might well be linearly (one-by-one) connected, but this was neither a necessary, nor a sufficient condition for what intuitively was felt to be textual coherence. Texts also have some overall unity, which makes sure that local coherence between sentences has some direction or continuity. So, the next step was to introduce the notion of *macrostructure*, namely, as a semantic structure that would describe, at a more global level, this overall unity and coherence. At the same time, the notion of macrostructure would be able to account for such important intuitive notions as topic, theme, gist, upshot, summary, and similar notions so abundantly present in everyday English, and hence apparently important in language use.

Incidentally, the notion of macrostructure had been used before, namely, by the prominent (then East) German linguist Manfred Bierwisch (Bierwisch, 1965). However, he used it to describe the conventional overall structure of stories—the kind of schematic (formal, categorical) structure I later called *superstructure* to distinguish it from the semantic macrostructure that defines the overall meaning of a text (van Dijk, 1980a).

At this point, current sentence grammars were left behind, because there was no theoretical concept in syntax and semantics that was similar to that of macrostructure. Macrostructures were related to their (local) *microstructures*, that is, to the propositions expressed by the sentences of the text, by mapping rules (e.g., those of deletion, generalization, and construction) that theoretically simulate the types of information reduction that characterizes the process of abstracting or summarizing a text.

In the early 1970s it was virtually impossible to sell outlandish products such as macrostructures to linguists, and even less to transformational grammarians.

Even my own text grammar colleagues in Germany (the Konstanz group), for whom formal theorizing was imperative in order to be able to compete with generative grammar (and be credible or persuasive as an alternative, serious grammar), macrostructures were still a rather strange element in grammar (see, e.g., Petöfi & Rieser, 1973). However, intuitions about text structures proved to be too powerful, and leaving the rigid mold of the then prevailing theories of grammar, I went looking for allies elsewhere.

And that is how I met Walter.

TEXTS AND PSYCHOLOGY

Why Walter? Why, indeed, psychology? The late sixties and early seventies had more to offer for text analysis in the emerging semiotics or in structural theories of narrative (Communications, 1966). However, semiotics was hardly explicit enough: It had provided ideas about narrative schemata and about the structural semantics of stories (Greimas, 1966), but there was nothing like the notion of macrostructure or, indeed, a general theory of discourse. A more general approach was necessary, and in order to prove the existence of macrostructures, the psycholinguistic mood of the time suggested looking for empirical evidence of grammatical structures in cognitive processing. So, if macrostructures were real, they also would have to show up in theories of text understanding.

In 1972, however, there was no ready paradigm to provide such theories of text understanding. Psycholinguistics was still wholly absorbed in testing the psychological implications of generative grammars, and of course did not talk about text or discourse (Jakobovits & Miron, 1967). After Chomsky's onslaught on Skinner, psychology itself was barely beginning to reject its behaviorist shackles, and the cognitive revolution was still in its infancy. Three of the books marking that watershed—namely, Lindsay and Norman (1972) and Tulving and Donaldson (1972), both appearing in the same year, and Anderson and Bower (1973), appearing a year later—had little to say about text processing: The terms *text* and *discourse* do not appear in their indexes.

Theories and experiments of understanding and recall of that time were still focused on lists of words or at most on sentences. Processing language was largely verbal learning, although problem solving, question answering, propositional representations and notions from rediscovered Gestalt theory already provided some of the theoretical instruments that later proved to be useful in the development of a cognitive theory of text processing.

Even Walter, in his extensive contribution to the Tulving and Donaldson book (W. Kintsch, 1972), did not yet go beyond the conceptual structure of lexical items and propositions, but translated the then-popular generative (sentence) semantics into a theory of memory representations. In sum, psychology in the early 1970s was still discovering the basic semantic units of language, understanding, memory and recall, and text was certainly not one of them.

Yet, the history of the cognitive psychology of discourse did have important forerunners who did speak about texts, and their work would soon be rediscovered by psychologists and the scholars in the then-emerging new field of artificial intelligence (AI) alike. Bartlett (1932), as is now recognized, was the most important and most influential of them all. Quibbling over theoretical sophistication and experimental adequacy instead of focusing on major new ideas, Anderson and Bower (1973) were reluctant to recognize the relevance of Bartlett's work, whereas Lindsay and Norman (1972) only referred to his book in their bibliographical recommendations. In that respect, they hardly followed the lead of Neisser (1967), whose *Cognitive Psychology* not only introduced the new cognitive paradigm, but also extensively discussed Bartlett's work, especially the soon popular notion of "schema," although without saying much about texts or semantics.

The hesitation in the new cognitive and semantic paradigms of the early 1970s to use stories and other texts as experimental materials or as objects of theoretical speculation also ignored other scattered but interesting work in the previous decades, sometimes directly influenced by Bartlett. Thus, already in the early 1940s, Cofer (1941, 1943) had done experiments with verbatim and "logical" learning of prose passages, as well as with long-term recall of stories. After another early study by Slamecka (1959), most other work on "learning from text," however, began to appear in the 1960s and early 1970s (see, e.g., Dawes, 1966; Dooling & Lachman, 1971; Frase, 1969, 1972; Frederiksen, 1972; King, 1961; Koen, Becker, & Young, 1969; Lachman & Dooling, 1968; Lee, 1965; Pompi & Lachman, 1967; Rothkopf, 1972).

It is not surprising that many of these studies came from educational psychology, the field that also later proved to be particularly receptive to studies on text processing, given the obvious need to understand the processing of textual learning materials. Indeed, our later article in the *Psychological Review* (W. Kintsch & van Dijk, 1978) would be most widely quoted in educational psychology.

Again, 1972 appeared to be a crucial year for these early ideas on learning from text to appear in the form of a book, namely, Freedle and Carroll's edited book on language comprehension and the acquisition of knowledge (Freedle & Carroll, 1972). Here, both "text" and "discourse" appear in the Subject Index, and several papers discuss text structures and processing extensively, such as those already mentioned by Frederiksen, Rothkopf, and Frase, as well as those by Chafe (1972) and Crothers (1972). Chafe's contribution in this book is especially interesting in light of later AI developments on the role of knowledge in text comprehension: He showed that many properties of discourse (such as pronouns and definite noun phrases) not only may presuppose previous information in the text but also systematic knowledge of the world. Similarly, Freedle (1972), following Dawes (1966), was among the first who explicitly aimed to study the comprehension of topics of texts, without presenting a theory of the textual nature of such topics, however (he abstractly associated topics with what he called "the set of possible alternatives"). Crothers (1972), in his formal account of text structure, was much more explicit about the structure and the role of topics, and defined them in terms of hierarchical conceptual structures that resemble the outline of a text, and thus came close to the notion of macrostructure. Frederiksen (1972), also influenced by Dawes (1966), focused on a formal model of "veridical," "inferred," and "elaborative" information that results from text processing, thus focusing on the semantic structure of recall protocols.

In sum, in the Bartlett tradition, this book seems to be the first in the new cognitive psychology to explicitly think about the role of texts and their structures in comprehension and recall. Most explicit, as is the case elsewhere in psychology and linguistics, is the new propositional semantics for sentences. Typical textual structures beyond the sentence level are either ignored (in which case texts are simply treated as sequences of sentences or propositions) or still dealt with in more or less informal terms. Similarly, despite special interest in the structure of text recall protocols, this work still tells little about the kind of actual processing strategies and representations of text in memory. Making up for a lack of revolutionary new ideas, it is surprising to see how much these and similar studies, following the linguistic trend, were couched in arcane logical, mathematical, and graph-theoretical jargon.

THE PSYCHOLOGY OF TEXT PROCESSING

From this brief history it becomes clear that the early 1970s have been pivotal in the emergence of the psychology of text processing. Thus, the year 1972 was an important temporal point of crystallization, namely, when many of the earlier ideas appeared in book form. Incidentally, this was also true, more or less independently, in several related disciplines dealing with discourse, such as artificial intelligence (Charniak, 1972; Newell & Simon, 1972), linguistic pragmatics (Wunderlich, 1972), sociolinguistics (Labov, 1972a, 1972b), and the ethnography of speaking (Gumperz & Hymes, 1972). Apparently, sometimes the *Zeitgeist* can be pinpointed to a rather precise period of change.

In this context and against this background (that is, between 1972 and 1974), Walter and I, at first independently, discovered the mutual relevance of discourse and cognition. This is especially clear in Walter's first book, which deals extensively with text meaning (Kintsch, 1974). Whereas this book already refers to my 1972 dissertation on text grammar, I had little to say about the psychological nature of text grammars. Again, due to the influence of TG psycholinguistics, which always wanted to prove grammatical rules in cognitive terms, I had briefly speculated on the psychological nature of macrostructures. With little knowledge about the barely emerging cognitive psychology, I nevertheless had the inexplicable intuition to read and refer to the three most relevant books of that time to support my ideas (Bartlett, 1932; Neisser, 1967; but see also Miller, Galantner, & Pribram, 1960, a seminal but at first rather ignored book on plans and understanding, which provided abstract ideas—TOTE units, etc.—that later proved to be very relevant for theories of macrostructures and other structures of the organization of discourse).

As soon as I read Walter's new book (W. Kintsch, 1974), I knew that the marriage of text linguistics and the psychology of text processing was imminent. Whereas many earlier studies were close encounters of the first kind, Walter's book initiated, for a broader public, the second phase of the courtship of the two neighboring approaches to discourse. Beyond the prevailing linguistic and cognitive semantics of the time, this monograph explicitly took texts as a major object of study for experimental cognitive psychologists (and not only as arbitrary materials of "prose recall" experiments). Thus, while retaining his earlier ideas of propositional structure (W. Kintsch, 1972), and still under the spell of TG semantics, Walter explicitly construed these propositions in a "textbase." This notion of a textbase had also been used by the Hungarian-German text grammarian Petöfi (1971) in the first book on text grammar, but Walter probably did not yet know this work. Walter emphasized that psychologists should also proceed to take texts as the basic units of their studies. Many unsolved issues in linguistics and psychology, such as the resolution of ambiguity, could then be easily accounted for in a theory of texts: Problems arise because "linguists write sentence grammars instead of text grammars, philosophers analyze isolated sentence examples, and little psychological work has as yet been done with complete texts and proper contexts" (W. Kintsch, 1974, p. 11).

After this programatic statement, Walter then goes on to specify the nature of a textbase in terms of proposition sequences made coherent by argument repetition, whereas macrostructures can be defined as higher order propositions subsuming underlying propositions. Despite his discussion of macrostructures, Walter largely focused on the microlevel of propositions, obviously the more concrete material evidence of text structure, both in psychology and in linguistics. Macrostructures are more abstract, and cannot be "seen" directly—unless in summaries or other expressions of abstract underlying structures—and are therefore less easy to pinpoint in an experiment: They must be inferred from texts.

Despite our enthusiasm for the program of a new psychology of text processing, this focus on propositional linkage due to argument overlap also produced our first theoretical disagreement. In my view, such overlap was indeed rather typical of discourse, but neither a necessary, nor a sufficient condition, and hence a derived property of more fundamental conditions of coherence. Instead of merely relating arguments of propositions, the entire propositions should be related by coherence links. However, Walter's experiments seemed to nicely confirm argument overlap, and I had only linguistic evidence and intuitions to offer (see also van Dijk, 1976).

The fact that in 1980 we dropped the practical (while easily testable) argument-overlap criterion, also shows how sometimes successful experimentation may initially induce psychologists to keep looking for epiphenomena instead of searching for deeper regularities, and how linguists and psychologists sometimes remain at odds when trying to explain discourse structures and their processing. After all, linguists have little to offer to empirically test their theoretical ideas: Many of their constructs may have no psychological processing reality at all.

Also, Walter soon convinced me that theoretical simplification is often unavoidable when running an experiment, if only for a feasible analysis of textual test materials or recall protocols. For instance, his practical method for propositional representations of texts worked nicely to assess text recall, but would probably be an intolerable simplification for formal philosophers and linguists, whose theories of propositional structures, however, were too complex and abstract to be used in practical experiments and analysis.

After the publication of his book, I had sought contact with Walter and made my first pilgrimage to Boulder, which initiated the beginning of nearly a decade of close collaboration. From the start, our discussions were exciting, stimulating, and fruitful (and that is not a typical preface formula): I went home with a lot of ideas about how to test some basic features of text grammars, or indeed, of theories of discourse more generally. Parallel to working on my next and last book on text grammar (van Dijk, 1977b), I thus started to do "memory experiments" with my own students (departments of literature have no labs), using stories from Boccaccio's *Decameron*, materials that were also used by Walter and later by others, simply because they were short and had canonical narrative structures. Our first paper, therefore, focused on story structures and recall (W. Kintsch & van Dijk, 1975). Interestingly, this paper was not published in English (although the English text circulated widely) but in a French version, which proved to be a major obstacle for references: Many people who referred to that paper mentioned the (linguistic) journal *Language* as its source, instead of the French journal *Langages*, which also shows something about the practice of referring in psychological articles.

One major theoretical point of this more (in Walter's case) or less (in my case) experimental work was to show the relevance of narrative structures on the one hand, and of semantic macrostructures on the other hand: Subjects typically show not only that they actively recall only a fragment of the original stories (typically between 10% and 25% on immediate reproduction), but also that what they reproduce is not just a fragment of the earlier text, but rather a higher level, abstract version of it, that is, something that looks much more like a macrostructure of the text. Indeed, immediate summaries of a story (theoretically expressing the—subjective—underlying macrostructure) nicely predict what subjects will recall later. We thus had a much clearer picture of the relationship between texts, their semantic macrostructures, and the mental processes and results involved in understanding and recall (W. Kintsch, 1977b; van Dijk, 1979).

At the same time, besides macrostructures, narrative schemata (superstructures) play a role in understanding and recall. This hypothesis would soon spark the famous "story grammar" row, which opposed story grammarians such as

Mandler (1978, 1984), and AI approaches to stories formulated in terms of action structures, plans, goals, and related notions (see the discussion in the issue of the *Behavioral and Brain Sciences* about Wilensky, 1983; see the special issue of *Poetics* on this topic: van Dijk, 1980b).

Our theory around 1975 assumed that texts are processed in cycles, due to the limited size of the short-term memory buffer, and that in this way a text representation (or textbase) is gradually construed in episodic memory. This textbase, however, does not merely consist of a connected sequence of propositions, but also features a hierarchical structure of macropropositions, corresponding to the major and minor topics or themes of the text, as assigned to (inferred from) the text by the reader. Delayed recall, in that case, involves this textual representation, but in such a way that, in general, primarily the higher (macro) nodes would still be available, plus an incidental lower node if representing information that was salient for other reasons.

At the same time, however, something was still lacking: knowledge. In order to be able to establish links between propositions in the episodic textbase, and to derive semantic macrostructures, vast amounts of knowledge were involved and applied by the reader. It was at this time that also the first AI work on knowledge and text comprehension began to appear, so that we readily introduced notions such as knowledge frames, and later "scripts" into our theory (Schank & Abelson, 1977; van Dijk, 1977a). However, we did not further explore the nature of the representation or the application of such knowledge in text processing: It was simply assumed that in order to construct a textbase readers would activate relevant scripts or other knowledge structures to infer "bridging" propositions or macropropositions to establish local and global coherence. Walter, however, continued his earlier work on lexical memory, and continued to battle with the AI people on the nature of knowledge and lexical structure (W. Kintsch, 1977a).

Around 1977, the theory had developed up to a point where rather specific predictions could be made about text recall. Several experiments had been devised and carried out, also by Walter's students, and we were ready to submit a paper to a serious journal, which became the much-cited 1978 *Psychological Review* paper. The text being used this time was not a story but an (informal) scholarly paper from social psychology: "Bumper Stickers and the Cops." The paper was about a social experiment in California in which subjects that had Black Panther bumper stickers were more harassed by the police than other drivers. Again, both the macrostructure and the superstructure hypothesis were tested, and the theoretical predictions Walter had developed in a more or less formal theory were nicely confirmed (for other work along these lines, see, e.g., the special issue of TEXT; van Dijk, 1982a).

As predicted, the overall macrostructure of this scholarly text was recalled best, whereas its abstract genre schema helped recall. Interestingly, especially in immediate recall, subjects also recalled a number of salient details. For instance, the fact that one of the people who was often stopped by the police was described as a "blonde girl" was one of those seemingly irrelevant "details" of the text my subjects in Amsterdam remembered quite well. After longer delays, however, that detail was also forgotten. The moral of that finding was that macrostructural (topical, important) information is indeed crucial for understanding and recall, but that also other factors may influence attention, prominent representation, and, hence, recall. That is, information may be salient, well-organized, or better re-trievable for other (social, personal) reasons, such as remarkableness, vividness, or other vague criteria that need better theoretical analysis.

THE THEORY OF STRATEGIC TEXT PROCESSING

After the success of the 1978 *Psychological Review* paper, it was time to write up our theory of text processing in a more ambitious and extended form—in a book. So many elements of the theory never got a detailed discussion in the earlier papers, and a book would give us the opportunity to do just that.

In the meantime, however, our core theory was also undergoing significant change. We were both feeling that the theory up to 1978 was too "static," too linguistic: Propositional text representations in memory were hardly different from the abstract semantic representations of sentence and text grammars, and the only difference with a formal description were some necessary elements of the process model: Processing in short-term memory, assumptions on the size of the short-term memory (STM) buffer, and cyclical construction of a text representation in episodic memory. Also, of course, the role of implicit information in understanding (derived from knowledge scripts) was a genuinely psychological dimension.

However, such an approach was too neat, too structuralistic, and seemed to reflect too little the actually ongoing mental processing. A proper theory of text comprehension and production would have to embody the more dynamic, ad hoc, online, tentative nature of understanding. Instead of rules (e.g., for the account of macrostructure derivation), therefore, we needed more flexible ways to represent the process. We thus introduced the crucial notion of *strategic* proc-essing: an online, context-dependent, goal-driven, multilevel, hypothetical, par-allel, and hence fast and effective way of understanding.

Thus, for each partial process involved—such as decoding surface structures, analyzing syntactic structures, interpreting local and semantic meaning, estab-lishing (co-)reference, and interpreting speech acts, among other things—various strategies would be needed to effectively do such a specialized job. The same would be the case for the activation and application of knowledge in the con-struction of the meaning of the text. That is, the strategic approach at the same time presupposed a modular conception of processing.

The various strategies would be monitored by the specific goals of the reading (or production) process, and hence by contextual (interactional, social) information. Readers should be expected to make mistakes, if only to account for garden-path sentences, and for other likely mistakes they would make, online, when reading the respective words and sentences of a text. All this would make the theory much more flexible, more psychologically valid, although at the same time theoretically more fuzzy. Instead of precise rules, we now needed complex, more or less strategic operations being fed by information from knowledge scripts, representations of context, various textual levels, and so on. When processing syntax, semantic, pragmatic, or other information would help, and vice versa. Modularity, thus, did not imply independence of respective processes involved.

This vastly complex process could only be centrally managed by a mental supervisor, that is, a Control System that would coordinate the various tasks being accomplished at the same time, that would do the bookkeeping of the information being activated and deactivated, and that would match the ongoing processes with the overall goals of the process, such as those of understanding and production. The Control System would also take care of another theoretical problem: If the STM buffer is limited, say to seven plus or minus two units of each level of analysis, then it is hard to imagine how STM itself would not only be busy decoding incoming talk or text (letters, sounds), analyzing syntax or assigning semantic and pragmatic interpretations, but also at the same time deriving macrostructural propositions (topics), schematic structures ("this is a story," "this is an argument," etc.), macro speech acts, contextual information (overall goals), and so on. With our understanding of the limitations of STM, we could not imagine how STM could handle all these tasks. Therefore we assumed that all control tasks had to be taken care of by a different system, which would guide the process—metaphorically speaking—"just below the surface" or "across the horizon," and be less conscious than the actual processes being worked on. However, such control information would need to be immediately available, and activated as soon as it was needed for STM processing (e.g., when problems arise or questions are asked that pertain to the control process: "What are you doing?"). Although this control system plays such a central and prominent role, we were unable to provide a detailed description of its precise internal structures or of the management processes involved. As far as I know, no other theorists have been working on the precise nature of such a system, either theoretically or empirically. Here is one of the many unfinished elements of our theory that needs further attention.

For the book we also abandoned the local theory of coherence based on argument repetition, which in light of theoretical advances was no longer tenable, and had been criticized from various points of view. Instead, we further focused on propositional coherence, namely, as a relation between whole propositions, of which argument overlap is a special case.

Our major example, discussed throughout the book, was a news article: a text on the situation in Guatemala published in *Newsweek*. This article was analyzed systematically, and its understanding by real readers was explicitly simulated for all levels: syntax, local semantics and coherence, macrostructures, schematic superstructures, and context. In addition to our earlier focus on comprehension, we also added a chapter on text production, which would at least tentatively fill another major lacuna of the theory.

I had proposed to extend the theory also to what was increasingly becoming known as "social cognition," that is, with a component that would account for opinions and attitudes (van Dijk, 1982b). So far, the theory of text processing was rather narrowly cognitive, and hardly any social contexts, or specific sociocultural information beyond knowledge, was involved to account for understanding. However, when people read a news report in a weekly like *Newsweek*, opinions, attitudes, ideologies, emotions, norms, and values are involved. Readers may evaluate the miserable situation in Guatemala, and it is plausible that processing and recall are also a function of such and other social cognitions shared with other readers (e.g., an anti-U.S. point of view, a pacifist attitude, etc.).

Although Walter found all of this quite likely, his caution made him veto this hazardous extension of the theory, for which we had neither theory nor experimental data. We already had more than enough complex and at times hazardous hypotheses and ideas to defend in the book. Going all the way would probably make the book less credible. For me this was fine, but it meant that something was still on the agenda. So during the 1980s, I have, though from a different perspective, tried to develop some of these ideas on the relations between discourse and social cognition; these are crucial to understand real discourse understanding, namely, as a function of the mentally represented social position of the reader(s).

MENTAL MODELS

One of the key concepts of the new theory was the notion of a *situation model*. A model, as we saw it, is a construct in episodic memory that represents the event or situation a text is *about*. That is, for the first time, we would build in a true referential dimension. Texts no longer would be interpreted relative to reality, but to the subjective representation of a fragment of reality in the reader's mind. The overall goal of text understanding in that case would no longer be, as we had assumed until the end of the 1970s, the construction of a textual representation (textbase) in episodic memory, but rather a model of the event or the situation referred by the text. The textbase would merely represent those meanings expressed by the text—those relevant for local, online understanding—but real understanding would involve the construction of a new model, or the updating of an activated old model. Such models would of course be subjective: It would feature personal associations, inferences, and fragments of other models (i.e., previous experiences). Hence, the model of a text would be personal, ad hoc and unique, and define one specific interpretation of one specific text at a specific moment.

Most importantly, models would feature the activated and instantiated information derived from knowledge. Indeed, the resulting model of a text would be much richer than the representation of the text itself, which would merely express relevant new information, and some pointers to old or otherwise known information (e.g., in the form of presuppositions, expressed or signaled by, e.g., definite articles, relative clauses, or sentence order). In other words, the text and its episodic representation are merely the tip of the vast iceberg that constitutes the model, featuring bridging propositions, fragments of personal knowledge, fragments of general social knowledge, and so on. Thus, models are the ideal interface between shared social information such as knowledge, on the one hand, and the personal, unique semantic interpretation or production of a specific text, on the other hand.

Models for us had many uses. We listed at least a dozen independent arguments concerning why models were indispensable. Thus, models were also necessary to explain what most psychologists had ignored, and what was crucial in a theory of discourse: reference, co-reference, and referentially based coherence. With a model, all this was easy, elegant, and transparent: Texts are simply interpreted relative to a model. Argument overlap, hence, was no more than a strategic surface expression of underlying continuity of discourse referents in a model. This use of the notion was of course hardly new in logic and formal linguistics: Formal semantics had introduced possible worlds and models some time ago, though in very abstract terms, in which model structures consist of sets of individuals, and other elements needed to interpret sentences relative to a formal model. Some of these ideas were soon also applied in the formal interpretation of (some) discourse structures, such as anaphora (Kamp, 1981; Nash-Webber, 1978; Stenning, 1978; see also van Dijk, 1977b, 1987b).

The functions of models were many. Thus, they also allowed us to put some distance between propositional representations of texts and memory and intuitions about possibly analogical representations of textual information people may have stored. That is, once one has the notion of a model, one may also explain how it is that after a period of time people no longer remember whether they have read about an event, seen it on TV, or actually participated in it. Whatever the mode of perception, the results in all cases would be a model of the event. Also, models allow a much better understanding of how spatial information is processed and stored. (See also recent work in Van Oostendorp & Zwaan, 1994.)

The introduction of the notion of model implied that for the first time we had a starting point for processes of production. Comprehension theories are not only easier because we can manipulate input texts, and then measure the results of understanding by recall protocols, question answering, priming, or other methods. For production, it was never quite clear where to start: with lexical items, knowledge, or semantic meaning representations. With the text-independent notion of a model, talk and text production begins with a representation of a personal experience (as in a story), or other specific, personal knowledge about the world, represented in a model. Indeed, the point and intention of much informative communication is to convey our models to others, or to realize models expressed by others, as is the case in commands, plans, recommendations, instructions, or similar discourse types and speech acts.

Finally, as suggested earlier, models are also the missing link between texts and general, socially shared information such as knowledge. That is, whereas scripts are about stereotypical or prototypical events and episodes, and hence feature general and abstract information (typically represented by variables), models represent concrete, specific events, and hence feature constants representing specific people, places, or time. What was usually referred to as knowledge instantiation could now be formulated in terms of specifying general information as particular information in a model. Conversely, learning would involve processes of generalization and abstraction based on (sets of) models, thus linking episodic memory with semantic memory. This view suggests that besides specific models of unique situations, people probably also have generalized models in episodic memory: These may be personal, and hence feature specific individuals (for instance myself), and at the same time abstract from specific time, place, or circumstances (as in the models I have of my daily work or weekly shopping).

As with other useful theoretical concepts, the idea of mental models as the basis for textual interpretation was discovered more or less at the same time by Johnson-Laird, whose book *Mental Models* (1983) appeared in the same year as our *Strategies of Discourse Comprehension*, but who had already published earlier articles on models (Johnson-Laird, 1980). However, Johnson-Laird had other motivations, goals, and uses for these models, which, in line with his earlier work on inferences, especially served to explain otherwise strange contradictions between logical and psychological inferences. Furthermore, Johnson-Laird did not specifically focus on discourse comprehension (but see Johnson-Laird & Garnham, 1981).

Thus, although there were many differences in the ways we used the notion of a model, the fundamental idea was the same. Both Johnson-Laird and I were obviously inspired by developments of model theories in formal semantics and linguistics, which also began to find their ways into theories of formal discourse structures, as I (imperfectly) had tried to provide in my 1977 book. I remember having written an unpublished note for a conference in Paris in 1981 in which Johnson-Laird also participated, and whose work on models I still had not seen. This note was about "text representation and world representation" in a psychological theory. Although the basic idea of models was there, I still had no idea how rich and useful the notion of a model would eventually become in the theory developed with Walter soon after that.

Indeed, at first Walter was not readily convinced by these premature ideas to introduce a totally new form of representation in our theory. Rereading the hundreds of letters that constitute our contacts of that time (long-distance cooperation has the advantage that one has a record of it in the form of letters), I found the following, poetic passage in a letter from Walter of December 12, 1980, reacting to my "text-world" paper:

> My first reaction to this paper was something like a shock. I sat outside in the noonday sun, which was so strong that both dog and cat had retreated into some shade; only I, being considerably older, was still soaking up the warmth; everything was utterly quiet, except for some birds rummaging around in the dead leaves under the trees. In the midst of this pastoral scene burst this manuscript, stepping right into the middle of the learning issue. This is, of course, acknowledged as a fine problem, but hardly anybody dares touching it these days. Wasn't it too presumptuous?
>
> On the other hand, of course, it is certainly the case that you are talking about real problems. Are we obliged to hide them, just because we can't properly solve them? Just as a little breeze came up which drove the cat and me inside, I realized that I was shocked for nothing. What you do here is merely to say that such-and-such are the outlines of a problem that is very important; take note psychology, and start worrying how to solve it.

After his initial shock and hesitation, Walter, practical as ever, then goes on to propose how "world representations" in memory might be modeled and experiments run to test it. At the same time, he warns against the notion of "pictures" of the world.

This was typical of our cooperation. I might come up with a crazy idea, or one of these other linguistic inventions or objections, and Walter would think, hesitate, and see the useful elements in the idea. Then he would propose how to deal with it in a way that would be acceptable to psychologists. More than that, once the notion of a "situation model" became part of the theory, he came up with many of the arguments as to why it was so useful; and I had introduced it primarily to account for coherence, (co)reference, and as a bridge between social knowledge and semantic representations of texts.

The success of the notion of mental models was considerable. In different branches of cognitive science and psychology it was being used more and more, also because it allowed nice links with formal approaches to language and discourse, AI representations of "reality," and so on. Soon, also the first experiments were carried out to test some concrete predictions of the model, for example, by Morrow and his associates, who nicely showed that information close together in the text, but already "old" or "distant" in a mental model (e.g., when in a story the storyteller continues to talk about Mary when it has just been said that Mary left the house) was more difficult to retrieve than information about individuals still "present" in the now-active model (or model fragment) (Morrow, 1986, 1990; Morrow, Greenspan, & Bower, 1987). Also in British psychology, much interesting work was done on text understanding making use of the notion of a model (Garnham, 1987). One of the theoretical differences was/is that for Walter and me it was clear that models were needed besides textual representations (which have their own role in understanding and production), whereas others only admitted models as interpretations of discourse.

There was one major point where all model theorists so far failed to deliver the goods: No one had any clear and explicit idea about what such models looked like. We knew what they should do, we knew a lot of their functions, and what was probably in them (like representations of our personal knowledge about persons, objects, events, and situations), but how such information was to be represented, we had as yet no clue. With Johnson-Laird, and others, we agreed that some model information might be analogical, but that opened the well-known Pandora's box of visual versus propositional (or other abstract) representations that had inspired earlier theoretical disputes in psychology (Paivio, 1971). Also, using the term *analogical* begs the question of representation formats, and may lead to more questions than it answers. So, despite their central role in text processing, we still know very little about the internal structures of models, as well as about the detailed strategies of their construction, change (updating), activation, de-activation, and other processes relating them to the rest of the memory system. I come back to the problem of model structures later.

The limitation of cognitive psychology to knowledge-based processing also implied another restriction on the view of models. That is, as I remarked about the processing of our *Newsweek* text about Guatemala in the *Strategies* book, what was lacking in the model were other forms of personal beliefs—that is, *opinions*. Readers of that text not only represent what is going on in Guatemala (following the textual leads persuasively expressing the "preferred model" of the writer), but also have evaluative beliefs about that situation. That is, in the same way as they bring to bear general knowledge about civil wars and oppression from their scripts or frames in semantic knowledge, they also activate and apply socially shared attitudes and ideologies, for example, about the role of the United States in Central America. The concrete personal opinions that result from the instantiation of such group attitudes are also part of the readers' model of Guatemala, so that models can also be seen as the interface between personal and social cognitions, and between individual and group-based understanding of a text. Possibly, models might even feature a representation of personal emotions, such as hate, fear, or jealousy. If so, this would nicely explain the well-known finding, already familiar in Proust's *A la recherche du temps perdu*, that emotions sometimes may be used to retrieve specific models about past events (Bower, 1980).

Finally, people not only construct models of events they read or speak about, but also of the communicative events they are engaged in. An ongoing conversation, reading the newspaper, or watching TV are such events, and while processing the information these discourses are about, language users also activate, construct, and continually update the *context model* of the present communicative situation in which they participate. Such special situation models are relevant because they represent the context, including speakers or readers, the author or the listener, the newspaper one reads, the goals of the interaction, and other pragmatic information relevant for understanding and production. Context models, thus, are in turn the interface between event models and the concrete text: what speech act to select, what style to use, what event model information to express or what to presuppose (given the knowledge of the reader/hearer, also represented in the context model), and so on. In other words, whereas much of the meaning of texts is controlled by the event model, much of the variable surface structure of the text will be monitored by the context model. Unfortunately, Walter and I had no idea either how to represent context models and their interactions with event models, and how context models influence the actual semantic and formulation strategies in text production, or the biased interpretation of texts in understanding, that is, as a function of the contextual position of the reader. This was another of the fundamental questions we had to leave open for future research.

All these theory fragments, experiments, and the writing of the respective chapters of the *Strategies* book obviously took a lot of time. Ideas for chapters going back and forth over the ocean (e-mail at that time was not yet operative— although in our correspondence I saw that we briefly used a precursor system called Plato), and finally Walter retreated to the Stanford Institute for Advanced Study, and I took the opportunity of a stay in Berkeley to commute to Stanford in order to discuss the finishing touches of the last version.

As with all the discussions we had during my trips to Boulder, and Walter's occasional visit to Amsterdam or Austria, our debates were always exciting. Unlike much experimental work in psychology, my own work in text grammar and discourse analysis was usually a rather isolated activity, with only occasional close collaboration with others. So, my joint work with Walter was also a rather new experience in jointly producing ideas and a book. Despite our differences of theory, our frequent working sessions were mutually inspiring and very productive. It is only due to this form of close cooperation that I learned so much about the psychology of text processing, if not about experimentation. Discussions would often continue at home with Eileen Kintsch, who after her earlier work in linguistics and German began to make a career in psychology herself, and whose many comments and hospitality made my trips to Boulder more than just a business trip to see a colleague. Soon, she also became a co-author of some of the work at Boulder on story comprehension (Poulson, E. Kintsch, W. Kintsch, & Premack, 1979).

FINAL EPISODE: NEW DOMAINS AND APPLICATIONS

It is now 10 years ago that our book *Strategies of Discourse Comprehension* appeared. Although I sometimes see references to it, I have been unable to follow the relevant psychological and related literature in order to see its academic fate.

Checking our citation scores, I see that even 10 years later dozens of our citations are still based on this common work.

In the meantime, and as usual, I have moved to other domains of research, trusting that hundreds, if not thousands, of psychologists over the world would continue to work on the psychology of text processing. Increasingly interested in the social and political dimensions of discourse, I turned to the study of news in the press, and especially to the analysis of the reproduction of racism and other forms of inequality through discourse and communication. However, also for this research I have immensely benefited from my earlier work with Walter, and our theoretical framework has served me to formulate research questions in these new areas that otherwise would have remained vague. Let me therefore finally summarize some of my own applications and extensions of our theory in these new areas.

News Analysis

As is often the case in the humanities and the social sciences, everyday phenomena tend at first to be ignored by scholars. Such was the case for everyday interaction and mundane conversation in sociology and for everyday memory in psychology. It is also true for the genre of text most adult citizens (in rich societies) are confronted with daily and most intensively: the news reports of our newspapers. In a series of studies, I therefore turned to a systematic analysis of the structures of news reports, and to the processes involved in their production, comprehension, and uses by the readers (van Dijk, 1988a, 1988b).

Obviously, processes of news production and comprehension not only involve social interaction of journalists and news actors, or patterns of communication more generally, but also cognitive processes. Thus, in the daily production of news reports, journalists are confronted with the formidable task of processing large numbers of source texts from other media, informants, interviews, press conferences, press releases, phone calls or documents, and of reducing that vast amount of information to the relative short news report one reads in the paper. The mental strategies involved in this routine process of information reduction obviously need to make use of macroprocesses of information reduction: Just like the reader of the newspaper, journalists also must reduce many input texts to a manageable story, which is in fact a relevant combination of the journalist's (subjective) macrostructures of the input texts.

Also involved are the mental models of news events journalists construct and update on the basis of the source texts they process. They combine new information with already-present information about the same topic or issue, and thus daily update their models of important social and political events. As is argued in somewhat more detail later, these models may be unique, ad hoc, and personal, thus representing the personal experiences and opinions of the journalist. But they also feature instantiations of general knowledge, beliefs, attitudes, and ideologies, namely, those shared by other journalists of the same newspaper, or by other (mostly white, male, middle-class) citizens. Thus, the mental basis of each individual news report is an event model that is strategically (i.e., depending on the constraints of the context model) expressed as a news text. Conversely, the structure of a news text reveals the combined influence of the underlying structures of event and context models: Headlines and leads express the (subjective) macrostructures of the models—the information the journalist finds most important, relevant, interesting, or otherwise newsworthy—and similar remarks may be made about the major news actors and their actions, as well as their evaluation by the journalist. Thus, different news accounts are socially and ideologically variable versions of reality as they are represented in underlying models of journalists. This way of framing the well-known problem of truth or bias in news reports allows the formulation of research programs and analytical techniques that go beyond the traditional approaches to news and the media.

Similar remarks may be made for the other side of the communication process (i.e., reading, understanding, and memorization of news reports by the readers). In the 1980s, an increasing number of experimental studies have paid attention to the details of the cognitive processes involved in this important domain of research, and some of these studies also make use of our work (Bruhn Jensen, 1986; Graber, 1988; Gunter, 1987; Robinson & Levy, 1986). Invariably, readers or viewers of news recall very little in (uncued) immediate recall and even less in delayed recall. Most of these findings can rather straightforwardly be explained in our theoretical framework: Readers recall on the basis of their subjective models of events and not on the basis of some kind of text representation, and of these models they have mainly access to the higher level macrostructures. This process is in turn influenced by preexisting specific knowledge ("old" models), by general sociocultural knowledge about the issue in question, as well as by shared, group-based social attitudes and ideologies. Finally, reading and understanding news is of course monitored by the context model of the ongoing communicative event, featuring recipient goals and interests and opinions about the newspaper or television program. Although many questions still need to be answered, the main processes of reading, storage, and recall are rather well-understood.

The Reproduction of Racism

Possibly even more relevant, especially in the framework of increasing racism in Europe, is the study of the ways ethnic or racial prejudice, discrimination, and racism are reproduced in Western societies. Many of the structures, processes, and institutions involved in this process are social, political, and cultural. However, from the start I have emphasized the role of discourse and cognition in this process. That is, prejudices and racist ideologies do not come about spontaneously, and are not merely confirmed by observation of, and participation in discriminatory or other interethnic interaction. They are acquired also through discourse and communication. Thus, in a series of research projects, I have studied the structures and strategies of everyday conversations, textbooks, news reports, political debates, and scholarly and managerial discourse, and how these persuasively influence and are controlled by the minds of members of the majority (van Dijk, 1984, 1987a, 1991, 1993a).

This again requires an analysis of the relations between discourse and cognition. Fortunately, due to my work with Walter, I had learned much about such relationships. Thus, in order to analyze racist stories or news reports, I now knew these should be derived from models, in this case of perceived, experienced ethnic events (van Dijk, 1985a). Similarly, the well-known social-psychological processes of group categorization, polarization, overgeneralization, and other ways to process information about other groups, could now be reformulated in terms of the relations between input discourses, models, and more general social cognitions, such as ethnic and racial prejudices. That is, it is now known (at least more or less) how racist readers go about understanding ethnic issues and events, or how the media contribute to prejudging readers in the first place. Obviously, the processes involved here are extremely complex, but at least there is a framework in which they can be studied with some precision.

Social Cognition and Ideology

Racism is one prominent form of group power and dominance. In the same way, other forms of social inequality, and the processes of their social reproduction, may be studied. Again, discourse and cognition are involved, although such a subjective or "mentalist" approach to racism and social inequality is often felt by social scientists to be reductionist. I obviously do not agree at all. The rather widespread misunderstanding among many social scientists is that psychology is only "individual" psychology, which leads to the understandable rejection of an approach that ignores the fundamental social dimension of dominance and inequality.

However, if one focuses attention not merely on general properties of human cognition, but on social cognition, there is no reason to see such an approach as individualistic. On the contrary, just as discourse is social so also is the mind: Knowledge and other beliefs are formed, changed, and used in social situations, about other groups, social issues, and societal structures. In my most recent work on critical discourse analysis, which focuses on the discursive reproduction of dominance and inequality, therefore, I emphasize the fundamental, mediating role of social cognitions such as group-based and sociocultural knowledge, attitudes, group goals, ideologies, norms, and values (van Dijk, 1993b, 1994).

Indeed, such social representations and the mental strategies that manipulate them are needed to relate acts and interactions (including discourse) of social members with social conditions and sociocultural structures and institutions—for instance, newspapers and the media, journalists as a group and profession, and newsgathering routines, on the one hand, with concrete news reports on the other hand; or structures of racial dominance and racism, on the one hand, and individual acts of everyday discrimination against minorities on the other.

A more detailed study of this well-known missing link between the macro- and microlevel of societal analysis shows the relevance of a combined sociocognitive and discursive approach (van Dijk, 1990). New developments in the study of social cognition (see, e.g., Fiske & Taylor, 1991) provide some of the background for these analyses of the links between discourse and social cognition. Again, models play a central role in such an analysis because they relate individual and personal experiences with general, socially shared beliefs, which are in turn related to group goals, ideologies, the moral order, and the interests of different groups and institutions that give rise to such shared social cognitions in the first place. A sociocognitive account also emphasizes (and analyzes!) the well-known sociological fact that social reality for social members is relevant only in so far as it is subjectively construed by them, that is, as a function of (shared) social representations in the mind. Thus, a systematic analysis of social and public discourse might show how to reconstruct individual members' models, as well as the general social representations that control many of their structures.

In sum, in my later work, models continued to play a central role in the account of many social phenomena, such as the production and reception of news in the press, the reproduction of racism and other forms of inequality, or as part of a theoretical account of the process of the "manufacturing of the consent" in critical political studies (Herman & Chomsky, 1988). Thus, power, political socialization and cognition, agenda setting, public opinion, prejudices, and many other issues in the social and political sciences can be much better understood if we recognize the relevance of the cognitive interface between individual actions (discourse) and societal macrostructures such as groups, group relations, and institutions. Models are the core of that cognitive interface, because they underlie individual experiences and action, while at the same time embodying the instantiations of general, shared social representations.

One other notion regularly appearing in these new studies is that of *ideology*. Although widely studied in the social and political sciences, vagueness and disagreement about the nature of ideology are rife. Rejected as merely meaning coherent (political or social) belief systems, or as merely denoting negative (biased) forms of consciousness, most proposals in this area replace one vague approach with another, although all seem to retain at least some aspect of the truth.

In a new project that aims to explicitly link discourse and ideology, I propose to examine in detail the structures and processes of ideologies seen as the basic systems of social cognition. Just like attitudes, group goals, norms, and values, ideologies are both mental and social. They are not individual, but shared by the members of a group. Their function is to provide coherence to the system of social cognitions, and to relate systems of social cognitions with the goals, interests, and social-political conditions of the group sharing that ideology. Despite undeniable personal and contextual variations (to be accounted for in terms of event and context model), at least some internal coherence in social cognitions is needed, given the vast complexity of relevant social attitudes. To develop and apply relevant social attitudes (e.g., about abortion, multicultural education, or the civil war in Bosnia), social members need an organizing system that monitors the many mutual links between different attitudes (e.g., between those about abortion, and those about the freedom of women), as well as between attitudes and the interests and goals of the group(s) to which social members belong.

Ideologies have precisely that role. At present, I surmise that they are probably built up from basic sociocultural units, such as norms and values that represent the social and moral order of a society or culture (e.g., equality, freedom, etc.), as well as by self-group schemata that represent the social position of the relevant group. This construction of ideologies is a function of processes of selection, emphasis, and construction that are biased by group goals and interests. It will be the task of the new project to spell out these structures and strategies of the ideological organization of the social mind, and to explain, thus, how discourses (indirectly) express, signal, form, or confirm such ideological systems. One way to do so is to make explicit the links between mental model structures and the social cognitions that underlie the personal opinions of such models, more or less in the same way as personal knowledge may be studied as a function of more general, sociocultural knowledge.

Despite vast numbers of recent studies on social and political cognition, and despite the enormous amount of work on attitudes in traditional social psychology, most of the relevant structures and strategies involved here are still unknown. Here are other challenging tasks for joint projects of cognitive and social psychologists, sociologists, political scientists, and discourse analysts, and more generally for a social extension of the currently rather narrowly conceived field of cognitive science.

On Models and Model Structures

Let me finally return to mental models. I have argued that although it is pretty well known what theoretical role and tasks they have or should have, psychologists are more or less groping in the dark about their precise internal structures. Walter and I, Johnson-Laird, and others working, theoretically or empirically, with the notion may have had some general clues about such *model structures*, but these were no more than well-educated and, especially, rather vague guesses. Thus, unlike episodic text representations consisting of propositions, models are assumed to also feature analogical information, whatever this may mean in a precise representational language. It was mentioned earlier that when I first developed my own idea of models, I metaphorically spoke of "pictures of events," a terminology resolutely rejected by Walter. Yet, if analogical structures are involved, one needs to somehow find, first of all, the theoretical language in which to speak about such structures without somehow reducing them again to propositions or other objects that are verbalized in natural language or translated into some kind of formal language. Eventually, maybe developments in the neurophysiology of the brain might come up with suggestions that can provide ideas for such a language of analogical representations (e.g., in order to explain model memories for faces, persons, objects, places, and other visual information).

If I leave aside for a moment this complex and at present unsolvable question, I may nevertheless make some suggestions about the nature of model structures. As a discourse analyst, I tend to search the evidence for such structures in their expression (i.e., in text and talk), the kind of evidence most psychologists also use, albeit indirectly, in their experiments. Thus, semantic structures are traditionally represented by propositions of which the respective arguments have various roles or functions, such as agent, patient, experiencer, object, and so on, which are in turn syntactically expressed or signaled by word order and different syntactic categories.

If it is assumed that at least the basic principles of such functional semantic structures are more or less universal, they may be interpreted as evidence of an underlying model structure—that is, as semantic coding in natural language for the schematic structure of an underlying model, consisting of a limited number of fixed categories. The relevance of such a model schema resides in the fact that people are forming and updating thousands of models each day, of each of their personal experiences and events (and of discourses of such events). This means they need a very fast, flexible, effective, and strategically relevant schema by which to mentally represent such events, or rather, the *structure* of such events.

For instance, in the representations of actions, it is necessary to represent the persons involved in the action and their roles (e.g., as agents, etc.). Similarly, for the representations of settings of such events, categories are needed for time, place, distance, space, as well as of objects and their relational role(s) in the event. Note that the content of the models is then filled in by instantiated information derived from frames, scripts, or other schematic structures of persons, objects, and actions, as they are available in the general knowledge system. In other words, much of the functional semantics of sentences may be based on, and explained by, the functional, categorical structure of underlying models.

However, not only sentences describe (or prescribe) events, actions, or situations. Discourses, such as stories, news reports, or conversations do so as well. That is, whereas semantic sentence structures may give clues about corresponding microstructures of models, structures of discourse may yield clues about the local and global structures of models of complex events. That is, a car accident, going to the movies, or a civil war are events usually described by several or many propositions (although they may, at higher levels, be summarized by macropropositions). Thus, local coherence relations between propositions may express relations of temporality or causation that may be assumed to order event structures in models. Similarly, the order of propositions in sentences or texts may be interpreted in terms of distance versus proximity, whole versus parts, direction or movement, and other basic properties of complex models. It was argued that models also involve personal opinions, that is, evaluative beliefs, which are multiply coded in topics, local semantic relations, the lexicon, style variations, and the rhetoric of texts. Similarly, sentence and discourse structures may express or signal relevance, importance, and other relations between people and the events they witness, participate in, or read about, and hence represented in mental models. We have seen that argument continuity in discourse signals underlying identity of participants in concatenated micromodels that form the overall model of an event, as does tense for temporal relations (see the work by Givón on these links between discourse grammar and cognition, e.g., Givón, 1989a, 1989b).

Note though that the links between event models and discourse are indirect, and a function of the many factors represented in context models, such as goals, interests, impressions or "face," and mutual knowledge and opinions of the discourse participants. To wit, when many of the white interviewees in Amsterdam and San Diego in my earlier project on conversations on ethnic minorities routinely told the interviewers "I have nothing against Blacks [Turks, immigrants, refugees]," such statements need not be interpreted as a straightforward expression of true opinions in their models. Rather, they are a socially and interactionally constrained expression of norms and values applied to, and represented in the context model of, the present situation, that is, as a disclaimer within an overall strategy of positive self-presentation. How do we know that? Well, one clue is that such statements are invariably followed by *but* and (only) negative opinions about the others (van Dijk, 1987a). In sum, a discursive approach to the study of the structures of models obviously needs to take into account the interactional, the social, and the cultural constraints of text, talk, and their underlying event and context models.

In other words, besides investigating the fundamental psychological constraints on the general structures of models and the strategies of their formation and change, systematic discourse analysis may yield hints about actual models as they are used and expressed by language users (for suggestions about a large variety such discourse structures, see, e.g., van Dijk, 1985b). Just as cognitive psychology provided many insights into the nature of discourse structures and their processing, it might be useful to take explicit grammar and discourse analysis seriously in the quest for the properties of model structures.

CONCLUDING REMARKS

As may have become obvious from the last paragraphs, I tend to finish (and sometimes begin) with speculations, programmatic statements, and other fantasies. These are all products of the mind. They are all strategically manipulated by cognition and persuasively formulated to entice the more adventurous of my colleagues. I realize, however, that it is a long way between speculation and testable and applicable theories. My cooperation with Walter has shown me how this is done, and how one may persuade skeptical colleagues of one's new proposals.

To conclude this brief and incomplete personal history of our theory and our cooperation, I would like to say that the obvious success of the psychology of text processing in cognitive and educational psychology and related areas is not only due to the urgency, the relevance, and the interestingness of the topics involved. Also the originality and the quality of the work of the many women and men who developed this domain have been decisive. There can be no doubt that for over 20 years Walter Kintsch has been one of the inspiring leaders of that group.

REFERENCES

Anderson, J. R., & Bower, G. H. (1973). *Human associative memory.* Washington, DC: Winston & Sons.

Bartlett, F. C. (1932). *Remembering: A study in experimental and social psychology.* London: Cambridge University Press.

Bierwisch, M. (1965). Poetik und Linguistik. In H. Kreuzer & R. Gunzenhauser (Eds.), *Mathematik und Dichtung* [Mathematics and Literature] (pp. 49–66). Munich: Nymphenburger.

Bower, G. H. (1980). Mood and memory. *American Psychologist 36*, 129–148.

Bruhn Jensen, K. (1986). *Making sense of the news.* Aarhus: Aarhus University Press.

Chafe, W. (1972). Discourse structure and human knowledge. In R. O. Freedle & J. B. Carroll (Eds.), *Language comprehension and the acquisition of knowledge* (pp. 41–70). New York: Winston.

Charniak, E. (1972). *Toward a model of children's story comprehension.* Unpublished doctoral dissertation, MIT.

Cofer, C. N. (1941). A comparison of logical and verbatim learning of prose passages of different lengths. *American Journal of Psychology, 54*, 1–20.

Cofer, C. N. (1943). Recall of verbal materials after a 4-year interval. *Journal of General Psychology, 29*, 155–156.

Communications 8 (1966). *L'analyse structurale du recit.* Paris: Seuil.

Crothers, E. J. (1972). Memory structure and the recall of discourse. In R. O. Freedle & J. B. Carroll (Eds.), *Language comprehension and the acquisition of knowledge* (pp. 247–284). New York: Winston.

Dawes, R. M. (1966). Memory and distortion of meaningful written material. *British Journal of Psychology, 57*, 77–86.

De Beaugrande, R., & Dressler, W. U. (1981). *Introduction to text linguistics.* London: Longman.

Dooling, D. J., & Lachman, R. (1971). Effects of comprehension on retention of prose. *Journal of Educational Psychology, 88*, 216–222.

Fiske, S. T., & Taylor, S. E. (1991). *Social cognition* (2nd ed.). New York: McGraw-Hill.

Frase, L. T. (1969). Structural analysis of the knowledge that results from thinking about texts. *Journal of Educational Psychology Monographs, 60*(2), 1–16.

Frase, L. T. (1972). Maintenance and control in the acquisition of knowledge from written materials. In R. O. Freedle & J. B. Carroll (Eds.), *Language comprehension and the acquisition of knowledge* (pp. 337–360). New York: Wiley.

Frederiksen, C. H. (1972). Effects of task-induced cognitive operations on comprehension and memory processes. In R. O. Freedle & J. B. Carroll (Eds.), *Language comprehension and the acquisition of knowledge* (pp. 337–357). New York: Wiley.

Freedle, R. O. (1972). Language users as fallible information processors. In R. O. Freedle & J. B. Carroll (Eds.), *Language comprehension and the acquisition of knowledge* (pp. 169–209). New York: Winston.

Freedle, R. O., & Carroll, J. B. (Eds.). (1972). *Language comprehension and the acquisition of knowledge.* New York: Winston.

Garnham, A. (1987). *Mental models as representations of discourse and text.* Horwood: Halsted Press.

Givón, T. (1989a). *The grammar of referential coherence as mental processing instructures.* Unpublished manuscript, University of Oregon, Linguistics Department.

Givón, T. (1989b). *Mind, code and context: Essays in pragmatics.* Hillsdale, NJ: Lawrence Erlbaum Associates.

Graber, D. A. (1988). *Processing the news* (2nd ed.). New York: Longman.

Greimas, A. (1966). *Semantique structurale.* Paris: Larousse.

Gumperz, J. J., & Hymes, D. (Eds.). (1972). *Directions in sociolinguistics: The ethnography of communication.* New York: Holt, Rinehart & Winston.

Gunter, B. (1987). *Poor reception: Misunderstanding and forgetting broadcast news.* Hillsdale, NJ: Lawrence Erlbaum Associates.

Herman, E. S., & Chomsky, N. (1988). *Manufacturing consent: The political economy of the mass media.* New York: Pantheon.

Jakobovits, L. A., & Miron, M. S. (1967). *Readings in the psychology of language.* Englewood Cliffs, NJ: Prentice-Hall.

Johnson-Laird, P. N. (1980). Mental models in cognitive science. *Cognitive Science, 4,* 72–115.

Johnson-Laird, P. N. (1983). *Mental models.* Cambridge, England: Cambridge University Press.

Johnson-Laird, P. N., & Garnham, A. (1981). Descriptions and discourse models. *Linguistics and Philosophy, 3,* 371–393.

Kamp, H. (1981). A theory of truth and semantic representation. In J. A. G. Groenendijk, T. Janssen, & M. Stohof (Eds.), *Formal methods in the study of language* (pp. 277–322). Amsterdam: Mathematical Centre Tracts.

King, D. J. (1961). Scaling the accuracy of recall of stories in the absence of objective criteria. *Psychological Record, 11,* 87–90.

Kintsch, W. (1972). Notes on the structure of semantic memory. In E. Tulving & W. Donaldson (Eds.), *Organization of memory* (pp. 249–308). New York: Academic Press.

Kintsch, W. (1974). *The representation of meaning in memory.* Hillsdale, NJ: Lawrence Erlbaum Associates.

Kintsch, W. (1977a). *Memory and cognition.* New York: Wiley.

Kintsch, W. (1977b). On comprehending stories. In M. Just & P. Carpenter (Eds.), *Cognitive processes in comprehension* (pp. 33–62). Hillsdale, NJ: Lawrence Erlbaum Associates.

Kintsch, W., & van Dijk, T. A. (1975). Comment on se rappelle et on resume des histoires [How stories are recalled and summarized]. *Langages 40,* 98–128.

Kintsch, W., & van Dijk, T. A. (1978). Toward a model of text comprehension and production. *Psychological Review, 85,* 363–394.

Koen, F., Becker, A., & Young, R. (1969). The psychological reality of the paragraph. *Journal of Verbal Learning and Verbal Behavior, 8,* 49–53.

Labov, W. (1972a). *Language in the inner city.* Philadelphia: University of Pennsylvania Press.

Labov, W. (1972b). *Sociolinguistic patterns.* Philadelphia: University of Pennsylvania Press.

Lachman, R., & Dooling, D. J. (1968). Connected discourse and random strings: Effects of number of inputs on recognition and recall. *Journal of Experimental Psychology, 77,* 517–522.

Lee, W. (1965). Supra-paragraph prose structure: Its specification, perception, and effects on learning. *Psychological Reports, 17,* 135–144.

Lindsay, P. H., & Norman, D. A. (1972). *Human information processing.* New York: Academic Press.

Longacre, R. (1983). *The grammar of discourse.* New York: Plenum.

Mandler, J. M. (1978). A code in the node: The use of story schema in retrieval. *Discourse Processes, 1,* 14–35.

Mandler, J. M. (1984). *Stories, scripts, and scenes: Aspects of schema theory.* Hillsdale, NJ: Lawrence Erlbaum Associates.

Miller, G. A., Galantner, E., & Pribram, K. (1960). *Plans and the structure of behavior.* New York: Holt, Rinehart & Winston.

Morrow, D. G. (1986). Places as referents in discourse. *Journal of Memory and Language, 25,* 676–690.

Morrow, D. G. (1990). Spatial models, prepositions, and verb-aspect markers. *Discourse Processes, 13,* 441–469.

Morrow, D. G., Greenspan, S. L., & Bower, G. H. (1987). Accessibility and situation models in narrative comprehension. *Journal of Memory and Language, 26,* 165–187.

Nash-Webber, B. L. (1978). *A formal approach to discourse anaphora.* (Tech. Rep. No. 77). Cambridge, MA: Bolt, Beranek & Newman.

Neisser, U. (1967). *Cognitive psychology.* Englewood Cliffs, NJ: Prentice-Hall.

Newell, A., & Simon, H. A. (1972). *Human problem solving.* Englewood Cliffs, NJ: Prentice-Hall.

Paivio, A. (1971). *Imagery and verbal processes.* New York: Holt, Rinehart & Winston.

Petöfi, J. S. (1971). *Transformationsgrammatiken und eine ko-textuelle Texttheorie.* Frankfurt: Athenaum.

Petöfi, J. S., & Rieser, H. (Eds.). (1973). *Studies in text grammar.* Dordrecht: Reidel.

Pompi, K. F., & Lachman, R. (1967). Surrogate processes in the short-term retention of connected discourse. *Journal of Experimental Psychology, 75,* 143–150.

Poulson, D., Kintsch, E., Kintsch, W., & Premack, D. (1979). Children's comprehension and memory for stories. *Journal of Experimental Child Psychology, 28,* 379–403.

Robinson, J. P., & Levy, M. R. (1986). *The main source: Learning from television news.* Beverly Hills, CA: Sage.

Rothkopf, E. Z. (1972). Structural text features and the control of processes in learning from written materials. In R. O. Freedle & J. B. Carroll (Eds.), *Language comprehension and the acquisition of knowledge* (pp. 315–335). New York: Winston.

Schank, R. C., & Abelson, R. P. (1977). *Scripts, plans, goals, and understanding: An inquiry into human knowledge structures.* Hillsdale, NJ: Lawrence Erlbaum Associates.

Slamecka, N. J. (1959). Studies of retention of connected discourse. *American Journal of Psychology, 72,* 409–416.

Stenning, K. (1978). Anaphora as an approach to pragmatics. In M. Halle et al. (Eds.), *Linguistic theory and linguistic reality* (pp. 162–200). Cambridge, MA: MIT Press.

Tulving, E. T., & Donaldson, W. (Eds.). (1972). *Organization of memory.* New York: Academic Press.

van Dijk, T. A. (1972). *Some aspects of text grammars: A study in theoretical poetics and linguistics.* The Hague: Mouton.

van Dijk, T. A. (1976). Discourse meaning and memory. Review article of W. Kintsch, *The representation of meaning in memory* (1974). *Journal of Reading Behavior, 8.*

van Dijk, T. A. (1977a). Knowledge frames, macrostructures and discourse comprehension. In M. Just & P. Carpenter (Eds.), *Cognitive processes in comprehension* (pp. 3–32). Hillsdale, NJ: Lawrence Erlbaum Associates.

van Dijk, T. A. (1977b). *Text and context: Explorations in the semantics and pragmatics of discourse.* London: Longman.

van Dijk, T. A. (1979). Recalling and summarizing complex discourse. In W. Burghardt & K. Holker (Eds.), *Textverarbeitung/text processing* (pp. 49–118). Berlin/New York: de Gruyter.

van Dijk, T. A. (1980a). *Macrostructures. An interdisciplinary study of global structures in discourse, interaction, and cognition.* Hillsdale, NJ: Lawrence Erlbaum Associates.

van Dijk, T. A. (Ed.). (1980b). Story comprehension [Special triple issue]. *Poetics 9*(1/3).

van Dijk, T. A. (Ed.). (1982a). New developments in cognitive models of discourse processing [Special triple issue]. *Text 2*(1/3).

van Dijk, T. A. (1982b). Opinions and attitudes in discourse comprehension. In J. F. Le Ny & W. Kintsch (Eds.), *Language and comprehension* (pp. 35–51). Amsterdam: North Holland.

van Dijk, T. A. (1984). *Prejudice in discourse.* Amsterdam: Benjamins.

van Dijk, T. A. (1985a). Cognitive situation models in discourse processing. The expression of ethnic situation models in prejudiced stories. In J. P. Forgas (Ed.), *Language and social situations* (pp. 61–79). New York: Springer.

van Dijk, T. A. (Ed.). (1985b). *Handbook of discourse analysis.* 4 vols. London: Academic Press.

van Dijk, T. A. (1987a). *Communicating racism.* Newbury Park, CA: Sage.

van Dijk, T. A. (1987b). Episodic models in discourse processing. In R. Horowitz & S. J. Samuels (Eds.), *Comprehending oral and written language* (pp. 161–196). New York: Academic Press.

van Dijk, T. A. (1988a). *News analysis: Case studies of international and national news in the press.* Hillsdale, NJ: Lawrence Erlbaum Associates.

van Dijk, T. A. (1988b). *News as discourse.* Hillsdale, NJ: Lawrence Erlbaum Associates.

van Dijk, T. A. (1990). Social cognition and discourse. In H. Giles & R. P. Robinson (Eds.), *Handbook of social psychology and language* (pp. 163–183). Chichester: Wiley.

van Dijk, T. A. (1991). *Racism and the press.* London: Routledge.

van Dijk, T. A. (1993a). *Elite discourse and racism.* Newbury Park, CA: Sage.

van Dijk, T. A. (1993b). Principles of critical discourse analysis [Special issue]. *Discourse & Society, 4*(2), 249–283.

van Dijk, T. A. (1994). Discourse and cognition in society. In D. Crowley & D. Mitchell, *Communication Theory Today* (pp. 107–126). Oxford: Pergamon Press.

van Dijk, T. A., & Kintsch, W. (1983). *Strategies of discourse comprehension.* New York: Academic Press.

Van Oostendorp, H., & Zwaan, R. A. (Eds.). (1994). *Naturalistic text comprehension.* Norwood, NJ: Ablex.

Wilensky, R. (1983). Story grammars versus story points. *Behavioral and Brain Sciences, 6,* 579–623.

Wunderlich, D. (Ed.). (1972). *Linguistische pragmatik.* Frankfurt: Athenaeum.

Epilogue

Suzanne Mannes
University of Delaware

It still amazes me that little more than a year and a half has passed since Chuck and I embarked on this adventure. In an unexpected series of fortunate (and timely) events, both the conference in Walter's honor and this volume have somehow come to serve as a tribute to him. During the course of this project, I have learned many things about editors, publishers, deadlines, those who do not meet them, and the like. I have also learned what a large, friendly family the academic world can provide. Gathered together with other participants and attendees for two days, on the campus where pleasant memories were made for many of us, gave me a real appreciation for the maxim, "it's a small world." In the rooms where meetings were held, meals eaten, and discussions had, there were representatives from many corners of the world—from California to Massachusetts, and from Minnesota to Georgia (not to mention Europe). All of these colleagues came to acknowledge Walter's contributions to the field of psychology, and to impart inspiration for his continued success.

We had always suspected that Walter's influence was far-reaching, but to see these suspicions so heartily confirmed was enlightening and rewarding. It is obvious from the work presented at the conference and included in this volume that Walter's work with Tuen van Dijk continues to inspire and inform cognitive psychologists, and that his newer construction-integration theory has already had a large impact on many aspects of psychology. This model has already found a wide range of applications and promises to endure as an important and influential model of cognition. One criticism of many cognitive theories is that they do not

411

apply to a wide range of cognitive phenomena (Newell, 1987). The construction-integration model has already shown wide-reaching impact, consistent with that expected for a general theory of cognition.

In this volume alone, Walter's models have been applied to some traditional findings in the area of cognitive psychology, such as primacy, recency and priming, and to the areas of planning, acquisition of knowledge, and medical diagnoses. The broad scope of his work is additionally evidenced by references in journals of varying foci and distinct readerships. In the past 3 years, citations to his work have appeared in the *Journal of Gerontology*, the *American Journal of Mental Retardation*, the *Review of Educational Research, Artificial Intelligence*, the *International Journal of Man-Machine Studies*, and many major journals with a psychological, educational, or cognitive science focus (e.g., *Cognitive Science, Memory & Cognition, Journal of Educational Psychology, Journal of Experimental Psychology*, and the *Journal of Personality and Social Psychology*). Walter is a tough man to keep up with, but fortunately for many of us, he gives us reasons to keep trying.

Author Index

Subject Index

A

ACT*, 309
Action planning, 307
Activity of minimal predication, 216–221
Affordances, 68–79, 84–85, 91–93
Anaphor, 111, 395
Argument filling, 31
Array model, 36–44
Artificial intelligence, 6, 66, 197, 311, 387,
    388, 412
  expert systems, 66
  human–computer interaction, 5, 361

B, C

Bottom-up processing, 25
Causal relations, 77, 164
  causal chaining, 317, 319
  causal coherence, 173, 213–215
  causal links, 171
  causal path, 213
  causal reference, 172
  causal structure, 163–168
Classification, 36, 47, 65–66
Cognitive development, 65
Cognitive effort, 157, 179, 184

Cognitive science, 1, 2, 5, 65, 397, 412
Coherence, 97, 104, 106–111, 123–127, 157,
    163–165, 186, 213, 251, 399, 352–355,
    375, 385–395, 405
  causal coherence, 173, 213–215
  co-referential coherence, 215–216, 219
  local coherence, 100, 227
  temporocausal coherence, 217
Collaborative activation-based production
    system, 338
Combinatorics, 5
Compound cues, 128, 135
Connectionism, 5, 127, 212, 228, 340, 361
  distributed-memory models, 53–55
  parallel processing, 98
Construction-Integration model of discourse,
    2, 5–6, 17, 31, 36, 61–62, 105, 127,
    134, 191, 208, 212, 221, 227, 233–236,
    240–249, 257, 260, 280, 307–309,
    313–322, 330–337, 338–355, 357,
    360–372, 378, 411–412
Constructionist models of comprehension,
    97–99, 103–108, 123–127, 135
  reconstruction in recall, 172
Context checking, 100
Context model, 398–401
Convergence principle, 131
Convolution, 53–57

423